J. C. H. Aveling was born and educated in Grantham, read history at Cambridge before World War II and then, after a short period of research, was trained at Lincoln and ordained as an Anglican clergyman. After five years in this profession he became a Catholic and was a monk in the Benedictine monastery of Ampleforth in Yorkshire from 1946 to 1967. During these years he also taught history in Ampleforth College, researched and wrote a number of historical works. In 1967, after a crisis of conscience, he left the Benedictine Order and the Catholic church. The following year, while studying at Cambridge, he married. He was received back into the Catholic church as a layman in 1974, and is now teaching history in a large comprehensive school in Berkshire. He is already the author of several books on English monastic history and the history of English Catholicism and of an article on mediaeval Westminster in the standard modern history of Westminster Abbey.

THE HANDLE AND THE AXE

The Handle
and the Axe

**The Catholic Recusants in England
from Reformation to Emancipation**

J. C. H. AVELING

Blond & Briggs

First published 1976 by Blond & Briggs Ltd
London, and Tiptree, Colchester, Essex

© Copyright 1976 J. C. H. Aveling

SBN 85634 047 2

Printed in Great Britain by The Anchor Press Ltd
and bound by Wm Brendon & Son Ltd
both of Tiptree, Essex

CONTENTS

To my wife, and to the Ampleforth
Benedictine Community, without whose
constant patience and support this
book would not have seen the light of day.

Introduction

'. . . so dismaying a subject as history.' (T. C. Smout, *A History of the Scottish People, 1560–1830*, p. 337)

'The Church is ever ailing, and lingers on in weakness, "always bearing about in the body the dying of the Lord Jesus, that the life also of Jesus might be made manifest in her body." ' (J. H. Newman, *Via Media*, vol. I, lecture 14.)

I have a much cherished old axe: I call it 'old', though I am well aware that the adjective is part true, part false. Years ago the original handle broke and was replaced. Then the original blade wore out and was replaced. So now none of the material substance of the original axe remains. But its replacement, in some odd way, has a real continuity with it and shares in its identity.

My axe in a crude way can stand as a symbol of the much more mysterious workings of human identity and continuity. We experience these constantly and are so accustomed to them that it is only occasionally—when we are confronted by their most startling manifestations—that we pause to reflect in a bewildered way on the mysteriousness of the whole complex process. Thus the scientists tell us that the physical substance of our bodies is continually wearing away and being replaced. In an average life-span a human body is totally renewed seven times. Yet, obviously, our body's identity and its real continuity remain. In the children of a family we can often detect family identity and continuity in bewilderingly diverse ways: shatteringly exact reproductions of the physical characteristics, physical mannerisms, or traits of character of earlier generations. I have a vivid memory of seeing a friend standing in the hall of his house directly beneath a portrait of a seventeenth-century namesake and ancestor. The house was crammed with relics of his family's continuous occupation of it since the fourteenth century. My friend accepted, and revelled in, this tremendous (and even claustrophobic) weight of family history. In almost every detail of physical appearance and stance he reproduced his ancestor in the portrait. Yet a study of the family pedigree showed that he could only have had 1/32nd of the blood of his ancestor, much diluted by generations of intermarriage. Or there is that different experience we have in meeting suddenly by chance an old friend after many years of total separation. At first sight we do not recognise her at all: she is physically altered beyond all ordinary recognition. But then, like a flash, comes the shock of identification, generated by seeing her very distinctive walk or laugh and hearing her voice.

When we pass from individuals, families and races to communities and institutions, the basis of whose unity is primarily a faith backed up by an organisation and old buildings, the workings of identity and its continuity appear, at any rate at a first glance, much less mysterious, more planned and manmade. Surely there is a monolithic clarity about the enduring identity of, say, the Papacy, the British Parliament, the American Congress, Oxford university, or the Society of Friends. Their physical, historical continuity is, indeed, indisputable, as is their general character viewed broadly. But historians have no difficulty in demonstrating that they have undergone immense, successive changes of ethos and function in society —so great that their founders would find it hard to recognise them. Ronald Knox explored these processes of change in his brilliant series of imagined dialogues in the same Oxford college commonroom at various dates between the sixteenth and twentieth centuries. With great artistry he conveyed an impression of the successive profound breaches of mental continuity underlying an amazing but superficial continuity of buildings, organisation, academic functions and even mannerisms. Yet even so, Knox suggested that the community of the Fellows of Simon Magus College still had, albeit ever more tenuously, an enduring 'focus of identity' (and so of real ideological continuity). To his mind this was provided by their constant relationship, partly of attraction and partly of repulsion and mostly unconscious, with a 'point of reference' outside themselves, namely the Catholic Church.

To a good many educated non-Catholics, Catholicism still does, consciously and unconsciously, serve as just such a point of reference helping to give meaning and direction to the flux of life. It does so largely because it is supposed that Catholicism is somehow immune from the historical transmutations which afflict all other ancient institutions. Even Macaulay, the great Whig historian, writing at the height of Victorian self-confidence in technological progress, and himself sure that Catholicism stood for medieval superstition, could not help imagining a remote future in which London was in ruins while Papal Rome still stood intact and triumphant. Until the 1940s, Church historians, Catholic and Protestant alike, assumed as self-evident the monolithic unchangeability of the Catholic Church. The Protestants had always, it is true, insisted that Catholicism was an evil mutation from the purity of the Christianity of New Testament times; but they admitted that this mutation took place once and for all in the third and four centuries, and that thereafter Catholicism remained fundamentally unchanged. Catholic apologists retorted both by asserting boldly that no such mutation took place, and by charging the Protestant Churches with successive fundamental variations and changes of belief since the sixteenth century. In the 1850s John Henry Newman propounded a fresh line of Catholic apologetic. This was not merely an intellectual theory: it represented the organic development of his own life, from a very English compound of Evangelical Protestantism and Whig Liberalism into Romantic Catholicism. He suggested that Catholicism had undergone a continuous and remarkable process of organic growth and change down the ages, baptising and appropriating large elements from non-Catholic sources, and suffering periodical autumns and winters of weakness followed invariably by springs of new life. To Newman's mind this progressive development was clearly foreseen by St Paul in his Epistles and reflected the profoundest insights of nineteenth-century secular thinking. It was certainly a bold and fascinating hypothesis. But Newman was, in reality, never as radical as he seemed to alarmed Catholic and Protestant traditionalists. He always assumed that the successive transmutations of Catholicism down the ages were, if in sum impressive, still superficial and in detail small. He thought of Catholicism in the same way that Edmund Burke, the Whig political thinker, thought of the English Constitution—as a seed growing immensely slowly and organically into an oak tree, preserving throughout the dramatic process a massive and obvious symmetry and continuity of identity.

Of late years Church historians, while preserving Newman's idea of development in general, have increasingly challenged his assumption of simple linear or biological progressive growth. (Indeed Newman himself, in his old age, showed signs of becoming much less optimistic.) Even in the 1930s Church historians were suggesting that, at least since the fourteenth century, Catholicism had been a beleaguered and shrinking city, whose successive revivals had been less and less effective. By the 1940s they were tending to regard the Church's progress since the fourteenth century as a long series of shotgun marriages with alien cultures. Now they are ready to admit that, in quite fundamental matters of faith and morals, the Church has made no ascertainable progress at all, or has actually suffered a loss of understanding by tarrying for centuries in mistaken paths. Research into, and the patient reconstruction of, religious history is, of its nature, a very slow and difficult work. The interpretation of the evidence is always speculative, and sometimes outright impossible. Inevitably therefore it is a happy hunting-ground for both conservative dogmatists and impatient radicals. Still, modern research has provided enough solid ground for a far-reaching revision of many features of the history of Catholicism.

Take, for instance, the long-cherished view of French, Polish and Irish nationalists that, from the sixteenth to the nineteenth centuries, their nations were overwhelmingly monolithic Catholic communities with a simple, straightforward continuity with the medieval past. At least we can now be sure that the historical reality was much less simple. In all three countries late medieval Catholicism was far from romantic normality—least of all in Ireland, which contained two rival but overlapping religious set-ups: a degenerate and anachronistic Gaelic, and a corrupt and decrepit Anglo-Irish, culture. In the course of the sixteenth century, all three countries saw medieval Catholicism reduced to rags and tatters. By the 1560s in France large areas of the country and its educated people had passed over to strong Calvinism; near-agnosticism was rife, and Catholicism in rapid decline. The aristocratic landowning families who by the nineteenth century were generally rigidly Monarchist-Catholic, in the later sixteenth century were often divided in religion or Calvinist. Poland was riddled with Protestantism (Lutheran, Calvinist or sectarian) and the first seed-bed of Unitarianism. Sixteenth-century Ireland was in religious chaos; the hierarchical structure of medieval Catholicism was in ruins, a Protestant ordering of religion was still barely a reality, and the landowners (Irish, Anglo-Irish and Scots) changed their formal religious allegiances at the drop of a hat to suit the wildly changing political situation. In seventeenth-century France and Poland there were massive recoveries of Catholicism. Traditionalist Church historians have concentrated their attention almost exclusively on the spiritual and clerical elements in these remarkable resurrections: on missionaries, Jesuits, contemplatives, bishops, writers, genuine conversions from Protestantism and agnosticism. More recent historians have attempted to sketch in the political, social and economic background which clearly provided much of the dynamic of these movements. Thus in a Poland at war with Sweden and Russia, Protestants and Orthodox were a dangerous potential 'fifth-column'. In France the Protestants formed a powerful, armed nation, which, in constant alliance with foreign Protestant powers, threatened civil war and the dismemberment of France. The re-Catholicisation in both countries was accomplished with all the brutality of discriminatory laws, armed force, compulsory conversions and deportations.

Although this resurgent, militant Catholicism was, in principle, Papist, it showed little disposition to obey Papal directives, and its thoroughgoing efforts owed most to very local vested interests. It would be false to deny that the astonishingly uniform mass Catholicism of the early eighteenth-century French and Polish countrysides owed something to survivals of medieval religiosity and something also to a genuine rediscovery of Catholic faith after the sixteenth-century trauma. Moreover, it seems that most features of the new baroque Catholicism (for instance its theatrical, Italianate church architecture and decorations, its operatic liturgy, its elaborate devotions, its reformed religious Orders, its ultra-systematic manuals of devotion and theology) can be traced back to roots and tendencies in late medieval Catholicism. Baroque Catholicism at first sight does look like extensively repaired medievalism. But penetrate below its surface and you find plenty of indications that a gulf separated it in spirit from the early sixteenth century. The sixteenth-century trauma and the very widespread impact of Protestantism and agnosticism was like a violent earthquake, leaving a deep fault across the line of continuity. Also in the course of the sixteenth and seventeenth centuries the whole temper of secular society grew markedly more modern—unsettled, sceptical. The new Catholicism, consciously and unconsciously, part protesting, part accepting, was carried along by the stream of these changes. It failed to check them or to baptise and influence them: it became increasingly self-conscious, artificial, precarious. Protestantism had undoubtedly failed to achieve the radical rejuvenation of Christianity at which it had aimed. Resurrected Catholicism failed also: it merely won itself a new and limited lease of life and power over society, at the cost of surrendering to become the moral policeman and buttress of the social order required by dominant political and economic interests which believed less and less in the Catholic faith.

In seventeenth-century Ireland, successive English governments made a massive effort to destroy the remnants of Catholicism by methods closely akin to those used by Catholic governments in France and Poland. Traditionalist Irish Catholic historians have used legend and the obvious fact that the effort failed in the long run to conceal from us the extent to which it had come near to success by the early eighteenth century. By 1700 very possibly more than a third of the population was Protestant. Nonconformity flourished in Ireland, even in the west, and Wesley was later to find the country a profitable mission field. The Irish and Anglo-Irish Catholic landowning gentry were near extinction by forced exile, expropriation, bankruptcy and conversion to Protestantism. Mixed marriages were common. Irish Catholicism was at a low ebb. Its clerical resources (diocesan bishops,

religious, secular missioners and thirty-one small seminaries scattered widely over Europe) were too much wasted abroad and too
badly deployed in Ireland. Nationalist feeling was at a discount.
Middle-class Catholics were commonly Unionists: often the most
genuine nationalists were Protestants. What saved demoralised and
disorganised Catholicism? According to Catholic legend it was a
mixture of ardent Catholic nationalism and the heroic endeavours of
poor missioner 'hedge-priests'. Modern historians are not so sure. To
their minds more potent factors were the gross mistakes by the English governments and a substantial increase in Irish prosperity and
population in the eighteenth century. The policy of destruction of
Catholicism was carried out brutally at first, but then more and more
inefficiently and half-heartedly. Whigs and Irish Protestants slipped
into an attitude of quasi-toleration of Catholicism. A colonialist
government policy produced in Ireland much the same effects that
it roused in contemporary America. So, almost by accident, Irish
Catholicism got a reprieve. Yet it was so unreformed, disorganised
and demoralised that in 1800 it was still an open question whether
it had any real future. The age of baroque had largely passed it by,
for good or evil.

Between the 1780s and 1815 French and Polish Catholicism underwent shocks even more severe than those of the sixteenth century.
The whole material and clerical structure of French Catholicism
was smashed by the French revolutionaries between 1791 and
1799. The artificiality and precariousness of the baroque political
new Catholicism was laid bare. The forced regimentation collapsed,
and a large section of the people abandoned Catholic belief and
practice. Yet between the Napoleonic Concordat with the Pope of
1801 and the end of the nineteenth century there came a vast Catholic
resurrection. Traditionalist historians have stressed heavily its links
with the baroque and even medieval religious past, the genuineness
of many conversions from scepticism or revolutionary Republicanism, the magnitude of the task of building up the structure of the
hierarchy, the seminaries, the religious houses and Catholic schools,
the high level of religious practice achieved and maintained in some
rural districts. None of this is in doubt. But recent historians have
started to fill in other, contradictory and disturbing features of the
picture of the age. This second 'new Catholicism' was even more
artificial and precarious than the first. It never regained huge sections
of the population, in the cities, industrial areas and certain wide
peasant areas. The economic and church-going support it received
so strongly came from *bien pensant* influential sections of society
(rulers like Napoleon I, Louis XVIII, Charles X, Napoleon III,
royalist aristocratic landowners, *haute bourgeoisie* and prosperous

peasants), who saw Catholicism as a buttress of their political power and social dominance. French Catholicism by the later nineteenth century was oddly constituted. It contained a hard central core of ultra-Papalist, ultra-clericalist, ultra-Establishment clergy who lived in a strange, escapist mental ghetto. Alongside this core was a secret, guerilla band of dissident 'Modernist' seminary professors who challenged the whole doctrinal and structural development of the Church since the later middle ages. Typical of them was Turmel, who retained his professorship for years, making many gestures of conformity, while publishing a shower of deeply radical articles under many different assumed names. Surrounding these clerical groups and their lay admirers were millions of more or less *pratiquant* French Catholics, whose mental life and beliefs bore little relation to the religious structure they acknowledged. So, for instance, modern historians of contraception have pointed out that nineteenth-century France was unique in Europe in having a stationary population: even the *pratiquants* used abortion and contraception widely. Clearly this second resurrection of French Catholicism was living on borrowed time. Around 1903 there began its third collapse in modern history, from which there are still no signs of another resurrection.

Polish baroque new Catholicism was largely shattered by the destruction of the government by the late eighteenth-century 'Partitions' of the country, and by foreign occupation, which lasted until 1918. Especially in its latter days, baroque Catholicism was feeble and riddled with formalism and scepticism. After 1815 there came a painful resurrection. This owed much to genuine religious forces, but possibly more to *bien pensant* social conservatism and romantic nationalism opposing the rigid anti-Catholic policies of the Prussian Protestant and Russian Orthodox occupying powers. Nineteenth-century Polish Catholicism shared many of the features of its French contemporaries, the rigid clericalist, Papalist core, the radical Liberal Catholics, the huge iron collar of *bien pensants*. The religious views of, say, Chopin and Joseph Conrad were fairly typical of the age. In the free Poland of the 1930s and the largely enslaved Poland of the years since 1946 the element of *bien pensant* support has eroded. Catholicism survives, sustained (much more precariously than might appear at first sight) partly by the strength of its clerical organisation, partly by its small minority core of genuine spirituality, and largely by the popular force of nationalistic, anti-Russian sentiment amongst millions who have little real spiritual affinity with official Catholicism.

Irish Catholicism went through a prodigious sea change in the course of the nineteenth century. It began the century as possibly the most disorganised and depressed Catholic community in Europe, living on sufferance and uncertain of its future. It ended the century as perhaps the strongest Catholic community anywhere, in terms of numbers practising fully, of numbers of vocations to the priesthood and religious Orders, of domination of social life by the clergy. To cap all this it had established a unique Catholic Empire overseas, in the United States, in Australia, in England, Wales and Scotland, quite apart from wide areas of the African and Far Eastern mission fields. To Irish Catholic traditionalists the reasons for this astounding change are obvious: they attribute to late medieval, sixteenth-, seventeenth- and eighteenth-century Irish Catholicism a size, steadiness and vigour which are largely legendary; this was an ideal springboard for nineteenth-century efforts by a perfectly uniquely spiritually-gifted and passionately nationalist people. But, as modern Irish historians are (still somewhat cautiously) showing, the truth must be vastly more complex and mysterious. The French Revolution destroyed most of the elaborate Irish clerical structure on the Continent, and forced the bishops, religious and secular clergy to retreat to Ireland. There the social and economic situation was drastically altered by the Potato Famine, massive emigration, impoverishment and the collapse of the landowning aristocracy of the Protestant Ascendancy. Simultaneously, Liberal policies of the English government progressively withdrew support and resources from the Protestant Church of Ireland, and gave subsidies and full tolerance to Catholic institutions. By the 1860s, led by Cardinal Cullen, an extremely efficient reform and reorganisation of clerical and parochial structures was effected. The clergy were batting on a very easy wicket: Irish society was mostly backward and rural; it lacked a real aristocracy or *haute bourgeoisie* to offer anti-clerical resistance; Irish society contained few intellectuals, and they were mostly non-practising Catholics. The new Irish Catholicism was built on small-town lower-middle-class peasant respectability. It certainly was not built out of nationalist sentiment. The hierarchy had a record of steady Unionism. Nineteenth-century Irish nationalism was very much a small minority movement, manned by non-practising Catholic romantics, men of violence and Protestants. The achievement of Dominion status and then full national independence in the 1920s was due far more to a sudden throwing-in of its hand by the English government and to accident than to any widespread desire for independence amongst the Irish, least of all among devout Catholics.

The post-Reformation history of Scots Catholicism bears all the familiar marks of death and strange, unsatisfactory resurrection. We know very little about later medieval Scots Catholicism, largely be-

cause of the lack of interest shown to this day by post-Presbyterian
Scots historians. It must have been in an unhealthy and demoralised
state. By the 1580s it had almost totally collapsed: there remained,
protected in a few areas by landlords, no more than some 2000
Catholics. In the seventeenth century came an intensive missionary
effort by Presbyterians and Episcopalians, and, to a lesser extent, by
Catholic priests trained abroad in the few Scots colleges. By the early
eighteenth century the Catholic community was tiny (the Kirk
estimated its numbers as less than 1000 adults). Its gains by individual
conversions from Presbyterianism and, in the Western Isles and
Highlands, from near-paganism, were more than offset by losses
through emigration and lapse. In 1800 the community appeared to
have no viable future. Yet by the 1860s it had been magically transformed. A massive Irish Catholic immigration to the new industrial
areas of the south-west, together with Highland Catholic settlement
in Glasgow, produced the heaviest concentration of Catholics in the
British Isles, outside Ireland. This concentration of itself enforced a
practical toleration and social acceptance which made possible the
creation of an Irish-type clerical control. Simultaneously Walter
Scott's Romanticism and the effects of Tractarianism produced, by
conversion, a small but respectable Scots Catholic aristocracy and
upper middle class. This new Scots Catholicism had practically no
continuity with the medieval past (except in the romantic medievalist
fantasies by the convert Marquis of Bute) and little with pre-nine-
teenth-century Scots Catholicism.

The late medieval Welsh Church bore many similarities to the
Irish Church. Its native Celtic culture was depressed; the Anglo-
Welsh official Church was corrupt and ineffective. Even nineteenth-
century romantic Welsh Catholic converts could find little in its
records to inspire them. In the sixteenth century, as was to be expected with so remote an area, Catholic sentiment hung on strongly
in Wales. But by the early seventeenth century Welsh Catholic
missioners, trained abroad in English colleges, had only succeeded in
recreating Catholic communities on a small scale in a few areas.
Meanwhile a very successful English and Welsh Protestant missionary effort conquered most of the country for (Welsh-speaking)
Anglicanism. By the 1830s Welsh Catholicism appeared to be dying.
It was rescued in the 1860s and 1870s by a large Irish Catholic immigration into some industrial areas of South Wales. But this, in its
turn, coincided with the remarkable efflorescence of Protestant
Dissent in both industrial and rural areas, and the great age of
'ranters' and 'revivals'. Catholicism has, narrowly, survived in Wales,
in the teeth of respectability and Welsh nationalism.

But what of the fortunes of post-Reformation English Catholi-

cism? According to its most distinguished modern historian, Bishop
David Mathew (in his *Catholicism in England: the Portrait of a
Minority, its Culture and Tradition*), the story is essentially simple
and clear-cut. Present-day Catholicism is a direct prolongation into
the modern world of late medieval English religion, continuing its
characteristic temper and virtues. He is, naturally, prepared to admit considerable successive changes of style and ethos, immense
losses to Protestantism and scepticism, and large gains by conversions
and Irish immigration. But, to his mind, these fluctuations have been
superficial: the converts were successfully absorbed, and even the
Irish either absorbed and essentially Anglicised, or, where found
indigestible and alien, left apart in separate groups. It is significant
that Bishop Mathew was himself an Anglicised Celt. For him the
clothes, idiom and emphases may alter from age to age, but all the
Catholic leaders in England, whatever their origins, reproduce the
same distinctive 'Englishry', cool, stubborn, humorous, pragmatic
—from Langland, Chaucer, Dame Julian of Norwich and Richard
Rolle of Hampole to Thomas More, Campion and Persons, Cardinal
Allen, Augustine Baker, Benet Canfield, Dryden, Challoner, Wiseman, Newman, Faber, Manning, Bourne, Hinsley, Eric Gill to
Cardinal Heenan. To Bishop Mathew as to Ronald Knox, English
post-Reformation Catholicism is not an alien ghetto or backwater:
it has been one integral facet of the whole of English life. More
than that, they would insist that it has somehow been *central* to
'Englishry'—more central than the comparatively recent phenomenon of English Protestantism.

This is a grand and moving vision: in its way it is just as
impressive as the Catholic nationalist historical traditions of the
French, Poles and Irish. Even a complete outsider can be moved by
its power, perhaps by reading Evelyn Waugh's novels, or by visiting
such old Catholic mansions as Coughton Court (Warwickshire),
Harvington Hall (Worcestershire), Oxburgh Hall (Norfolk),
Stonyhurst (Lancashire) or Lyford Grange (Berkshire). A recent
writer who was himself a prisoner-of-war at Colditz Castle has
sketched the impression made on him and his fellows by one
prisoner who was a peer and head of a family with a long Catholic
history. They noticed (or thought they did) his detached, priestly
manner, and attributed his quiet, aristocratic contempt for the
Germans' prison regulations to a hereditary Catholic nonconformist
spirit. Hence, when he was sentenced by the Germans to a spell of
solitary confinement, his fellows escorted him to the cells with a
mock-serious fancy-dress procession of an Elizabethan kind, with a
'headsman' carrying an axe, its blade turned towards the prisoner.

But, moving or not, does this version of English Catholic history represent the truth? We have seen that similar nationalistic Catholic traditions have existed in other countries, and have been proved to be legendary. Is it not obvious that there is at least a *prima facie* case for the prosecution? There seem to be several impressive pieces of evidence. In the first place there is personal discontinuity: exceedingly few English Catholic families can trace their Catholicism back in perfect continuity to the sixteenth century. Secondly there is institutional discontinuity: between 1534 and the 1580s English Catholicism hardly existed at all as a coherent, organised community; it was utterly recreated in the later years of the century. Moreover, manifestly, the differences in character between, say, pre-Reformation, seventeenth-century, late nineteenth-century and modern English Catholicism are so profound as to make real continuity in spirit and organisation seem very tenuous indeed. What did the 'long-established', all-pervasive, taken-for-granted, shabby unreformed English Catholicism of 1534 have in common with the small, scattered, rustic nonconformist sect of the seventeenth century, self-conscious, defensive, almost Puritan in its worship, dominated utterly by its lay aristocracy and squirearchy? And what did either have in common with the highly organised, very clerically-run, baroque, mostly Irish and urban Catholicism of 1900? A third piece of evidence for the prosecution of the nationalist legend is the sheer size of the intake of Irish immigrants and converts. Thus in 1851, the year of the only census so far to make enquiries about religious practice, practically two-thirds of the Catholics in England had been born in Ireland, and well over four-fifths must have had Irish blood. Today, since the massive further Irish immigration after 1945, the proportions cannot be much different. Study the *Catholic Directory* and note the extent to which recruitment to the Catholic clergy in England still depends on Irish seminaries. As for converts, at most periods English Catholicism seems to have owed most of its leaders, its verve, colour and ideas to them. Very clearly, nineteenth- and early twentieth-century English Catholic history is studded thickly with converts: for instance Newman, Manning, Faber, William George Ward, Ullathorne (of convert parentage), George Tyrrell, Eric Gill—not to speak of the Irish or part-Irish, like Nicholas Wiseman, Bourne, Heenan. Before the nineteenth century and the Irish influx there abounded converts such as Cuthbert Mayne, Margaret Clitheroe, Edmund Campion, Robert Persons, Guy Fawkes, Augustine Baker, Benet Canfield, Charles II, James II, Dryden, Richard Challoner. If English Catholicism had merely consisted of native born-Catholics it would have been, and would certainly be now, a tiny, insignificant, colourless and inbred nonconformist sect.

The case for the prosecution of the nationalist vision is impressive. Yet, in England as in the other countries, there must have been *some* profound, enduring and underlying forces to give real identity and continuity to Catholicism. Without something definite and very strong of this kind, how could Catholicism have survived such great material damage, ostracism, persecution, disorganisation and so many strains of adaptation to huge changes in personnel and ethos? As we try, in the course of this book, to trace the history of English Catholicism since 1534, we must primarily be concerned to try to discover the nature of its underlying identity. Almost every suggested ingredient of that identity is open to question: 'medievalist Englishry'; a highly authoritarian Church government anchored on the Papacy; a deep, mystical sacramentalism of sacraments, blessed objects, images, shrines, rituals; a profound other-worldliness stemming from a profusion of monasteries, convents and contemplatives. For a great many years during the history of English Catholicism most of these features were practically non-existent, or in short supply: even at the times when they were most evident, they were diluted and affected large sections of the Catholic community relatively slightly.

Whatever the answer may be, the question is of very practical and urgent concern for the English Catholics of today and interested outside observers. Since 1960, even at a most conservative estimate, the Catholics have been faced with a torrent of change more severe and radical than at any time since the mid sixteenth century. Almost all the distinctive features of both baroque and post-1850s Catholicism are fading away and under a heavy fire of Catholic criticism: the clerical-authoritarian-paternalistic structure based on Rome, the rigidly exclusivist attitude towards Protestantism, the sharply authoritarian and Puritan moral orthodoxy, the stereotype Latin services, the proliferation of religious Orders. More radical observers claim to detect clear signs of a spiritual and intellectual landslide threatening to upset fundamental levels of belief and organisation which were untouched by the sixteenth-century cataclysm, barely challenged even by Protestantism, and intact since the very early centuries of Church history. The Catholic Church has always carried in her bosom a sizable minority of secret dissidents (the early monks, the early Franciscans, the sixteenth-century Catholic radicals, the seventeenth-century eccentric radicals, the eighteenth-century English 'Catholic Committee', the Catholic Modernists of 1900–14) as well as an unnumbered host of sceptical priests and *bien pensant* or nominal Catholics. Is today's widespread Catholic dissidence and agnosticism in any way new in character and extent?

As we have seen, Catholicism in Poland, France and Ireland has owed much of its strength and style to its association with national-ism or anti-Establishment nonconformity. We shall have to ask our-selves to what extent English Catholicism since 1534 has gained strength from the same source. Perhaps it was not only the Quakers, Congregationalists and 'ranters', but also the Catholics, who served as a haven for the nonconformist conscience. Perhaps it was this charac-teristic of Catholicism which attracted to it so many of the Irish (who otherwise gravitated for preference to the sterner forms of Protestant Dissent) and so many converts from both Established Protestantism and Puritan Dissent.

1. Catholicism in Ruins, 1534–70

The traditional Catholic view of the English Reformation is bold and clear. Up to 1534 England was a profoundly and traditionally Roman Catholic country. In 1534 its clergy and religion had weaknesses and faults which were, for a folk-religion in a still rustic and primitive country, natural and excusable: in any case the Church would, in its own good time, have set its house in order. But then a small minority of cynical politicians, headed by the grotesque figure of Henry VIII, carried out a skilful revolution. For motives of political power and economic gain, they played on the natural ignorance, greed and anticlericalism of the upper classes to secure their consent to a breach with the central authority of the Church, the Papacy. This made possible a wholesale pillaging of Church and monastic property, which was further disguised as an overdue measure of radical Catholic Church reform. It was inevitable that now, as in most major revolutions, power should pass from moderate revolutionaries to radicals. After 1547 the 'Jacobins' or 'Bolsheviks' of the time—in this case radical Protestants—intrigued their way to political power and used it to carry out a second, more extreme, Protestant religious revolution by force. Thus the vast majority of the English people were tricked, and eventually brain-washed, out of their traditional faith. However, this faith was so deeply rooted that various degrees of residual Catholicism remained the only real religion in many parts of the country well into the later decades of the sixteenth century. Hence, even to the end of the seventeenth century, the restoration of Catholicism as the national religion remained a real possibility: Protestantism, until then, had not made any profound impression on the bulk of the population. (Indeed, Catholics have suggested that it never did, and that the sixteenth-century revolutionaries were chiefly responsible for the massive collapse of Christianity in England by the nineteenth century.) Evelyn Waugh frankly suggested that if the Tudors had stayed Catholics, or if

James II's 'Catholic counter-revolution' of 1685–8 had succeeded, a strong national Catholicism would have tempered the asperities of the modernisation of England in the nineteenth century, checked the rise of unbelief and made modern England a far happier place to live in.

According to the traditional Catholic view, Catholicism was preserved from 1534 by the majority of the population passively, and by a continuous golden thread of ardent leaders actively: Thomas More and his family, clerical Catholic intellectuals in exile abroad, and numerous country gentry and priests covertly at home. By the 1570s this band organised a marvellous and heroic Catholic Resistance, officered by self-sacrificing priest-missioners trained and ordained abroad, and sustained by an elaborate organisation of secret hides, reception committees of ardent young men, and underground channels to forward priests and information. The Anglican Establishment was rightly terrified by the size and strength of the Catholic menace. It was controlled by men who were partly genuine Calvinist fanatics, and partly post-Catholic agnostics, grown wealthy on monastic, episcopal and parochial Church property. They used Gestapo-type methods to suppress Catholicism: propaganda, smearing, spies and double agents, torture (especially implemented by the fiendish Topcliffe, who would have been at home in Germany in 1939–45) and concentration camps. In the seventeenth century the threat offered to the Protestant Establishment by a Stuart monarchy which was swinging steadily back towards Catholicism provoked the ruling class to further revolutionary action, in 1642–60 and 1688. After the final revolutionary ejection of the Stuarts (now openly Catholic) in 1688, the monarchy, machine of government and Protestant clerical organisation fell under the complete control of the triumphant Whig aristocracy. Perhaps the most typical of its class was the Russell family, the Dukes of Bedford. Their palace was Woburn Abbey, originally a Benedictine monastery suppressed by Henry VIII when its mild but courageous abbot was hanged for daring to disapprove openly of the King's religious policy. From Woburn the Dukes were masters by patronage and ownership of scores of church livings. Elsewhere, in East Anglia and the west country, they held sway over vast estates, originally monastic.

Like the French, Polish and Irish nationalist Catholic interpretations of history, this English view has had tremendous strength. From the first English Catholic apologists writing at Louvain in the 1560s to Pugin, the convert neo-Gothic architect, and on to Hilaire Belloc and Evelyn Waugh it has been orthodoxy for a host of writers. For all of them, especially the sixteenth-century apologists, it has been no mere historical judgment or opinion but an integral part of the Catholic faith. Thus, for instance, to Hilaire Belloc writing in the early twentieth century, 'Europe is the Faith', the true tradition of Western civilisation and decency is only to be found within Catholicism. He was reproducing, in a different idiom, the views of William Allen, who wrote in the 1580s. To Allen a universal Catholicism based on the divine right autocracy of the Papal monarchy and exercising a paternalistic control over all Christian governments was the will of God and also the only ordering of society which accorded with right reason and men's natural inclinations. Therefore revolt against Catholic authority was essentially irrational and unnatural: it was the ultimate, demonic evil, the fruits of which were inevitably in the long run unrestricted 'private judgment' (religion reduced to every man's human opinion), mass immorality, and the rise of a chaotic democracy in politics. Since this Catholic truth was so essentially obvious, denial of it could be due only to malice and was invariably in bad faith. Hence to Allen, as always to traditional Catholics, lapse from the faith must always be 'falling' or 'apostasy' (another Judas), resistance to the known truth and gravely sinful. Hence also came the old Catholic belief in a kind of divine law of gravity bound to draw back to the Church eventually all but the most malicious apostates.

But it would be wrong to imagine that this Catholic outlook was triumphalist. Writing in his study in the university of Louvain in 1589, the Sussex and Oxford Catholic theologian Thomas Stapleton expressed it in stark terms which became part of its orthodoxy. He compared Europe in general, and England in particular, to a woman in travail who cannot give birth and who lies tossing in agony and growing exhaustion: 'Why is it that there is no birth and no end to the travail after sixty years of effort and warfare?' He sees the darkness fast increasing. Protestant heresy is triumphant, and, once the walls of Catholic unity have been breached, a flood of evil has poured in: revolt of children against parents, of subjects against rulers, gross immorality, a massive increase in the volume of witchcraft and black magic. But the dark heart of the storm is not outright Protestant heresy or the advances into Europe of the Ottoman Turks: it is 'the *politiques*', 'feigned Catholicism'. In Catholic countries like Flanders these are the many who feign practising Catholicism simply to procure jobs from a Catholic government or to avoid persecution. In England they are 'the many thousands' who profess a vague attachment to 'the old religion', but who frequent Anglican services and behave like Protestants for social and economic reasons. Clearly true Catholics in England, and everywhere, are a small minority. To Stapleton's mind this menacing situation must portend the end of the world and second coming of Christ. All the signs of the times (even the appearance of Christ among the natives in the new worlds of the African, American and Far Eastern missions) fit the prophecies in the Book of Daniel. In the 'last days' is to appear—and surely has now appeared—the very ultimate horror of evil, 'the abomination of desolation' seated in the holy of holies: a *woman*, Queen Elizabeth, Supreme Governor of the English Church, and seated in the place of the Pope. God will, indeed, give a final deliverance to his Catholic faithful at the End: but it will be utterly miraculous and they must suffer terribly before it comes.

It is noticeable that this traditional Catholic outlook—at least in its stern, classical form before the onset of modern romanticism and sentimentalisation—was frank about the small numbers of Catholics and the hosts of the lapsed and nominal. Above all, it did not romanticise the medieval Catholic past. Allen and Stapleton place the blame for all the suffering squarely on the faults of *Catholics*, and especially on the failings of the pre-Reformation English Church and clergy. The most forthright expression of this is in the writings of Robert Persons, a Jesuit leader and probably the ablest mind amongst the Elizabethan Catholics. He was unimpressed by the thousand-year-old tradition of pre-Reformation Catholicism. To his mind a person became a Christian only as the result of a profound personal religious conversion. The conversion of the Anglo-Saxons was incomplete and its effects had worn off swiftly. He was equally unimpressed by the 'Tridentine' reformed Catholicism in Latin countries of his own days. It was, he wrote, 'full of accommodations to the weakness of the age and the decayed state of Christendom'. Writing with the Evangelical intensity common then to both devout Catholic reformers and Protestant Puritans (from whose ranks he had most likely come), he demanded 'a perfect Reformation', 'a perfect restitution of the ancient Christian Church' of the first three centuries. In his private letters Persons included under a blanket condemnation most of the English Catholics of his day. Most were unconverted or feigned: even the seminary priests and students were commonly riddled with faction and secular attitudes. He thinks it little wonder that eminent cardinals in Rome (a place which he privately criticised severely for its permissiveness and laxity) insisted that the English are a faulty race, full of violence and 'hatred of the magistrate': even the most apparently zealous English Catholics and martyrs had no true spirit of religion.

How near does this traditional Catholic view come to the historical truth? Modern historians of pre-Reformation English religion frankly confess themselves defeated. Contemporary or sixteenth-century writers are almost exclusively Catholic or Protestant reformers. It is impossible to make out from their uniformly adverse judgment whether late medieval religion was really unusually corrupt or whether it was of average or even above-average standard but still falling short of the reformers' perfectionist standards. The matter is not decided by the mass of ordinary surviving evidence—cases in Church courts, devotional works, chronicles, jottings and graffiti, architectural and archaeological traces. Like Russian icons they come from an age when very personal self-revelation was somehow psychologically and practically impossible. As with icons and art historians, the Church historian attempting to interpret these formalised religious evidences is tempted to take refuge in wildly speculative and imaginative theories. It is safe to say that pre-Reformation English culture was complex and deep-rooted, nevertheless offering little direct or effective resistance to its own dissolution in 1534–70. At the base of the social pyramid was the great majority of the population, the illiterate poor. They apparently had a subculture of their own, of a barbaric kind. Specialists in folk-history, in popular music and dance traditions and in the history of witchcraft and the occult have often worked over the scanty surviving evidence of this subculture. But it is no use pretending that we know, or will ever know, much about it. Some elements of it (legends, ballads handed down by oral tradition, dances and mummeries, corn-dollies and witchcraft—mostly white) had nothing to do with orthodox religion, and contained a strong flavour of mockery of it and of the 'possessioners' ('haves') of society with which it was associated. But it would be very unwise to exaggerate the solidity and coherence of these elements and to imagine that they formed a real opposition religion. It is likely that the poor were always too undernourished, too preoccupied with the struggle to live and the long hours of heavy manual labour, too effectively regimented by their betters and employers ever to be able to maintain a strong underground counter-culture.

Nor can we guess the strength of the relative pulls on their mentality of, on the one hand, feudal loyalty, and, on the other hand, internal withdrawal into silent, secret dissidence. No doubt the composition of the mix varied greatly from time to time and area to area. Other elements of the subculture (shrines, holy wells, wonder-working images, relics, charms and prayer formulas) were, though baptised into the fringes of orthodox Catholicism, still barbaric and often wildly superstitious. The reactions of the poor were probably like those of Russian peasants in 1905–22, ultimately mysterious to their betters. Individuals and groups could display, on occasion, a simple and profound Christianity; others could react with indifference and savagery towards the clergy. Most of the time the majority probably showed an outward servile respect for the Church rituals and for the clergy as wonder-workers. We must presume that mass church-going by the poor was a strong habit reinforced by immemorial custom, public opinion and the organisation of life; but we can suspect that there was always an undertow of laxity and non-attendance. The evidence provided by old parish churches is scanty and misleading. The survival of so many of them, and so many fragmentary structural relics of the pre-Reformation past, is deceptive. We tend to forget how many churches have vanished, and how many have been restored out of all recognition. The Victorian Gothic revival, neo-medievalist restorations or reconstructions produced a tidy, aseptic, romantic result which bore little resemblance to the late medieval actualities. In 1534 the big, elaborately decorated churches of wealthy parishes, ecclesiastical corporations and religious communities with literate worshippers were, for all their home-made, garish fittings, images and wall-paintings, mud and dirt, fine centres of local pride. But many churches and chapels of poor rustic or town communities must have been dirty, ramshackle and uninspiring.

Higher up the social pyramid came the twenty per cent who, by their wealth and modicum of literacy, stood to some extent apart from the poor subculture. Just as the poor were divided by many slight but powerful clefts between area and area, types of employment and degrees of poverty, so the literate must have been elaborately divided and cross-divided by distinctions between clergy and laity; aristocracy, gentry and plebeians; town and country; employers and employees. By modern standards, Tudor English society was very thin on the ground indeed, and yet elaborately hierarchical and intensely class-conscious. To a modern mind there is a puzzling contradiction about the attitude to life of the Tudor literate. On the one hand the material place which religion occupied in their lives seems to have been enormous. The average amount of church-going they took for granted far exceeded that of even the very devout today. There were a great many holidays of obligation, the respectable often went to Mass on ordinary weekdays, all Fridays were black fasts and Saturdays fish-days, Lent was kept with great rigidity and austerity. Ordinary conversation and letters were habitually thickly laced with religious expressions. Yet, on the other hand, their daily lives were so uninhibitedly secular, so intensely preoccupied with the material business of living, that both Catholic and Protestant modern historians have often accused them of gross materialism or 'an incapacity for sustained conviction'. Here surely, say the historians, we have all the signs of a real religious culture in decay, something parallel to, say, the religious formalism and Puritan earnestness of mid-nineteenth-century sceptics, or the Irish attitudes revealed in James Joyce's *Ulysses* and *The Dubliners*. This is a dangerous assumption. It romanticises the religious culture of the high middle ages, which was not nearly so simple and other-worldly as we imagine. Religious cultures and human psychology are immensely complex and changing things. When Thomas Cromwell, the arch-political boss and man of affairs of the sixteenth century, was under grave stress, he was found in a window-recess in floods of tears, 'saying our Lady Mattins'. We have no real reason to believe that his gesture was insincere.

Another apparent contradiction about the behaviour of the Tudor literate lay in their deserved reputations in Europe both for violent dissidence and for respectable conformism. In the early fifteenth century they had given Europe Wycliffite Lollardy, its first genuine heresy for some centuries; yet English polite society had driven it underground very successfully. Continental visitors to early sixteenth-century England noted both the violence and the outstanding decency and seemliness in the practice of religion amongst the literate. They actually queued for Mass, they kept relatively quiet during it, saying their rosaries or conning their books of devotion, they crowded to sermons, which they adored. We can guess that two forces contributed to produce this orderly seemliness. The first was a strong desire amongst the literate for respectability, all the stronger because of the underlying current of violence and dissent. The respectable held aloof from the barbarities of the poor. If they were Church administrators they waged an unending (and usually unsuccessful) battle to prune away the more glaring and scandalously disorderly habits of the poor: for instance drinking, dancing and mumming in churchyards and even churches, mockery of the clergy, sexual irregularities. The respectable were afraid, with good reason, of popular movements uncontrolled by the clergy and magistrates. They struggled, with some moderate success, to keep the poorer parochial clergy from becoming totally assimilated to village communities, by insisting on clerical celibacy and a modicum of clerical education and professional competence. The respectable insisted on the duty of unquestioning obedience to constituted authority. Whatever their private opinions about the ultimate basis of royal, episcopal and Papal authority (as the law of God, or simple social necessity), they set a high value on it as an essential reinforcement of local officialdom. Religious faith and practice, and the continued existence of a powerful, well-organised, property-owning Church (as employers and auxiliary local officials) was then a vital part of the backbone of law and order. The respectable idea that a well-organised, richly-endowed Church was the main buttress of civilisation was then hard commonsense, and by no means necessarily a dilution of genuine religious faith.

The other force making for seemliness amongst the literate was 'devotion'. In a sense pre-Reformation Catholicism was one vast monastery, organised so as to inculcate in and demand of everyone an intense devotional life. The clergy—perhaps 35,000 in number—of whom half lived in religious houses and a good many others in colleges of canons, teachers, or chantry priests, were all bound to celibacy, an austere life, and the choir recitation of the Divine Office at great length. The laity, as we have already seen, were bound to church-going and ascetic devotional practices on a scale which would make most moderns wilt. For the vast majority, clergy, monks and laity alike, this great burden of ritual could be tolerable only because long practice had made it utterly familiar, because they expected that serving God would be at least as physically arduous and full of repetition as their daily manual work, and because the official Latin services had long ago forced into them an unofficial people's part. During the Mass or the Office the illiterate and semi-literate were expected to say the Rosary and perform their devotions before images; the fully literate could pray from English books of devotion; the priest at the altar served God by the sheer labour of getting through the difficult Latin; the simple monk in choir was expected to have the same attitude to the endless psalmody, or, per-haps, to meditate on truths of the faith while voicing the Latin. This formed the ordinary basic devotion. We have simply no idea how far it was really executed in practice, or how effective it was in pro-ducing real prayer. Manifestly it could, and did—especially in ill-run monasteries and convents—produce boredom and distaste. Since the twelfth century, sophisticated and well-educated people had sought both to get the collar of servitude of the long liturgy substantially reduced, and to develop new forms of unofficial devotion, either of systematic meditation or of meditative reading of Scripture. Hence in 1534 there were a good many different types of the devout in England. There were very simple illiterates who flourished on the ordinary devotion. There were deeply pious innocents who, like Margery Kemp of King's Lynn, spent their lives in incessant pil-grimages to shrines. There were, both inside and outside monasteries, innocents who were given to dreams, portents and visions; such were Elizabeth Barton, the 'nun of Kent', the Carthusian monk-visionaries of Mount Grace in Yorkshire, or Thomas Parkinson, the Yorkshire small-town butcher who abandoned married life after a highly sym-bolic vision and became an anchorite. There were highly educated men like the judge, Thomas More, who became detached from, and severely critical of, ordinary devotion, and pinned his faith in systematic meditation and Scripture reading, preferably in Greek.

So pre-Reformation English Catholicism meant a complexly inter-woven structure, incorporating the subculture of the poor, respectability, and the many forms of devotion. It was hardly surprising that different strands should have overlapped and influenced each other. Even the poor, to some degree, must have felt the influence both of orthodox respectability and of devotion, much as, in nineteenth-century parishes earnest Evangelical or High Church incumbents sometimes made an impact on the normally silent withdrawnness of the poor parishioners. The respectable and the devout must often have overlapped. Even so intellectual a man as Thomas More could display at various times in his career, or even simultaneously, the radical new devotion of *Utopia* or the *Letter to a Monk*, and the traditionalism of occasionally putting on a surplice and taking his place with the clergy in his Chelsea parish church choir for the Office. There are distinct traces in his writings of popular religious superstition, and ferociously respectable defences of the Catholic Establishment against Lutheran heresy. This Catholicism was apparently a strange mixture of soggy inertia and passionate dynamism, of unthinking and incoherent conservatism and of searching radicalism or savage dissent. It was a phenomenon about which there could never be any simple clear-cut judgment.

The reaction of this Catholic society to Henry VIII's breach with the authority of the Pope, destruction of the major religious shrines, and dissolution of all the monasteries and convents probably caused less surprise to contemporaries than it has done to modern historians. The poor (eighty per cent of the population) appear to have shown no coherent reaction at all. That is hardly surprising, since there was practically no change in religion as they experienced it. The dissolution of the monasteries did produce a massive change in land-ownership, but neither this nor the dispersion of the relatively small staffs of monastic servants can have had any major effect on the lives of most of the poor. But the literate minority—or, at least, very large sections of its lower grades—reacted sharply to the changes. Between 1534 and 1547 there were demonstrations, a great deal of angry talk, and even the furtive distribution of seditious handbills over wide areas of the country. A few hundred clergy departed to Scotland or the Continent. Typical of these was perhaps the Dominican Prior of Newcastle-on-Tyne, who fled to Scotland, leaving behind him on his desk a strongly-worded letter of protest against the King's religious policies. The Crown had to use armed force to suppress four major demonstrations in arms, in Lincolnshire and in Yorkshire and Lancashire in 1536, in Norfolk in 1537, and again in Yorkshire in 1541. The risings of 1536 very likely involved most of the literate and semi-literate of the large counties concerned. We can hardly be in any doubt that some fifteen per cent of the population (and three-quarters of the important literate class) voted for the retention of the main features of traditional Catholicism, and were intelligent enough to perceive the issues involved. This is an impressive fact. But just as impressive are other features of the protest. Relatively few of the top five per cent of the population, the landed gentry and aristocracy, took any part in the protest. Their absence deprived it of natural leaders and, more than any other reason, doomed it to failure.

The protesters were relatively mild in their objections. Few of them were prepared to die for the Papacy. Even amongst those many who had some feeling for it, the great majority simply could not see it as a matter of fundamental religious faith: humanly-established and long-proved bulwark of the traditional order, yes: but not a divinely-given absolute. The northern demonstrators of 1536 assembled a Parliament of learned clergy at Pontefract. Their debates on the Papacy showed wide differences of opinion. The demonstrators also clearly felt strongly about the dissolution of the monasteries. The Lincolnshire men would have been content to halt the process of dissolution, and did not defend the smaller houses which had already gone. The northern men however wanted all the houses retained or restored. As they explained, in their remote and very thinly populated part of the country religious houses fulfilled a good many purely social and economic functions, as safe-deposits, hotels, churches for local people where parish churches were few and far-between, havens for younger daughters without adequate dowries, burial places where graveyards were few and distant. In general the protesters simply saw monasteries as bulwarks of a traditional socio-religious order. From a purely religious point of view they were simply super parish churches, maintaining the ordinary devotion of the serving of God by the hard labour of the liturgy.

Of the few hundred people who, during these years, defended the Papacy to the point of dying or suffering exile for it, only a small minority seems to have held to what is the modern official Roman Catholic view of the Papacy. Most of them took their stand on the traditional Catholic principles of the organic, international unity of the Catholic Church, and the authority of the clergy over religious matters. Even Thomas More basically took this position. For him so important a change as a rejection of Papal authority could be decided only by the clergy (not by a lay Parliament), and ultimately by the supreme international clerical authority, a General Council of the Church. As a royal judge of distinction, his whole training impelled him to defend order and the due courses of law at any price. The breach with Rome was clearly a unilateral repudiation of the traditional legal framework of European society, and that by Parliament, the jurisdiction of which in such matters was, by traditional law, *ultra vires.* As a younger man More had been a radical: he had considered that the Papal monarchy over the universal Church was merely based on Positive Church law (that is, a human contrivance based on consent and utility), and that its utility was now gravely in doubt. Later in life, and as the Crown's chief law officer faced with the disruptive influence of Continental Protestantism in its early days, he had come to believe that the Papal monarchy had much more to be said for it on grounds of utility: its very legal existence seemed to provide the only possible defence against religious chaos. Nevertheless More went to his death still asserting the primacy of Church General Councils over the Pope, and, at any rate by inference, refusing to say that the Papacy was established directly by the law of God.

The bishops, learned and ordinary parish clergy, the landed gentry and the peers, who formed the official and best-educated sections of the literate, offered practically no resistance to, or vocal criticism of, the King's religious policies. This was not because they were, to any really major or serious extent, already affected by radical Catholic Dissent or Protestantism. As early as the 1560s devout Protestant publicists were researching into the origins of their religion in England. It was their cherished belief that, at least in an embryonic form, Protestantism must have had a substantial, if underground, existence throughout the middle ages. John Foxe, whose *Acts and Monuments* ('Foxe's Book of Martyrs') became standard Protestant family Sunday reading for the well-to-do down to the nineteenth century, put a good deal of time and energy into research, drawing upon bishops' court registers and upon living witnesses whose memories carried back to the 1530s. Yet even he could not make a mountain out of a molehill. In 1547, when Henry VIII died, convinced Protestants were relatively few amongst any section of the literate. Protestantism was not, as Foxe would like to have believed, original Christianity, but a new, German ideology. The English who felt its influence up to 1547 were mostly academics, merchants and workers in the cloth industry, who all had natural links with the Continent. Admittedly, by 1547, some catch-phrases (describing the old devotion as 'Mumpsimus' or 'Pharisaism' or 'popery') common to both radical Catholic reformism and Protestantism were tending to become fashionable amongst the literate. But this fact in itself did not necessarily—any more than certain fashionable Left-wing phrases today—mean that the users had gone over to full-blooded, dogmatic dissent.

But if the English official class had not, in the main, gone Protestant, why did it offer no resistance to Henry VIII? Some historians have suggested a religious degeneracy or slump, which rendered

B

them 'incapable of sustained conviction'. Others have maintained
that this entire class, and even the peerage, were demoralised by
contemporary spiralling inflation and by their dependence on the
Crown for a great part of their livelihood. But neither of these
theories seems to get to grips with the real complexities of the situation. Ignorance, slackness and cowardice certainly existed, perhaps
more intensely than we can readily imagine, precisely because traditional Catholicism demanded so stiff a standard of devotion. But
there also certainly existed, as the essential background to these
faults, a general social climate of religiosity, of moral and spiritual
principledness of an intensity and thoroughness quite beyond our
own experience. Considering all this, it is surely very likely that the
official class judged that the King was not upsetting the fundamentals
of their religion: he was pruning away what contemporary radically-
minded Catholic intellectuals called *adiaphora*, that is details to be
fixed by human convenience (the Papacy, shrines and religious
houses). In the main the official class could not conceive of true
religion *without* some equivalent of these details, but they would not
feel bound in conscience to make an ultimate stand about retaining
the traditional forms of them. Hence they must have had very mixed
feelings about the King's policies. There is plenty of evidence that
they were in real doubt.

The monasteries could, pretty certainly, never have been dissolved
if their inmates had stood fast and joined in with a general lay movement of protest. But when it came to the point, the overwhelming
majority of the monks, friars and nuns displayed the same temper of
mind as the rest of the official class. They quietly acquiesced in the
Dissolution, refused outright to give countenance to the lay protests,
and made little effort, then or thereafter, to return voluntarily to
monastic life. A handful of them protested vocally; a few travelled
abroad to continue community life in a Catholic country; perhaps
half of them would have opted, if the Dissolution had been partial, to
continue community life in their own or some other religious houses
in England. Was this the result of a massive loss of nerve and prodigious moral and spiritual collapse? The greatest modern historian
of the Dissolution believes that it was. But his judgment was much
coloured by the fact that he was himself a Catholic monk of an extremely austere and contemplative cast of mind. Other historians
have suggested that ignorance and fear played a large part in the
surrender. The religious must have been, in the main, mentally
more dependent than any other class. We know that the government
played skilfully on their occupational weak points by a mixture of
offers of pensioned retirement, threats, and imposition of an un-
bearable discipline on those who stayed. This is all true, but such

methods would not have had so complete an effect if the bulk of the religious had not been already consciously or unconsciously persuaded that it was impossible to defend their way of life with absolute conviction. It is noticeable that the few small groups of religious who *did* display absolute conviction all belonged to very untypical communities. All of them were relatively recent foundations, populated by an *élite* who, in a modern fashion, had chosen their calling freely in adult life, and whose common rule of life had about it usually a radically new devotion flavour. The Carthusian monks, Observant Franciscans and Bridgettines specialised in contemplation. Syon was a wholly unusual new devotion community of scholars. But the vast majority of religious in the older Orders were wedged immovably into a highly complex traditional setting binding them to an antiquated way of life, to the old devotion, ancient disciplines, multiple ties with local society, huge loads of plant and buildings. With reduced communities and more fast-moving minds than their ancestors they had long ago slipped into a host of semi-official mitigations and relaxations. The weight of their obligations, social custom and the vested interests of the secular clergy barred them from any comprehensive and large-scale modernisation. They were in a very real dilemma. Throughout Europe, sixteenth-century experience was to prove conclusively that there was no totally effective way of modernising this host of old Orders. Church legislation and grass-roots initiatives could and did found many new, modernised Orders, or create within the old ones certain half-modernised groups of communities. But, even in Catholic countries, many of the old houses had their problems eventually solved only by natural collapse or dissolution by Church authority.

To some extent the Dissolution *was* tragic: as the demise of a very old English institution, of many fine buildings and a host of local arrangements and loyalties. A visit to the ruins of Tintern or Rievaulx is a depressing experience. Even convinced Protestants have, since the later sixteenth century, felt the depression. In the early seventeenth century Sir Henry Spelman wrote a book to show that the Dissolution was sacrilege, and that a curse had fallen on all the families who bought ex-monastic property. Eventually Protestantism fostered legends of monastic loose-living and long underground tunnels connecting monasteries with neighbouring convents. But it also fostered an equal number of local legends of the benevolence and skills of the old monks. Long before the fashionable romantic medievalism of Scott's day, there were solid Protestants who saw the Dissolution as the cause of inflation and rampant commercialism. On the other hand we can be certain that, had England remained a Catholic country, the religious houses would have undergone at least some radical change eventually as they did, for instance, in Italy or France. Today the abbeys of Tintern and Rievaulx would have vanished totally or would have been replaced by baroque or nineteenth-century stucco and brick monasteries. Moreover the tragedy was hardly final. We tend to forget that today, relative to the population then and now, England contains more religious houses, Catholic and Anglican, than it did in 1534. Lastly the Catholic-minded showed little reluctance to join in the sixteenth-century rush to buy ex-monastic property. The average Catholic landowning family of the seventeenth century, and its picturesque mansion, rested, to some extent, on profitable exploitation of such property. Some Catholic gentry of the sixteenth and seventeenth centuries showed a religious feeling for ruined monasteries and shrines: a few (for instance St Winifred's Well in Wales and the Lady Chapel at Mount Grace in Yorkshire) were restored to Catholic religious use. But it was only in the mid nineteenth century, under the influence of romantic neo-medievalism, Walter Scott and Pugin, that some Catholic landowners began to have scruples of conscience and sell, or convey to religious Orders, ex-monastic property in their possession.

As we have suggested, at the death of Henry VIII in 1547, the great majority of the English literate would most probably have thought of themselves as genuine Catholics. But in England as very widely on the Continent, religious distinctions must have been very blurred and uncertain. Traditional Catholicism shaded imperceptibly into reformist Catholicism, and that into a Protestantism which was still a very divided and tentative movement, by no means decisively separated from radical Catholicism. In one sense England still was a Catholic country: in another sense (as seen in terms of the strict letter of Roman Canon Law) Catholicism had ceased to exist: there must have been exceedingly few worshipping communities of English in full communion with Rome either in England or abroad. In the next thirty years (1547–77) the country underwent no less than four religious revolutions carried out by successive governments. The first, in 1547–9, replaced traditional Catholic worship by a new, English liturgy which modern dogmatic Protestants and Catholics see as a mongrel halfway house between traditional Catholicism and pure Protestantism. The second revolution, in 1550–3, imposed a religion and worship which we today would regard as sharply and austerely Protestant. The third revolution, of 1553–8, ordered a return to traditional Roman Catholicism. Lastly, in 1559–6, Queen Elizabeth's government ordered a settlement which lay halfway between the Catholic–Protestant compromise of 1547–9 and the extreme Protestantism of 1550–3. Long ago Church historians who were ardent protagonists for either Protestantism or Catholicism have analysed and sifted the scanty evidence of people's reactions to these rapid changes. Indeed it was often the protagonists who took care to collect and preserve the documents. Looked at objectively, it is clear both sides found the evidence very disappointing. It appears that the majority of the people simply sat out all the changes without strong reaction. Even by 1561 Protestantism was still not a united force, sharply and totally distinct from radical reformist Catholicism. It achieved no major breakthrough. A prominent Yorkshire politician, who had occupied important positions throughout the revolutionary years and had known Catholicism and Protestantism from the inside, gave it, in the 1560s, as his considered judgment that Protestantism was much less forward then than in the 1550s. Catholicism was also beset by doubts, divisions and a hazy frontier with moderate Protestantism. Even amongst the most educated we repeatedly come across cases of confused reactions and marked changes of opinion.

For instance, John Jewel and Thomas Harding were west country schoolfellows and contemporaries at Oxford. In the 1530s, as young Fellows of Colleges, both moved through reformist Catholicism to acceptance of the government policies of the 1540s and 1550–3. When the Catholic reaction began in 1553 the friends met at Salisbury to discuss their religious beliefs. Jewel, hitherto a pupil of Peter Martyr, an Italian Protestant academic, had been the more extreme Protestant of the two. He now confessed lurking doubts, declared that Providence (by bringing a Catholic to the throne) had declared His will, and professed himself now a traditionalist Catholic. Harding, on the contrary, now professed a very resolute Protestantism and readiness to suffer for its beliefs. Yet, within months, Jewel reverted to strong Protestantism and left England, eventually to return in 1559 to be Bishop of Salisbury and to write a classical defence of Anglicanism. Harding, for his part, declared his conversion to orthodox Catholicism, retired into exile in 1559 and wrote, in Louvain, a classical defence of his new faith. The most socially distinguished English cleric of the age (and perhaps its most widely-known theologian) was Reginald Pole, a cousin of Henry VIII. In the 1530s, in his university rooms in Padua in Italy, he simultaneously condemned Henry's breach with Rome and defended something so akin to the new German theology that he was later delated to Rome for Protestant heresy. Yet by the 1550s Pole was the Pope's Cardinal-Legate in England and a pillar of traditionalist Catholic orthodoxy. Robert Pursglove, a Yorkshireman, head of a religious Order, and a suffragan bishop before 1540, readily accepted the breach with Rome and dissolution of the monasteries. Throughout Edward VI's reign, when Catholic reformists generally (but by no means universally) expressed doubts about government policy or resisted it, Pursglove cooperated fully as an active bishop in the new order. During Queen Mary's Catholic reaction he readily went over to orthodox Roman Catholicism. In 1559 he refused cooperation with a Protestant order rather less extreme than that of 1550–3 which he had accepted. For the rest of his life he stuck to a reformist Catholic position which allowed occasional conformity to Anglicanism and aloofness from the Papacy: it is by no means clear that he died in communion with Rome. We could easily prolong our list of people whose religious opinions wavered: what of Archbishop Cranmer (whose many elaborately—if obscurely—documented changes of front offer an insoluble historical puzzle), Bishop Hugh Latimer (who at least twice recanted the Protestantism for which he eventually died at the stake), Bishops Tunstall, Gardiner, Thirlby and Cheyney (whose variations used to fascinate historians), Thomas Cromwell (whose real religious opinions are still debated), John Dudley, Duke of Northumberland (who was responsible for the extreme Protestant revolution of 1550–3, but who shortly afterwards professed himself a Catholic on the scaffold)?

As religion in England settled down in 1559–70, after the revolutionary years, we get two reports by highly intelligent and educated observers of the moral and spiritual state of the bulk of the population. Though one observer, Augustine Baker, was a Catholic convert from Protestantism, and the other, William Perkins, a very Puritan Protestant, their findings are in substantial agreement. Perhaps this may not be so surprising, since comparatively little divided their outlooks and even their doctrinal views. Both wrote in the 1590s, but looking back to the days of their youth. As converted Christians and intellectuals both, in spite of some humane sympathy, had little that was good to report: very many, both landowners and poor, were fast sinking into being 'beastly neutrals' or even 'atheists'. As Perkins put it, they commonly grumble: 'that it was a good world when the old Religion was, because all things were cheap.' Under stress 'they still swear, By the Mass! B'our Lady!' In their cups they say 'a man eats his Maker in the Sacrament'. But this is only talk, and perhaps contains a dig at parsons and officialdom. Indeed they admit freely that it now means nothing 'since the Mass is gone and our Lady is gone'. As for the Sacrament, neither before nor after the Reformation were they what Thomas Hardy the novelist called 'Communion folk'. Their real religion is, says Perkins, respectability: salvation is automatic provided you put in a fair number of church-attendances, avoid murder, serious theft and open adultery. 'Devotion' is for parsons. Baker, as a Catholic could not help taking a somewhat more hopeful view of this post-Catholicism, since he knew of some cases (for instance his own father) where the Catholic habits opened the way to a death-bed reconciliation with orthodox Catholicism. But, on the other hand, as a converted Roman Catholic he felt that post-Catholicism was a gross scandal and, to his view of the workings of Providence, sin and human psychology, usually more toughly resistant to Catholic conversion than outright Protestantism. The devout then were very pessimistic about human capabilities. Hooker (an Anglican divine) and Persons (a Jesuit), contemporaries of Baker and Perkins, judged the English, in spite of all outward appearances of church-going, to be probably the most irreligious of nations; even their religious enthusiasms were often inspired by secular motives.

The Church legal court-books give some local colour to these reports. The old subculture was still alive. Here is an Anglican archdeacon on religious practice in Weaverham, Cheshire:

> Ther is in the church an altare standing undefaced. There lacketh a lynnon cloth and coveringe for the Communion table. The parishioners refuse the perambulacion. The people will not be staied from ringinge the bells on All Saints Daie. They frequent alehowses in service tyme. Great Talkinge used in the churche. No levyinge for the poor of the absents from the churche. Morres Daunces and rushe bearinge used in the churche. Jane, an old nun, is an evell woman and teacheth false doctrine. They refuse to communicate with usuall breade. None cometh to the Communion iij tymes a yere. They refuse to bringe ther yowth to be catechised. Crosses are standinge in the churche yearde.

Compare Sherburn, in the East Riding of Yorkshire, where, in 1569, parishioners insisted on performing the old dances and mummeries inside the church. Their ring-leader was a housewife, Katherine Lacy, who certainly, like all the rest, attended church regularly. But she 'conveyed away' the Sacrament when she communicated (rarely) and dropped it furtively on the floor. She insisted that 'it was a good tyme when the old religion was', and would not give up praying to our Lady and the saints, kissing the font stone when she came to be purified after childbirth, and kissing the paten or Communion book when 'she made her offeryng'. Or there was the great minster church at Ripon in Yorkshire, where the authorities in 1567 found the outlying parts of the building tightly packed with the old Catholic fittings, preserved though dismantled. The parishioners were notoriously oldfashioned in behaviour and the five clergy went along with them. They used forbidden wafer-breads at the Communion and were suspected of occasionally saying Latin Masses. One cleric was 'of very dissolute life and lewd conversation; he useth very undecent apparell, namelie great britches drawen unto with sarcenett and taffitie and great Ruffes laid upon with laces of golde and silver'. He 'useth to daunce verie offensivelie at alehowses and mariages in the presence of Comon people'. He combined his post at Ripon with a private chaplaincy to a northern peer, Lord Latimer. Latimer was rated as a scurrilous atheist. Several ladies of his family, including his wife, appear to have been convinced Protestants. He had another chaplain to whom he was devoted, and who was in trouble with the authorities for rampant extreme Protestantism. Yet Latimer was currently being prosecuted in the York Church courts for maintaining no fewer than eleven concubines.

What had happened, by the 1570s, to the old tradition of respectable and devout Catholicism? Manifestly, early English Protestantism grew up within this tradition and then burst out of it, carrying away a good many of its most lively and ardent spirits. If the Catholic protest movement of the 1530s and 1540s contained a full quota of innocents, visionaries and devout persons, the Protestant 'Marian martyrs' of the 1550s surpassed it with their array of the same psychological types. Manifestly also, once in political power, Protestantism clothed itself in the mantle of Establishment respectability. Many Catholic-minded respectables succumbed to Elizabethan Protestant use of this mantle and conformed outwardly to Anglicanism. A sectarian existence seemed to them intolerable, a Catholic military revolution practically impossible and morally repulsive, and a decent conformity to the single national religious Establishment a grave duty in conscience. Most of the thin and patchy documentary evidence for this period shows that 'Church-papistry' (as it was then called) of this kind was extremely widespread, and 'Papist recusancy' (complete refusal to go to Anglican services) comparatively rare.

The vast majority of the clergy had Catholic Orders; relatively few of them quitted their Church livings as a matter of Catholic conscience. It is true that almost the entire bench of Catholic bishops in 1558 did refuse to serve the Elizabethan Protestant Church Establishment. Admittedly most of them spent the rest of their lives in a state (often allowing of much contact with society and some freedom of movement) of house-arrest. Yet, as a class, they were very far from being martyrs for the cause of orthodox Roman Catholicism. They made no effort whatever to build up an underground, sectarian Catholic organisation; they did not protest against Catholic-conformism (indeed some of them appear to have connived at the practice). They waited passively for 'a change of religion'. They proved a serious embarrassment to the militant Catholic minority. So far as we know the great majority of the clerical managerial class carried conformism much further. So, for instance, John Woodward was a priest-fellow of Merton College, Oxford, throughout the official Protestantism of Edward VI's reign. By 1560–1 he was very comfortably wedged within the Anglican Establishment. He held in plurality a canonry of Gloucester Cathedral, benefices in Essex, Kent and elsewhere, and a private chaplaincy to a peer, Lord Petre, who was ostensibly a Catholic-minded conformist. In 1565–6 Woodward voluntarily resigned all his posts except the chaplaincy, and in 1577 he left England to join a colony of English Catholic exiles in France. Richard Petre, a son of his patron, was a massive pluralist, who retained canonries at York, Salisbury and Peterborough Cathedrals until 1571, when he was deprived of them for flight abroad to a Catholic country. Francis Mallet was a priest with an unusually consistent record of devoted, orthodox Roman Catholicism in Henry VIII's and Edward VI's reign. He served Mary Tudor as chaplain before and after her accession to the throne, and was made dean of Lincoln Cathedral by her. Yet he demonstrated sufficient conformity to Elizabeth's Anglican Establishment to ensure his tenure of the deanery, undisturbed, to his death in 1570. Thomas White was a highly successful academic, who retained the wardenship of New College, Oxford (together with an archdeaconry, two canonries and a benefice) solidly from 1553 to 1573. We can be reasonably sure that these cases were normal, and that, throughout the religious revolutions of 1534–70, resignations of, or deprivations from, clerical posts for religious reasons were exceptional.

It is very unlikely that the parochial clergy behaved otherwise. Recent patient detective work, helped by unusual good luck, has unearthed a very full documentary record of one such country priest in East Yorkshire. He served his cure faithfully, without protest or rebuke from his superiors, throughout all the religious revolutions and died ostensibly a good Anglican pastor. He subscribed to a succession of doctrinal formulas, some Protestant, some Catholic. He was a man of lively intelligence and some education. His extensive private papers show that he consistently and strongly favoured the Catholic side. So far as we know he never felt serious qualms of conscience. Some of these clergy secretly celebrated Latin Catholic services, but it seems that this was a rare practice.

The lay counterpart of these Church-papist clergy was an unknown, but apparently fairly substantial, number of landowning peers and gentry of conservative religious views. In England, as throughout Europe, some degree of religious nonconformity was made easy

by the long-standing custom (with a legal backing) that such people,
their households and servants, might worship privately in house- or
manorial-chapels, provided they attended their parish churches on the
major festivals. Moreover the greater landowners were inevitably
peripatetic, so it was very hard for authority to keep a check on their
religious practice. Can we therefore imagine that, in 1559–70, a
multitude of manor house private chapels throughout England supported islands of complete Catholic worship and sacraments in a
Protestant country? The evidence is exceedingly thin and shadowy.
We should most probably be right in thinking that such islands did
exist, but that at this period they were unusual. Possibly the Catholic
nonconformity in most chapels even of families with Catholic leanings were limited to an occasional Latin Mass celebrated with extra
secrecy while the normal course of services followed the English
Book of Common Prayer, and perhaps daily family prayers from a
Latin Primer while devout older people read Our Lady's Mattins or
said their rosaries. Moreover the overwhelming majority of such
families obeyed the law and attended Anglican services at their
parish churches. Strongly Protestant officials called people who
practised such things 'the Lady Mattins lot' or, simply, 'Papists',
distinguishing them from real Protestants (who would use the *Book
of Common Prayer* with very Evangelical extras). Beneficed clergy
(who not infrequently earned extra money by doubling as house-
chaplains to local gentry) had everything to lose by indulging in
systematic nonconformity. There was a small 'pool of clerical
labour', unemployed, poor curates who, on occasion, scraped a
living not only by supplying Anglican services for sick incumbents,
but by secretly saying Latin Masses or sacramental rites for real, or
superstitious, conservatives. There were genuinely recusant unemployed clergy (definite Catholics). They were usually living under
police supervision. Some of these very likely conducted Latin
Catholic worship on occasion, but they had, perforce, to live in a
society where degrees of conformism by Papists were utterly usual,
and they seem to have accepted the situation philosophically. They
had no real hope of establishing completely Catholic worshipping
communities on any scale. As we have seen, they were very likely
unsure whether it was right even to make the effort to do so. The
Papist landowners were living in a time of economic stress, when they
were dependent on the favour of their betters and the government in
multiple ways, for offices of profit, advancement, and favourable
verdicts in lawsuits. In the long run, even in that very laxly-
administered England, these considerations and the slow, complex
grindings of the mills of authority, made it practically difficult to be
a landowner and a complete Catholic recusant. Indeed, both at this

period and later, the sheer force of social respectability seems to have made Catholic nonconformists feel that they must somehow compensate for their nonconformity by an extra show of civic obedience in affairs that they deemed just less than fundamental.

The number of Catholic recusants (those who refused to go to church), complete and obstinate nonconformists who cut themselves off totally from Anglicanism, seems to have been tiny during these years. They were the focus of official attention and investigation, so there is a disproportionately large body of evidence of their behaviour and views compared with that of the ordinary conformist Papists. It obviously required an out-of-the-ordinary strength of mind, courage or perversity to embrace a course of action which the vast majority (and even the Papists) regarded as spiritually and morally dubious. It seems clear that most recusancy during these years when it was unfashionable was the result of an intense religious conversion from conformism or Protestantism. The convert was a lonely person, with an impulsion to justify his behaviour both to himself and to his friends (mostly conformists), and to prove that he was not an antisocial anarchist or rebel against all law and authority. Henry Cumberford was perhaps a fair example. He spent all his early life as a student and teacher at St John's College, Cambridge, a very large and lively college at the centre of academic discussion of the religious issues of the day. He compromised repeatedly, while puzzling over the problem of truth in religion. By 1559 he was ready to commit himself to uncompromising Catholic orthodoxy. He lost his university and Church posts and became a wanderer, dependent on the charity of Papist landowner patrons. In 1571 he was arrested in the mansion of the Dowager Countess of Northumberland at Sheffield in Yorkshire. In a legal statement he defiantly affirmed 'the Masse to be good and saieth he will mayntayne the same even untill deathe . . . he affirmeth the Pope to be the supreame Head of thuniversall Churche.' The ultimate basis of his faith was not theological principle established intellectually or by historical analysis. He seems to have come back into the pre-Reformation stream of devout Catholicism, to which the heart of religion was an intense personal evangelical experience of Christ and His Grace, strengthened or mediated by both Bible-reading and visions.

To Cumberford the Latin Mass and liturgy, especially Holy Communion, were, in his personal experience, what the burning bush was to Moses, the 'fearful place' of face-to-face meeting with God. From experience of conformity he clearly knew that, for him at least, the English services of the *Book of Common Prayer* had no such charismatic effect. In his cell in a York prison, he had a vision in which he was told to read and ponder well on 'the third

chapter of Danyell'. This is the great description of King Nebuchad-
nezzar's golden image and fiery furnace. The application of its
imagery to the contemporary situation seemed obvious. In the vision
Cumberford had been told that the fiery trial of the truth in England
was 'nere an end'. He and his like were the three Hebrew children
cast into the fire for refusing to worship the golden image (Queen
Elizabeth, set over English religion in place of the Pope). Her evil
Protestant advisers would themselves be cast into the furnace, and
the recusants exalted to high power over the kingdom. Moreover
Cumberford believed that a final, cosmic struggle between Catholic
truth and Protestant evil was beginning. For instance, the old
Countess of Northumberland (very likely a conformist Papist) had
been seized by a demonic fit, from which Cumberford had sought
to release her by exorcism.

Thomas Bell's recusancy was just as remarkable. In 1569 he was
a recently ordained Anglican curate of his native parish, Thirsk in
Yorkshire. According to his own account he was not yet twenty
years old. He seems to have had no more than a grammar school
education. He and a neighbouring fellow-curate, influenced by reading an old Catholic Latin devotional book lent to them by a Thirsk
tradesman, Thomas Parkinson, began to have grave doubts whether
their Anglican ordination and the English services were true and
spiritually effective. Parkinson, who was later imprisoned for
recusancy, maintained that he had been a conformist, but had been
sacramentally reconciled to the Roman Church by some unnamed
priest. He insisted that the spiritual validity of Roman Catholicism
and the falsehood of Protestantism could be established by experience, and that a Communion bread, consecrated at a Latin Mass,
would shed real blood when pricked with a pin. (This was a very
old, pious folk legend.) Bell and his friend abandoned their cures,
and travelled to London to seek work as laymen. Failing in their
purpose, they drifted back to Thirsk and were arrested, apparently
not for outright recusancy, but for speaking against Anglicanism.
When interrogated, both young men wavered and were ready to
admit that they had been wrong. Bell's companion recanted fully
and returned to the Anglican ministry. But Bell, perhaps influenced
by Parkinson and by Cumberford, to whom he talked in gaol,
eventually swung round to defiant recusancy and professed that
'the Pope is the Byshop of Rome and supreame Heade of the
Catholique Churche and that he wolde sticke to that opynyon by
Gods grace untill deathe'. Getting tired of imprisonment, with the
help of a recusant schoolmaster-graduate who was a fellow-prisoner
and aided by books probably supplied by Cumberford, Bell decided
to challenge the York Anglican Establishment—not with any

evangelical purpose, but to force them either to sentence him to death or to release him. He wrote out his version of a dialogue between himself and his interrogators, and smuggled copies out of gaol to his friends round Thirsk. Five years later he escaped from York Castle, reached the Continent, was formally reconciled to the Roman Church and ordained priest. After a long, eventful and even dramatic career as a secret Catholic missionary in Yorkshire and Lancashire, he returned to the Anglican ministry and launched a fervent Protestant literary attack on Catholicism.

The legal statement made in 1570 by Anthony Travers explains the mere physical difficulties encountered by a would-be recusant gentleman. Travers was a landowner living near Preston in Lancashire. Until 1568 he was a complete conformist, though once, in 1564 ('in Preston churchyarde on the backside of the churche, to Sir Edmunde a blinde preiste dwellinge at Brindley'), he went to Confession, presumably in the old Catholic form. When he began to have doubts about conformism, he continued to go to church but abstained for six months from Communion. Then he took the plunge into complete Catholic recusancy. During his conformist years he had occasionally attended secret Latin Masses in private houses of friends and relations. In the two years of his recusancy, by his own acount, he managed only to attend three Masses, each time in a different house, and once he talked of religion to a 'priest'. Clearly even in the parts of Lancashire which, ten years later, contained a substantial number of recusants and Mass centres, in the 1560s there were practically no Roman Catholic worshipping communities which a recusant could join.

We can take four other fairly well documented cases of recusancy amongst landowners. Thomas Percy, Earl of Northumberland, has been traditionally regarded by Catholics as the finest example of Catholic recusancy in the 1560s and as a pure martyr for his faith. Tradition assumed that the English landowning class was essentially medieval Catholic to the core; at a time when this basic characteristic was temporarily obscured, Northumberland reasserted its spirit with unique clarity and dynamism, and rallied to 'the Revolt of the Northern Earls' in 1569 the tacit support of the bulk of the landowners and active support of all the northern ones. But the documents of his case show a far more complex and confused situation. The overwhelming majority of landowners gave no support whatever. Even in the circumscribed northern areas where Northumberland could expect major support, he and his few associates only mustered their immediate dependants (relatives, household and tenantry). Indeed, statistically the majority of the rebel force consisted of the 'musters' (local militia) of jurisdictional areas the leaders controlled only as royal officials. Although the rebels as a whole displayed papist feelings (they tore up Anglican service-books and had Mass celebrated), after the rising, with exceedingly few exceptions, they recanted, swore to accept Anglicanism, and returned to their original complete conformism. Most probably a great many of the rank and file of the rebels had only vague ideas as to the purpose of what they were doing, and were brought out by the summons of their 'muster-masters' and by the force of a strong current of economic and social unrest then flowing through the north. The country was full of alarmist rumours, anonymous broadsheets and vaguely dramatic prophecies of imminent change.

Northumberland and his associates revolted in a panic. They had prospered in Queen Mary's reign from government offices and favours. Since 1558 they had felt left out in the cold politically, and had gravitated into ineffective opposition. In 1569 they feared proceedings against them for disobedience. They were in touch with two other centres of disaffection. One was in the south and at court around the Duke of Norfolk. The other was overseas amongst a small band of English Catholic clerical exiles plotting the overthrow of Queen Elizabeth's Protestant government. Northumberland associated himself with both, though neither movement had got beyond the stage of discussion, and he himself was unsure of both their aims and the degree of his own support of them. He was a complete religious conformist until two years before the rebellion, and had then, according to his own account, been reconciled to the Roman Church after reading books written by the clerical exiles and consulting two agents sent by them. His recusancy may well have been limited to occasional conformist non-communicating. When the rebellion broke out his published declaration of intent was grandiose but vague. It makes clear that he was fighting for government office. It leaves a reader quite uncertain whether (as is more likely) he intended merely to make a demonstration of force to compel changes in the government, or whether he meant to achieve something much more revolutionary. As far as religion was concerned, the declaration hovers between merely securing toleration for (Papist or recusant) Latin Masses in private chapels, and replacing Elizabeth's Protestant government by a Catholic one headed by Mary, Queen of Scots. The rebellion was not pushed home with real determination: Northumberland fled abroad, and was only captured by an unlucky accident. He then redeemed his follies and hesitations by a gallant death, rejecting an offer of his life in return for conformism.

Sir Thomas Cornwallis of Broome in Suffolk was a prominent royal official whose family owed their wealth and station in life to commercial drive and careful conformity to prevailing government policy. Rather like Northumberland, even this conformism (political and religious alike) failed to safeguard his status after 1559, and he was similarly pushed by circumstances into contact with currents of political (the Duke of Norfolk, his local patron) and religious opposition. In 1569 this led to his arrest and interrogation. He was able to clear himself of the political charges without much difficulty. As for religion, he professed himself as now having genuine and profound difficulties of conscience. Up to 1569 he had conformed to all changes of government religious policy without fuss or real scruple of conscience. This, it seems, was for a complex set of reasons. As a layman and official, he had felt himself justified in leaving fine points of doctrine to clerical experts, and, since they were undoubtedly much divided and confused, in supporting the established principles of respectability and conformity to set a good example to the lower orders. As a thinking man, his own religion found its natural food in books of the Catholic new devotion. Like many others of his kind, he had for a long time thought it quite possible that this private religion of his would harmonise with Anglicanism. But as Anglicanism settled down and tended to acquire its own distinct form, moulded by a rising generation of clergy who were too young to have had a Catholic upbringing, Cornwallis became alarmed. On the one hand he continued for life to regard conformism to the religion of the government and society as an essential spiritual and moral principle: he detested sectarianism and abhorred rebellion. He had no sympathy with the Catholic clericalism of the exiled revolutionaries. His religion was now devout to the point that he felt no particular affection for the Latin Mass or sacramental system. But, for him, a large query stood over developing Anglicanism and its alienation from the current of Catholicism. By 1571 he brought himself (and the government) to a compromise: he conformed outwardly to Anglicanism without communicating, and he was set free from prison. By the 1580s he had again become a complete Catholic recusant. It seems certain that this was not so much due to any growing sympathy with contemporary aggressive political Catholicism as to the hardening of the aggressively Protestant temper of Anglicanism.

Sir Thomas Metham of Howden, and William Hussey of North Duffield, both in the East Riding of Yorkshire, were landowners who became recusants in the mid 1560s and who lived for some years in gaol or under house arrest in York. As such they were rarities. Metham most possibly owed his recusancy to the influence of his private chaplain, Philip Sherwood, a learned priest who had left England by 1567, and to the reading of books by the Catholic clerical exiles. The Metham family's recusancy was not entirely clear of conformism. After Sherwood's departure, although the family refused to frequent their parish church, they did invite the Anglican incumbent to perform Protestant churchings in their house-chapel. When Lady Metham gave birth to a child while under arrest in York, it was baptised by Anglican rites in a parish church. As we shall see later, the peculiar arrangements and common outlooks of sixteenth- and seventeenth-century English society always made it impossible for even the most determined of Catholic recusants to avoid some forms of participation in Anglicanism—for instance weddings, Protestant family prayers for Protestant visitors or servants, the appointment of Anglican incumbents to parishes of which the Catholic landowner owned the 'advowson', the payment of tithes and Anglican church-rates. William Hussey is a far more shadowy figure, save for the known fact that he was an extensive reader of Catholic books, both of the (now old) new devotion and of the Catholic exiles.

Cumberford, Bell, Metham and Hussey were all probably acquainted in York with a man who apparently had the distinction of being the only Catholic recusant in the 1560s in a city of some 10,000 inhabitants. This was Thomas Vavasour, a distinguished physician, and a graduate of the universities of Cambridge and Padua. He specialised as a gynaecologist, had an ante-natal clinic in York and a large practice amongst the Yorkshire country gentry, to many of whom he was related. By the 1580s he had a remarkable reputation amongst both Protestants and Catholics in the area. They attributed to him stubborn and complete Catholic recusancy since 1559, a very active lay-priesthood in York which created a recusant Catholic group of some sixty tradespeople, a lively part in the 1569 revolt of the Northern Earls, acting as agent for the militant Catholic exiles abroad, and sending abroad for training as a missionary priest his medical auxiliary, John Mush.

The reality was probably more modest. The evidence suggests that Vavasour and his wife developed gradually from conformism in 1559–67 to occasional conformity in 1567–70 (Mrs Vavasour was capable of lapsing back into non-communicating conformism temporarily even in the later 1570s), and thence to stubborn recusancy. It is unlikely that the doctor's part in the 1569 rising went beyond verbal sympathy. He certainly did not do any effective Catholic evangelism in York or elsewhere before 1570–1. The court records of 1574–80 suggest that by then he had acquired from Cumberford and the apologetic books of militant Catholic exiles, and passed on in a simplified form to some of his York patients, the same attitudes we noted in Cumberford's confessions. For all of this handful of 'Catholic nonconformists', solid experience of Protestant worship and preaching generated a rediscovery of Catholicism. They did not join any existing worshipping community of Roman Catholics with complete continuity to the medieval past: no such thing then existed. It seems unlikely that most of them (at least before 1570) were, in a legal and sacramental sense, received into (or back into) the universal Catholic Church. Such a formal reconciliation could only be performed by priests coming from overseas with special Roman authorisation: there was as yet no definite or systematic effort to send such agents to England. Again, as we have seen, it is very likely that these Catholic nonconformists had attended secret Catholic Masses—but very rarely and infrequently. In fact their Catholicism was, in 1570, largely an aspiration by individuals, and still inchoate. Its future cannot really have been very evident to intelligent observers of the English religious scene. English Protestantism was still in the making. It was quite conceivable that, by the 1580s, Catholic Nonconformity would have settled down into a High Church or Anglo-Catholic wing of Anglicanism, and that Roman Catholicism, as an organised, separate body, would have practically vanished. This is what happened in Sweden. Perhaps it was then England's natural and normal course. It is the disturbance of that course in the 1570s and 1580s which must seem extraordinary and call for special explanation.

If an English Roman Catholic community, as an organised and strong opposition to Anglicanism, was to be created in the 1570s, two factors must come into operation. The first would have to be a far larger spontaneous reaction towards Catholicism amongst conformists or definite Protestants inside England; the second a large and well-organised missionary movement to be mounted by the militant English Catholic exiles abroad. There was little sign in the 1560s that the first factor would ever operate: the second seemed equally unlikely. In the early 1560s there appeared in university towns abroad, chiefly in Flanders, small groups of English Catholic clerical exiles. They were a few hundred in number. The strength and definiteness of their rejection of Anglicanism certainly varied, as did their adhesion to Roman Catholicism. A good many of them had been ousted from university posts or canonries in England in 1559 only because of political chance: Protestant academics whom they had themselves supplanted in jobs in 1553–4 had successfully secured reinstatement by Queen Elizabeth's government. Others of the exiles, with fairly secure posts in England, had only slowly and reluctantly decided on voluntary resignation. Many of them were tonsured clerks—legally clergymen, but not ordained priests by either Catholic

or Anglican rites—when they arrived abroad. Their main preoccupation was to secure university lectureships, canonries or chaplaincies
—by no means an easy task in Catholic countries which already had
a surplus of native clergy and a prejudice against foreigners. They
had no plans for the future except to wait patiently in the hope that
yet another political revolution in England would bring the return of
the Catholic religion to control of the Church Establishment, and
so their own return to good places on the English ladder of preferment. They felt rather like lucky survivors after an atomic explosion
which had shattered their world. Hence the largest single group lived
in the university town of Louvain in two hired lodging-houses, which
they called 'Oxford' and 'Cambridge'. They filled in their abundant
leisure by reading for higher degrees and accumulating qualifications
(the priesthood amongst them) for Church posts in Flanders. A few
had also published (for export to England by the usual academic
booksellers' channels) controversial works attacking Anglicanism
and answering Anglican apologetics. (To a large extent this 'paper-
war' was narrowly personal: the English academic world was small
and the protagonists on both sides had often known each other well;
both sides were competing for the same plums of their profession.)

The intellectual and spiritual standard of this Catholic apologetic
was mediocre. Its style, tone and arguments reflected the limitations
of the writers, their mental world and their material preoccupations.
We can take as a fair example Nicholas Sander. He was a Winchester
and New College, Oxford, man, trained in Church law. But he had the
misfortune to graduate in law at Oxford in 1551, at the height of a
Protestant revolution which threatened to abolish the Church legal
system and so deprive him of his profession. The turn of fortune's
wheel in 1553 brought a Catholic revolution; his profession was
again assured. In 1558-9 the wheel turned again, and he left for
Rome with others of his trade. There he soon gained a post as secretary and legal adviser to a Cardinal, and travelled round Europe
with his master for three years. By this time he was probably well
aware that Englishmen, however able and equipped with patrons,
had a very hard road to tread to reach bishoprics on the Continent.
So he closed with an offer from his patron to find him a professorship at Louvain university. In the event the only professorship offered
was a supernumerary one in the elementary courses of theology,
not his subject. He very hastily went through the formalities of
graduating in theology and was appointed professor before the
course was finished. He had already entered the controversial lists
with a series of published attacks on Anglicanism. There is no reason
to doubt that Sander was, by now, a sincere Catholic. He was a
charitable man (at least outside legal pleadings and the lists of

theological controversy). There are fine passages and impressive arguments in his books. As we have seen, copies of them were undoubtedly used and found intellectually helpful by educated Catholic nonconformists in England. Nevertheless his work is a barrister's special pleading. If we are to believe him, his traditionalist, Catholic respectability arguments are self-evident truth; a traditional Catholic, clericalist version of the ancient respectability is the whole truth; Protestantism is obviously self-contradictory, and the source of every possible immorality. Sander's contribution to the rescue of English Catholicism was limited strictly to propaganda calculated to cause a mass withdrawal in England of obedience to Queen Elizabeth, and so a Catholic political revolution. As such it could not possibly succeed, if only because its arguments were over the heads of most English people, and ultimately only really conclusive to the narrow class of men who shared Sander's professional training and professional vested interest.

2. The Elizabethan Resurrection, 1570–1603

By 1570 Queen Elizabeth's government had good reason to feel that the real danger of major religious dissidence in England was passing, most probably for good. Catholicism was practically dying. At the other end of the range of the religious spectrum, extreme, radical Protestantism (Puritanism) appeared to be a declining, powerless minority group. Then, unexpectedly, through the 1570s, came a religious ferment or revival which gave simultaneously great accessions of manpower and ability to both nonconformist extreme parties. The Puritan movement, which was to make a profound impact on English (and eventually American) society and to play a revolutionary political role in the mid seventeenth century, owed some of its ideas to early English Protestantism, had pioneers in the 1560s, but really began life as an organised movement in the 1570s. Post-Reformation English Roman Catholicism similarly had pioneers before 1570, but its career as a coherent movement started in the 1570s. The religious ferment was hardly a mass phenomenon; its impact seems to have been limited to the universities, to graduates, the devout and the urban middle class. Yet it was a reality. Its main feature seems to have been a surge of religious idealism and sharp discontent with established Anglicanism, all of which produced vigorous discussion and numerous conversions. In Oxford and Cambridge colleges religious debate, which had been languid in the 1560s, waxed intense, and violently opposed parties divided common-rooms. Papist undergraduates could undergo a conversion to Puritanism, or Puritans swing over to Popery. The famous case of the two brothers, John and William Reynolds, who began as, respectively, a Papist and a Puritan, and then, in the heat of argument and prayer, converted each other, is possibly apocryphal. But such things could and did happen in the debate of the 1570s.

The ferment was, as is usual with such matters, by no means simply an operation of the Spirit blowing where it listed. In those years the universities, which had been in a depressed state due to the upsets of the previous quarter of a century, rapidly recovered: the numbers of admissions of students soared quickly; the proportion of young graduates queuing for fellowships and lectureships swelled and created intense friction with the university Establishment. With bewilderment and alarm, the English Catholic academic exiles found their Shangri-La invaded by crowds of opinionated young graduate and undergraduate emigrants from Oxford and Cambrige. The new-comers sometimes flourished copies of the books of Sander, Harding or Dorman (the main exile writers) and claimed to have been con-verted to Catholicism by reading them. Others talked in a confused way and their Catholicism seemed very self-made. Some grew dis-illusioned, and returned to England to seek Anglican ordination, or drifted round the Continent for years in a state of religious in-decision. Others sought reconciliation with the Catholic Church: few had had the time or occasion to take this step before leaving England. The established Catholic exiles were forced to undertake relief work —to find religious instruction, housing, money and university en-trance for the new arrivals. In 1568 a group of the original exiles, headed by William Allen, had founded a small hostel or 'English College' at the brand-new university of Douai in Spanish Flanders. The original purpose of the hostel was to copy the Oxford and Cambridge houses at Louvain, to provide cheap lodgings for English Catholics teaching or studying at university and to create a base for scholarly work and writing.

William Allen, who was later in life to be a Cardinal, Archbishop of Malines, and the official clerical head of the English Catholic Church, has occupied a special place of honour in Catholic tradition as the saviour of the English Church. In fact he seems to have been a man of very moderate ability. He was born in 1532, two years before Henry VIII began the English Reformation. He grew up inside the Henrician Church of England, went to Oxford in 1547, and as an Arts undergraduate was a conforming member of Edward VI's very Protestant Church. When Queen Mary formally reconciled England with the Pope in 1554, Allen was taking his M.A. In 1556 his college, Oriel, gave him the wardenship of a college annexe, St Mary's Hall, which housed young 'exhibitioners' (aged fourteen to eighteen). He was thus in effect a schoolmaster, engaged in keeping discipline and teaching the Arts course. In 1559, when Queen Elizabeth re-established Protestantism, Allen resigned his warden-ship, but remained in Oxford at the task of freelance tutoring poss-ibly until 1563. In that year he visited Louvain briefly and matriculated there at the university. For the next two years he was moving around England, apparently earning his living by tutoring boys. He was still not in Orders. Then in 1565 he finally went abroad, joined the ranks of the exiles permanently, and was ordained priest at Malines that year, obviously without much formal theological preparation. This is the man who, in 1568, became head of the Douai College and, willy-nilly, in the 1570s, responsible for housing, disciplining and coping with hundreds of English students and ordinands. He was forced to improvise money, teaching and accommodation in a Flanders which was deeply disturbed by civil war and in a town where the English influx was bitterly resented by the inhabitants. Meanwhile the College gradually changed its character, much more by force of circumstances than by any deliberate design on Allen's part. It became a seminary for training ordinands and despatching them to missionary work in England.

To the end of his life, Allen took a very gloomy view of the prospects of Catholicism in England. Like most of the original exiles, he held the respectable Catholic view that there was no sane and natural way to organise society other than traditional, established, compulsory Catholicism; a cloak-and-dagger, underground existence of Catholicism as a sect always seemed to his mind incomprehensible, unnatural and distasteful. He saw no real hope for the survival of the faith except through political revolution and the capture of the government, which required armed invasion by the Spaniards and an English Catholic revolt. Hence his original idea for dealing with the pack of unruly convert students foisted on him was to turn them into academics like himself, so that they would reinforce the exiles, awaiting return to staff the universities, schools and parishes of England after a successful revolution. But the flow of converts was too large for the number of university places, chaplaincies and College accommodation available in Flanders. Moreover many of the converts were (not surprisingly, considering their background) allergic to academic discipline. They had carried with them overseas not only their rooted distrust of academic authority, but their internal quarrels—between moderates and radicals, Englishmen and Welshmen—and these quarrels festered within the narrow confines of the English College and the existence of exiles. Allen tried desperately to improvise solutions to his many problems. He met the lack of money by soliciting subsidies from the Pope and, more hopefully from Philip II of Spain. The Spanish subsidy, once granted, became both essential and intensely embarrassing. Other English Catholic exiles already on the Spanish payroll complained bitterly that the College drained away most of the limited Spanish funds. Other exiles, who were either refused Spanish pensions or who disliked the

Spaniards, gravitated to the French political camp and loudly accused Allen and the College of having sold out to Spain. The English government and Protestants naturally made the same charge, and by the 1580s English law made Catholic ordination abroad and landing in England thereafter automatically treasonable. This put Allen in a fix. He personally, from his earliest days to his death, consistently supported Catholic revolutionary activity, the fomenting of rebellions in England and Spanish efforts at invasion. He saw this simply as his Catholic duty. Yet simultaneously he insisted that the College, its students, teachers and seminary priest missioners were totally innocent of involvement in such political action. Indeed, in his pamphlets defending them, he clearly stated in general that it was the Christian duty of English Catholics (especially clerics) to endure Queen Elizabeth's rule patiently, eschew rebellion, and merely await the judgment of God. Rebellion and regicide, he wrote, were the typical crimes of Protestants, who, by embracing heresy, automatically lost their hold on all decent principles. Allen's double-think was all too characteristic of good men caught in revolutionary situations. It convinced no one but Catholic militants, helped to build up the English Protestant image of Catholics as fundamentally treacherous and dishonest and badly damaged the Catholic mission to England. Nevertheless it is difficult to see how a man in Allen's place, and with his distinctive training and prejudices, could have acted differently.

Allen's solution to the problem of discipline was to streamline the College courses. Students who were already university graduates of a good standard and well-behaved were entered for higher degrees in theology at Douai university. They were destined to become teachers in the College or university. Their courses automatically qualified them for ordination as priests. As was then usual throughout Europe, they combined their studies with part-time teaching. The less capable or more fractious students received improvised crash-courses inside the College. When money was especially short and numbers large, or when students were especially troublesome, this course could last a year or even less to ordination. These ordinands were packed off to England with a small *viaticum* (journey-money) immediately after they were priested. By the mid 1580s the original flow of university converts naturally dried up, and the needs of the English mission for manpower were met by recruiting boys and young men who had had no university education or who were incapable of it. For many of these the College had to devise simplified Humanities courses and even more simplified versions of the theology crash-course.

These academic improvisations have won for Allen, in Catholic legend, the reputation of being the creator of the modern Catholic seminary courses: some historians have called the English College the first modern seminary in Europe. In reality Allen was a complete academic traditionalist. He had been bred to an old system which provided a lucky minority of ordinands with a highly academic university course and ordained them solely on the strength of this and a private short course in ritual and rubrics; the great majority was ordained after no more than a practical apprenticeship in rubrics and *pastoralia* gained from living with a poor and uneducated priest. The background to such a system was a mass practice of religion served by numerous clergy who were regarded primarily as ordinary officials, chosen with no particular regard for spiritual vocation, and ordained as a formality. This religious and social set-up remained the norm for the Catholic and Protestant parts of Europe down at least to the nineteenth century. Long before the Reformation, Catholic reformers had suggested that the system needed certain minor modifications, and had experimented with the provision of textbooks and hostels to give condensed theology and *pastoralia* courses. The large-scale clerical disarray produced by the Reformation in wide areas of Europe created for Protestants and Catholics alike an urgent need for rapid, short courses. The textbooks and experience of the pre-Reformation reformers came in handy here. Allen was simply following suit. Neither he nor the many others then training ordinands (and not even Protestants whom we might have regarded as ideologically committed to an utterly new and modern view of the Christian ministry) thought of themselves as fundamentally changing the ancient system. Both they and society, into which they were sending their newly-trained clergy, maintained and took for granted the ancient view of the position of clergymen. Indeed it is only very recently that Church authorities have begun to realise how unmodern the seminary system of 1560–1960 was, and how, in fundamentals, it reflected the religious and social state of a past age now departed.

Catholic legend has also made Allen the founding father of another feature of the seminary system, a very strict, monastic discipline enforced by spiritual sanctions. In the early days of the College, when it still contained a good many convert-graduates, Allen wrote that they had no more formal discipline than, say the Fellows' common-room of an Oxford or Cambridge college. But, by the 1580s and 1590s, things had changed. Rules were very strict; little free-time was allowed; every student had to have a spiritual director (confessor and mentor) allotted to him by the superior; reading matter and letters were censored; 'delation' (informing) by students was strongly encouraged and even made systematic; spiritual exercises abounded (highly formalised and standardised meditation, retreats carefully tailored to produce life-changing). This was not devised by Allen, but a consequence of his friendship and partnership with Robert Persons S.J. It cannot be said that if Allen had never met Persons and indeed if the Society of Jesus had never existed, the English College would have remained a relatively libertarian institution. The rather advanced new educational methods introduced by Allen were very closely associated with strict, ascetic discipline and the use by students of systematic spiritual exercises to induce a more receptive and docile frame of mind. But the new Society of Jesus was far out along this same line of development. Its short-courses were widely used even by Protestants. Its disciplinary system was secretly admired by Puritans, and Jesuits much sought after by Catholic bishops and superiors responsible for running institutions. Thus Allen quite naturally sought Jesuit help with College discipline.

Robert Persons still awaits a modern biographer, not least because his career was so very controversial. Looked at objectively, he was an ideal partner for Allen. On the one hand the two men had much in common: both were blunt country men (Allen from rural Lancashire, Persons from rural Somerset); both had been Oxford dons; both were basically traditionalist in outlook and frank supporters of Catholic revolutionaries (though both concealed this fact in writings meant for public consumption); both were converts to Catholicism. On the other hand, Persons's experience and abilities supplied deficiencies in Allen's make-up. Persons was a younger man and himself one of the wave of converts of the 1570s, knowing by experience their restlessness and ardour. As a Jesuit, Persons was trained to be flexible and adaptable; he had far more organising ability than had Allen. His Jesuit superiors allowed him much latitude and he built up a small organisation of English Jesuits with an efficient network of patrons, contacts, highly placed benefactors and informers. He had especially strong influence at the two most crucial Catholic centres in Europe, Rome and Madrid. But, like Allen, he had his difficulties. Both Catholic and Protestant tradition have credited him with great backstage power. He himself was obsessed with a feeling of powerlessness. He wanted to build up a strong English Province of the Society of Jesus. But, as a seventeenth-century English Jesuit historian lamented, the English were almost the last of the northern European countries to have a Jesuit national Province and noviciate. Even in 1600 their numbers still fell far short of the necessary total. Why were the English so reluctant to become Jesuits? Catholic tradition has laid the blame squarely on Persons's own shoulders, for his political policies, his double-think, and his reputation for underhand methods of gaining influence. Persons himself attributed the blame equally to English pragmatism or lack of intense religious fervour, and his own unselfishness in helping the English secular priest mission without deliberate recruiting for the Society from its ranks. Thus, in his view, by a self-denying ordinance, he allowed the vast majority of available English Catholic clerical manpower to be turned over to the secular priest mission run by Allen. Meanwhile the relatively thin dribble of English Jesuit vocations, for lack of a national provincial organisation, passed under the control of foreign Provincials and was, by them, scattered far and wide singly in places remote from Persons and England. So, for instance, Father William Good, a Somerset man who entered the Society in Flanders in 1562, was sent to work in Ireland, Flanders, Rome, Sweden, Poland, and Rome again, before dying in Naples in 1586. Father Thomas Derbyshire spent a long life as a Jesuit teaching in France. Father Adam Brooke was for many years rector of a Jesuit college in Vilna, Lithuania. Father Richard Storey taught in Germany, Italy and Vienna. Father John Rastell spent all his Jesuit career in Germany. Father John Stephen was sent to India, and spent thirty years in Goa. Father John Yate was sent to Brazil.

In his private letters Persons revealed what he could not in published apologias, the hair-raising difficulties of getting anything effective done for the English Catholic cause in a Rome and Madrid where it roused little interest most of the time, where governmental action was clogged by innumerable departments and factions, and in a Europe constantly upset by war and served by appallingly slow and uncertain channels of communication. Moreover the very strength and efficiency of the Society of Jesus roused everywhere a far stronger weight of virulent Catholic criticism and opposition. In such a situation, and bereft of helpers, what could Persons do but rely heavily on moral strength, on influence, superior information, careful planning and propaganda?

Allen asked for his help with the English College. Persons was able, with difficulty, to supply him with English and Flemish Jesuit spiritual directors. Then the war in Flanders and anti-English hostility in Douai forced Allen to transfer the College to Rheims in France. The Spanish subsidy was temporarily lost; it was replaced by one from the French Catholic leader, the duc de Guise. But France was in the thick of religious civil war and life there for the English students was uncomfortable and insecure. Persons gave constant help in founding overflow colleges at Rome, and at Valladolid, Madrid and San Lucar in Spain; he founded a Jesuit-run, pre-seminary school, first at Eu in Normandy, and then at St Omer in Flanders; he made arrangements for backward Rheims students to do courses of Humanities at Flemish Jesuit schools. Persons was so closely involved in rescuing and building up the whole system of clerical training that it was natural that, after Allen's death, he should have stepped into his shoes as main director of the English Mission. With good reason Persons could feel that, without his energetic work and Jesuit help, the whole seminary system and mission would have foundered. But the more its fortunes became identified with him and the Society of Jesus, the more virulent and disruptive became the anti-Jesuit movement amongst English Catholics. Certain as Persons was of the purity and integrity of his own motives and the rightness of his policies, the more certain he became that he was facing, not merely ordinary human jealousy and English factiousness, but the ultimate mystery of iniquity, the final apparent triumph of the supernatural forces of Evil which, according to Christian tradition, would precede the end of the world and the second coming of Christ.

If the life of the English clerical students in the colleges was a curious mixture of acute boredom (as Robert Southwell, a Jesuit poet and spiritual director of the English College, Rome admitted), tight discipline, ebullient revolt, intense religiosity and illness (the loss rate from consumption, fever and mental breakdown was high), what was life like on the mission for seminary priests? By 1603 some 800 priests had been sent to England, and a permanent clerical work-force of some 300 established. The first hazard to be overcome was the landing in England. In the earlier years of the mission priests were left to make their own arrangements: some chose to attempt entry through the main ports; others were dumped ashore haphazardly on south coast beaches at night. They could rely on the notorious inefficiency and venality of Tudor government officials, and take cover under an already large volume of ordinary illegal exit and entry and smuggling. Later, both the Elizabethan government and the Catholic Mission superiors developed their organisations. The government employed a small network of agents on the Continent (even planting some inside seminaries) to give advance warning of departures of priests for England, together with descriptions of their appearance. Justices of the Peace, especially in coastal areas, and customs officials were expected to maintain extra vigilance. On the Catholic side, priests were directed to especially safe entry points; coastal reception areas were sometimes organised (especially on the north-eastern coast), passes and bribes arranged. In the earlier years, once in England, priests had to depend on their own wits and resources to establish themselves in some area of work—usually in their home county. Later, a rough but fairly effective mission organisation was built up.

The country was divided into county areas, each set under the authority of a senior priest. It was his responsibility to organise a network of stations. Certainly in Yorkshire, and very likely in other areas, the normal layout was as follows: the county was divided into circuits; each circuit consisted of a number of manor- or farm-houses of families willing to receive the ministrations of priests and to contribute towards their upkeep; the circuit was served by a couple of priests who used as their base between mission tours a hired house in a central but remote place, and who made the rounds of the houses regularly. The priests were usually disguised as travelling gentry or 'chapmen' (dealers). In Yorkshire at this period it was un-usual for a priest to reside permanently in a manor-house as a family chaplain. Catholic legend has concentrated attention heavily on the family chaplains and paid little attention to the peripatetic circuit missioners. The hold of the legend has been strengthened by the publication of contemporary accounts of the mission methods of a few Jesuit priests (who undoubtedly founded 'house chaplaincy missions' in the midlands and south), and by the discovery of a good many priests' hiding-holes in country mansions presumed to have been Catholic stations. There are in existence contemporary accounts of a small team of carpenters, led by a Jesuit laybrother, Nicholas Owen, who created numbers of very ingenious hiding-holes. Modern investigators have certainly made a few remarkable finds: in Yorkshire a long walled-up garret still containing a wooden table altar with priest's vestments; in Berkshire a wax *agnus Dei*, blessed by the Pope in Rome in 1579, brought to England by Edmund Campion, a celebrated Jesuit missioner, and found by electricians in the rafters of an Elizabethan mansion visited by Campion in 1580; in Worcestershire a hide still containing a chair, Catholic books, and clothing. Obviously there were resident priest-chaplains in some man-sions: hides did exist and were occasionally used. But the great majority of mission priests can never have been house-chaplains nor have seen the inside of a hide. Moreover, legend has been too ready to attribute all hides to Catholics. It is very likely that non-Catholic propertied people had long been accustomed to having secret rooms for valuables.

As we have seen, up to 1570 English Catholicism was an amor-phous phenomenon, in no real sense an organised community. By the mid 1580s and 1590s it had become a community, at least in an ecclesiastical sense of the word. The mission priests arrived with legal and sacramental authority derived from Rome through the seminary superiors to reconcile people, both Papists (in the pre-1570 sense) and Protestants, to Rome. The lay people (and old priests—possibly some 200, who were usually grafted into the sem-inary priest organisation as auxiliaries or even, in a few cases, retrained abroad in seminaries) so reconciled were thus linked to a common, united clerical body and so, at least very locally, to their Catholic neighbours.

The published memoirs of the Jesuit missioners give a vivid impression of considerable success, of finding everywhere a host of schismatics (conformists with a bias towards Catholicism) ready to listen to priests, shelter them and be reconciled. They suggest that the large size of landowners' households, the strength of their multiple connections by marriage and their hold over the loyalties of their servants and immediate tenants all provided natural channels for spreading Catholic influences and procuring almost mass conversion in some areas. The Jesuit missioners mention, by name or discreetly by inference, a great many aristocratic families; they imply that, at this rate of progress, the conversion of a large part of the English governing class was becoming a solid possibility. The backcloth to this seductive picture is made up of the common people (barely mentioned, except for occasional anecdotes of passing encounters which imply schismatic sympathy for the mission), and the Calvinists—gloomy, demonic bureaucrats, Anglican clergy and powerful men, who are constantly outwitted and outargued. All this represents a contemporary Catholic point of view, but it is very questionable whether it squares with the overall realities of the Catholic Mission, or the realities of the life of the average non-Jesuit mission priest.

A recent effort has been made to produce files on the mission careers of all the 800 priests; the results are impressive in their mass of detail, but they leave a great deal unexplained. On the one hand the priest's life in England was dangerous. Approximately half of them were caught by the authorities sooner or later. 123 were executed, and many others remained in gaol for long periods with death sentences hanging over their heads. Some were certainly tortured, usually by Topcliffe, to whom English Catholic legend gave the place which was occupied in English Protestant legend by Torquemada. On the other hand a large number of priests worked for years in England without ever being caught, and the majority of those arrested were eventually released on condition that they went abroad. From 1580 the law imposed the death penalty automatically on every priest ordained abroad and caught in England: in practice the execution of the death sentence depended partly on the political views of the prisoner, and partly on the military situation of the moment. Imprisonment could often be exceedingly unpleasant, with chains, dungeons, ill-treatment and gaol-fever (typhus). But at other times and places it could mean startlingly easy conditions. By the 1590s the government had created concentration camps for Catholic priests at Wisbech and Framlingham in East Anglia, where the inmates formed a community, had Mass, and were able to exercise an apostolate amongst their visitors. In the London prisons it was often quite possible for priests to celebrate Mass fairly regularly for themselves and fellow-prisoners, and sometimes go out on parole. Hence priests' prison experiences could differ greatly.

At one extreme was the case of Christopher Bagshaw, a convert parson, who had been principal of Gloucester College (now Worcester), Oxford, and a canon of Lichfield. He was arrested within a few months of his landing as a seminary priest in England in 1585. After short periods of imprisonment in the Tower of London and the Marshalsea, he was paroled for a visit to his home town of Lichfield. In 1588 he was returned to gaol, this time to Wisbech Castle. Here he remained until 1601 and his exile abroad, forming a leading member of a community of some forty priest-prisoners who employed their own servants, managed their own community affairs, received visitors very freely, wrote and transmitted letters frequently and played cards. Bagshaw filled in his abundant free time with gossip, intrigue and taking an active part in clerical politics. At the other extreme was the case of Alexander Rawlins. The archives of the English College, Rome, contain a bundle of his letters written in gaol, together with his own very detailed account of his interrogations and trial. Some priest-prisoners deliberately composed 'final letters' in the form of pious, rhetorical exhortations, meant for publication. Rawlins occasionally slipped into this style, but, for the most part, his writings are unpolished, frank and uninhibited.

Rawlins claimed that he was always a Papist, though throughout his childhood and education at Winchester College, and perhaps for some years after that, he was a complete conformist. After a mere fifteen months as a student at Oxford, he went to serve an apothecary in London, became a recusant, and volunteered to act as guide and servant to two mission priests working in Berkshire and Buckinghamshire. He was arrested with them, and although apparently liable to the death penalty for aiding them, was eventually released and sent into exile abroad. He was ordained priest and despatched back to England with a group of priests directed to work in the north-east. After a hazardous landing by night on a beach under the cliffs of Whitby in Yorkshire, he contacted his appointed local superior, Richard Holtby, a Jesuit, and was conducted by him to his circuit —a round of six or seven stations on the east Yorkshire moors. After his arrest, he was interrogated for several hours on end in York Castle while being kept kneeling on one knee. Where so many others in his situation had been sent to Wisbech Castle, he, for no very apparent reason of law or policy, was condemned to death and executed. He arrived in York Castle in secular dress, a cloak and riding boots, and had 10s. 11d. in his purse. He begged the other Catholic prisoners (who had a common fund and table, though Rawlins was kept apart from them) for food and 'anie gowen or longe cassocke'. He was able to get out of prison two letters to his 'father', confessor and superior, Richard Holtby, and five to his 'children' (penitents), 'uncles', 'brothers' and 'sisters'. These were all members of his scattered congregation, whom he clearly regarded as his family. (His will does not mention his natural family, who lived around Oxford.)

His base of operations had been a farmhouse, of which the legal tenant was Thomas Warcop, a married man who, like Rawlins in earlier life, had undertaken the dangerous job of being housekeeper and guide to missioners. Rawlins and Warcop had been captured in the garret of the base, along with the priest's Mass kit, his breviary and most of his books. From his cell the priest slipped a short letter of comfort to Warcop, his penitent, and assured him that some day Warcop's desire to embrace a contemplative life would be satisfied. (In the event Warcop soon escaped from York Castle, but was later recaptured and executed.) The circuit funds and the priest's reserve fund (in the form of two gold and two silver rings), spare altar-linen, a second breviary and other goods were distributed round the stations in safe-keeping. Rawlins, even in the middle of the terrific tension which makes his style and grammar sometimes fall asunder, did not forget even small, well-loved details—such as the pot of 'hunny' being kept for him by a woman parishioner. There is no shadow of doubt about his simple Christianity, his strong devotion to his Jesuit superior and his parishioners, and his indignant rejection of the charge that he was disloyal to Queen Elizabeth.

The casualty rate of the missioners by execution and imprisonment was very high. But on top of this came other losses. Of the 800 priests ordained abroad by 1603, about 150 never returned to England: they either died while still in a seminary, were adjudged (by their superiors or themselves) unfitted for the labours and dangers of the mission, stayed in the seminaries as teachers, or entered religious Orders. We have already noted English Jesuits working in Lithuania, France, Italy or America. There were also English secular priests who were promoted to bishoprics, canonries or university posts in Flanders, France and Italy; some were Army chaplains to English regiments in the Spanish forces in Flanders; one or two served as naval chaplains in Spanish fleets operating against England; others became chaplain-secretaries to foreign prelates; three or four were actually trained for the priesthood in the German College in

Rome and worked as missioners in Germany; a few ended up as missioners in Ireland. Then there were some fifty other English seminary priests who either formally became Anglicans while in England (about forty), according to known records, or lived a shadowy life under Church censures as being notoriously disobedient, or suspected spies for the English government. Finally there were another eighty priests of whom there is, as yet, no trace after they set out for the English Mission. Some of them may well have lost heart and remained on the Continent; others must have died by accident or disease, yet others have lapsed and ceased to practise as priests or Catholics, and certainly some quietly worked as missioners, evading the attention of spies and informers, and dying before the first known Catholic lists of missioners were compiled, late in the century.

The resurrected convert-Catholicism of the years after 1570 was violently hostile to Protestantism, and officially regarded it as so absurdly false and unnatural a religion that sincere adherence to it by an intelligent person was practically impossible: for a Catholic priest to become a Protestant was called apostasy (the sin of Judas Iscariot) and regarded as gravely sinful. The apostate priest could not possibly be in good faith. Moreover the natural gravitational force of Catholicism, as the true faith, must tug hard at the soul of the wretched apostate: so, at the end of his life he had either to yield to the truth and die seeking, or finding, reconciliation to Catholicism, or make the supreme, demonic act of final repudiation of what, in his heart, he must know to be divine truth. Hence, in some mysterious way, Catholicism must retain its empire even over the mind of the apostate, even though that mind is wilfully averted from it. After all, as Robert Persons insisted, Protestantism as such could not be a means of divine grace: Protestants could not really *pray*. (He was outraged when an Anglican canon of York pirated, and published in a doctored version, a devotional work of his own.) It was a common opinion amongst devout Catholics that Anglican ordination was 'the mark of the Beast'; so the converted clergyman ordained as a Catholic priest was, to such people, suspect; he could be expected to apostasise; it was a rare grace if he did not. No doubt the force of these Catholic ideas did account for the fact that a number of apostate priests eventually sought reconciliation. But most of them clearly did not. Of course it is ultimately impossible for a modern, even a strictly traditionalist Catholic, to get inside the minds of Elizabethans. We simply do not know how many of the apostate priests remained powerfully 'Catholic-minded' and so knowingly fell into outward conformism to Protestantism through human weakness, while retaining a deep sense of guilt. Nor do we know how many of them genuinely underwent a conversion to Protestantism: remembering that a committed Elizabethan Protestant regarded Catholicism as patently absurd untruth. Or was it really then possible for an apostate priest to subside thankfully and sincerely into a conformism which concealed a middle way, agnostic about the dogmatic absolutisms of both sides?

How effective was the English Mission? If it had not existed, nostalgic conformist Catholicism would undoubtedly have faded away almost completely by the 1580s and 1590s. But the spontaneous Anglo-Catholic or convert-Catholic revival of the 1570s, which begot the seminaries and English Mission, would, even without a supply of missioners trained abroad, have no doubt created a very small network of lay Catholic groups. These could have been supplied (very minimally though) with Mass and the sacraments by converted old priests for the rest of the century. There were, in fact, some such priests who lived on into the 1580s and 1590s ministering to Catholics in Cheshire, Lancashire, Yorkshire and Hampshire; a handful remained alive and on the strength of the English Mission as late as 1603–10. Catholicism has survived, minimally, for long periods with few priests and in hostile environments—for instance the USSR; in Japan it survived from the 1650s to the 1850s without any priests at all.

But how could the small numbers of seminary priests available up to 1600 do any more than apply mild stimulants to a moribund patient? None set foot in England before 1574; by 1580 only one hundred had arrived. In the face of a tremendous casualty rate, their numbers reached 300 by 1600—an average of six per county, and to be contrasted with the 10,000 Anglican clergy. Yet sixteenth-century European history showed that aggressive evangelisation, initially by a mere handful of able clergy, backed by an effective literary propaganda campaign, could gain quick and sweeping successes, at least amongst the educated and propertied minority. Once a substantial proportion of the landowning nobility, gentry and townsfolk of a province was won over, a hostile royal government would find it impossible or exceedingly difficult to stop the rot. Moreover, as society was then constituted, revolutionary religious influences could produce a landslide effect by sweeping along the many private channels of communication provided by family bonds, the bonds between lord and tenants, and trade arteries. So the English Mission had a sporting chance of creating so large a Catholic minority by the 1590s that, like the Protestant minorities in France and Poland, it could wrest legal toleration from a hostile government.

The records of Elizabethan lay Catholicism after 1570 lie very widely scattered all over England in libraries and private houses;

C

they form a huge jig-saw of a multitude of tiny pieces, the place of which in the whole pattern can be determined only by laborious, local research. The sections for merely a few areas (Yorkshire, Cheshire, Hampshire) have so far been pieced together in any real detail. So we can only guess at the shape of the whole pattern for England. Government fining records for 1593–1600 list some 5000 Catholic recusants, rather oddly distributed. 3000 of them were to be found concentrated in the north (and thickest in Yorkshire and Lancashire). Of the other 2000, 650 were in the midland counties, 500 in Wales and the Welsh borders, 350 in East Anglia, 350 in the south-east, and 300 in the west country. In seventeen counties they were very few indeed. Yorkshire had a very unusually high number, but otherwise its Catholics probably displayed characteristics shared by most of their fellows elsewhere. In 1580–2 the government carried out a strong drive against popery in Yorkshire, Cheshire and Lancashire. The spontaneous Catholic convert movement was still alive, but seminary priests were still few on the ground and undistinguished. The drive dredged up some 4000 Catholic recusants and noncommunicants, 3000 of them in Yorkshire. Under pressure, the vast majority promptly conformed to Anglicanism, and half of the conformists apparently abandoned for good their new, open Catholicism. The results of the drive showed that the impact of Catholicism had been uneven. Overall it touched no more than one per cent of the population, but almost twenty per cent of the middling and poor landowning gentry, their servants and immediate tenants. It affected the mass of the country poor and townspeople only slightly, and not at all the peers and major landowners. Obviously the new Catholicism was still a feeble plant, but something very unusual had happened to jerk so considerable a section of the cautious minor landowners out of their habitual conformism. It was only a dozen years since these same people had studiously avoided giving support to the botched Catholic revolt of the northern Earls.

Thus the build-up of the sketchy circuit organisation of the seminary priests in the 1580s by Thomas Bell (the individualistic convert-parson whom we have already met) and John Mush (a devoted pupil of the Jesuits) came at a time when the new Catholicism appeared to be in danger of collapse. A provincial government, the Council of the North established at York, directed by the Earl of Huntingdon, hunted the missioners with considerable success, and harried Catholic lay recusants incessantly. By 1594 a competent Jesuit organiser arrived in the area. This was Richard Holtby, himself a member of the gentry who were the backbone of the Catholic community. He built up the mission organisation into a tighter and more efficient thing covering a triangular area with the Mersey, Humber and Tyne at its corners. By 1600 the results were impressive. There was a hard core of constant recusants—some 1500 in Yorkshire, and possibly 2000 or more in Lancashire and Cheshire and 600 in the remoter north. Surrounding the core was an amorphous mass, perhaps double the number of recusants, consisting of fellow-travellers, who supported the mission and hoped to die in the communion of the Roman Church even if they lived normally as Anglican conformists. Though overall only one and a half per cent of the population was affected, Catholicism now had a hold on some twenty-five per cent of the gentry, and was beginning to penetrate the families of a few peers. In some limited rural areas—for instance round Northallerton and in Nidderdale in Yorkshire, and in some coastal areas of Lancashire—the majority of the local landed gentry families contained Catholic members. Elsewhere in England and Wales in 1600 there was no single area of Catholic strength to compare in size and numbers with the north. But, at least in miniature, the same community structure and vigour existed fairly widely in South Wales, Staffordshire and Herefordshire, and in small pockets in many other counties. English Catholic legend has long made much of a string of mainly southern, western, midland and East Anglian gentry recusants of these years—Francis Tregian of Cornwall, Sir Thomas Tresham and Lord Vaux of Northamptonshire, the Gages of Sussex, the Stonors of Oxfordshire, the Bedingfields of Norfolk, the Rookwoods and Timperleys of Suffolk. The best-known Jesuit missioners of the 1590s, John Gerard and William Weston, undoubtedly concentrated most of their attention on the midlands and south. Clearly, while both they and the Elizabethan government realised that the main power of Catholicism still lay in the north, both parties saw that the crucial battleground lay elsewhere. Gerard and Weston were superb journalists. Their mission memoirs pile up statistics of conversions or (more often) promised conversions; they are experts in name-dropping; they ceaselessly imply that English upper-class society was riddled with pro-Catholicism. Armageddon has begun, the stars in their courses are fighting for a Catholic revolution; the Devil and his angels are at work to save Protestant heresy. (Weston was deeply involved in the exorcism of witches and heretics.)

But we cannot safely take these memoirs at their face value. In part they were composed to strengthen the hand of Persons. He was struggling in Rome to convince the Jesuit General that the English Jesuits, scattered over Europe as members of foreign Provinces, should be gathered into an English Province dedicated to a massive reinforcement of the English Mission. In part also the memoirs were

designed to be read at meals in colleges abroad to English clerical
students to rouse in them an aggressively revolutionary, evangelistic
spirit. Moreover there is plenty of evidence that the Jesuit authors
were privately far from optimistic. Persons knew well the realities
from private reports and from experience of the students coming
from England to the colleges. The Jesuits in England were very
few—only a dozen by 1603. The seminary priests' ranks contained,
for every intelligent, well-informed, devout and energetic man, four
or five others who were more or less gravely deficient; grossly idle,
ignorant and scandalous priests were increasing in number. As for
the laity: indeed there *were* model Catholic recusant families,
through and through recusant and devout. For instance there were in
Yorkshire at Harewell and Hemingborough, or in Lancashire at Ince,
or at Newcastle on Tyne, Catholic gentry households run like well-
conducted monasteries. But the average Papist gentry family mixed
recusancy with conformism so much that clerical students, drawn
from that background almost entirely by 1600, arrived in the colleges
very ill-instructed semi-Protestants.

Over and above these pressing anxieties was the growth amongst
English Catholics of an anti-Jesuit opposition of a powerful and
virulent kind. To Jesuits, who honestly believed that the survival,
and perhaps triumph, of the faith in England depended utterly on a
great extension of their influence, this opposition was more than
suicidal. It was a far worse machination of the Devil than even
heresy and witchcraft. The quarrel was destined to rage for more
than a century within the English Catholic community; indeed today
its embers are still alight. Historians have been defeated by its
immense complexities of ecclesiastical intrigue and embarrassed by
its sheer ferocity. So, for instance, Robert Persons in his old age
constantly harped with satisfaction on the sufferings and (or so he
imagined) the painful deaths of his Catholic opponents. Some of
them, for their part, attributed unspeakable crimes and immoralities
to the Jesuits. To this day there is an English Jesuit school of
historians devoted to re-fighting the battles of the sixteenth and seventeenth centuries in immense detail to defend the honour of the
Society.

The quarrel began in earnest in 1594 in the curious concentration
camps for captured priests in East Anglia at Wisbech and Framlingham. There some thirty or forty priests were kicking their heels
under slack supervision by the gaolers. The arrival amongst them
of the Jesuit leader, William Weston, precipitated a vicious conflict.
The immediate issue was Weston's effort to secure the acceptance
by all of a set of disciplinary rules. The explosive reaction of a
minority of the priests showed that they already nurtured long-

standing resentments dating back to their student days in the colleges under Jesuit direction. But this was only the beginning. From 1594 to 1598 the English College, Rome, was rent by student disorder, and a considerable body of the students left, numbers of them to enter Benedictine monasteries in Italy and Spain. Then, in 1598, began the affair in England of the Appellants, which raged on until at least 1606.

The issues in all this fighting were tangled. First there was a politico-religious issue. The Jesuits' opponents attributed to them the view that Queen Elizabeth's Protestantism deprived her of all moral right to the throne, that Catholics had no obligation in conscience to be loyal to her, and, indeed, an obligation to support plots to dethrone her and replace her by a Catholic sovereign, perhaps even a Spaniard. The Appellants insisted that their moral duty was, even in defiance of Papal orders, to Elizabeth and to reveal to the government the plots of Catholic militants. One storm centre here was a book published abroad in 1594, *A Conference about the Next Succession*, widely (and, so it seems, rightly) thought to have been inspired by Persons. The book tactlessly discussed in detail the best Catholic successor to Elizabeth: it nowhere openly refused allegiance to her, but it implied that an English Catholic layman's political allegiance and policy must ultimately be controlled by the Pope through the Jesuits. At this point the first issue between the Jesuits and their opponents ran into a second, more down-to-earth one between clericalists and anticlericals. From the beginning of the spontaneous Catholic revival in the 1570s, some clergy had insisted that the faith had no future in England unless the clergy were under strict disciplinary control, and the laity (feeble, ignorant, given chronically to conformism) were under the thumb of the clergy. Since the ordinary, pre-Reformation structure of Church authority did not exist in England for Catholics, some effective substitute must be found. The supporters of the Jesuits assumed that a perpetuation and strengthening of existing Jesuit control was the only practicable solution. As spiritual directors of the colleges, they could gain an ascendancy over the minds of future missioners. On the mission Jesuits could control missioners by binding them to the Society— either by private vows of obedience to Jesuit confessors, vows to enter the Society some time in the future, or (as was then possible) secretly serving a Jesuit noviciate while working on the mission and being professed as Jesuits. Then, through Jesuit (or Jesuit-controlled) confessors, vows and so forth, the laity could be drawn into the same close and secret net.

A good many of the leading lay gentry had, ever since 1570, simply refused to enter such a net. They repeatedly professed their allegiance to Queen Elizabeth and repudiated any idea that the Pope or clergy could give them orders in political matters. In general the gentry regarded the clergy as their employees. They rejected any idea that they should take the services only of missioners allotted to them by clerical superiors, freely sent packing missioners who displeased them (one devout recusant gentleman dismissed a respectable priest for kicking a dog), and set light to canonical rules taken for granted by the clergy. Manifestly very many Catholic gentry were never persuaded that occasional conformity to Anglicanism was a grave sin. Some were quite prepared to carry this to the point of taking oaths which were formally anti-Catholic. For many of the lay Catholics, visits by priests were occasional and irregularly spaced, hence, especially in households containing conformists and Protestants, children might often be baptised at the Anglican Church, wives be churched there, marriages be celebrated there and the dead buried in church graveyards with Anglican rites. The difficult circumstances of the English Mission often produced complex cases concerning betrothal and marriage where the laity were unwilling to wait on the lengthy processes of Catholic Church law. Allen and Persons had long ago realised that English conditions made it physically or morally impossible to enforce the letter of pre-Reformation Catholic Church law. They had provided the college students with (sometimes clear-cut, sometimes subtle and obscure) instructions. Some priests, especially Jesuits, were inclined to be severe in their interpretation of the instructions: most were probably much more sympathetic and lax. The laity were well aware of these differences of attitude amongst the clergy. Hence it was not surprising that the mere suspicion that there was a Jesuit plan to control and discipline the entire mission should have aroused fear and resentment amongst many of the laity and clergy. If such a plan were effected, it would pretty certainly bring down on most of them censures and penances. For many Papist conformists it might well seem to be slamming a door in the face of their hopes of a tolerable reconciliation with the Roman Church.

To add to the confusion of the debate, the two sides were by no means themselves united. Experience of the mission field seems to have convinced some Jesuits and seminarist fellow-travellers that Persons's party-line was wrong. By 1600 at least one Jesuit missioner, Thomas Wright, had left the Society and, with the connivance of the government and Queen Elizabeth's favourite, the Earl of Essex, had embarked on a propaganda tour of the mission to beat up Catholic support for a deal with the Queen whereby a Catholic oath of loyalty to her (and a disowning of the Jesuits) would be traded for partial religious toleration. Moreover the Jesuit General in Rome on occasion received protests from English gentry against Persons and Jesuit militants and acted on them. Then there were divisions in the ranks of the anti-Jesuits. Some were clearly rabidly militant. Others, like John Mush, agreed with the Jesuits that the laity and missioners must have some form of clerical discipline. He proposed a confraternity to be spontaneously accepted by all the clergy and organised in local branches: this should be supplemented by some form of episcopal authority appointed by the Pope and binding on Jesuits and seminary priests alike. But, to Mush's mind, only a radical improvement in the system of recruiting and training the clergy could possibly win them more respect from the laity.

By 1598 a group of priest-opponents of the Jesuits drafted an appeal to the Pope for the appointment of an English bishop. By arrangement with the government (the policy of which was simply to sow confusion in the ranks of the Catholics and checkmate Persons's designs) they were allowed a safe-conduct for a deputation, including some prisoners from Framlingham, to take the appeal to Rome. The outcome was a disastrous muddle. Pretty certainly due to Persons's influence, the deputation was arrested in Rome and deported back to France. The Pope proceeded to give episcopal authority over the English Catholics to an Italian Papal agent resident in Brussels. The English Jesuits were excepted from his jurisdiction. The agent was to delegate his authority over the mission priests (not the Jesuits or the laity) in England to an Archpriest resident on the mission and assisted by twelve senior priests. The Archpriest was instructed to act closely in accord with the Jesuits. Rome chose for this crucial post George Blackwell. Ostensibly it was a wise scheme and an equally wise choice. Blackwell was a convert university don of considerable learning and independence of mind; he had a reputation for gentleness; he had hitherto remained aloof from the great quarrel; he had extensive experience of mission work and the inside of gaols. But in practice his rule proved disastrous. His efforts to impose discipline on the more ebullient Appellants roused their fury: as one of them wrote sourly, he made suspensions, censures and dismissals fly 'as thick as tennis balls'. The Appellants regarded him as a tool of the Jesuits. By further deputations to Rome they procured the reversal of his censures and the cancelling of his obligation to consult the Jesuits. By 1603 his credit and authority, always slender, were minimal. Yet, so far as can be judged from his letters, he saw through the complexities of the quarrel more clearly than most Catholics.

Thus, as the century ended, the more knowledgeable and responsible Catholics on all sides were only too well aware that their community was disorderly, devoid of central authority, sharply divided,

and an object of mockery to both Roman officials and English
Protestant administrators. Even before the quarrel the government
had, through spies and indiscreet Catholic prisoners, a pretty
detailed knowledge of the Catholic set-up. As the quarrel developed,
both sides leaped into print, as if unaware that Protestants would
read their many pamphlets. The leading Appellants had even given
the government astonishingly free access to their letters and papers.
The most distinguished recent Catholic historian of Elizabethan
Catholicism has summarised its record as 'from inertia to inertia
in three generations'.

But is he exaggerating? Catholic apologists have always done
their best to prove that recusants provided most of the glory of the
Elizabethan age. They have estimated recusant numbers as high as
a quarter of the population (including fellow-travellers); they have
credited them with a strong hold on the higher aristocracy; they have
made the Catholic martyrs the only heroes in a materialistic age;
they have attributed the Elizabethan breakthrough in literature to a
'golden succession' of recusant writers from Sir Thomas More to
Persons; they have claimed as Catholics Shakespeare, Marlowe,
Ben Jonson and Lodge; they have claimed as Catholics the cream
of Elizabethan musicianship, Byrd, Tye, Tallis, Philips; they have
valued recusant theologians (Stapleton, Sander, Dorman, Richard
Smith) above their Anglican contemporaries, and rated Robert
Persons (for his *First Book of Christian Exercise*) as the only great
spiritual writer of the age. Edmund Campion, the Jesuit martyr, has
been rated as the finest example of Elizabethan sensitivity and
heroism.

Manifestly a community which could produce such creativity
could only be superficially wounded by its weaknesses. But much
of this apologetic is special pleading. Catholic numbers were actually small; by 1603 the vast bulk of the higher aristocracy and its
patronage was solidly Protestant. The martyrs, like the victims of
modern Resistance movements, were sometimes political militants,
but much more often innocent sufferers for the mistakes and politico-
religious schemes of their superiors. Nevertheless a good many of
them were very genuine heroes. Recusant writers were mostly educated as Protestants; their undoubted literary flair, increasing as the
century wore on, simply reflected a general current in educated
society. No amount of special pleading can produce a really convinc-
ing case for the idea that Shakespeare and Marlowe were Catholics.
Jonson certainly became a Catholic in 1599, but later reverted to
Protestantism. John Donne, the brightest literary hope of the late
Elizabethan Catholicism, had become an Anglican by 1603. Of the
musicians, Tallis and Tye were conformists; William Byrd (un-

doubtedly the greatest Elizabethan composer) was certainly a Catholic, but as organist of Queen Elizabeth's Chapel Royal, he was necessarily a conformist and most of his religious compositions were for the Anglican liturgy; Peter Philips was a minor composer and, as a Catholic, could find patronage only abroad as organist to the Viceroy of the Netherlands. It was not a great age for English theology, but the Catholics produced no writer of the stature of Ames, Hooker and Perkins. In the field of spirituality both Anglicans and Catholics were, down to 1600, struggling to rethink their positions, and resorting to second-rate late medieval and early sixteenth-century manuals. Persons's best-seller owed its success amongst both Protestants and Catholics to his ability to summarise the manuals in a contemporary English style: but it has no place in the succession of classical English mystical writings. As for Edmund Campion, he must occupy an honourable, but surely subordinate, place in the large galaxy of Elizabethan nonconformist protest, mostly Protestant. On the whole, the creative achievements of the Elizabethan English Catholics are much what we should expect of a small, nonconformist community of people originally bred in the mainstream of a developing and vigorous national society.

3. Early Stuart Catholicism, 1603–60

(1) Jesuits, Monks, Friars and Nuns

In the early seventeenth century David Baker, a recent Catholic convert, looked back at the fortunes of British Catholicism (he was a Welshman) in the previous century. To his hindsight the established, traditional Catholicism which began to die in 1534, for all its faults—'ignorance . . . superstition . . . a few concubines of priests' —now seemed 'a Silver or Golden Age'. Then came 'an Iron Age' of heresy 'exploding all honesty and true goodness'. Catholicism had been miraculously resurrected in the 1570s and 1580s by 'brands escaped from the Protestant burning'. By the early 1600s it was only partly living, shot through with 'iron' corruption from the debased, Protestant society in which it had to exist. To Baker's mind its survival had been, humanly, due to its compromises with heresy, and such a survival was almost worse than the death of the community. Catholicism's only real hope must lie in a total transformation into a completely Catholic, completely contemplative Church.

This young Welsh convert's ideas were not in the least original, though they seemed to him to be a revelation of the will of God mediated through the private intensities of his conversion: a deliverance from polite, respectable Anglican conformism masking deep inner doubts and moral perplexities. In a sense all Christian Church history has been a constantly recurring battle between formalism and passionate Dissent. The sixteenth-century Protestant movement and the Catholic reaction to it (the Catholic Counter-Reformation) both sprang from a late medieval tide of this same fierce religious Dissent. As we have seen, educated English people in the 1570s experienced another tide, which begot the two opposed extremist minorities: Protestant Puritanism and the new Catholicism. By the 1590s the force of that tide seemed long spent, and both movements appeared to be fading into compromise with the Estab-

lishment: there began yet another, and bigger, tide. This religious ferment produced a multiplicity of dissenting minorities, a fiercer wave
of Puritanism, Laudian High Church Anglicanism, a neo-Catholic
movement amongst Protestants, a Catholic revival including some
striking rebels and eccentrics. Seventeenth-century English society
was to experience a second Protestant Reformation, and a second
Catholic Counter-Reformation, both more vigorous and passionate
than their sixteenth-century counterparts. The English Catholic
community was, between 1603 and 1642, to be both shaken and
strengthened by an intense religious revival bred out of doubt and
self-searching, and by an influx of converts, mostly intellectuals and
aristocrats.

This process coincided with the onset of a wave of cultural and
intellectual influence over England emanating from the Continental
Catholic Counter-Reformation monarchies, especially France. From
the 1590s the Counter-Reformation, which had hitherto operated
largely in Spain and Italy, began to gain ground aggressively and
fast, at the expense of Protestantism, in France, Germany, Austria,
Bohemia (Czechoslovakia), Hungary and Poland. Its spirit was
militant, its temper authoritarian; it set great store by carefully-
designed methods and systems calculated to produce fast results; its
art-forms were baroque, dramatic, emotive, though conventionally
classical Greek and Roman in style. The movement was so massive,
so well-organised, so psychologically appealing to people wearied of
the strife amongst Protestants, the governments adhering to it were
so militarily strong, that European Protestantism seemed doomed.

As early as 1608 local religious wars between Catholics and
Protestants broke out in south Germany; by 1618 war was general,
and was to last intermittently for the rest of the century. Although
England remained an officially Protestant country, there were several
reasons why it now became particularly susceptible of cultural influences from its religious enemy. One reason was certainly the age-
old tendency to copy one's enemy's methods. Another was the un-
deniably strong superiority of Latin Counter-Reformation culture.
Again, during much of the seventeenth century, both England and
France, for prudential reasons, remained technically neutral during
the religious wars, or even gave intermittent support to their religious
enemies. This tended to make relations between the two countries
unusually close. Lastly James I and Charles I chose to favour close
relations with France, and even with Spain and the Pope. James I's
Danish Queen was a convert to Catholicism, though she barely
practised her new religion after 1603. Charles I's Queen was a determined and devout French Catholic. Her advent to England in 1625
made permanent an already noticeable tendency for interest in, and

outright conversion to, Catholicism to become fashionable at court
and amongst the aristocracy. Inevitably these political and cultural
factors aided the purely religious ones, steadily strengthening English
Catholicism between 1603 and 1642. By the 1660s London was to
get a new Protestant Cathedral, St Paul's, which was a copy of the
baroque St Peter's, Rome. The English aristocracy were out of the
swim unless they had their portraits painted by French or Flemish
Catholic artists; unless their light reading was French novels or
English pamphlets in French styles; if their theatre was not full of
Spanish and French plots, their drink claret, sack or port wine, their
styles of clothing and wigs French, their military fashions (the
Household Guards, fusiliers, grenadiers, bombadiers and bayonets)
French, and their language used before the servants and in diplomacy
also invariably French. The English Catholic community could
hardly avoid basking in some reflected glory.

The Catholic revival manifested itself especially in the proliferation of foundations of English monasteries and convents. Before the
1590s the English Catholics betrayed a remarkable lack of interest
in such matters. Two small groups of English religious, of Carthusian
monks and Bridgettines (an Order containing both priests and nuns),
had narrowly succeeded in surviving in community through the dark
winter of 1534–70, in Flanders. They endured privations and had
to shift house several times; but few new recruits joined them until
1603. From the 1560s a thin dribble of English, largely converts,
entered foreign Provinces of the Society of Jesus, but even in 1590
overall numbers were quite insufficient to warrant starting an English Province and opening a separate national noviciate. Down to
the 1590s odd English people became Franciscan, Capuchin, Carmelite or Dominican friars, Benedictine monks and nuns, Oratorians,
but they were few and had to settle in foreign communities. This
English Catholic lack of interest is strange. The religious temper of
the Elizabethan age readily accepted the idea of a retired life of
devotion, perhaps all the more because of its restless activism. Even
strong Puritans like William Perkins, while condemning in principle
religious vows for life (as contrary to Christian liberty), valued a
retired life in community with promises of celibacy for those with the
gift of continence. Perkins went out of his way to write that he 'did
not condemn the ancient monks'. Also the organisation of family
life and landed property still made entry into a monastery or convent the only satisfactory solution to the two problems of preventing
younger sons from marrying (to conserve the unity of family inheritances) and providing for an excess of unmarriageable daughters.

On the other hand there is evidence that Elizabethan Catholics
(mostly converts from a Protestant upbringing) were severely critical

of traditional monasticism. In 1580 Robert Southwell, the Jesuit poet, wrote that throughout much of Europe 'monk' was synonymous with 'scoundrel and roamer'. The Jesuits were part of an effort to produce an entirely new form of monastic life, suited to the spirit of the age (and so mixing great activism with bouts of strict retirement, and limiting life-vows to a small, senior segment of the Society). In the later sixteenth century most religious Orders of men in Europe followed suit, usually by creating modernised houses or branches. It is significant that, when English Catholics did begin to overcome their prejudice and enter religion in large numbers, from the 1590s, they mostly chose modernised communities. Again, until the 1590s, the bulk of English Catholic male devotion was channelled through the seminaries towards a pastoral ministry in England: the students had to take a mission oath to follow this course. As for feminine devotion, as we have seen, to the 1590s there were few completely Catholic devout gentry households or Jesuit missioners to urge girls into convent life, and the prospect of living in a community of foreigners was daunting.

In the 1590s this situation began to change rapidly. There was a sharp increase in the number of clerical students and mission priests entering the Society of Jesus. In 1593 there were only forty-nine English Jesuits, of whom thirty were priests, and only nine in England. By 1610 there were fifty-three Jesuits in England and possibly 120 in the Society; the English Province was at last launched, with a feeder-school for boys at St Omer and a noviciate at Louvain. By 1620 there were 211 in the Province and 106 missioners in England. By 1641 overall numbers had risen to nearly 400, and missioners to about 180. The Appellants attributed this development to base motives. In their view Persons's long-maturing plans for a Jesuit take-over-bid for the mission had flowered naturally: the Jesuit hold over the seminaries had long ago created a fifth column of mission priests bound to the Society by vows of obedience; once the Province was started, its needs for manpower would inevitably make the Jesuit superiors call into the Society these supporters, for whom it had hitherto no room. There must be some truth in all this, but it does not entirely explain the remarkable rush into the Society after 1600. There are signs that the Jesuit superiors were surprised and embarrassed by its scale: their new training establishments had too few places and insufficient funds to accept all applicants; the applicants were not infrequently critical and troublesome, and the selection and screening procedures were inadequate. The new General of the Society in Rome in 1616, Vitelleschi, circularised the Provincial superiors complaining that the Society was expanding everywhere far too fast—the Belgian Province (to which a good many of the English Jesuits had belonged, and from which it still drew teaching staff to cope with the English Province's rapid expansion) had grown from 154 members in 1579 to 782 in 1608; in 1616 it had been divided into two Provinces, which had 1262 members. Hence Vitelleschi ordered a rigid screening of entrants and strict rationing of their numbers. Small Jesuit houses, which were being founded wholesale, were to be radically pruned. Manifestly, amongst both the English Jesuits and their Continental colleagues, Counter-Reformation drive, method and success partly accounted for the boom in vocations, but in part it came from a spontaneous, general religious revival.

Simultaneously the years between 1591 and 1610 saw serious waves of student unrest in all of the English seminaries, and the departure of a considerable number to offer themselves to the noviciates of modernised religious Orders other than the Jesuits, especially to the Benedictines. As the Appellants pointed out cynically, many of these student rebels were moved by detestation of Jesuit direction; they saw that the English Mission was rapidly acquiring a surplus of missioners, and that they themselves had to choose promptly whether to fall under Jesuit control and be assured thereby of a comfortable station in England, or to campaign in the seminaries for the dismissal of Jesuit directors and superiors, and (if they were ordained and not ejected from the seminaries for disobedience) pass as missioners to England to share the insecure and embattled life of the Appellants. According to the Appellants it was inevitable that some of the rebels, less constant or more escapist than the rest, would evade the hard choice by flight to monasteries, the only other refuges abroad willing to offer them subsistence, a continuation of their clerical education, and perhaps freedom from the discomforts of the mission. So, thought the Appellants, often such religious, devoid of a real vocation to their Orders, grew restive under monastic discipline and clamoured to be allowed to go to the mission after all. Once there they tended to be troublesome misfits. The Jesuit balance between monastic retirement and vigorous, adaptable pastoral work was delicate enough, and supremely difficult in English conditions; they had their extremists, laxists, and apostates. But at least the Society was designed expressly for such a task; dead wood could be expelled swiftly from the Society, since most of its missioners were only in temporary vows. But the older Orders, however much modernised, depended for their spirit fundamentally on a living contact with their monastic houses. Life on the mission deprived them of this. Even when they had local superiors in England and methods whereby missioners could, even there, keep up monastic observances to a minimal extent, the life was a severe strain. As we shall see, they were not helped by sharp conflicts within their Orders between activists and contemplatives (who regarded missionary life as dangerous and wrong). The Appellants regarded the Catholic 'rush into religion' with distaste and foreboding. As early as 1602 William Watson, one of their most vigorous writers, speculated gloomily on 'the rise and fall of great Empires':

> The rise and fall of Monasticall Orders in the Worlds Theater represent a mournfull tragedie of mens miseries; how like to flowers they have now one and then another Order, companie or societie, burgeoned, blossomed, bloomed and flourished and yet subiecte to the fates of freewill in all human wights and so loose their primitive spirit and decaie . . .

The Appellants' interpretation of the motives of the new religious certainly had a basis in fact. The behaviour of some of the student rebels desiring to be monks or friars was odd. Two Yorkshire brothers named Rayner arrived at the English College, Douai, in 1598. They later maintained that their parents were determined recusants, but the College authorities found it necessary to receive them formally into the Catholic Church after six months of probation and instruction. By 1601, after joining in the student demonstrations against the Jesuits, the brothers demanded to be sent to Spain to join a Spanish Benedictine monastery. They were sent to Seville, a small Jesuit-run college, apparently kept for difficult cases, and thence to the English College in Valladolid. Three years later they arrived back at Douai, asked to resume their studies, and wrote to the Spanish Benedictine monastery at Valladolid to say they had decided not to be Benedictines. They were received back, although Dr Worthington, the College rector, was generally severe with such cases (he had just expelled one recently ordained priest to his Protestant relations in England for 'paradoxical and phanatical opinions' and despatched an unsettled student to a Benedictine monastery in Spain). A year later Worthington flatly refused to re-enter three former students who had abandoned Benedictine noviciates, judging them totally unsettled. By 1606 the Rayners had reached the diaconate, but then proved so uncooperative and so set on being Benedictines that they were finally expelled. They took refuge in Rheims, were ordained priests there, and apparently spent another two years in the town before they took the plunge and entered a Benedictine noviciate.

Meanwhile, back at the College at Douai, Dr Worthington was at odds, first with an old College student who had been expelled from the mission for heterodox opinions, then with a dozen students who wanted to leave *en masse* for the Benedictines—seven were expelled, one of them by physical force—then with Bartholomew Roe. Roe was a recent Cambridge convert from Protestantism and a natural student leader. He incited his fellows to refuse penances, openly criticised College rules, and, when rebuked, answered the authorities: 'There is more trouble with a few fools than with all the wise; you pull down, and I will put up; you destroy and I will build.' He was expelled, and, after two years of wanderings in England and on the Continent, found his niche as a Benedictine. Yet, years later, when in England on the mission, his name occurred on a Catholic list of 'scandalous' priests, with the note: 'ill-famed because of his frequent drinking parties, gaming and the like'.

For the Jesuits the rush into Benedictinism was discredited not only because of its origins in student rebellion, but because the new Benedictine communities seemed riven with feuds, and their leading spirits appeared notoriously free-thinking. In 1600 Rome agreed to allow English Benedictines who so wished, and who were despatched by their superiors, to serve on the mission. Consequently there soon grew up groups of monks professed in the Italian (Monte Cassino) Congregation, and the Spanish (Valladolid) Congregation. Some of them strove to create an English Congregation, into which all could be gathered. The effort cost fifteen years of strife: strife with the Jesuits who flatly opposed the foundation of English monasteries anywhere near the seminaries (for obvious reasons), strife with the College superiors, strife amongst the Benedictines. In 1619 the English Congregation came into being, though a small group of 'Italian' monks never joined it.

But fresh controversies now arose. Some of these, the most bitter, were waged over the nature of monasticism. There were monks who regarded the mission with horror, and who wanted the Congregation to return to the strict enclosure, banning of outside works, and the austere discipline of the Primitive Observance they assumed to be the true, early medieval monastic tradition. In the end this school of thought was allowed a compromise: the establishment of the remotest of their monasteries, Dieulouard in Lorraine, as a house of Primitive Observance. The experiment lasted some twenty years before it had to be abandoned, not least because the health of the community broke down. Then there were monks, especially Augustine Baker, who also wanted to withdraw from the mission, but who utterly rejected Primitive Observance in favour of 'Bakerism': an almost Carthusian, eremitical monastic life heavily weighted towards long periods of individual, private prayer. The bulk of the Congregation eventually rejected both of these extremist policies, though, like ghosts, they have continued to haunt it down to today.

Between 1619 and 1633 another Benedictine controversy raged simultaneously. Its complexities and technicalities were perversely convoluted. Broadly speaking the issue was one of personalities: a strong group of ex-'Italian' monks in the Congregation suspected that their ex-'Spanish' colleagues meant to draw them all into the Valladolid Congregation. Behind this apparently lay a bitter clash between monks who were pro-French and others who were pro-Spanish at a time when France and Spain were fighting for mastery of the Counter-Reformation movement. The Spanish party stood for a rigid and narrow Catholicism, and, almost as a matter of Catholic faith, the subjugation of French national interests to Spain's leadership. There were French Catholics, as well as English ones, who regarded this point of view as the only one possible for a devout Catholic. The French party, on the contrary, saw disaster lying ahead of such a policy; for them France was the right leader of the Counter-Reformation. Inside the little English Benedictine Congregation this quarrel was carried to absurd extremes. In the 1620s, led by Francis Walgrave and John Barnes, two great extremists, members of the French party proposed that the Congregation enter the French Congregation of Cluny; indeed, they boldly suggested that it already was subject to it, since the English Congregation had no legal basis, and the English monks were leasing monastic properties belonging to Cluny. Barnes and Walgrave, with great panache, argued that the English Congregation was intended by Rome to be a simple resurrection of the medieval Congregation dissolved by Henry VIII; but, so they said, the pre-dissolution English monasteries had never been formed into a legal Congregation. The argument was eccentric and historically false. But the issue at stake—French or Spanish leadership—was an immensely live one.

These two debates by no means exhausted the mental energies of the most active-minded Benedictines. They plunged also into the thick of a series of general controversies which raged very widely amongst educated Catholics in the 1620s and 1630s in France, England, Belgium and Holland. The controversies all arose from separate and particular events—usually the publication of a radical book in one country and dealing with one complex issue. Yet invariably the repercussions of the local debate were felt strongly over the whole area and produced a shower of pamphlets. Moreover, though at the time few of the combatants realised it clearly, we can see now that the issues and controversies were all linked together in a common pattern: indeed European Protestantism was hotly engaged in its own internal debates, and we can detect the same pattern running through these also. To the leaders of the two embattled Establishments, Counter-Reformation Catholic and

Reformation Protestant, the dogmatic positions they had taken up were divinely-guaranteed ultimate truth, final and irreversible. To the radical, active minds, Catholic and Protestant, of the contemporary religious revival, this was doubtful. But most of the protagonists were so much the mental prisoners of a profoundly traditional education and of hardened party lines that their revolt was almost always curiously partial and muted. Nevertheless the English Benedictines repeatedly produced outstanding radicals out of all proportion to their numbers. The single most eminent early Benedictine was William Gifford. He had long been a rebel seminary priest and ardent opponent of Robert Persons, Jesuit policy, and Spanish Counter-Reformation ideas. During the later stages of the Elizabethan persecution of Catholicism he made no secret of his belief that the English Mission as conceived by Allen and Persons was a disastrous mistake. While firmly adhering to Catholicism, he corresponded in a friendly way with Queen Elizabeth's ministers. Expelled from Flanders by the Spanish government, and branded by Persons as a crypto-Protestant spy, he settled in France, became an English Benedictine, and, through his close association with leading French officials and clergy, became Archbishop of Rheims and Primate of the French Church. He was in such a unique position for a foreigner, and one with so stormy and rebellious a past, that it is not surprising that his pronouncements became largely conventional. But he never ceased privately to use his influence to support English Benedictine and French radicals.

Another Benedictine, Thomas Preston, while openly supporting conventional Counter-Reformation views, published under an assumed name a powerful attack on aggressive political Catholicism and denied the Pope's right to issue political directives binding in conscience on Catholics. Another, Leander Jones, a convert from Anglicanism, attempted to retain his Anglican friendships and promote discussion on reunion of the Churches. His ecumenism did not go very far, but at least he suggested that there was much more common ground than Rome and the Jesuits thought, and that there were many features of Catholicism which could be changed. Another Benedictine, Rudesind Barlow, long President of the Congregation, published a book on Papal authority which was formally suppressed by Rome. But these rebels were put in the shade by the radicalism of a small group of their colleagues led by John Barnes, Francis Walgrave and David Codner.

William Gifford has long been enshrined in English Jesuit tradition as the great betrayer of the true English Catholic cause. John Barnes, at least until historians recently studied his books and the shattering impact he made amongst the English Catholic clergy for a few years in the 1620s, was dismissed by the Jesuits and his own Benedictine community as a madman. He was certainly violently pugnacious and eccentric and he lacked all sense of discretion. On the other hand he had immense courage and a mind clear enough to escape much further out of the straitjacket imposed by custom and tradition on the thinking of the most perceptive people of his day. He was an East Anglian Cambridge convert from Protestantism (like most of his colleagues), and had been a student rebel in his seminary at Valladolid. As a Benedictine he found his intellectual freedom hemmed in on every side. He was under obedience to superiors who inspected his correspondence, decided his studies, and censored his writings. As so often in history in similar circumstances, rebels had to pass around their manifestos in manuscript secretly. If they went into print, it had to be under an assumed name. Barnes attempted to gain freedom of action within monasticism by a series of tortuous and ingenious stratagems, refusing to join the new English Congregation, dodging the superiors of his own (Spanish) Congregation, and ultimately trying to slip into the legal position of a detached foreign member of a French (Cluniac) Congregation. Humiliatingly penanced by his superiors, and expelled from university teaching by the English Benedictines, he faced the fearful problem of finding some decent source of income and independence. For a time he was able to shelter under the secret influence of Archbishop Gifford and French sympathisers in a kind of English Benedictine rebel monastery at Chelles. Then the Benedictine superiors closed in on him, had him delated as a fugitive monk, arrested by the French police, put into an English Benedictine monastic private gaol and then deported under guard to the Holy Office's gaols in Rome. There he vanished from sight, apparently dying in custody thirty years later and officially classed as insane. Some of his writings are certainly radical *jeux d'esprit*. But he left behind him an immense (542 pages) published attack on contemporary official Catholic moral theology, and two long papers (unpublished in his day) dissecting both the official Protestant and Catholic doctrinal positions, discarding much in both that was mere theological accretion, and proposing grounds for reunion.

The silencing of John Barnes did not mean that the English Benedictines were soon to settle down into conventional respectability. As he was being removed to Rome the groundswell was arising in the Netherlands and France which would produce in the 1640s and 1650s the greatest storm of radical Catholicism, Jansenism. This storm was going to rage throughout the second half of the century. The English Benedictines were deeply involved in it from the start. The groundswell began in the last decades of the

sixteenth century in the university of Louvain with a violent attack
on Jesuit theology. Barnes, in his earliest years as a Benedictine,
itched to join in the attack. Some of his colleagues were just as eager,
but they were restrained by their superiors for prudential reasons.
Barnes and his colleagues were later in friendly contact with Pierre
de Berulle and Jean Duvergier, Abbot of St Cyran, leaders of radical
French Catholic clergy who supported the Louvain movement.
Cornelius Jansen, a Dutch Catholic theologian educated in France
and a close friend of St Cyran, was to precipitate the Jansenist
storm with a book published in 1640, but long circulating in manuscript before that date. Jansen's circle of friends and supporters
included numerous English and Irish priests, amongst them Benedictines and Appellants. The storm centre of Jansenism in France
was to be the radical community of Port Royal, near Paris, containing nuns, male solitaries and lay supporters. Port Royal had
English admirers. Its first director was an English Capuchin friar;
there were at least two Scottish nuns in the convent, probably
several English solitaries, and the English Benedictine monastery in
Paris supplied chaplains to the convent for a good many years.
Benedictine radicalism died hard.

If the English Benedictines were inclined to radicalism, their
fellow-countrymen who became Franciscans, Dominicans, Capuchins
or Carmelites from the 1590s were hardly less unconventional.
In their case this was perhaps unsurprising since the friars had
played a prominent radical part in Catholicism in the middle
ages and in the Reformation conflicts of the sixteenth century. The
reform and modernisation of their Orders thereafter produced multiple internal tensions: tensions between their traditional radicalism
and the authoritarianism and closing of the Catholic ranks incul-
cated by the official Counter-Reformation movement; tensions also
between friars enthusiastic for Jesuit methods of modernisation
and their colleagues who were passionately opposed to them. The
typical Englishman who entered this whirlpool from the 1590s was,
like the new Benedictines, a convert from Protestantism, a clerical
student or secular priest rebel, and certainly an independent-minded
idealist. This was a recipe for an explosive mixture.

The Franciscans were resurrected by John Gennings, a convert
from Protestantism who had trained as a missioner at the Jesuit-
controlled English College, Rome, at the height of the student dis-
orders. He nevertheless persevered, apparently remaining associated
with the Jesuits, and served as a missioner in England for fifteen
years. He crossed to Flanders around 1617, and, with the help of
Christopher Davenport, a far better-educated convert from a strongly
Protestant background, established a tiny English community of

Franciscans of the Stricter Observance in Douai. They recruited novices mostly from student rebels at the nearby English College. It is very likely that Gennings and Davenport wanted an austere life of retirement, contemplation and bare poverty, cut off as far as possible from both the English Mission and university studies (a path which led inevitably to immersion in contemporary controversies). They were soon compelled to modify their policy. Their original band of student novices was decimated by plague and consumption, brought on by strict enclosure and poor food. Recruiting from the English College became difficult: if the community was not to die out, it had to gain a following in England, and this required the despatch of missioners thither. Also Gennings had energetically founded two English convents of Franciscan nuns in Flanders and Franciscan missioners in England were urgently needed to recruit girls and subscriptions to support them. The training of Franciscan missioners meant involvement in Douai university studies. Thus, by the 1620s, although the friary remained very austere and unhealthy, its community emerged to play a small part in the affairs of the English Mission and its controversies. We know little of Gennings's opinions since he wrote nothing beyond a pious biography of his martyred priest brother and a short instruction, designed for Franciscan missioners, on the many spiritual and moral perils of the mission. His close associate, Davenport, eventually became a leading radical theologian who joined with the Benedictine, Leander Jones, in a determined effort to secure reunion with Anglicanism. Davenport's published major theological work, *God, Nature and Grace*, printed commendations from all of the most radical Benedictine and Appellant thinkers, was delated to Rome by the Jesuits, and only narrowly escaped condemnation by the Holy Office.

For an Englishman to be professed as a Dominican friar in those days automatically placed him in the forefront of opposition to the Jesuits. From the 1580s Dominicans throughout Europe (even in Spain) were locked in academic theological conflict with the Society. Around 1585 at least five rebel seminary students became Dominicans. Some of them became notorious collaborators with the English government or apostates. One, William Lister, was in Rome in 1596 and was accused of inciting students at the English College to revolt against the authority of their Jesuit directors. At that period an English Jesuit commented ironically that there actually existed, at San Lucar in Spain, Father Paul, an English Dominican who was the sole exception to the rule, 'a quiet man who . . . will not be drawn to any such faction'. Until the 1650s the situation remained unchanged, and there seemed no hope that there would ever be an English Dominican Province, with its own noviciate, officials and discipline.

Then, quite unexpectedly, a young English aristocrat became a Dominican in Rome. Philip Howard's family had such great influence and resources that Rome and the Order agreed to his establishment of an English friary at Bornhem, in Flanders. Howard realistically saw that, even with the prestige of his name and family behind them, the Dominicans would not recruit many young men of ability until Bornhem had proved itself as a centre of peace and solid discipline. They had much of the past to live down. Until that happened, in the 1670s, the Bornhem community suffered (as the early Franciscan foundation had) from small numbers, a high death rate from sickness, and the recruitment, perforce, of older men from any source, mission priests, Irishmen, Scots. It is therefore hardly surprising that, unlike the Benedictines and Davenport, the Dominicans produced no leaders and writers on the great controversies of the day.

The history of the English Capuchin friars and Carmelites followed the same course, except that the Capuchins by chance recruited very notable converts, and neither had a Howard to gain them a solid community base. Father Simon Stock (Thomas Doughty), the leading English Carmelite friar, repeatedly failed to found a noviciate. His sympathies in the controversies are clear. At one time he thought of competing with the English Jesuits on the mission in Maryland, America. Later he toyed with the idea of cutting free from the authority of his Order and getting the support of the Appellants for a 'free friary' under an English bishop. The Capuchins received two windfalls in the early 1590s: Archangel Pembroke (who, though himself a friar of no particular spiritual or intellectual distinction, was closely in with the French radical thinkers, Berulle and St Cyran, and with the Port Royal community) and a very remarkable spiritual guide, Benet Canfield (Benet Fitch).

Canfield was a convert. Apart from one visit to England in 1599, when he was arrested and found himself in gaol in the company of the Appellant priest leaders, he spent all his religious life in France, immersed in French Church affairs. Circumstances threw him constantly into association with French Catholic radicals, and his sympathies were with them and against the Spanish and Jesuit conception of the Counter-Reformation. But he was no pamphleteer or theologian. With his whole being, like the Benedictine, Augustine Baker, he knew that Christianity had no future unless its main energies were bent on establishing strong centres of contemplative prayer. No doubt the sacramental and clerical organisation of the Catholic Church at large, and the English Mission in particular, must be accepted, but he had little interest in them or belief in their spiritual efficacy unless backed by a host of contemplatives. His spiritual writings circulated amongst the *cognoscenti* in manuscript versions, often differing textually, and the greatest of them, his *Rule of Perfection*, was soon repeatedly produced by the printers in many languages (three English editions by 1609; twelve in French by 1640; five in Latin, two in Italian, four in Dutch, one in German, one in Spanish, one in Arabic). Some historians have exaggerated his importance in European religious history and, indeed, made him out to be the Catholic Counter-Reformation's greatest spiritual guide after St John of the Cross and St Teresa of Avila. His teaching was narrowly onesided, and even sometimes perverse. His writings had a great vogue in their day, particularly amongst would-be devout lay people seeking 'instant holiness' or an infallible short guide to contemplative prayer. Like John of the Cross and Teresa, he had to endure hostility from the Church authorities (in his case probably justifiably to some extent). The Spanish Inquisition forbade the faithful to use the *Rule*, and the Holy Office in Rome put it on the official *Index of Prohibited Books*. Canfield's career was a final proof, if any were needed, that the new English Catholic religious communities were all hotbeds of ebullient radicalism.

But surely, we may think, these male communities must have had their female counterparts, and *they* must have been conservative and peaceful? Historians have recently been noting that, amongst English Protestants, the religious and social ferments of the seventeenth century often had women participants. The Puritan movement owed a great deal to pious women, who sometimes gave a stronger lead than their menfolk. Even in the social protest marches and demonstrations of the 1650s women banded together and played an active part. They always paid lip-service to their traditional inferior place in society, but nevertheless explicitly claimed the right to their own opinions. It seems to have been presumed that Catholics were essentially conservative, and that therefore the seventeenth century cannot have known any similar demonstrations by their womenfolk. Yet the history of the new English Catholic women's religious communities upsets this presumption.

In 1600 there were no more than ten English Catholic establishments on the Continent. By the 1660s this number had swelled almost tenfold, and the increase is all the more impressive if we add to it the forty or more Irish Catholic and dozen Scots Catholic institutions. The Protestant Reformation had played havoc with Catholic institutions over great areas. Many monasteries and convents were wrecked or deserted by their communities, and other communities were much depleted. The Counter-Reformation brought everywhere a great wave of rebuilding, modernisation and new foundations. The English Catholic effort was of a piece with this activity. It

could, and did, get help (in subscriptions, legal assistance, the loan
of the services of expert modernised foreign monks, friars and nuns)
from it. It often followed the custom of the time in getting permission
to take over disused monasteries, or moribund ones, from which the
survivors of the original owners were legally removed. So for
instance Philip Howard was put to much trouble in 1657 to get a
moribund Flemish Cistercian monastic community to vacate the
buildings at Bornhem. The Jesuit house at Watten was a building which had already been appropriated by Flemish Jesuits. The
Benedictine foundation at Dieulouard in Lorraine occupied an
old deserted college of priests. Inevitably the English founders
followed the monastic fashions of the day in deciding their form
of life.

As we have seen, the prevailing note of the fashion was austerity
and modernisation, varying in degree. The English generally plumped
for an advanced degree. Thus by the 1660s their houses were scattered very widely across Catholic Europe. Not surprisingly the
thickest concentration was to be found in Spanish Flanders: half
their establishments lay there. Almost every town of any size in the
country had at least one English, Irish or Scots house, and a good
many had two, three or four. Douai remained the chief Continental
Little Britain, with the English College, its feeder boys' school, a
Benedictine monastery with its boys' boarding school, a Franciscan
monastery, house of studies and small postulants' school, Irish and
Scots seminaries. In spite of incessant seventeenth-century wars in
the area (which eventually made the town French), the forced evacuation of most of the British in the 1790s, and the devastation of two
world wars, the town even today bears many marks of the long alien
occupation. Brussels, the capital of Flanders, had three English convents of nuns, Louvain five establishments, Antwerp, Ghent,
Gravelines, Dunkirk, St Omer, Liège, Cambrai two each. France
came next to Flanders in popularity with the British founders, with
nearly forty establishments, and the second largest Little Britain at
Paris—a Benedictine monastery and house of studies, its chaplaincy
at Port Royal, the Arras College for secular priests' higher studies at
the Sorbonne, two English convents both with girls' boarding schools,
and Irish and Scottish houses. Spain was unpopular with English
founders, and houses were very few, no doubt because it was the
ideological centre of a version of Counter-Reformation Catholicism
that most of them found distasteful. The Irish had fewer prejudices
against the country. Portugal was under Spanish rule to the 1640s,
yet, probably because of its already growing English community
engaged in the port wine business, it acquired a group of English and
Irish houses at Lisbon.

Oddly enough Italy was also never popular with the British founders. The English have always found the climate of Rome trying. Hence, more for reasons of prestige and Church politics than natural inclination, there was an English seminary and convent, a Scots seminary, and a seminary and two monasteries of the Irish. There were English nuns at Naples and Perugia (directing communities mostly comprised of Italians), and Irish religious at Viterbo. Even the growth of a mostly Catholic English lay community of merchants at Leghorn never attracted the founders. The advance of the Counter-Reformation into northern and eastern Europe by the 1620s brought tempting offers from Catholic kings and princes who were even willing, in their desire to re-Catholicise captured territories quickly, to provide English, Irish and Scots religious with monastic buildings free of cost. Often unwisely, the British superiors succumbed to the temptation. The English Benedictines accepted from the Emperor monasteries at Lambspring, Cismar and Rintelin. Rintelin carried with it the burden of directing a new Catholic university. But the tide of the Thirty Years War turned swiftly and the Benedictines had to quit Cismar and Rintelin after a short occupation. War operations threatened Lambspring and led to the butchery of some of its community. But this isolated English monastery was destined to survive as an embarrassment to the Congregation. The community inherited, with the buildings, a medieval abbatial jurisdiction with the right to maintain a gallows and prison. There were English convents (with mainly German communities) at Munich, Cologne, Trier, Pressburg and Vienna, all of which eventually became wholly German. The Irish fought shy of Germany, but the Scots—very poor and with strong German connections— accepted five or six foundations there. There were even Irish Franciscans and English nuns at Prague, the capital of Imperial Czechoslovakia. Yet Slav eastern Europe was not by any means the most adventurous and risky field attempted by these early Stuart English Catholic founders. At various times English nuns set up underground convents in England itself—in and around London, at Dolebank in Yorkshire, and in York in the 1620s, 1630s and even during the civil wars. The English Jesuits established a missionary house in America, in Maryland, a proprietary colony belonging to a Catholic peer, Lord Baltimore. The Franciscans made several efforts to found houses in Maryland and the English West Indies, and, in the 1660s, the Dominicans briefly took over a house in Tangier, then an English colony.

In all this wide-flung mass of foundations, men played the major part. But women, in the teeth of innumerable social restrictions, taboos and outright male resistance, played nevertheless a far greater part than would have been possible in the Catholicism of earlier centuries. They established some forty convents. As early as 1582 the English Jesuits were considering what could be done with the devout women, who formed a disproportionately large majority of most recusant groups in England. By 1604 they had in circulation 'An instruction and direction for the spiritual helpe of such Inglish gentlewomen as desyre to lead a more retired and recollected life then the ordinarie in Ingland doth yeald'. The document suggested that, as was becoming fashionable in Spain and Italy, it might be possible to organise informal groups of women living together a secret life of devotion, each making, as the confessor directs 'some one vow, some two, some all three, some perpetually, some for a tyme . . .' The difficulty for the Jesuits, then essentially modern-minded men, was twofold. In the first place they were very doubtful of the wisdom of helping devout recusant women to found convents abroad, since experience had proved that such places rapidly became dumping-grounds for unwanted girls, centres of gossip and laxity. Secondly Jesuit rules did their best to discourage the Fathers from getting heavily involved with women: there was an absolute ban on the formation of convents of auxiliary 'Jesuitesses'. Yet the Jesuit system equally absolutely demanded that the laity, without regard for sex, should be directed by the Fathers, with all the apparatus of private vows to confessors. Moreover existing Church law required that convents be subjected very firmly to male authority, which could be either that of the local bishop (in which case the authority of Jesuit directors over the nuns would be limited), or of some male religious superior. In every way Jesuit furtherance of the foundation of convents faced a thorny path, and they generally fought shy of direct involvement.

Hence devout recusant women and girls in England by 1600 had to face a difficult choice. If they were of the school of thought which regarded Jesuit direction as essential, they must either stay in England as individual Jesuit penitents in private vows, or go overseas and be prepared to join an existing foreign, or create a new English, convent which would inevitably lie under episcopal control, and where steady Jesuit direction would most likely be in short supply. If the woman was anti-Jesuit, the path was a little easier. She might well persuade the contemporary English Benedictine, Franciscan, Carmelite or Capuchin groups in process of formulation to undertake the support and control of nuns of their Orders. After all, these Orders, unlike the Jesuits, had a long tradition of supporting auxiliary convents of nuns under the same Rule. Quite apart from these problems of ideology, there were complex economic and social restrictions imposed by the pattern of contemporary society. As respectable women, nuns had to be chaperoned and protected by men. They must have a secure endowment, in the form of a 'dowry' provided by their families or benefactors. As the seventeenth-century rediscoverers of monastic life found out by bitter experience, all houses, even of men, had to restrict entry constantly and at all costs, to fit the number of places available economically. It was not easy to convey sums of money, usually by notes of credit passing amongst merchant-exporters, overseas; dowries not infrequently remained unpaid because they were lost in transit, or because families in England, due to apostasy, conformism or the death of benefactors and the legal difficulties of carrying out testamentary bequests to 'superstitious papist uses', broke their promises to pay. Dowries were only payable after religious profession: novices could leave before profession, or, as they not infrequently did, die during the noviciate. For instance, Philip Howard launched a convent of Dominican nuns at Vilvorde in Flanders, starting with three borrowed Flemish nuns and one English novice, Mistress Antonia Howard, aged sixteen, his cousin. The novice died less than four months later.

There were other economic problems. Everywhere in Europe the law placed many complicated restraints on the ownership of money and property by women, either individually or in community. It was exceedingly difficult for an unmarried girl convert to Catholicism to persevere in her new religion; if she did succeed in escaping abroad, her entry into a convent had to depend on some generous benefactor, unless the convent could find her a vacant place as a laysister—that is, practically as a domestic servant. The position of convert widows was somewhat easier. The Franciscan convent at Brussels was founded by two widows of means of whom at least one appears to have been a convert. They were temporarily clothed in the religious habit in 1619, but allowed to live indefinitely outside the Flemish convent while they searched for English recruits. After two visits to England, one of them collected another widow and '6 virgens', with whom a start was made at community life. The two foundresses accepted the position of laysisters, to manage the finances of the convent outside the strict monastic enclosure: the other widow became the first Abbess of her teenage community. On her death-bed in 1642 the Abbess significantly promised to pray in heaven for the community firstly to continue 'in the Unity in which she left them till god came to Judg the world', secondly to continue subject to the Franciscan Fathers, and thirdly 'that God Allmighty Would enable them With sufficiency of temporall means'. Once an English convent had surmounted the formidable difficulties of foundation, it could still be destroyed by any one of three disasters: violent dissension within the community (usually over the Jesuits), breaking away from its shelter under a male Order (for the same reason), or financial collapse.

The battle over Jesuit direction certainly convulsed a good many convents. The Benedictine nuns were particularly afflicted this way. In 1598 an aristocratic lady, Lady Mary Percy, who had financial means and much influence with the Spanish Viceregal government, founded a Benedictine convent in Brussels. The English Benedictine Congregation did not yet exist, so the convent was put under local episcopal control and secular priest confessors. The community, because of the rank and connections of its Abbess and foundress, quickly increased in numbers, and soon had a large party of nuns who demanded and got an English Jesuit director. It now became impossible for the two parties to live together, so in 1624 most of the pro-Jesuit nuns hived off to found their own convent at Ghent. Unfortunately this still left a group of Jesuit-directed nuns at Brussels. A new secular priest chaplain there, a prominent Appellant, approached the bishop and secured the eviction of the Jesuit director. Violent dissension in the community followed, and the chaplain was charged with being an Appellant and a heretic. The bishop gave way, and, for the sake of peace, allowed the nuns freedom, if they wished, to resort to a Jesuit director.

By 1629 the community was totally split, and the 'Jesuited' nuns refused even to attend choir when the chaplain celebrated Mass. The affair became a great Catholic scandal and talking-point. In 1635 an effort was made to remove the 'Jesuited' by force to pro-Jesuit convents. Meanwhile the pro-Jesuit English Benedictine convent at Ghent had prospered, and it was eventually to give birth to four new foundations. But in 1623 the English Benedictines decided at last to enter the lists. They brought over nine young women from England, borrowed three anti-Jesuit nuns from the Brussels Benedictine convent, and started with this community a convent at Cambrai subject to the Congregation and its spiritual directors. Unfortunately the Cambrai community's director for its first nine years was Augustine Baker. He gained a great hold on the minds and affections of most of the new community; he not only turned them away decisively from Jesuit spirituality, but made them passionate adherents of his own peculiar system. He already had followers amongst his colleagues who were sowing dissension in the English monastery at Douai. The Benedictine superiors, disapproving greatly of his views, withdrew him from Cambrai (to the great distress of the nuns) to Douai, and eventually tried to quell the uproar both at Cambrai and Douai by despatching him to England permanently. Thus the eventual outcome of the controversies amongst the Benedictine nuns was their division into three separate groups, one (Brussels) adhering to the Appellants and direction by secular priests; one (Ghent, Pontoise, Dunkirk, Ypres) adhering to Jesuit confessors and direction and anti-Appellant; one (Cambrai and its later foundation at Paris) adhering to a middle road, neither pro-Jesuit nor pro-Appellant, devoted to the English Benedictine Congregation, and strongly marked for generations by the extremist teaching of Bakerism.

The Franciscan nuns were not to escape the infection. The Poor Clare community founded at Gravelines in 1609 owed its origins to Jesuit influence and was, from the start, Jesuit-directed. The English Franciscan Province was not yet in existence. It was a very successful community and grew rapidly to a strength of sixty-five nuns by 1625. It was able to make five daughter foundations by 1652. But the peace of the parent community at Gravelines was increasingly disturbed by a growing anti-Jesuit section of the nuns, who demanded subjection to, and direction by, Franciscans. The quarrel was still raging in 1660. Meanwhile the English Franciscans had riposted in 1621 by founding their own community of nuns (of the 'Third Order') at Brussels. It had a modest success, and made a daughter foundation at Paris in 1658. But the English Franciscan convents remained as divided as the Benedictine nuns.

In 1603 two of St Teresa of Avila's Carmelite nuns, Anne of Jesus and Anne of St Bartholomew, arrived in France from Spain. They found awaiting them many devout French Catholics who had read of their distinctive spirituality and of its great impact in Spain. Pierre de Berulle formed a special committee to assist the Spanish nuns in making French Carmelite foundations and to watch over their material needs. From 1607 French Carmels—all with very small communities, as they were obliged to be by St Teresa's Constitutions—were founded in a steady stream. In fact St Teresa was by no means opposed to the Jesuits; her methods simply passed through and beyond theirs. Nor were the French and English Jesuits hostile to the Carmelite movement: they quite often directed some of their women penitents to apply for entry into a Carmel. But there was a distinct danger that Berulle's committee and some women entering the Order would attempt to impose on it their own preconceived allegiances, pro- or anti-Jesuit. It was also likely that quite soon English Carmels would begin to appear and that they would suffer from the contemporary English Catholic quarrel. This fear proved justified. In 1618 an aristocratic English widow living in voluntary exile, Lady Mary Lovel, decided to use her money and influence to found an English Carmel at Antwerp. She herself had already tried to be a nun in the very divided English Benedictine convent at Brussels, and was strongly 'Jesuited'. Hence she proposed that her foundation should be Carmelite, but Jesuit-directed, and under the authority of the local bishop. In principle there was sense in this proposal, since Carmels were normally left very independent of outside authority, and simply under a light surveillance by the (male) Carmelite Order and the bishop. There was no English Carmelite Province. Hence the new Carmel of Antwerp started off under Jesuit confessors, much to the indignation of the few English Carmelite priests. Eventually, and slowly, Antwerp was to give birth to three other English Carmels, all Jesuit-directed. But the movement, the most austere form of religious life amongst the English Catholics, never attracted much attention amongst them or exerted much influence.

The familiar pattern of division runs on through the convents of English Canonesses. The convents at Louvain and Bruges owed much of their early recruitment to the Jesuits. The convent at Douai, later transferred to Paris, became one of the very few communties of nuns adhering wholeheartedly to the Appellants: in the 1630s it was practically their headquarters abroad. On the other hand the Canonesses of Liège and the tiny Dominican convent at Vilvorde seem to have been untouched by the great quarrel. The Liège community had benefactors from both sides: the Dominicans, though closely subordinated to the fathers of their Order, and so to the anti-Jesuit faction, were too struggling, austere and introverted a group to bother about faction outside their enclosure.

We have now considered just over half the English convents. The remaining seventeen or eighteen formed a closely united and peculiar group, associated with a remarkable woman, Mary Ward, who is the seventeenth-century female counterpart of John Barnes, the rebel Benedictine. Her life-story is fascinating, but still far too little known. Both in life and after death the records of her work suffered a mysterious eclipse. In her lifetime the creative work of this woman, who was very ardently devoted to the Papacy, the English Jesuits and their principles, was disowned by the Jesuits and officially dismantled by Rome: its records were suppressed. Shreds of her communities survived by a series of Church law stratagems, camouflage and dropping of all reference to Mary Ward. In modern times, when the ban seemed to be lifting, and historical studies of Mary were beginning, the bulk of her papers, long concealed in Germany, were said to have been accidentally destroyed; but enough is left, both from her side and (in far greater quantity) from the side of her virulent opponents, to show how extraordinary her achievement was.

Mary Ward grew up in a very unusual Catholic forcing-house: a small Yorkshire circle of intensely devout recusants closely associated with Fathers Holtby and Gerard, the greatest Jesuit missioners of the 1590s. It was an atmosphere of rather claustrophobic intensity and militancy. At the age of twenty she was passed overseas to Flanders by the Jesuits and directed by her confessor into a Flemish Poor Clare convent. But she persuaded him that she had a vocation which could not be fulfilled either there, or in an English convent of any existing kind. Back in England in 1610 she was made by the Jesuits the leader and headmistress of a school for girls planted at St Omer alongside a Jesuit boys' school. The Jesuit missioners passed over to her in the two years of her school's existence over fifty teenage girls and widows, who were almost all, after taking the 'Spiritual Exercises', directed on to the various English convents under Jesuit influence. Clearly the back-up organisation and the confessional direction were Jesuit. But, for reasons of policy already explained, the Jesuits were unwilling to assume formal control of the school. This was in the hands of Mary. She rapidly acquired a remarkable business sense and skill in handling women. Moreover, from amongst the young women who came to the school, she soon gathered a large group who were ready to follow her lead and diverge from orthodox, modernised conventual practice into something more radically experimental. Her experiment began to burgeon fast from 1614. Its original base consisted of houses at St Omer and Liège containing large communities, approximately seventy women in each.

Mary's 'Constitutions' provided for them an almost exact copy of Jesuit life. The whole organisation was to stand completely outside the normal Church law structure of monastic life: it was to be subject to Rome alone, and not to any bishop or religious Order, nor even to the Jesuit Provincial or General. This last provision was partly to accord with official Jesuit policy, and partly reflected Mary's own considered judgment that her relationship with Jesuits should be one of a relatively free association. Thus the members of the Institute were laywomen, not nuns; they wore ordinary secular dress, were not subject to the elaborate enclosure rules imposed then on all nuns, could engage in parochial and teaching work freely, and had none of the usual elaborate timetable of community worship. Like the Jesuits, the vast majority of the members were never to take anything except temporary vows, and so could leave or be summarily dismissed at any time. Broadly speaking, these ideas were not new: on a small, local scale, they had been applied in many places on the Continent by radically-minded Catholics for at least a century. In contemporary France several radical leaders were experimenting in the same way with their women supporters. But it was one thing to do this on a tiny scale, temporarily: it was quite another to propose to do it on a very large scale, permanently, and over wide

areas of Catholic Europe. Such an enterprise would, if it became
fashionable, draw away many women from entry into normal convents and so put the foundation movement in peril. On a small scale
it could pass as an exception and eccentricity: on a large scale it
could not fail to challenge directly some massive vested interests
and traditional prejudices. The opposition was clearly identified in
Mary's words:

> There is a report that Cardinals in Rome say 'they are but
> women and their first fervour will fade'. There is no such dif-
> ference between men and women . . . it is not because we are
> women, but imperfect women . . . there is not verity of man,
> nor verity of woman, but the verity of the Lord and this verity
> women may have as well as men . . . Fervour is not placed in
> feelings, but in a will to do well, which women may have as
> well as men. There is no such difference between men and
> women that women may not do great things, and I hope in God
> it will be seen that women in time to come will do much . . .
> Heretofore we have been told by men we must believe. It is true
> we must, but let us be wise and know what we are to believe
> and what not, and not to be made to think we can do nothing. If
> women were made so inferior to men in all things, why were
> they not exempted in all things, as they are in some? I confess
> wives are to be subject to their husbands, men are head of the
> Church, women are not to administer sacraments, nor preach in
> public churches, but in all other things, wherein are we so
> inferior to other creatures that they should term us 'but
> women'? but as if we were in *all* things inferior to some other
> creatures, which I suppose to be man! Which I dare be bold to
> say is a lie . . . I would to God all men understood this verity,
> that women if they will be perfect, and if they would not make
> us believe we can do nothing and that we are but women, we
> might do great matters . . . I know a missioner in England
> who said he would not for 1000 worlds be a woman, because he
> thought 'a woman could not apprehend God'. I answered
> nothing but only smiled, although I could have answered him
> by the experience I have to the contrary. I could have been sorry
> for his want of judgment, not to condemn his judgment, for
> he is a man of very good judgment, his want is in experience.

There were priests who were at least partly persuaded of the truth
of what she said. Augustine Baker wrote that in his experience 'In
these latter times . . . God hath as freely (perhaps more commonly)
communicated the divine lights and graces proper to a contemplative

life to simple women, endowed with lesser and more contemptible gifts of judgment, but yet enriched with stronger wills and more fervent affections to Him than the ablest men.' He noted that 'an experienced author says for 1 man nearly 10 women go to heaven'. However he judged that male contemplatives were 'more noble, sublime, exalted in spirit, less partaking of sensible effects, raptures, ecstasies and imaginary representations, as likewise melting tendernesses of affection, than women'.

Mary Ward despatched into England some thirty members of her Institute, who worked with missioners, mostly in London, searching out lapsed Catholics, helping the sick and establishing underground schools and catechetical centres in Spitalfields, the Strand and Knightsbridge. On the Continent, with the help of the Jesuits, and their influence with princes, houses were astonishingly quickly set up in Rome, Naples, Perugia, Cologne, Trèves, Pressburg, Vienna, Munich, Augsburg, Prague, Cambrai. Almost all of the houses ran large girls' schools. In these schools Mary adopted a slightly altered version of the Jesuit syllabus and method which was so immensely successful in their boys' Colleges. Latin was taught thoroughly, the humanities and—to the shocked horror of the Appellant priests— dogmatic and moral theology, 'in order, as they say, they may not be taken in by their confessors'. In this matter of teaching, Mary was again by no means innovating. Advanced educated parents for over a century had been giving their daughters through tutors an education much like that of their brothers. Even the girls' schools run by the orthodox English convents sometimes, depending on the abilities of the nuns and their pupils, went far beyond the usual ladylike education in music, needlework and a little French. Missioners in England had already begun to complain wryly that their educated women parishioners (who, by English custom, were commonly allowed to be sacristans and answer Mass) were far too knowledgeable about fine points of rubrics and theology. But before Mary, no English woman had ever been quite so blatant and open about her ambitions for girls' education, or so very capable in mass organisation of it. It was mass organisation; for instance the school in Vienna had 500 pupils soon after it opened. Indeed the sheer scale of Mary's success compelled her to take into the Institute an increasingly large number of Italian, German, Austrian and Czech women.

Trouble began very soon. The Appellants regarded the Institute as a Jesuit monstrosity, and showered Rome with demands that it should be suppressed. The English Jesuit Provincial feared for the good name of the Society. He had already bundled out of it one able Jesuit who had, on slight evidence, been accused by the Appellants of insulting the French government. He now instructed his men to

D

withdraw all support from Mary and her Institute, and in no way to defend it in word or writing. The numerous English Jesuits who had hitherto backed her warmly were dumbfounded: her confessor was removed to the English Mission; Father Gerard, her most important backer, was summarily silenced and removed to Flanders. Within the Institute, amongst Mary's original companions, there now appeared violent dissensions and opposition to her policies. Most probably one party demanded that Mary should avert trouble by compromise, and agree to accept at least a modicum of orthodox nunnery. In the heat of the quarrel Mary's picture was torn up, and one of her sisters left the Institute.

By 1629 Church authorities were starting to close some houses of the Institute. In 1631 a formal Papal Bull of total suppression was issued. The arrest of Mary was ordered as a 'heretic, schismatic and rebel to the Holy Church'. She was imprisoned by the Holy Office in a Poor Clare convent's gaol in Munich. (It was then perfectly normal form for religious houses to have their own private cells for the imprisonment of the disobedient and unruly. Mary herself had given as one of her reasons for having temporary vows that she infinitely preferred that unsuitable subjects should be sent away and released, rather than that the Institute should have the expense and trouble of maintaining prisons for recalcitrants.) Except in Germany, where the civil authorities winked at the survival of a few houses provided they conformed to orthodox patterns of monastic life, the Institute was quite brutally dismantled, its property seized, its members ejected. Some found their way back to their families and eventually married, others entered orthodox convents. Mary was eventually quietly released. She bowed outwardly to Papal authority and kept (for her) remarkably quiet: but there is no sign that she ever budged from her conviction that her plan had been directly inspired by God. After fruitless efforts to appeal against the sentence, dogged by spies and the ridicule of most respectable English priests and religious, pursued by the indignation of some families of the ejected sisters, she arrived back in England in 1639. A small body of sisters, camouflaged as nuns, remained in Munich: a still smaller group awaited her in London. After a vain and extraordinarily stubborn effort to recruit girls and restart the London schools, she was forced by the imminence of civil war to leave for Yorkshire. There sympathetic priests and relatives, under cover of wartime confusion, sheltered her until her death near York in 1645. Her companions dispersed, mostly to Munich.

Possibly upwards of 5000 English people entered religious life abroad between 1598 and 1642. By any standards, it was as remarkable a phenomenon as the contemporary Great Migration of some

20,000 others to the American and West Indian colonies. It would be naive to imagine that all of the 5000 English religious went abroad for purely pious reasons. The Jesuits, while sternly determined to develop purity of motive in themselves and those whom they directed, were sure that God's grace and calling of souls mostly worked obliquely, not directly: the average soul was childlike in its blindness and selfishness and could only, at any rate initially, be led to better things by rewards and punishments. Hence from the 1590s, English colleges and convents influenced by the Jesuits tended to enquire closely into, and record, the spiritual backgrounds of entrants. The chroniclers clearly expected to find, and stressed, the elements in these biographies of error, accident, human frailty, opposition: the moral was always clear—God's calling and preventing grace turns evil into good constantly. Perhaps they overdid things: perhaps the entrants exaggerated their stories in a human, or pious, desire to please. But there must be enough solid truth in the stories, and the impression they give of mixed motives is likely to be a true one. Thus a great many of the students entering the English College, Rome (a substantial number of whom later became Jesuits), admitted frankly that they had been either Protestants or very lapsed, conformist Catholics: they owed their presence in Rome, over and over again, to urgent persuasions by pious relatives or priests, or to fortunate accidents. The chronicle of the English Canonesses of Louvain is very explicit. Entrant after entrant comes due to pressures: ('her brother, a priest asked her whether she would not enter religion. She answered yes, though she did not then know what religion was'; 'her father had a great devotion to St Augustine; he promised that if he had two daughters, he would name one Mary and the other Anne, and give them both to God in religion').

A large section of the entrants into all religious houses was made up of 'family blocks'. Lady Constable, a pious patroness, seems to have looked over her very large flock of relations, especially the poor ones burdened with many children, with an eye to providing places in religion for them at her expense. The Louvain chronicler writes: 'Lady Constable saw that Mrs Lawson was burdened with children, so she offered a place in religion for one girl.' All twelve daughters of the Bedingfield family of Redlingfield, Suffolk, ended in convents, including one who first married. The Benedictine convent at Cambrai was largely started from three such family groups. By the 1650s the Radcliffes of Dilston in Northumberland had two daughters, four aunts and two nieces in convents. In Yorkshire there were two intensely pious family groups which acted as unofficial seminaries for future religious: the house of Mary Ward's grandparents, and the house of Sir Ralph Babthorpe at Howden. The

Babthorpe clan eventually emigrated *en masse* to Louvain. Sir Ralph started on a course of the 'Spiritual Exercises' to nerve his will to accept his wife's plan that they should, with Papal permission, separate into religious houses. The younger sons moved automatically to Jesuit and Benedictine noviciates along with nephews and cousins. The girls were already married, but their children were urged into religion, followed by the footman and the steward's daughter. It is very noticeable that this wholesale rush affected only certain families; others, especially if they were not directed by Jesuits, rarely if ever sent any member into religion.

But although the majority of the 5000 were pushed into arranged marriages with religion, and, once there, apparently remained docile spiritual children, manifestly the dynamic force which created and sustained the whole movement was much more profound. The English Jesuits had a peculiar, distinctive and strong regimental loyalty and discipline. They admitted (and even rejoiced in) the mixed motives and agonisings of their entrants; perforce they had to admit the complex, violent characteristics of those who left the Society or who were expelled from it. But serving Jesuits must appear to the world as docile, serene, supremely competent to deal with the doubting from a platform of complete assurance. The officially inspired autobiographies of John Gerard and William Weston give, as they were meant to do, just such an impression. Of late Jesuit historians themselves have began to breach tradition and show, from internal, secret correspondence within the Society, the large degree to which its leading spirits were driven by something greater than regimental discipline and docility. Weston, for instance, is revealed as a convert, neurotic, obsessed with a fear of witches and damnation, often deeply depressed, yet clearly struggling compulsively towards some strange divine mystery. Gerard (outwardly so self-assured, relaxed, self-confident) was also a convert in his teens, who had had exceedingly little formal Jesuit training. He was essentially an improviser and spiritually a late developer. The issue of Mary Ward, whom he strongly supported, most probably thrust him personally out of spiritual childhood. He dared to stand up for her, and was punished by his Provincial with banishment from his life's work in England to thirty years of stagnation abroad. Roger Lee, Mary Ward's chief Jesuit director abroad, appears to have been a docile, textbook man. Mary's quiet, respectful rejection of his guidance at first enraged and then overcame him; he passed out of his spiritual childhood under her direction, and very likely the passing was confirmed by his summary banishment from his lifework abroad to the English Mission as a punishment for his support of her. But admittedly the English Jesuits of these years produced no

leader of even the spiritual stature of Mary Ward, Augustine Baker
or Benet Canfield: no doubt they simply had not the human material,
and their peculiar discipline acted as a depressant and ejector of
originality. However it was not mere drill which powered the Province: there was enough spiritual maturity, albeit in chains.

Mary Ward's autobiographical writings are fascinating. On the one
hand she was, mentally and spiritually, all her life a perfect product
of official Jesuit training. Her very feminine love-attachment to the
Society went beyond, in its intensity, the romantic young-man devotion of the Campions and Southwells or the regimental spirit of older
Jesuits. In the highest flights of her mysticism, her revelations told
her, in the plainest Jesuit officialese, to copy the Society exactly. No
number of rebuffs by the Provincial could decrease her love for it.
This side of her mentality moved on a level of intense but practical
spirituality, of incessant religious exercises (she underwent the
'Spiritual Exercises' far more often than any Jesuit), rigorous physical asceticism (she whipped herself often with 'the discipline', an
instrument of penance much used in English religious houses),
frantically active organisation and hard work, docility to authority.
But with another part of her mind and spirit she began to break
painfully out of this pious cocoon. She argued with her directors
fiercely and repeatedly; she freely admitted that the orthodox courses
they enforced nauseated her. The 'Exercises', with their highly
skilful, 'preacherly' techniques to rouse the imagination and
emotions, and the equally colourful textbook meditations which
were compulsory community exercises, very soon upset her. She
did not cease to be highly imaginative and emotional and given to
fierce loves and hatreds, but she began to think that, at any rate for
her and any soul who wanted to progress, reliance on such techniques
was deadening and wrong. She knew, she wrote, a good many women
whose religion was built on their affections; they loved their directors,
loved being directed, enjoyed and sought 'sensible devotion': there
were the nuns in every convent who claimed, at their fortnightly
Communions (directors then deliberately rationed Communions), to
experience ecstasy, to taste and smell exquisite flavours and scents.
So long as this satisfied them and they remained in that state perhaps
it was good. But Mary knew numbers of them who, deprived of a
Jesuit director, crumpled up 'and fell into great tepidity or even athe-
ism'. She realised that she herself had 'placed my affections more in
the esteem of those that for the present guide me than in the verity
which is God'. She saw 'the large numbers of the damned and how
few are saved; the only cause of their damnation is the want of
cooperation with those impulses the good God gives'. Clearly it
seemed that God himself is the real director: when, sooner or later,

he chooses to withdraw sensible pleasure in religion and make detailed human direction end, you are thrown out into the dark to sink or swim; you swim only by expecting blindly, asking for, and relying solely on, direct divine directions (which come in the form of voices heard internally, or perhaps in unforeseen events), shutting out all reliance on emotion and feeling.

In this new, terrifying dimension, she felt the impact of temptations she had hitherto been sheltered from: 'Chastity is the gift of God, whether ingrafted in nature, or the contrary prevented by grace and due to many combats, always a peculiar gift of God and not conjoined to the nature of flesh and blood.' Her life was now an extraordinary mixture of light and darkness, blinding certainty and shattering doubt. She seemed to receive categorical, spoken answers from God to her questions. (Sometimes astonishing ones: speaking to God about the sudden death of a priest whom she suspected of spying on her, she said: 'Lord, I pardon him with all my heart and all that he has done against me, which appears to oblige thee, on the score of justice, to pardon him also', and the reply came: 'What he did was not against thee, but against me.') At other times she had visions—for instance of the Jesuit General in Rome, apparently smiling at her. Or, at other times, she had 'lights'—new, startling ideas which appeared, as from nowhere, in her mind. Or events could happen unexpectedly and so aptly that they must be divine answers (as when, in a reaction of doubt, she took a vow of obedience to Roger Lee until his death—and he was promptly ordered to England and died there suddenly). But these messages came fitfully, in bursts, interspersed between long periods of silence and agonising doubts.

Very early in the life of the Institute she went through a shattering trial. Sister Praxedes, a member of the Institute, raised up an opposition group who argued that Mary was deceiving herself: that her plan corresponded all too obviously with her natural affection for the Society of Jesus. However the opposition shared Mary's belief in divine inspirations: Praxedes claimed that she herself had received a message from God ordering the Institute to conform to orthodox convent life. It is worth remembering that Mary's Constitutions for the Institute required all members to give merely outward obedience to local superiors, but absolute submission of mind and conscience to Mary 'as to Christ', and that every member had to take an extra vow never to try to alter the character of the Institute. The tables were being turned on Mary. Her answer was to spend a month yet once more taking the 'Spiritual Exercises' and reviewing her whole life minutely. She emerged battered, sure that she was right, but somehow, as she wrote to John Gerard, 'still in a sea of uncertainty'. She suggested, unenthusiastically, a trial of strength with Praxedes, who should be made to ask God what he thought of Mary's plan. Then occurred a surprise, all too common in early seventeenth-century life. Praxedes was one day in blooming health, the next she was apparently at death's door. She herself now proposed her own trial of strength: she persisted in believing her own inspiration, but was ready to let God decide: if he let her die, then her party would take it as divine approval of Mary's plan. She died.

The ultimate trial of Jesuit rejection and Papal ban was far more severe: it even included Mary's imprisonment on a charge of heresy. Indeed, by selective quotation from Mary's letters, addresses to the Institute and private notes, they could easily have convicted her both of determinism of a Protestant kind (belief that God's predestination handles humans like puppets: had she not often said that freewill takes people to Hell, and talked of 'the marks of Predestination'), and of 'Illuminism' (the traditional and feared scourge of ultra-devout Catholic movements down history: revolt against hierarchical authority by those who claimed a superior source of divine lights). Fortunately for Mary she had constantly professed Catholic orthodoxy in the past, and continued to do so now, much more loudly; after some hesitation, she was acquitted and released. Henceforward her divine messages still came occasionally. The burden of what they said was, in effect: 'Conform, obey, be patient; this is a trial preordained to purify your motives; but you are right and your plan is God's, so your opponents are fighting God, and will perish if they do not repent.'

The story of the Capuchin friar, Benet Canfield, as set out in his *Autobiographical Writings* and reflected obscurely in his best-selling devotional books, is just as odd and extreme as Mary Ward's. He was brought up a conventional Anglican, and became a law-student at the Inns of Court in London at a time when the groundswell of the religious revival was beginning to stir the students. He found amongst his fellows a growing discussion of religion; some were in the throes of conversion to Puritanism, others to Catholicism. By the influence of Puritan friends he himself fell into an agony of doubt: he became convinced that London was 'an Egypt so dark that the darkness could be cut with a knife', and that his mild interest in dancing, theatres, playing cards and wenching was a mark of damnation. He fell into despair, could not sleep, wept incessantly, had appalling hallucinations, and a physical repulsion from religious practice. In his desperation, he had a mad impulse to receive the Catholic Eucharist, was hurried by a Catholic friend to a priest and received into the Catholic Church.

So far his story was not untypical; the path he was on generally led either back to Anglicanism, or abroad into a seminary. But he was convinced that he had a calling beyond ordinary courses. He pushed his confessor into letting him take, as a private act of devotion, the three religious vows of poverty, chastity and obedience, went to France and entered the noviciate of perhaps the most austere Order available there, the Capuchin friars. His noviciate was troubled; he had incessant visions, tears, ecstasies, weeks when he seemed paralysed. The community judged him a neurotic and advised against profession: the superior decided to overrule them. It was a risky decision. The Capuchins, after the Jesuits, were a great part of the spearhead of the Catholic Counter-Reformation in Europe. They were at least as active and adaptable as the Jesuits; had, like them, a rooted prejudice against mystical flights, and, perhaps even more firmly, a belief in the virtue of rigid austerity and scrupulous performance of religious set exercises. The Capuchin way of life was so peculiar that it never appealed to more than a tiny handful of Englishmen. How could someone like Canfield, with his old English emotionalism developed to the point of imbalance, ever knuckle under to the iron Capuchin discipline without psychological collapse or flight? Moreover he was profoundly provincial, starting with no knowledge of foreign languages, and now doomed to live in wholly foreign communities, being set to teach Italian novices, hear confessions in French parish churches and direct French nuns and pious ladies for practically the rest of his life.

He hints at the agonies of mind he endured steadily: for himself and his penitents he made ceaseless concentration on Christ's sufferings, a very far-reaching identification of oneself with Christ being spat on, beaten and tormented, lonely and depressed, a daily necessity. His devotional writings are full of the idea that humanity is deeply passionate and sensual, prey to strong emotions, wild fancies and imaginations, deep fears, depressions and tears. Life for the overwhelming majority, even of religious, is busy, strenuous, noisy, smelly, uncomfortable, painful and perilous. The average devout person keeps going spiritually by a mixture of rigid asceticism and application to a stiff daily programme of highly emotive and imaginative meditation from a textbook. All this is child's play. To remain at this stage of spiritual development for life (as he admitted most devout people did) was as monstrous as a circus dwarf. Everyone was called by God to the contemplative life, where, even in the midst of the hurly-burly of ordinary activity, a person is totally and perpetually at one with God, has no thoughts but God's, is 'attracted, illuminated, filled out, raised up, ravished, inebriated'. Such a person, by the drawing of God and their own acceptance and cooperation, normally remains within the ordinary framework of life and devotional exercises but only bodily so: within the mind he steadily retreats away from it all towards a silent, unfelt and permanent union with God. Outside that storm centre, his senses and imagination undoubtedly go on with their natural and devotional fireworks. He may well, at this stage, be afflicted with massive temptations, doubts, fears, ecstasies, tears, apparent neuroses: but all that will leave his inner peace utterly unmoved . . . or rather often unmoved. Canfield's map of the life of devotion allowed for *three* successive stages. Even contemplatives, he admits, cannot keep it up all the time. It is only in the third, highest stage, of supereminence, that union with God becomes total in reality; 'they are hardly in themselves at all, but in God'; they are already, while still on earth in the flesh, enjoying the beatific vision of God of the saints in heaven.

Reading between the lines, we can suspect that much of this is autobiographical, that Canfield's emotions and psychosomatic troubles remained with him, but that in the midst of the sufferings they and Capuchin life gave him, he clung doggedly to that inner light which had come to him in the Inns of Court and led him into such strange places.

Strangest of all is the story of David Augustine Baker, whose *Memorials* (edited by his Benedictine disciples from the heaps of autobiographical papers he left with them) and devotional treatises (later heavily digested and edited by them in one volume, *Sancta Sophia*) give almost as much fascinating detail as Pepys's *Diary*. Baker was brought up an Anglican and destined originally by his father to be a clergyman. He became later so fixed in views of human psychology, which were a highly individualistic version of the old amalgam of theology and medieval popular science then normal, that his detailed account of his upbringing needs treating with caution. He was probably one of the best, if not the best educated and most intellectual converts to Catholicism of this period. His mind was, like that of the English intellectuals of the day, wide-ranging; he was interested in history, science, theology, law, curiously impatient of dogmas and orthodoxies, always curious. Like most of his fellows he was an omnivorous, if not very profound, reader 'riding post through authors'; like them he had an original, speculative—though not a deeply intellectual—mind; like them he had an itch to write. As a London-trained barrister he came to know many leading intellectuals, mostly lawyers and administrators. He frequented the most celebrated salon of men of this type, in Westminster. Like them, in spite of his culture, he was curiously naive, obsessed with medicines and illness, a poor manager of his own money, clothes and affairs. By fits he was vastly laborious and then grossly idle; earthy and prurient and then smitten with intense remorse; by fits passionately religious and then slack. He had little or no sense of humour. Finally he was strongly Welsh, clannish with his fellow-countrymen, and given to confiding his most secret memoranda to the Welsh language. In fact he was very much of a piece with the large number of cultured Englishmen of the century—Bacon, Cotton, Spelman, Kenelm Digby, Pepys, Evelyn—a garrulous, 'ingenious' (their favourite word), able lot who nevertheless rarely achieved any real greatness. Very few of these men became or were Catholics, though most had personal contacts with Catholicism.

Baker's conversion, in 1603, was unusual. It took place while he was exiled from London society into the wilds of his native country. He attributed it entirely to a supernatural divine impulsion against all likelihood. Humanly speaking it was due to his disillusionment with Anglicanism, the effects of fashionable scepticism on his naturally religious mind, depression at the failure of his hopes of legal office in London, and a recent narrow escape from accidental death. His conversion, as he knew it would, effectively put an end to all hopes of any professional advancement. This, and, more important, an impulse (as he wrote, 'affection') as strong, if not as vulgarly emotional as Canfield's, drove him to seek a Benedictine life overseas. He entered an Italian monastery at Padua recommended to him, and his noviciate was a failure, though not because of any storms of emotion. He fell ill, as he generally did at crucial periods in his life, and he was not impressed with the monastic training.

He left for England, his great impulse reduced to a rather hesitant intention to complete his noviciate and be professed privately in England by English Benedictines of the Italian Congregation. His situation was highly anomalous: he was a layman, and he was proposing perhaps to undertake monastic life as a private devotion, remote from monasteries, while reverting to legal odd-jobbing to make a living and taking a part in London intellectual life. His father died at this point, and Baker inherited considerable private means. By 1607 he decided to go ahead with his monastic profession. The feelings of devotion aroused in him by the ceremony, which took place in London, led him to take lodgings in a quiet Catholic manor house in Warwickshire and embark on an experiment in prayer and the life of a hermit. He was very much a gifted amateur, with intense curiosity and a flair for picking up complex technical subjects rapidly. At Padua, perhaps overawed by his learning and restricted by his ignorance of Italian, the novicemaster had supplied him with books and left him much to his own devices. He became interested in the literature of Catholic spirituality, mastered the elements of the subject, and experimented with various forms of prayer, almost in the way that his contemporaries dabbled in scientific experiments.

The only result was a brief impression of ... something which shook him, deeply impressed him, and then vanished, to be replaced by an almost physical distaste for intense prayer. He dropped the experiment and, until his arrival in Warwickshire, had limited himself to formal use of a typical, childish meditation book. Now he re-read his books and launched out on a more intensive experiment, with that brief, mysterious impression at Padua at the back of his mind.

He certainly worked hard. As he wrote later, he spent over fourteen months at work, meditating, and then periodically moving to vocal acts, repeated over and over again, and finally to purely mental aspirations. Soon he was on his knees twelve hours a day. Suddenly that elusive impression fell on him out of the blue. He wrote: 'I was in a rapt. As far as memory now serveth I say that it was a speaking of God to the soul. I do not know whether the soul spake anything in answer to God or no.' After about fifteen minutes the experience vanished, and was followed by a deep depression, dryness and distaste for religion. He was exalted, and shattered. He dropped the experiment, and in great doubt threshed around for some answer. The priests whom he consulted shook their heads and professed ignorance of such matters. He even thought of approaching a Jesuit and asking to take the 'Spiritual Exercises'. Finally he left for the Continent, where without any theological training and solely on the strength of his monastic profession, he secured rapid ordination up to the priesthood. This was in no way with mission work in England in view, but simply as another experiment; perhaps ordination and saying Mass might solve his problem? After all, contemporary educated Catholics knew that Philip Neri had habitually been rapt into contemplation while saying Mass, for hours on end.

Back in England Baker now spent almost twelve years living in a succession of lodgings, mostly in London, paid for by his ample private means, saying Mass for one or two friends, and otherwise filling in his time with legal work for clients and historical researches. He reappeared at the Westminster salon. Once only did he take a station as a missioner, but was soon dismissed. According to his own account only Providential accidents prevented him from falling from Catholicism.

At last, in 1619, probably in desperation, he returned to his study of the books of spirituality and determined to try intensive prayer once more. He found quiet lodgings in the depths of Devonshire and set out more scientifically this time: he says he started with three solid months of formal meditation by the book, passed over gradually to acts and stayed on them for a whole year. Then came more and more aspirations, and then ... apparently no sudden impression, but distinct bodily mutations. He noted these down

exactly: palpitations, great weariness, icy coldness of the upper part
of his body and intense heat in the lower part, various pains. With
them went an exalted state of mind which seemed to bring height-
ened awareness of God and answers to difficulties. For the rest of his
life he maintained this state, where necessary topping up with
aspirations and acts. According to him he never again had a serious
bout of aridity. Now also he felt able to allow himself relaxations.
He undertook some spiritual direction rather selectively. He moved
back to London and, with hired clerks, embarked with his usual
thoroughness and speed on documentary historical research in the
Tower of London, in Mr Cotton's library at Westminster, at
Rochester and Peterborough cathedral libraries. This was not merely
filling in his time (by now he had settled down to a routine which he
found by trial and error to suit him—an hour of prayer morning
and evening, and another late at night, so leaving the rest of the
day free). He had theories about ancient monasticism and knew that
manual work was considered by the earliest monks to have a profoundly helpful effect on their prayer. Baker was too much of an
intellectual and hypochondriac to try gardening at his Gray's Inn
Lane lodging, so hard study and writing must do.

In 1624 he moved abroad, partly because of a wave of government
harassment of priests in London, and partly because he was beginning to feel he had something to contribute to the passionate debate
in the Benedictine monasteries about the form and nature of
monastic life. He arrived at the Douai monastery an odd and
formidable figure, swathed in thick clothing to keep his temperature
right for prayer, armed with masses of books, historical notes, half-
completed systematic treatises on prayer and monasticism. Nominally
he now belonged to the English Congregation, and to the strength
of the little monastery in Dieulouard. But Dieulouard was then dominated by monks who believed in strict observance and rigid austerity
—with which Baker utterly disagreed. The superiors hastily
despatched him to be confessor at their one nunnery at Cambrai.
There he spent the next nine years. Inevitably a section of the nuns
became passionate adherents of Bakerism, and others detested it.
The debate spread to Douai, and Baker's manuscript treatises started
to circulate there amongst the young monks. In 1633 the superiors
withdrew him to Douai, thinking that they could there more easily
bind him under obedience to keep silence or moderate his views.

He now made little secret of the fact that he regarded his method
of prayer and way of life as divinely inspired—much as Mary Ward
regarded her plan. To him all other methods were childish and
faulty. Like Canfield he believed that everyone—religious, secular
priests, the laity—was called to contemplative prayer. If only people

could accept this view, disputes would cease in religious houses and the dreadful controversies rending English Catholicism as a whole cease too. Baker, from his own experience in England, was convinced that the simple example and teaching of contemplative prayer would do what energetic evangelism (especially by Jesuits) and anti-Protestant controversy had so signally failed to do: convert to Catholicism masses of Protestants. As for the English Benedictines, divine inspiration was clearly calling them to a purely monastic life devised to turn them all into contemplatives. Their part in the English Mission should be limited severely to small, chosen communities of sound contemplatives abstracted from ordinary priestly work in order to exercise their own special witness. But the point in Baker's teaching which roused much the most violent opposition from the superiors concerned divine inspirations. Even more definitely than Mary Ward and Canfield, Baker believed that the contemplative would be automatically and infallibly guided by divine inspiration. Though he, with very long-winded subtlety, demonstrated to the satisfaction of himself and his band of monk and nun disciples that such an inspiration could never fundamentally contradict the principle of submission to rightful Church authority, the superiors smelled trouble. Past and contemporary history and the appearance within the Congregation of a Bakerite party set on a collision course with authority made the dangers of Baker's theory great.

We get a vivid picture of Baker during his five years' residence in the monastery at Douai. He was now rising sixty, gaunt, grey-bearded and frail. He stuck rigidly to the rule of life he had devised in England, spending most of his time praying, studying and writing in his cell. He did not attend the community's services in chapel, but could be heard singing the Office alone in his room. He never came to the refectory to community meals, but had his food brought to his cell. He did not attend community recreations or Chapters; instead, when the notice on his door warning off visitors was down, he received a steady stream of monks and outsiders in the cell. They found him voluble, fascinating and odd. He was always swathed in flannel wrappers and blankets, and in summer his cell was infested with fleas.

The President of the Congregation tried arguing with him in vain. Baker loftily refused to distract himself with controversy: but he gave the President personal and unsolicited advice on his own spiritual life, and treatises (all in Baker's distinctive, bold and clear hand) flowed in a thick stream round the community. The President desperately tried to force him to leave the monastery by cutting his food supplies. Then, in 1638, he ordered him to England. In a secular suit, cocooned in flannel, seeming (as his priest companions wrote) like a man in another world, loudly calling out strings of aspirations, he crossed the Channel by an ordinary passenger ship. A year later Mary Ward was to pass the same way. His disciples found him lodgings in Holborn in London. He was now too frail to venture out to his ingenious Westminster friends, and stayed in his room, praying, ceaselessly writing treatises, singing the psalms of the Office in a high, cracked voice, playing with the house cat, and slobbering over his meals. Occasionally he had holidays in the country. In one house in Berkshire he visited, a psychic American some years ago distinctly heard, at midnight, a cracked voice singing in Latin. Baker died in Holborn in August 1641, just before the outbreak of the civil wars.

4. Early Stuart Catholicism, 1603–60

(2) The Secular Clergy

The English Catholic secular clergy of 1600–42 must inevitably seem a depressed minority. Between 1570 and 1600 they had had their classical age of vigour and glory: now they were crushed between two great millstones. The upper stone consisted of the Orders of religious, who drew to themselves much of the available Catholic talent and devotion, and monopolised the clerical limelight in England and abroad. The lower stone consisted of the laity, massively dominated by the aristocracy and country gentry. They controlled appointments to most of the mission stations, were the clergy's patrons and employers, and, as the foundation movement created its web of colleges, religious houses and schools, the clergy's financial dependence on the gentry became even greater and more crucial. Now it was the religious who alone had any hope of exerting a real clerical influence on the lay patrons.

It is perhaps not very surprising that in these years the secular mission priests came close to total demoralisation. All too often they had to struggle to find places in England. Such pastoral work as they could find usually lay in poor missions or in dependent stations. A poor mission was a wide circuit, usually of remote moorland, where a priest travelled incessantly, serving a scattered congregation of freeholding smallholders. Such congregations existed mainly in Lancashire, Yorkshire, Northumberland and the north midlands and owed their existence to an unusual combination of local circumstances, chiefly the break-up of gentry estates, and the scantiness of Anglican pastoral care. Such missioners were dependent on the goodwill of their poor parishioners, who were not infrequently anticlerical, fractious and untrustworthy, and on Mass collections. In most cases the priest really lived on his own private means. A dependent station was an arrangement made by a landowning gentleman whereby he awarded his house chaplaincy, or at least his main financial support, to religious, while giving jobbing pastoral work amongst his servants and tenants to secular missioners.

From the 1590s to the 1660s the secular clergy, banded together in county Brotherhoods almost like Trade Clubs, fought hard in the pastoral field to save themselves from this subservient position. The rules of the Brotherhoods pointed out that, whereas the religious were supported by their Orders, seculars had no such financial security; they lacked also 'Church livings, the support of all Pastors'. Hence all members must subscribe to a common purse, from which those entering the district and without places and those unemployed through misfortune, sickness or old age might receive alms. Clerical unemployment was a much feared reality. The seculars ceaselessly complained that the seminaries poured new priests into England without regard for the acute shortage of stations. Foreign Catholic observers in England in the 1630s all reported that London was full of unemployed priests. Yet the Jesuits and other religious retorted bitterly that, so far from having a monopoly of the best stations, they quite often lost them to seculars; that their men were sometimes unemployed, and that a sizable proportion of seculars were much better off than they were.

The truth was that there was as yet no really solid parochial structure. A large number of even stoutly recusant gentry showed a marked reluctance to employ chaplains or endow missions: they much preferred (even in cases where the family had links with a religious Order) to make *ad hoc* arrangements to get themselves and their dependants served as cheaply as possible by visiting priests on circuit. Even recusant gentry with chaplaincies not infrequently treated their priests inconsiderately, dismissed them (as in the case of Augustine Baker) summarily, and appointed whom they pleased without fixed contracts. Even a station where the priest had respect, good living conditions and some security could vanish suddenly due to the apostasy or conformity of the patron, or his death and replacement by a Protestant, conformist or hostile recusant heir. Patrons could dismantle a station because of their bankruptcy, or if they decided to discontinue residence in the house. On the other hand conversions of gentry or the succession to properties of recusant heirs could suddenly create new stations. Again as the older missioners knew, the network of stations was very vulnerable to changes in the political climate. In their writings they list successive periods of boom and slump, peace and trouble. On the whole, between 1603 and 1642, the English government and society were astonishingly tolerant, if not kindly, and increasingly so. By the 1630s senior priests were amazed and alarmed at the change in climate: things were *too* easy. Nevertheless there were regular political storms at Westminster, which always meant harassment of Catholics, the gaoling of priests, and occasional execution of a few of them. At such times the mission structure crumbled, priests dispersed into hiding, stations ceased to function in some areas, a good many patrons took evasive action, moved house or conformed. The crisis might only last a few months: it could last two or three years. When peace came, the structure surfaced, battered and somewhat altered.

In the midst of such circumstances seculars and religious alike had to struggle for security, and their common foe was often the recusant lay patron. The seculars slightly outnumbered the religious; by weight of numbers and strenuous efforts they probably increased their hold on the mission structure by 1660. Yet they blamed their insecurity and discomforts largely on the Jesuits, reserving most of their spleen for the Ignatians—that is, secular priests trained by the Jesuits, suspected of secret affiliations with the Society, and attempting to pass as members of the secular priest body. It was this series of local battles for stations in the seventeenth century which, more than the public controversies between seculars and Jesuits, etched as with acid into secular priests' minds a violent animus against the Society and all its works. The private letters of seculars at this period are full of virulent abuse of 'the counterfeit brethren' (Ignatians), 'Ignatian cheats and underminings . . . the smooth operations of a lying Jesuit's tongue'. There is a strange and unhappy letter from an Ignatian in gaol in York Castle in 1618. He had found himself in the company of six other priests, Benedictines and seculars 'in the lowe Jaole in irones'. To him they are 'six supposed Preists . . . silly men, God knowes . . . All the Preistes reiecte me as Jesuited, and howe well soever I love Jesuites, I could wishe we had a learned Jesuite in stead of them all, for the good of the common cause . . . God grante our Frendes never prefarre any more such silly unfitt men, for yt harteth our common cause verye muche.'

The secular priest leaders also fought hard during these years to oust the Jesuits from the direction of the seminaries. By doing so, they hoped to achieve several objectives: to control and ration the flow of new priests to the mission; to train a new generation of secular priests in the true principles of the Brotherhoods, and put an end to the supply of Ignatians; to build up boys' boarding schools associated with the seminaries and so win away from the Jesuit and Benedictine schools the sons of the patrons; to create a body of well-educated secular priests and so raise the level of seminary studies. (They were painfully aware that the aristocracy sneered at the seculars as so lacking in culture and spirituality as to be fit only for the servants' quarters and kitchen.) Incidentally, such a body of professors could win much honour for the seculars in the battle of books with Protestants and the religious, and perhaps undertake the spiritual direction of nuns. By the 1640s this battle for the seminaries and learning was in progress and the seculars had won some notable, if small victories. They won exclusive control of the seminaries at Douai and Lisbon. The Douai College boys' school was a modest success with the gentry. Two convents of nuns were directed by secular priest confessors: one, at Paris, had the most fashionable aristocratic girls' school of the day. There were half a dozen secular priest scholars writing hard. But the battle was far from won. The Jesuits still controlled four seminaries and turned out Ignatians, in smaller numbers. The secular Colleges were in grave financial difficulties. There was, as yet, no sign of any improvement in the level of education of secular priests.

The small band of secular priest scholars contained some remarkable minds. It was typical both of English intellectual life at that time, and of the climate of the Catholic revival, that they were extremists with little sense of discretion, and that their considerable talents were either poured out in savage controversy or spread brilliantly but thinly over far too many different fields of study. Like Augustine Baker, they threw up ideas and speculations in a dazzling profusion, talked and scribbled incessantly, were curious about everything. Richard Smith was a Lincolnshire man and an Oxford convert to Catholicism. He was trained by the Jesuits in Rome, and he and a fellow-student, Thomas Preston, were accounted by Robert Persons as admirable material, likely to be very useful. Other Jesuits were not so sure, detecting in Smith a disturbing radical independence of spirit; Preston they thought docile. (In the event Preston turned to rebellion, left for the Benedictines and became a thorn in the side of the Jesuits.) Smith was sent by the Jesuits to Valladolid. There he spent eight years, acquiring higher university degrees and teaching, followed by a stint of teaching at the then still Jesuit-directed College at Douai. He passed to the English Mission in 1603, ostensibly a model Ignatian. During his years in England he went over to the cause of the secular priests, and proved to be their most ardent and capable advocate. In 1613 he was back in Rome as their spokesman, to the intense annoyance of the Jesuits. Then he moved to Paris, where he took a leading part in founding Arras College, a house of writers for secular priest scholars. He was short, young-looking for his age, a fascinating talker and so able a linguist that his many French friends called him a *bon français*. He became a friend of Armand du Plessis, Cardinal de Richelieu (whom he coached in theology), Pierre de Berulle and St Cyran. He was pious, a friend of

Carmelite nuns, a successful spiritual director and writer of devotional books. As a Sorbonne professor of theology he was brilliant, if lacking in depth. But, as we shall see, his tremendous mental energies were to find an unfortunate outlet after 1625.

Thomas White was probably, after John Henry Newman, the most original thinker as yet produced by modern English Catholicism. He was young enough to be Smith's son, came from Essex, and like Smith, began his clerical career as an Ignatian at the Jesuit school of St Omer and the Jesuit College at Valladolid. He was so able a scholar that he was moved to the College at Douai, acquired extra degrees there and taught philosophy with a brilliance and originality which alarmed other professors in the College and led them to delate him for unorthodoxy. He survived and they were dismissed. In 1624 he moved on to the Sorbonne in Paris to take yet another higher degree (this time in law). By now he had turned against the Jesuits and was lending his immense ability to forwarding the secular clergy cause. He served them briefly as their agent in Rome, acted as their first Rector of the English College, Lisbon, when they ejected the Jesuits, taught at the Sorbonne, and eventually retired to live in lodgings in Drury Lane in London. Like Augustine Baker, he was ingenious, immensely curious about many subjects—philosophical, mathematical, scientific, theological, mystical, political thought. He was astonishingly fertile in speculative ideas. Books poured out of him: some forty (mostly under assumed names, Blacklow, Blackloe, Albius, Anglus, An Englishman) were printed and others circulated in manuscript amongst his friends and disciples. The titles of a few of them will give some idea of the man: *Institutiones Sacrae* (censured by the Theological Faculty of Douai university, and by Papal decrees twice); *De Mundo*; *De Origine Mundi*; *A Theological System on Digbean and Aristotelian Principles*; *The Problem of Grace and Freewill*; *On Purgatory: the Middle State of Souls*; *Grounds of Obedience and Government*; *A Contemplation of Heaven: with an Exercise of Love and a Descant on the Prayer in the Garden*; *Euclid's Physics, or the Principles of Nature*; *A Geometrical Exercise*; *A Catechism of Christian Doctrine*; *Controversy Logic*; *Devotion and Reason*.

One of White's difficulties was that many people were frightened of him and quite unable to understand what he wrote. His two closest friends were equally feared and disliked. One was Sir Kenelm Digby, a strange ingenious aristocrat, a Catholic, and a propounder of vast speculative systems. The other was Thomas Hobbes, the Protestant philosopher, commonly regarded by most educated English people as an atheist and a thoroughly bad influence. White was an intimate companion of Digby in Paris for some years and later in London. Hobbes and White were often in each other's company in London in White's latter days.

Few people can ever have read all of White's works and studied them closely in their context: the task was too formidable for ordinary mortals. The secular clergy were at first flattered by his espousing of their cause, but later bewildered and mostly hostile. 'Blacklowist' by the 1660s amongst English Catholics became, like 'Hobbist' amongst Protestants, a blanket term of abuse, pretty well equivalent to Machiavellian or atheist. White only had one genuine disciple, his Douai pupil Henry Holden. Holden was a solid Lancashireman, acutely intelligent, well able to follow his master's flights of speculation, loyal to him, but far more moderate, less volatile, less omnivorous of new ideas. He was capable of writing gently to White criticising his books, though in 1657 he bravely published a *Defence of Blacloe*. In any case Holden, a full-time professor at the Sorbonne in Paris for many years, was busy and devout. He was ordinary confessor at a busy Paris parish church, Vicar-General in attendance on the Archibishop of Paris in diocesan business, and director of an English convent in Paris.

What were these new ideas of White's? It was an age of intellectual ferment in Europe. The beginnings of the Scientific Revolution were challenging many traditional ideas. Scientific study of history, along with the study of texts was adding to the ferment, not least because Scripture was coming to be treated with the same care as other historical documents. As always, when such changes happened, the uneducated or half-educated majority was long unaffected and continued to live in a medieval mental world; the educated reacted variously. All of them were willy-nilly affected; a few became *avant garde*, many tried to retreat into a frightened conservative reaction. Even the *avant garde* few had minds in which modern-seeming views were strangely mixed with medievalisms. It seems that White's work was an *avant garde* period-piece, as interesting and irrelevant today as, say, an early steam-engine. He tried to sketch out a view of Catholicism in terms of the scientific and philosophical ideas he saw emerging. He insisted that the fundamentals of Catholicism were embedded in, and ought to be disengaged from, many antique, obsolete arrangements and views. In particular he challenged some exceedingly cherished and deep-rooted medievalisms, like the absolutist Papal monarchy and the centralisation of the Catholic Church round it, or the necessity of a State establishment of religion with repression of other faiths. There was a scepticism and rationalism about his thinking. It is not surprising that traditionalists should have feared him as almost an alien from outer space.

The bulk of the energies of the leaders of the secular clergy was spent on what was to them the most vital of all their objectives: the establishment in England of a normal Catholic hierarchy of bishops. These bishops would be drawn from amongst the secular priests; they would have coercive authority over the two great powers then dominating English Catholicism, the aristocratic lay patrons and the religious Orders. Once this episcopate was established, both powers would be cut down to size: the patrons would lose their untrammelled right to appoint, dismiss and bully their priests; the Orders would have to become auxiliaries of the secular priests, or, if they would not, leave England. The great campaign to secure all of this began in the 1590s with the Appellant effort, which secured nothing more from Rome than Archpriests without episcopal authority, and certainly without power over patrons and religious.

From 1606 the production by the government of a new Oath of Allegiance, binding on Catholics under pain of life imprisonment and financial ruin, produced furious arguments amongst them. The Oath was wordy, the issues could be debated for ever by theologians. Priests were by training mentally conditioned to have exceedingly tender, scrupulous consciences. Put broadly and bluntly the Oath said that no Pope could ever give political orders to English Catholics. There is no doubt whatever that the vast majority of the laity and most priests, secular and religious alike, thought this proposition right. The secular clergy had all along believed this: their dislike of the Jesuits in part stemmed from stubborn Jesuit adherence to the traditional Catholic view of the Pope's power to decide disputed political questions. The secular priests honestly believed that the Jesuits had inspired Papal support of English Catholic plots against the Protestant government, and fomented the plots. For years affronted secular priests had actually gone out of their way to let the government know that they dissociated themselves from such action and were utterly loyal citizens. Hence it would seem natural that all secular priests should cheerfully take the new Oath of Allegiance. The Appellants had already suggested some such Oath, and that those who took it (the laity and secular priests) should, in return, be granted a limited religious toleration and freedom from recusancy fining. The Jesuits and their Ignatian and lay supporters would, of course, reject the Oath, be clearly identified as disloyal citizens, bear a great weight of persecution and probably have to leave England. That was the plan. Unfortunately the new Oath was worded in such a fashion that it could easily be interpreted to mean a complete rejection of Papal authority. Some secular priests, for this reason, dared not take the Oath or evaded doing so. In fact the Oath proved to be an embarrassment to the secular priest leaders, and they ceaselessly petitioned the government for the sub-

stitution of a simpler, more limited form. They also wanted from the
government an express promise of toleration to accompany such a
new form. The government puzzled over the political problems involved in the scheme. They were formidable. Though advanced
Protestant thinkers favoured the plan, no one could deny that the
violently Protestant lobby against it would be tough and dangerous.

Down to 1625 there was a succession of Archpriests, the last of
whom was actually in episcopal orders, but their power was only
decorative. Nevertheless now there existed all the forms of episcopal
government, a real bishop (if only one), a Chapter of canons to advise
him, Vicars-General, local Archdeacons and Rural Deans. Prelim-
inary talks with the Benedictines had shown them favourably disposed towards episcopal government. All that was required was a
Papal order to activate the forms. Then, in 1625, seemed to come
suddenly from God an answer to the secular priests' prayers. A
marriage was arranged between the young Charles I and the Catholic
Henrietta Maria of France. Intense backstage secret negotiations
took place involving the English, French and Papal governments.
The secular priest leaders were consulted. In the course of the year
of the wedding marvellous things happened. Rome appointed an
English bishop with all the powers of a bishop. The man chosen was
Richard Smith, then the intellectual leader of the secular priests.
Once in England, and ensconced in an aristocratic patron's house
in Bedfordshire, Smith circularised the patrons and the religious,
announcing that he intended, by using his power to grant or with-
hold sacramental authorisation to all missioners, a purge of the many
unemployed, lazy and disobedient clergy, and planned to exercise
a fatherly control over all appointments. Meanwhile the government,
carrying out the terms of its secret treaties, instructed magistrates to
stop imposing the Oath of Allegiance and the penal laws forthwith.
The new Catholic Queen arrived in England with a train of French
priests, including a bishop and a whole community of Capuchin
missionaries. Already architects and workmen were hastily converting rooms in all the main royal residences into open Catholic chapels.
Catholic worship began in them with considerable musical splen-
dours and courses of sermons for prospective converts. Enraged
Puritans noted the traffic jams caused by crowds of curious courtiers,
aristocrats, men about town and local Catholics going to Mass in the
new chapels. There were rumours of wholesale conversions at court.

Little more than two years later the golden bubble was punctured.
A violent Protestant backlash drove the King to expel from England
most of the Queen's French priests. Worship in her chapels continued, but under police harassment. The fining of Catholic recusants was resumed, though the fines exacted were compounded down

to a more realistic figure, and those fined were guaranteed freedom from police molestation. Meanwhile Richard Smith had overplayed his hand. He had a strong hand, and, played modestly and tactfully, it might possibly have succeeded in bringing peace and order to the Catholic community. In fact he sailed into his job with all the arrogant, aggressive panache of a radical university professor in theological debate with his seniors. The Jesuits contested his orders, maintaining their legal exemption from episcopal interference, and pointing out clauses in his Papal document of appointment which made his powers liable to summary limitation by Rome. A tug-of-war took place in Rome between Smith's agents and Jesuit influence. It lasted six years and was level pegging until, in 1631, Rome deprived Smith of the power to control missioners' sacramental acts.

This was defeat indeed. Rome also tried to stop the tremendous mass of controversy which had been roused by the quarrel. It had begun with an offensive of books backing Smith from learned secular priests abroad; these were answered hotly by two Jesuit champions. Smith's French theologian friends joined in the fray enthusiastically on his side. Smith's case, put by himself with typical bluntness and virulence, was that the ordinary, divinely guaranteed authority in the Catholic Church was that of diocesan bishops: Papal authority was merely supervisory and extraordinary, hence the Pope had no power to deprive England of normal episcopal government or, once it existed, to interfere with its workings. At this point in time Smith's case had an international importance. For at least two centuries throughout Europe there had been a strong Catholic radical movement of opposition which bitterly resented Roman Curial authoritarianism. The Catholic Counter-Reformation had been very much a grass-roots movement, created by the efforts of local groups of devout enthusiasts. Some, including the Society of Jesus, were strong supporters of Curial authoritarianism. Indeed the Jesuits, bitterly opposed in every country by local bishops, universities and secular priests, had pinned their faith in victory through Roman backing. Opposition to the Society in every country was closely identified with anti-Curialism. In Holland, during these years, Dutch Catholics were locked in battle over much the same issues which convulsed their English co-religionists.

The Dutch battle was eventually to lead to a schism away from the Catholic Church of a sizable body of anti-Jesuit, anti-Curialist priests and people. In France and Germany the quarrel was less dangerous, but just as violent. There is little doubt that most English priests and laity had long privately thought on the same lines as Smith; this was even true of most of the religious Orders (excluding the Jesuits and their friends). But Smith threw away his chances of rallying behind him wide English support. His sheer tactlessness alienated the Benedictines and Franciscans, though some of them abandoned him only with reluctance. His rigid authoritarianism and extreme views seemed, to a good many scrupulously devout people (including some secular priests) to challenge the Papal primacy and put in doubt the validity of all priests' ministrations. His petty and vindictive sniping at individual Jesuits—for instance he accused John Gerard of fomenting the Gunpowder Plot, and forced the Jesuit Provincial to dismiss from the Society a tactless Jesuit—slammed the door against any compromise with the Society. His authoritarian clericalism outraged most lay patrons. Even though most of them were anti-Jesuit and anti-Curialist, they readily signed a round-robin demanding his removal from office. On top of this, Smith's activities helped to increase the force of the Protestant backlash. The government ordered his arrest and deportation, and he became a fugitive. Eventually, he slipped back to Paris in disguise and never appeared in England again. His friend, Cardinal Richelieu, provided him with a living from French Church benefices. Smith also acted as assistant bishop in the diocese of Paris.

Smith left England finally in 1631 and died in Paris in 1655. His gravestone in the little cemetery of the English convent of 'Blue Nuns' in Paris has on it a grim quotation from the Scriptures: *a falsis fratribus vendito* (betrayed by false brethren). During the quarter century of exile he in no way accepted defeat. Rigidly, to his death, he refused to resign his episcopal authority in England or admit that his flight was the equivalent of resignation. He maintained an agent in Rome, showered the Pope with memoranda about his cause, and sent a stream of exhortations and orders across the Channel to his Chapter of Canons in England. The Chapter exerted spiritual authority in his name, through its Archdeacons and the fairly regular meetings of the local secular clergy Brotherhoods, over the 300 seculars in England. It did not matter to them that Rome regarded Smith's jurisdiction as ended and the Chapter as without authority. The Papal decree of 1631, depriving Smith of spiritual power over all missioners was equally disregarded by the Chapter. Yet, oddly and realistically, Rome was unwilling to use legal and spiritual sanctions (suspension from clerical duties, excommunication) against this overt revolt. Rome had no desire to provoke even a tiny clerical schism from the Church, especially since the acutely embarrassing quarrel was public knowledge amongst English Protestants. Charles I himself intervened, with letters to Rome suggesting that Smith had theological truth on his side. A succession of Papal agents visited England in the 1630s; some favoured the Jesuits, others the seculars, but none came up with a viable solution to the problem.

If the quarrel had reverberations in France, it also affected the English colony of Maryland in America. The proprietor of the colony, Lord Baltimore, was a convert. Originally he had proposed to provide secular priests for his colony. By 1629, apparently for no more profound reason than that he found it easier and quicker to deal with the Jesuit Provincial, he contracted to send out a band of English Jesuits. The Jesuit missionaries, once in Maryland, found themselves in the thick of difficulties. Baltimore made no special financial provision for their upkeep, so they were compelled to become shareholders in the enterprise, find and import English settlers and negroes, and engage in the management of large estates. In no time the Jesuits found themselves farmers and businessmen. John Lewger, Baltimore's deputy in Maryland and a convert Anglican parson, exerted over the Jesuits the dictatorial authority of an English patron, made far more oppressive by the special, almost military, conditions of early colonial life. Thus the Jesuits were forbidden to found missions or chapels except by Lewger's express permission; they were heavily taxed and liable for military service; since women were few in the struggling colony and required to marry, the Jesuits were forbidden by Lewger to direct them into private vows of chastity or into conventual life. When the Jesuits appealed to Rome, Lord Baltimore and Lewger did their best to thwart the appeal. Then Baltimore approached the superiors of other religious Orders and the secular clergy Chapter, proposing to make over to them, or to any of them willing to accept them, the Maryland missions. After long hesitation, Rome did not forbid the change. As the civil war broke out in 1642 the first two secular priest missioners sent by the Chapter embarked for Maryland. Meanwhile the Jesuits published to the world their complaints against Lewger (they tactfully kept silence on Baltimore's part in the affair).

By 1642 the idealist clericals amongst both secular priests and religious had uniformly suffered defeat. In spite of their vigour and increasing numbers the real control of the English Catholic community, its organisation and policies, remained firmly in the hands of the Papist peers and gentry.

5. Early Stuart Catholicism, 1603–60

(3) Court Catholicism

The expansion and diversification of English Catholic clerical institutions, their internal squabbles and passions, may be an interesting human study for us; but for contemporary Protestants it was a matter about which they cared (and, indeed, knew) little. It was a small backwater in the life of the nation. But Protestants were preoccupied with, and excited about, another Catholic development in the early seventeenth century: the rapid and dramatic growth of Catholicism among the upper classes, both at court and in the country.

In the seventeenth century 'the court' was often used as an emotive term of abuse. Few then dreamed of attacking patronage, the almost universal system whereby preferment (offices of profit, promotion in them, government contracts and licences to practise trades, manufactures and professions or to be exempt from government regulations) was in the gift of influential persons whose favour had to be humbly solicited or bought. Until the mid nineteenth century the patronage system operated in England as much as it did in the old Chinese Empire. Few early seventeenth-century people attacked the right of the Crown to be the supreme dispenser of patronage, and so to be the centre of a court of servants, Household officials, Ministers of State, civil servants, guards, chaplains, musicians and artists. It was philosophically accepted that the court would often be peripatetic (showing the flag round the royal residences), crowded, rather disorderly, and infested with applicants for patronage and undesirable hangers-on such as adventurers, confidence-tricksters, thieves and prostitutes. Even the Pope's court at this time had all these characteristics in abundance. But from 1603 many people thought that the English court, and its normal setting, London, was growing far too large, powerful and corrupt; it was waxing into a monster swallowing up the just rights of lesser patrons and the provinces. It was in process of transformation from a useful, natural thing into an organ of destruction, a cancer in the body politic of society. Seventeenth-century country peers and gentry cursed the court and courtiers in language we reserve today for Whitehall and the bureaucrats and for much the same reasons. Courtier had become the name for a hanger-on or minor official at court who made a handsome living fixing appointments, contracts and licences. At a price he could fix anything and dispense with any law or regulation. Titles—peerages, baronetcies, knighthoods—government offices and contracts had become commodities freely put up for sale to the highest bidders.

Before 1603 most propertied Catholics had to frequent the court occasionally. It was an inflationary, highly competitive age and patronage was essential for the preservation of property rights and the successful conclusion of lawsuits. But relatively few Catholics lived at court to make a living by it and none could exist in its mainstream. Recusants, and even men with recusant wives, were expressly excluded from court employment. Royal Proclamations regularly ordered particular searches of Westminster for Catholics and their banishment thence, along with tricksters and prostitutes. In the sixteenth and seventeenth centuries however Catholics had discovered that the most public places were sometimes their safest havens from observation. Jesuits and missioners haunted the rabbit-warren of lanes and lodging-houses in London and Westminster just as Catholics lodged in the close of York Minster and established reception bases for priests on coastal properties leased from Anglican bishops. But physical proximity to the court was not involvement in it.

The advance of Catholics into real court life began in 1603 with the accession of James I. He was an 'original', a freakish example of that radical seventeenth-century ingenuity we have already noted in Catholics like John Barnes, Augustine Baker, Richard Smith, Blacklow and Mary Ward. In an age which was restless, critical, physically uncomfortable, the best minds were struggling to recover a sense of identity, as Protestants, Catholics or just as human beings. James was haunted by the idea that royal authoritarianism alone could end the conflict of classes, interests and factions, that the clash of Catholic and Protestant could be solved by diplomacy and the swallowing up of Catholicism into a widened and reformed Protestantism. The idea was magnificent, the man and the execution base. James was acutely intelligent and superbly able; he was also idle, indiscreet, corrupt and an openly practising homosexual wide open to exploitation by the unscrupulous. His court and government tottered from scandal to grosser scandal. He positively welcomed known Catholics to his court and service, insisting that they performed a basic minimum of conformity to Anglicanism in outward show. He used and tolerated Councillors and Ministers (like the Earls of Northampton and Arundel and Sir George Calvert) who had Catholic pasts, close Catholic connections and personal sympathies with Catholicism. James's last 'friend' and favourite was a vain and handsome nonentity, George Villiers, Duke of Buckingham. Buckingham was a conventional Protestant, but his pronounced tastes in the arts were international and Catholic, and petticoat-influence in his family was heavily, if foolishly, Catholic. His wife was a Catholic bullied into apostasy but to revert promptly to her old faith after her husband's death; his doting and unscrupulous mother (also styled Duchess of Buckingham) was a Catholic convert separated from her Church-papist second husband. Buckingham also had a sister, sister-in-law and niece who were all converts.

James I had not prevented the Catholic conversion in Scotland of his Queen, Anne of Denmark, though he allowed her no facilities for the practice of her religion. To her death in 1619 she was no advertisement for Catholicism, but her existence gave it prestige at court and her influence helped to strengthen its acceptance there. Moreover the King was determined to marry his heir to a foreign Catholic princess, even if the price were the open, legal practice of Catholicism at court and semi-official relaxation of the penal laws. In 1625 just such an arrangement was concluded with the French government on the marriage of Charles, Prince of Wales, to Henrietta Maria, a devout Catholic.

Partly because of this change of royal policy, and partly because of the growing corruption of the court, known Catholics received offices and favours in other fields. Church-papists slithered into offices hitherto guarded jealously by Protestants; the Presidency of the Council of the North was held for years by Emmanuel Scrope, Earl of Sunderland, a clear (if slackly conformist and horribly corrupt) Papist; Sir George Calvert, Secretary of State, made a Church-papist his clerk and the man's equally Papist brother Clerk of the Peace to the West Riding of Yorkshire Justices; Henry Spiller, a Papist with a recusant wife, was made Exchequer Receiver of Recusancy Fines; the Mastership of the Ordnance Office at the Tower of London went to Sir Edward Sherburne, a prominent Papist. The Mastership of the King's Works went to the great architect Inigo Jones, the Papist son of a London Catholic recusant tradesman. In the Chapel Royal the doyen of royal musicians remained the great William Byrd, a very definite Papist to his death in 1622. His almost equally distinguished colleague, the Papist John Bull, overstepped the mark by becoming a practising Catholic in 1614; he had to resign and seek employment as organist of Antwerp cathedral. The Papist lutanist, John Dowland, in 1612 grew tired of exile in German and Danish courts, conformed, and took service in the Chapel. The rest of the cream of English musicianship, Peter Phillips and Richard Dering, preferred full practice of their Catholicism and employment at Brussels to Church-papistry in London. But the tone of Jacobean court music became distinctly Italian and courtiers thronged to the performances of the Ferraboscos (the grandfather a Catholic returned to Milan, the son and grandsons Anglican cathedral organists) and Giovanni Coperario (really John Cooper, a totally Italianate Englishman of indeterminate religion). Court literature had the same Catholic tinge. Taste was dominated by 'the sons of Ben' (disciples of Ben Jonson), the dean of St Paul's John Donne, and William Shakespeare. All three men seem to have been living down the Catholic influences of their youth.

Peerages were for sale at the Jacobean Court. Ambitious Papists were not lacking to face the conformism, servility and bribery required for success. In 1603 there were eight or nine Papist peers and in 1625 eighteen. The Catholic peers, both old and new, had few, if any, characteristics distinguishing them from their Protestant colleagues. Three were exceptional. The first of these was a secular priest missioner who, by the pure accident of family succession, inherited the wealthy Earldom of Shrewsbury from his Protestant fourth cousin. The priest was resident in Munich, and he stayed abroad the rest of his life. The second exception was a recusant country gentleman who likewise accidentally inherited the Earldom of Rutland. He remained busy in Catholic affairs but was especially protected from harassment by the marriage of his daughter to the Duke of Buckingham. The third exception was Lord Vaux, probably the only Papist peer to inherit a genuinely continuous family tradition of heroic Elizabethan recusancy. But he figured hardly at all in Catholic and national affairs since he chose to court social ostracism by living with the Protestant wife of the Earl of Banbury. Apart from these three cases, the Papist peers were a tough and acquisitive lot, striving desperately to maintain some connection, however tenuous, with Catholicism, and also to keep in with the Protestant Establishment and Crown patronage. Thus of the old Papists, the 2nd Lord Montague had a largely Protestant education, bought letters of protection at court, and sent his son and heir to Eton College. Lord Abergavenny had been educated at Oxford, was heavily in debt and ready to try anything short of total

apostasy to avoid bankruptcy. Of the new Papist peers, the 1st
Lord Arundell of Wardour was a Church-papist mercenary soldier
and persistent courtier, whose charm and accommodating temper
finally won him a free peerage in 1605, the year of the Catholic
Gunpowder Plot. The 1st Lord Teynham was a Church-papist
Judge, who had his heir educated in Protestant schools; in extreme
old age, in 1616, after years of bribery and intrigue, he acquired
his peerage. Lord Dormer bought his peerage in 1615 for £8000
which he could ill afford. The Papist peers provided high society
with one scandal even greater than that of the unfortunate Lord
Vaux. The Earl of Castlehaven, an Anglo-Irish Papist, drifted into
a fatal course of immorality and orgies; he was finally tried by his
peers, convicted and executed for a very thoroughgoing effort to
have his teenage wife corrupted by his servants.

At his accession in 1625 Charles I therefore inherited a court
which was already notorious for its size, corruption and openness to
Catholic influences. In the eyes of devout Protestants, it was totally
discredited by the Catholic tone of the Buckingham régime, the
Vaux and Castlehaven scandals, and the recent case of Lord Baltimore. In 1624 Sir George Calvert, long Secretary of State, had
driven a remarkably hard bargain with the Crown. He had decided
to retire into private life, a retirement which made possible full
practice of the Catholic religion. He turned this transaction into a
personal triumph. He surrendered his State offices into the Crown's
hand freely—by court custom they were his freehold property
which he could have sold to his successor. In return he received
free an Irish peerage, full letters of protection from recusancy proceedings, the confirmation of large land grants in Ireland (confiscated from Irish Catholic landowners), a substantial pension, and
the grant of proprietorship of the colony of Maryland in America,
with the rights of 'palatine lordship' over its entire area and
settlers.

Between 1625 and 1640 Catholic influences at court increased
steeply. They did so in the royal family due chiefly to the character
of the new Queen, Henrietta Maria, and the stupid complaisance
of Charles I. Henrietta Maria, sallow, plain, *petite*, but vivacious
and always exquisitely dressed, was a devout Catholic of an unin-
telligent sort. Her religion found its stay in pretty devotions, to our
Lady of Liesse, the three Kings of Cologne, relics of saints and
scapulars. Many factors eventually made her formidable. After the
assassination of Buckingham in 1628, the King became passionately
attached to her and would hardly leave her side. He was mentally
incapable of anything but a wooden continuation of his father's
policies without finesse or moderation. Although he was positively

repelled from Catholicism by his wife's devotions, he was easily persuaded by her to grant ever more sweeping concessions to Catholics. The Queen's separate Household and open Catholic chapels allowed by treaty, together with her exquisite French taste, made a profound impression on many in high society. She imported Richard Dering from Brussels to be her chapel organist at Somerset House; the chapel was created by Inigo Jones. Her Household became an artistic and literary salon, attracting the best poets and artists and wits, Protestant and Catholic. The well-known series of royal and court portraits painted during these years by the Flemish Catholic Sir Anthony Van Dyck express sharply the ambiguity of the situation. To Charles I and his Protestant courtiers they showed how Continental Catholic graces were successfully absorbed and conquered by a homely Englishness and a High Church Anglicanism, florid and baroque in style. To the Queen and Catholic courtiers the portraits expressed how, like the Greeks in the Trojan horse, they were engaged in a subtle conquest of Anglicanism and the Crown for Catholicism. Meanwhile, strategically placed in the Queen's Household were Catholic ladies and priests, all themselves converts, engaged in proselytising amongst courtiers. The prejudices of the English against Jesuits and Spaniards were respected; the priests were mostly aristocratic English converts trained in France (the King's cousin, Le Sieur Ludovic d'Aubigny, Toby Mathew, Walter Montague, and two Oratorians). A particular set was made at the heirs and wives of peers and at the brightest younger clergy and university dons of the High Church Anglican party.

The most successful lay proselytisers were Endymion Porter, gentleman-in-waiting to the King, and his wife Olivia, lady-in-waiting to the Queen. Endymion had been brought up in Spain. He was a man of many parts, a minor poet, a dealer in Italian paintings, a very skilled fixer of every kind of honour, licence, dispensation, contract and industrial scheme, a perfect courtier. His wife Olivia, the Duke of Buckingham's niece, was a convert with many aristocratic relations. The Protestant newsletter-writers followed the rumours of the Porters' activities with morbid interest. Thus in 1636 they reported the dramatic reconversion in the Porters' house of a lapsed Catholic celebrity, Sir Kenelm Digby; the tutoring of two sons of an unnamed Protestant peer by a Jesuit, and the designs of the Dowager Duchess of Buckingham to get custody of her children. In 1637 the news was that Mrs Porter had persuaded her old father, Lord Boteler, to become a Catholic on his deathbed, and that she had converted her relation, Viscount Purbeck (then suffering from a nervous breakdown because his

convert wife had left him), the Marchioness of Hamilton and the
Countess of Newport (wife of a Puritan Lord-in-waiting to the
King). Mrs Porter had also that year converted Sir Robert Howard
(a courtier with whom the Catholic Viscountess Purbeck was living)
and the son and heir of the Earl of Berkshire, secretly married,
with Mrs Porter's connivance, to a Catholic daughter of Viscount
Savage. In 1638 a newsletter-writer lamented:

> Our Grate Women fall away every day, now 'tis said my
> Lady Manners is declared a Papist, and also my Lady
> Katharine Howard, but 'tis love that hath bin the principall
> agent in her conversion, for, unknown to her father, the Earl
> of Suffolk, she is, or wilbe, maryed to the Lord D'aubigny,
> second brother to the Lennox . . . in France where he hath
> bin bred a Papist.

The Queen must also probably be credited with a hand in the
King's astonishing choice of Ministers of State. The assassination
of Buckingham cleared the way for promotions. The new Lord
Treasurer, until his death in 1635, was Sir Richard Weston, created
1st Earl of Portland. He was allowed to take the post although his
second wife was an ardent Catholic. Portland was received into
the Catholic Church on his deathbed. Francis Cottington moved
to the Council from a long career as a diplomat in Spain, where
he had become a Catholic. He was created Lord Cottington and
eventually became Lord Chancellor. While in office he conformed
minimally to Anglicanism, but his sympathies were evidently
Catholic. One of the two Secretaries of State was Sir Francis Windebank; like Weston, he was dispensed because he had a strongly
Catholic wife. Like Weston also, he was to die a Catholic.

Ranged in the Council beside these three Papists were three
Anglican bishops, whose appointment owed nothing to the Queen.
Her instinct, if not her intelligence, told her that her greatest rivals
for control of the King's mind were a High Church party of
Anglican clergy led by Archbishop William Laud. This party,
conscious of the growing strength of Catholic Counter-Reformation
ideology, aimed to save Anglican Protestantism, prevent the wave
of conversions to Catholicism, and rescue the King. Their plan was
in many ways a clerical version of that of James I, to reform
Anglicanism and take into its system as far as possible the good
points and methods of the Catholics. They were for ever asserting
that true Anglicanism was 'pure, primitive Catholicism', they
stressed episcopacy, priesthood, the sacrifice of the Eucharist, altars,
and the practice of Confession. One of their brightest spirits, John

Cosin, dean of Durham, filled his cathedral with lighted tapers at Candlemas. Archbishop Laud was the King's confessor. The King systematically promoted High Church clergy to a good many bishoprics and deaneries. Archbishop Laud and two other High Church bishops sat on the Royal Council, and one of them succeeded Portland as Lord Treasurer.

The Queen had neither the learning nor the spirituality to tackle the Laudians. She clashed with Laud's influence in the King's closet. Her priests and ladies found their proselytising efforts at Court opposed by High Church chaplains. There was a battle-royal for the soul of the Duchess of Buckingham, culminating in a theological tournament between Archbishop Laud and a Jesuit; Laud won the first engagement but eventually lost the battle. Then came similar, more backstage battles for possession of the Duke and Duchess of Lennox (many of whose relations were already Catholics) and the Marchioness of Hamilton. This time Laud was victorious and actually converted Lennox to High Church principles. Meanwhile the war was continuing outside the court. At Lincoln, Catholic missioners converted a High Church dean. At Lambeth they even converted one of Laud's chaplains. At Oxford they won a dozen High Church dons and undergraduates, including the poet Richard Crashaw and William Chillingworth. There were battle fronts everywhere in the provinces. In Yorkshire the High Church divine Bramhall invited Catholic missioners to public debates. Here and there the Catholic warriors gained scalps: the minor poets William Alabaster and James Shirley were both young Anglican curates converted to Catholicism at this period. The radical Bene-dictine writer, Leander Jones, was a convert who had once been a High Church pupil of Laud's at Oxford. He and the Franciscan Christopher Davenport made strenuous but unsuccessful efforts to secure a full-scale conference of Catholic and Laudian divines.

Encouraged by the Queen and sustained by the wave of fashion in their favour, Catholics began to gain entrance to most of the main artistic and intellectual circles at court. Their musicians were now rigidly excluded by Laud's influence from the Chapel Royal. But Richard Dering, the Queen's organist, gained a considerable following. John Wilby, an eminent Catholic instrumentalist and composer, had to rely on Catholic gentry patronage in Suffolk, but the Queen secured his appointment as music-teacher to the royal children. Inigo Jones was still the doyen of architects, the builder of the Queen's House at Greenwich, the Banqueting Hall at White-hall (for the royal family), Wilton and Coleshill Houses (for Protestants) and Basing House (for his most munificent patron, the Catholic Marquis of Winchester). The King and Queen attracted

E

to court a small army of mainly Catholic foreign painters, Van Dyck, Jordaens, Gentileschi, Rubens and Briot. Their German Protestant engraver, Hollar, may possibly have become a Catholic in England. The Queen's salon at Somerset House attracted poets, the Protestants Davenant, Suckling, Lovelace and Carew along with the Catholics Edymion Porter and William Habington. The 'Gray's Inn Circle' drew Massinger, Ford, Randolph and May along with the Catholics Habington and James Shirley (the most prolific and fashionable playwright of the day) and the apostate Catholic Benedictine, Sir Robert Stapleton. At his house in the Tower of London, the Catholic civil servant Sir Edward Sherburne kept open house for poets and amateurs of science. Of Sir Edward's seven sons, also Catholics, Edward was a junior civil servant, Henry an engineer, and both Edward and John minor poets. Sir Edward and Henry had an *entrée* to the main fashionable meeting-place of amateur scientists and mathematicians, Gresham College, where they were quite liable to meet other Catholics, such as Lord Lumley (who endowed a course of scientific lectures), Lord Herbert (who headed a west-country circle of scientists based on his father's seat at Raglan Castle) and Christopher Towneley, a Lancashire squire (leader of a northern circle mostly of Protestants). At Sir Robert Cotton's library in Westminster met the historians and antiquarians, and there Augustine Baker could be seen in lively conversation with Cotton, Spelman and the Anglican Archbishop Ussher.

Moving backwards and forwards between the Exchequer and the City of London were the projectors, industrialists and courtiers engaged in fixing contracts and licences. Sir Edward Sherburne was well-known in the City company boardrooms. He had been secretary to Francis Bacon, Lord Verulam and then to the Board of the East India Company before taking on the Ordnance Office. The Catholic Lord Mounteagle and Morley was a member of the boards of both the Virginia Company and the East India Company. Lord Herbert of Raglan, with his Shropshire Catholic partners in the iron business, Sir John Winter and Sir Basil Brooke, was often at Westminster Hall and in the City. By 1640 the Queen and Endymion Porter had managed for the Shropshire syndicate a Crown lease of the charcoal in the Forest of Dean, and Sir John had been appointed the Queen's secretary. Lord Maltravers, heir to the Papist Earl of Arundel, was angling through Porter to get a share in the proprietorship of an American colony to be called Carolina. Lord Baltimore had often to be in the City and at Westminster on the business of launching his colony in Maryland and his abortive journey to Newfoundland.

Almost at every turn at court and in London a visitor would thus run into Papists mixing fairly freely with Protestants in every current enterprise. In the 1630s the Puritans tried to start an uproar and pious strike against the use of 'Popish Soap'. They discovered that the Queen and Endymion Porter had managed a patent giving a monopoly of soap-manufacture to a syndicate mainly of Papists but including some Protestant merchants. In court taverns you might occasionally meet university poets like John Milton and Andrew Marvell. They both seemed steadily Protestant. But Milton's father had once been a Catholic recusant, and the family background perhaps helped, many years later, John's lawyer brother, Christopher, to become a convert. Andrew Marvell, bred in a Yorkshire Puritan parsonage, had become a Catholic while an undergraduate, had left the university for London and there had been caught by his father and persuaded to revert to Protestantism. London's most successful private school had as its headmaster Thomas Farnaby, also a distinguished classical scholar. He had become a Catholic in his youth and studied for the priesthood under than his patriotism, which had led the Papist Lord Mounteagle to Anglicanism. When Parliament was in session, Westminster was crowded with members of the Lords and Commons. A surprisingly large number of them had close Catholic relations, or were even themselves Church-papists. It was this fact, perhaps even more than his patriotism, which has led the Papist Lord Mounteagle and Morley to betray the Catholic Gunpowder plotters in 1605. Unless, like Lords Castlehaven and Vaux, they were disqualified by crimes, Papist peers were not yet excluded from sitting and voting in the House of Lords. By 1640 almost forty Papists had the right to sit amongst the other 120 Protestant peers. Moreover the most prominent Protestant peers often had Catholic connections. The Earl of Strafford had a Catholic uncle, aunt and cousins and two secretaries with recusant wives. Viscount Falkland had an aggressively Catholic convert mother, brothers who were priests and sisters who were nuns. Even Puritan peers suffered the same family embarrassments. The Earl of Essex had a Papist half-brother, Lord Clanricard. The Earl of Manchester had a younger son, Walter Montague, who was a convert secular priest chaplain to the Queen. Lords Denbigh and Newport had convert wives. As for the House of Commons, repeated efforts by Committees of the House to list known Papists or suspects in the House or in government offices had never succeeded in ousting a number of lax but determined Church-papists. Sir George Calvert occupied a seat in the House steadily until his elevation to the peerage; Jerome Weston, 2nd Earl of Portland, sat in the House before his accession to his father's title. Charles Howard, heir to the Earl of Berkshire and a convert in 1638, was sitting in the House in 1640–2. William Widdrington, a Church-papist with a recusant wife, was MP for a Northumbrian constituency, the Walmesleys of Dunkenhalgh (with recusant wives and children) were steadily members for Lancastrian ones.

By 1640 the roll of Papist peers gave an impression of considerable Catholic political muscle and aristocratic splendour. There were, in order of precedence, the two Duchesses of Buckingham, the Marquises of Winchester and Worcester, the Earls of Arundel, St Albans, Shrewsbury, Castlehaven, Portland and Rivers, the Countesses of Rutland (Dowager) and Newport, and the male heirs of the Earls of Berkshire and Powis. The titular Earl of Banbury was trying to establish his legitimacy in the courts. The young Earls of Carnarvon and Peterborough had been originally brought up as Catholics, and then, by pressures exerted by Crown guardians and Protestant relations, had been persuaded to apostatise. It was possible that they still had Catholic leanings: Carnarvon, indeed, perhaps returned to Catholicism at the end of his short life. There were the Papist Viscounts, Cashel, Dunbar, Fairfax of Walton and Montague, and the Viscountesses Falkland (Dowager), Newark and Purbeck, and the Papist Barons Abergavenny, Aston, Arundell, Baltimore, Brudenell, Cottington, Eure, Fauconberg, Lumley, Molineux, Mounteagle and Morley, Petre, Stafford, Stourton, Teynham, Vaux and Windsor. The courtesy Lords Maltravers and Herbert had Baronies in their own right. There were the Baronesses Mordaunt and Wotton and the heir of Lord Carrington. Political observers would have extended the list of Papist aristocrats still further, to include, for instance, Scots and Irish peers (like Lords Clanricard and Antrim) who frequented the court, and a queue of Papist gentry awaiting eagerly the grant of peerages.

Court Catholicism combined menace and fragility in so confusing a way that the soberest observers found it difficult to gauge its real strength. Charles I's attitude to Catholicism was oddly compounded of tolerance and sharp intolerance. The Queen's influence was at once an impressive asset for the Catholic community and a considerable handicap. Her narrow, superstitious piety grated on the King and undoubtedly confirmed most of her children in their Anglicanism. The Princes Charles and James endured their mother's crude proselytising unshaken and veered towards Catholicism only much later in life, for reasons which were unconnected with their mother. Henrietta Maria eventually became friendly with a considerable number of courtiers. It was notable that her greatest friends (Lucy, Countess of Carlisle, Lord Goring, Harry Jermyn, Susan, Lady Denbigh) either never became Catholics or, if they did, were converted very late in their relationship with the Queen, painfully, and by influences outside her control. The raffish little band of Catholic proselytisers (the Porters, Walter Montague, Toby Mathew, Sir Kenelm Digby) who made the Queen's Household their head-quarters aroused distrust amongst confirmed Protestants and were manifestly using the Queen's prestige merely as an instrument to accomplish their own cloudy designs. For the most part their relatively few converts were obvious psychological or moral drop-outs from solid Protestantism. Protestant observers naturally made the most of the moral failings of Household Catholicism, but their mark was genuinely as broad as a barn door. The Papal Agents at the court made dismal reports to Rome about the morals of the Queen's French Capuchin chaplains, several of whom apostatised. The King and Queen had great difficulty in trying to regularise the marital life of Sir Anthony Van Dyck, separate him from his mistresses and marry him off to a Scots Catholic. Though he came from a warm, affectionate and very Catholic family in Flanders, he did not practise his religion much in England and, many years later, his Anglican grandchildren, removed to Antwerp, had difficulty in accepting Catholicism. The Porters' Catholic sons all eventually lapsed from their religion, some scandalously.

The Queen's party—the Papist Ministers of State—were also poor advertisements for Catholicism. Portland, in his lifetime, displayed little favour for, or interest in, Catholics. His eldest child died insane. Of the other four children, only one married a Catholic. Jerome Weston, the 2nd Earl, had the slightest of attachments to Catholicism. He sat in the Commons in 1628–9; in 1635, after his accession to the title, he had no scruples in taking the anti-Catholic Oaths required by his new office as governor of the Isle of Wight. In 1641 he went on record as saying that 'he would live and die a Protestant as his father did'. Cottington made hardly the faintest gesture of Catholicism before his exile in 1642. Windebank behaved in the same fashion. Of his four sons, three were certainly Protestants. Of his four daughters, two married Protestants (one became the mother of a future Anglican bishop), and the two youngest, who accompanied their parents into exile in 1642, became nuns in a French convent.

The Anglican High Church party, ostensibly natural allies of the Queen and the Catholic community, in reality were their enemies. In the battle of books, sermons and influences between the Laudians and the Catholics, the Laudians gave as good as they got and possibly came off the victors. They probably gained from Catholicism (by conversions from it and reconversions of men like Chillingworth and Farnaby) more than they lost to it. Richard Crashaw's conversion, Anglicanism's biggest loss, was offset by the fact that his friends did not follow him, and he found no more employment amongst Catholics than as chaplain to the 'Holy House' at Loretto in Italy. The conversion of the bishop of Gloucester, Godfrey Goodman, was no triumph for Catholicism. Goodman was an eccentric and no High Churchman. He was suspended by Laud for gross irregularities and omissions in his episcopal administration, came to live in London, was apparently received into the Roman Chuch by a secular missioner and promptly and permanently became a Church-papist.

The weaknesses of the new Catholic peerage were evident. Its increased numbers were largely a natural consequence of the brisk selling of titles since 1603. As the wealthier gentry moved up into the peerage, it was inevitable that Church-papists, who already were fairly numerous in that class, should have taken their share of the loot. They took places in a peerage which was in process of being much swollen in size and watered down in political and social importance. The sale of titles included especially cheap and insignificant ones. Scots and Irish peerages were granted to Englishmen who did not own a foot of land outside England, and who were now entitled only to seats in the Houses of Lords at Edinburgh and Dublin, which they rarely occupied. A third of the new Catholic peers had this inferior status. Even before 1603, when peers were far fewer and more highly regarded, their status had been no automatic passport to high government office and political power. A peer who was idle, incompetent or spendthrift could easily end up in a limbo of unemployment and bankruptcy. After 1603 the large increase in numbers meant more intense competition for jobs, and a far higher number of losers. In this rat-race a Papist peer was handicapped, and a practising Catholic one at a severe disadvantage. It was significant that, in spite of the quite lavish royal graces awarded to Papist peers, none of them ever held high office in Charles I's governments (if we accept the enigmatic Portland, Cottington and Arundel) or played a significant part in the intense political jockeying in 1640–2. Although a good many Papist peers had seats in the Westminster House of Lords, their contribution to the anguished Parliamentary debates of those years was either absence or backbench silence. It was evident that the graces and posts they enjoyed were regarded by both the Papist holders and the Protestant Establishment as strictly conditional. Certain Catholic aristocrats were allowed a subordinate place in the Establishment and court society on condition that they accepted the Protestant ascendancy, practised their Catholicism with the utmost discretion, and bowed to their fate as second-class citizens.

The three most prominent Papist peers, the Earl of Arundel and the Marquises of Winchester and Worcester, were all, in varying ways and degrees, caught in this Protestant spider's web. Thomas Howard, Earl of Arundel, was hereditary Earl-Marshal of England (doyen of the peerage and official guardian of its rights, privileges and rules of precedence). His family had been impoverished by the execution of its head, the Duke of Norfolk, in 1570. Arundel's life was dedicated to resisting the watering-down of the peerage, collecting *objets d'art*, and intriguing to regain the lost Duchy and its estates. Although he and his children had strong Catholic leanings, they simply dared not become Catholics openly. Arundel's livelihood and hopes for his family were strictly dependent on his keeping in with the Establishment. His eldest son, Lord Maltravers, was an MP, a Councillor for Ireland, Lord-Lieutenant of Sussex, grantee of the proprietary colony of Carolina in America, and member of the very Anglican Court of High Commission.

Henry Somerset, 5th Earl and 1st Marquis of Worcester, was an altogether more daring and colourful figure. His family had fought its way into the aristocracy in the sixteenth century. Together with their great rivals, the Herbert Earls of Pembroke and Montgomery, they were the great aristocratic power in Wales and its border counties. The power of both families was built on a complex structure of landed property, vigorously exploited industrial enterprises, crucial marriage alliances, and key local government posts. The Somersets were always Lords-Lieutenant of Monmouthshire and Glamorgan and prominent members of the Council of Wales at Ludlow Castle. The good order of large areas of Wales depended on them, and their influence in turn depended on strong and constant government backing. Their main country seat, Raglan Castle, was a miniature court for the Welsh gentry, a busy centre of local administration, and the head office of a thriving iron-forging business based on government monopolies of the charcoal of the Forest of Dean and government contracts. Edward Somerset, 4th Earl of Worcester, had been a Church-papist married to a Protestant wife, a daughter of the Puritan Earl of Huntingdon. Edward had been converted to outright Catholicism by Jesuits, as was his heir, Henry Somerset, who was married to a Russell, sister of the Puritan Earl of Bedford.

The Somersets trod a tightrope. On the one hand they aimed at a Dukedom (after his succession to the Earldom in 1628, Henry was created 1st Marquis) and so cultivated a reputation for loyalty and absolute dependability. On the other hand they boldly championed the Catholic cause, within limits. Their London residence, Worcester House, sheltered Jesuits and was the main aristocratic Catholic centre there. Raglan Castle maintained a widespread Jesuit mission in Wales. By Somerset influence, the Catholic gentry minority in Glamorgan and Monmouth was safe, and even aggressive. The Somersets rarely married Protestants after 1615. They were a prolific family, and their marriage alliances (to Lord Petre, Lord Arundell of Wardour, the Howards, the Herberts, the Dormers, Irish Catholic peers and English Catholic gentry) formed the largest single relationship block in the Catholic community and helped some conversions—for instance of the heir of the Herbert Earl of Powis.

John Paulet, 5th Marquis of Winchester, was a millionaire His family had profited more than most from the dog-fight of Tudor politics. When he succeeded to the Marquisate in 1629, he was forced to live for a decade in rustic seclusion to nurse the family estates, which had been upset by his father's gross extravagance. John's business acumen soon rebuilt his fortune. From the profits he lavishly rebuilt his seat at Basing House in Hampshire as perhaps the finest Inigo Jones mansion owned by anyone other than royalty. He had grown up as a conventional Anglican under the influence of his mother's family, the Cecils, bulwarks of the Protestant Establishment. Although his first wife was a Catholic, he remained a complete conformist to 1629, an MP and holder of government offices. In 1631 he remarried, to a girl who was the daughter of an Irish peer and whose mother was the only surviving child of Sir Francis Walsingham, Queen Elizabeth's Secretary of State and a renowned hunter of Catholic priests. Helped by the country seclusion and the influence of his convert wife and her Jesuit chaplains, the Marquis became a devout practising Catholic. By 1640 he was the ideal Catholic aristocrat in the eyes of the mission priests, the supporter of missioners and provider of a haven in London for them (Winchester House); he was also the author of several translations of French Jesuit books of devotion He was left undisturbed by the government, which gave him letters of protection; in return he lived in such seclusion that he made practically no impact at court or even amongst the Catholic peers, with whom he had very few close marriage-connections. He held no offices even locally and played no active part in Catholic politics.

The rest of the new Catholic peerage cut insignificant figures. Most were so anxious about their standing with the Establishment that their Catholic practice was cautious. On the other hand, those of them who sought few favours were often either financially embarrassed or ostracised by society for eccentricity or immorality. As we have seen, George Calvert, 1st Lord Baltimore, plumped for full Catholic practice and retirement from office. But his continued prosperity depended on Establishment graces for his Maryland

colony, his Irish lands and his pension as well as his letters of protection. He had an understanding with the Jesuits, to whom he
owed his conversion, sent his sons to their school at St Omer,
supported them against Bishop Smith, and offered them the Catholic
chaplaincies in his projected colony in America. The Jesuits were
enchanted. They envisaged an exclusively Catholic colony (or, at
least, a Catholic one in which Protestants would be penalised) in
which the missions would have a privileged position and large State
subsidies: it would be a Catholic Utopia. But Baltimore, a former
Secretary of State, was a realist. His Maryland charter did indeed
give him extensive (palatine) rights as Lord, but the colony was
necessarily subject to ordinary English law, the Protestant Establishment and penal restrictions on Catholics. By private agreement he
might give limited graces of toleration to Catholics; he dare do no
more if he were to keep the charter; and he could not afford subsidies to the Jesuits at least until the colony's balance sheet showed
a profit. He died in 1632 before Maryland was started. His sons,
the 2nd Lord Baltimore and Leonard Calvert, perforce carried
out his policies. The Jesuits were outraged and accused the Calverts
and their agent, John Lewger (a convert clergyman, later himself
a secular priest) of Protestantism. How could Catholics support
an Anglican establishment, deny Catholic priests privileges, compel
them to do military service, dictate where missions should be
placed, and ban vows of celibacy by women?

By general clerical standards another score of the Papist peers
were Catholics only in name. Lord Vaux and Lady Purbeck were
openly living in concubinage. The 2nd Earl of Portland dodged
between Anglican churches and Catholic chapels. Lord Eure was
pious but scandalous. He was bankrupt, repelled the High Sheriff
and bailiffs of Yorkshire from his house with cannon-fire, and
carried on for years a lawsuit with his Catholic relation, Lord
Arundell. Lord Mounteagle, another bankrupt, had apostatised in
1626 and then returned, somewhat dubiously, to Catholic practice.
Lord Wotton had died in great debt, and his principal heiress had
married a Protestant and apostatised. The Earl of Castlehaven had
a Protestant wife and himself lived loosely at court, Lord Fauconberg had become a Catholic in his youth, but later conformed. By
1640 the observant rated him a Papist at least in mind, but he still
made no outward act of Catholic loyalty, and his children were
mostly lost to Catholicism. The 1st Lord Fairfax of Walton had
also been through a Catholic phase. His rejection of Catholicism
had been sharp. He persuaded a Jesuit son to apostatise, and did
his best to disown his heir, who remained a Catholic. Hence by 1640
the 2nd Lord Fairfax was a steady, quiet Catholic, impoverished

by his father's spite, unable to get letters of protection, and threatened with legal proceedings to carry out his father's testamentary wish that his eldest grandson should be taken away from his parents and brought up a Protestant. Charles I and the Catholic Master of the Court of Wards, Cottington, were embarrassed by the case, but in the end the law took its course.

Lord Dunbar was a new Papist peer in whose featherweight mind intense social ambitions were at odds with sincere Catholic feeling. For generations the ladies of his family had been ardent Catholics. Under their influence his father had wobbled between Catholic practice and conformism. Dunbar twisted and turned and intrigued on the fringes of the court, ready for any short-cut, legal trick or evasion. He bought a Scots peerage and then embarrassed the court with abject appeals for an English peerage and comprehensive letters of protection. He posed as the great stay of Catholics and priests in east Yorkshire, but defaulted on payments to missioners. Lord Molyneux was a man of the same type, though even less scrupulous. He had been a recusant, but conformed in part to win the lucrative Receivership of the lands of the royal Duchy of Lancaster and a peerage. Outright recusancy would endanger his slim hopes of getting the Earldom he craved to set him beside the Earl of Derby, the acknowledged head of Lancashire society. Molyneux's wife and younger children were recusants, but his eldest son was a conformist with a Protestant wife. Lord Brudenell was an intensely acquisitive Northamptonshire landlord, turned over to Catholic practice because he obtained letters of protection, but avid to get an Earldom and government favours. Lord Aston was a courtier-diplomat and conformist who bought a Scots peerage and then became a Catholic obscurely while on duty as ambassador in Spain. The young Lords Teynham and Petre were minors who had fallen into the hands of the Court of Wards. Their anxious relations were moving heaven and earth at court to buy their wardships and so preserve them as Catholics. The outcome was long in doubt.

Indeed every Papist peerage was at risk. Minors could be turned into Protestants by the Court of Wards or Protestant relations and trustees who bought the wardship. This had happened to the Earls of Peterborough and Carnarvon and was to happen to the 3rd Lord Fairfax. If a Papist peer died leaving no son, the peerage could (as in the case of the Catholic Lords Wotton and Stafford) become extinct or pass to a Protestant heir. The Papist peer could, by sheer improvidence, die bankrupt (as happened to Lord Windsor), and the Catholic heir be so landless as to have to relinquish use of the title. Even if a peerage avoided these perils, there was no sure guarantee that the heirs of Papist peers would choose to remain Catholics. The heirs of both Catholic Marquises were to apostatise.

The court Catholicism of Charles I's reign remains an oddity. Contemporaries found it hard to account for its steady growth. In 1642 in the ranks of the queue of gentry agitating to get peerages, some sort of Catholic leaven was already at work in numbers of people still outwardly (or even vocally) Protestant but destined soon to be converts: Lady Denbigh, Harry Jermyn, George Digby, Lord Gerard, Sir Arthur Aston, Roger Palmer, Viscount Strangford, Viscount Carlingford, Sir Marmaduke Langdale, Sir William Widdrington, Henry Bard (traveller and linguist, later Lord Bellomont), John Bellasis, the Earl of Derby (if he did become a Catholic before his execution), Lord Carnarvon. Catholicism had a peculiar fascination for aristocrats. The fascination was not for the otherworldly side of Catholicism. There were a few small islands of aristocratic pietism, at Basing, Wardour, Drayton House in Northamptonshire, Cowdray, Raglan, but they mostly centred on unusually quiet peers (Winchester, Wotton, the 2nd Lord Fairfax) or, more often, devout widows (Ladies Rutland, Wotton and Montague). The average Catholic aristocratic family was only Catholic in part, pushing, ambitious, given to compromise.

Oddly enough Protestants rarely seem to have accused the new Catholic aristocracy of conversion simply to gain political power, office or honours. The Jesuits were suspected of aiming at power, but not the laity, who were such manifestly feeble politicians. As we have seen, the average Papist peer was either (and more usually) a Church-papist who perceived that now a peerage and the practice of Catholicism could be safely combined, or a Protestant, for whom conversion invariably meant trouble and loss of offices.

Discerning Protestants thought that most conversions were caused by fear, that frequent contemporary phenomenon, a gnawing anxiety about personal salvation and yearning for some absolute assurance of it. William Chillingworth favoured this view. Like Persons and Hooker before him, he thought the English were conventional and superstitious but not naturally religious. There is plenty of evidence that scepticism was rife. Many felt insecure. Moreover it was common to look back nostalgically to the religious certainty of the past and to feel a sense of guilt over the absence of steady faith.

On the contrary, another ex-Catholic, John Donne, suggested that it was snobbery, political and social conservatism which attracted aristocrats to Catholicism. In his satirical poem *On Religion* he wrote:

> Seeke true religion. O where? Mirreus
> Thinking her unhous'd here and fled from us,
> Seekes her at Rome; there, because hee doth know
> That shee was there a thousand yeares agoe,
> He loves her ragges so, as wee here obey
> The statecloth where the Prince sate yesterday.

Was not Charles II soon to say that he preferred the Catholic religion because it was the only suitable one for a gentleman? Antiquarianism and romantic medievalism were much in fashion. The seventeenth-century sections of gentry family archives always contain largely fanciful efforts to trace descent from medieval barons. But this climate of sentiment existed widely amongst Protestants (and even Puritans) who were never attracted towards Catholicism. There were many devout Protestants, including Charles I, who regarded Anglicanism as the only fit religion for a conservative gentleman and Catholicism (along with Presbyterianism) as subversive of the natural ordering of society.

Lastly there was another seventeenth-century explanation of court Catholicism. This was the theory that Dissent was a posture always favoured by the English; that they had a rooted tendency to turn 'against the magistrate' (as Robert Persons had written) whenever they felt deprived of their just due or disillusioned with the Establishment. On this theory Catholicism and Puritanism alike were bound to attract drop-outs in an age which was overproducing aristocrats and university graduates. For these unfortunates competition was so hot that embracing Catholicism must have been a subconscious way of seeking compensation: it expressed a protest against the Establishment, it was unlikely to make the convert's position any worse, and it just possibly might win future advantages. It is, indeed, very likely true that the average court Catholic was motivated partly by superstitious fear and partly by Dissent.

6. Early Stuart Catholicism, 1603–60

(4) The Gentry and Lower Orders

We can now turn from that new, exotic and delicate shoot, the pre-civil war court Catholics, to the solid trunk of the Papist community, the country Catholics or landed gentry. Traditionally this was their age of maximum strength and glory. The Catholic clergy then, we feel, were gravely weakened by their eccentricities and factions, and the court Catholics by their scandals and compromises with Protestantism, but the Catholic community was redeemed by its firm base, the gentry. Indeed there is a magnificence and solidity about the roll of names of their leading families: Bedingfield, Jerningham, Paston, Walpole, Arundell, Gifford, Heneage, Meynell, Mannock, Preston, Blundell, Anderton, Walmesley, Towneley, Sherburne, Clifton, Trafford, Plowden, Huddleston, Haggerston, Ratcliffe, Sheldon, Tempest, Gascoigne, Vavasour, Constable, Pudsey, Riddell, Fleming, Gage, Shelley, Thimbleby, Thorold, Monson, Eyre, Burlacy, Carey, Turberville, Pole, Trevilion, Morgan, Biddulph. For those who have a taste for visiting the mansions of such families, examining their seventeenth-century memorials in old churches, or reading their family histories, the wide penetration of Catholicism into their class seems obvious. With a shock of surprise we find seventeenth-century portraits of Catholic priests and nuns in the houses of families well-known for their rigid Protestantism in the eighteenth and nineteenth centuries, or in their churches memorials of the seventeenth century asking for prayers for the family dead in old Latin terms (*cujus anima propitietur deus* or *R.I.P.*).

But what kind of people were these Catholic gentry? Their exact numerical strength will never be known. There are too many gaps in the surviving records of recusancy convictions, and an unknown but apparently large number of Papist gentry avoided conviction by legal tricks. But contemporaries agreed that their numbers were

much increased and now alarmingly large. All over Western
Europe the minor landowning nobility then proliferated as never
before or since. They were avid for status and privileges and politically active to defend their class-interests against monarchs and
aristocrats. In England and Wales there were some 9000 gentry
families whose right to bear coat armour was officially registered by
the College of Heralds (that is to say some 50,000 persons). They
manned the lower echelons of Westminster officialdom, local
government, the learned professions and executive management of
industry and foreign trade. Approximately another 50,000 persons
belonged to families of minor gentry who were unregistered by the
Heralds. They were descendants of cadets of registered families,
gentry 'on the wrong side of the blanket', or, most often, middle-
class aspirants to gentry status while already sharing its standard
of living and some of its privileges. Clearly if the Catholic community could win over a large slice of this 100,000 (as the French
and Hungarian Calvinists had won up to forty per cent of their
gentry) they would be well on their way to winning effective control of English society. In the north Catholic gentry were astonishingly numerous: in some county divisions of Yorkshire, Lancashire
and Northumberland they actually outnumbered Protestant gentry;
in Yorkshire as a whole probably one gentry family in four was
more or less Papist by 1630. On the other hand the distribution of
Catholics was patchy. There were counties in the south and midlands (for instance Surrey, Leicestershire, Cambridgeshire and
Huntingdon, Bedford) and areas even in the north where they were
very thin on the ground. In 1638 the Queen inspired an effort to
organise a voluntary Catholic collection of funds to help the King.
The list of 148 local collectors, county by county, shows that eleven
were needed for Yorkshire, eight for London and Middlesex, six
for Lancashire, four each for Cheshire, Hereford, Northumberland,
Warwick, Gloucester, Dorset, Devon, Suffolk, Norfolk and Rutland.
Eighteen counties made do with only one or two collectors, and
four (three of them in Wales) had none. Overall estimates of the
proportion of Catholics amongst the gentry, major and minor together, have varied between twenty-five per cent and less than ten
per cent.

The fact that these Papists were *gentry* meant that they accepted
involvement in a social and economic order as strongly controlled
by Protestantism as that of Eastern Europe is today by Communism.
Landlordship and gentry status were then so absolutely essential a
pillar of the governmental and social structure of England that,
since 1560, numerous Acts of Parliament had tied them indissolubly
to the Protestant Establishment. To start with, in an inflationary,

highly competitive and obsessively litigious age, it was utterly necessary that a gentry family's landed property should be legally registered and their ownership protected from attack in every direction. Legal succession to property was usually secured by mounting a collusive lawsuit to get the details into court records. But the culmination of such processes had to be sealed by a livery, and the livery was only granted if the heir took the anti-Catholic Oath of Supremacy. Some Catholic heirs never took out livery; most certainly did, a few of them bribing Westminster officials to forego the Oath; the majority took the Oath and later went to Confession to missioners who had to treat the act as scandalous apostasy.

Just as inevitably Papist gentry were closely involved with local church affairs and church property. Most of the major Catholic gentry owned ex-monastic lands. A few actually lived in mansions which were remodelled medieval monasteries: the Bellasises at Newburgh Priory in Yorkshire, the Careys at Torre Abbey in Devon. The Catholic Prestons owned the ruins and lands of Furness Abbey in Lancashire, the pious Earl of Rutland Rievaulx Abbey, the Constables Drax Priory in east Yorkshire. In Nidderdale in west Yorkshire much of the moorland grazing land had belonged to granges of the Cistercian monasteries of Byland and Rievaulx. In the early seventeenth century all the gentry families in the dale except one were Catholic, and all owned great stretches of grange land. The Papists were not exactly unmindful of the medieval Catholic past, nor were their consciences easy. Here and there they made efforts to restore old monastic shrines to Catholic use: for instance the Cwm and St Winefrid's in Wales, and the Lady Chapel of Mount Grace in north Yorkshire.

The major Catholic gentry frequently had property rights over Protestant churches. They were often lay rectors of parish churches, a position which carried the right and duty of appointing (and sustaining) Anglican vicars, keeping in good repair the chancels of the churches and rectorial chapels or pews in them. It was not unusual for a well-to-do Papist squire to be rector of three or four churches. In a few places Catholic rectors actually owned side-aisles (as at Arundel in Sussex) or large chapels within Anglican churches. Such arrangements were commoner in Germany where brick walls were built across churches and the buildings used for both Protestant and Catholic worship. In England things were never carried so far. Catholic rectors normally occupied and took the profits of the bulk of the parish church lands, paying the parson a stipend, dining him in their kitchens on Sundays and allowing him favours and perquisites like game and fuel. The rectory pew was commonly a dominant feature of the church and was sometimes even in the chancel. Even if the Papist rector never occupied it at services, his Protestant relations and servants might use it, and he and his family were automatically buried under it or beside it, in the chancel, by legal right. Indeed Anglican churches and church-yards were the only legal places of burial and even missioners were buried in them, of course by the parson and with Anglican rites. Scrupulous Papists smuggled priests and coffins into the churches and yards by night illegally: most Papists acquiesced in Protestant burial.

The physical connection of Catholic squires and Anglican chur-ches was not infrequently even closer. In places the old parish church was beside the squire's mansion and well away from the village. Where a squire had emparked his grounds, the church might lie beside his house and in the centre of the large enclosed park. At Coughton in Worcestershire the Gunpowder Plot conspirators probably met in the mansion towerhouse which was within a stone's throw of the parish church within the great park. At Englefield in Berkshire the pious Catholic Marquis of Winchester lies buried in the parish church, which is within the park and beside his mansion. But some Catholic squires lived in large parishes and far from the parish church. They usually had manorial chapels adjacent to their houses. These chapels were Anglican chapels-of-ease for outlying Protestant parishioners' normal Sunday worship and supposed to be served by the parson. Occasionally (as at Hengrave Hall in Suffolk, Carlton and Hazelwood in Yorkshire) Anglican use had ceased, and the squires treated the chapels as their private property and family mausoleums. They were rarely, if ever, used in the seventeenth century for Catholic worship.

The average Catholic squire, whether he was a rector or not, also leased the tithe rights of local Anglican incumbents. He went through the considerable legal and practical business of collecting the tithes in kind or money (involving frequent lawsuits in Anglican bishops' courts to coerce non-payers), pocketed the proceeds and paid the parson a fixed rent. This was a highly profitable business and few squires could afford to dispense with it. Most were tithe-farmers in a big way: the Prestons of Furness farmed tithe in half a dozen parishes; the Constables in as many. It was common for Papists to lease Anglican cathedral or episcopal lands by arrange-ments which lasted for generations. The Catholic Gascoignes were in this business in a big way and provided the stone with which York Minster was kept in repair. The pious Papist 2nd Lord Fairfax farmed a York Minster prebend and was aggrieved because his recusancy cost him the family's long lease of the Crown lands of the former monastery of St Mary at York. It was notorious that

Papists swarmed as tenants of episcopal lands. They were thick at Ripon in Yorkshire, where Mary Ward's father was a tenant of the Archbishop of York. By 1640 it was noticed that Papist tenants were congregated in York especially in the houses of the Bedern (cathedral close). It was the same at Durham and Winchester.

The ramifications of Papist involvement in Protestant church affairs went further. It was by no means unknown for Papists to be parish churchwardens, even if they normally exercised only the considerable secular, local governmental duties of the office. Church-papists sometimes even functioned as advocates or judges in Anglican ecclesiastical courts, though they seem to have kept to the more secular side of the courts' business—wills and church property. The Anglican courts at York and London had an especially Catholic tinge. In the 1640s Thomas Read, a Protestant church lawyer and nephew of Secretary Windebank, became a Catholic and was ordained priest. Later he combined mission work in London with practice as an advocate at Doctors' Commons and surrogate in the Archbishop of Canterbury's Prerogative Court. Admittedly his case was a rare and extreme one. Baptisms and weddings with Latin Catholic rites and by Catholic priests had long been crimes punishable with large fines. Also the courts normally treated Catholic marriages as null and void because the missioners were illegally ordained. Thus the only sure, legal proof of a Catholic's age and legitimacy were the records in Anglican church registers of his parents' marriage and his baptism. Papist gentry took a grave risk if they married secretly with Catholic rites and had their children (especially elder sons) baptised by missioners. The more pious and scrupulous took the risk. But a great many Papists compromised in a variety of ways. Some had Catholic rites and then tried to get complaisant Anglican ecclesiastical court judges to register the ceremonies as valid but gravely irregular. Others had Catholic rites and tried to bribe friendly parsons to make false entries in their church registers. Others had two ceremonies, Catholic and Anglican, in some cases paying poor unemployed Anglican clergy to go through the charade of a clandestine Anglican ceremony in a private house. Others simply had Protestant rites, intending at some later date to square the matter with the Catholic missioners. It was not surprising that the Papal Agents resident in London reported to Rome that many laxities occurred and that the sacramental and marital status of many Catholics was in doubt. Hence ill-educated missioners tended to connive at the laxities.

The other great preserves of the Protestant Establishment, the public and grammar schools, the universities and Inns of Court, the

great professions, and government offices, were ostensibly barred
to Papists. In practice, like the structures of the Church of England,
they were all widely infiltrated by them in 1640. In the field of
education there was, indeed, a gulf between the Protestant and
Catholic systems. But a surprising amount of traffic flowed both
ways across the gulf. Apparently solidly Protestant gentry families
occasionally sent their sons to private schools which had Church-
papist masters and Catholic pupils; they could not prevent them
falling, at Oxford or Cambridge, under the influence of Church-
papist private tutors, Papist undergraduate friends or even missioners. Sometimes they sent them to France and Italy to university
or to travel. Even within mainly Protestant gentry families there
were Catholic relationships which, in the chances of seventeenth-
century life, could have a decisive influence on the children's education. Thomas Churchill, later an eminent secular priest and missioner in Jamaica, wrote: 'I am a gentleman born of a more ancient
stock than the present duke of Marlborough. My grandfather, audi-
tor and judge in the court of wards in the reign of King James I,
raised the duke's ancestor to be his clerk . . .' His grandfather died
of the plague, leaving Thomas's father an orphan in the hands of
dishonest trustees who stole the property. Thomas's father married
a girl of a partly Catholic family, but she was a Protestant. The
husband departed to the Indias to seek his fortune and was drowned
at sea. The widow died of the plague in 1637. Thomas, then a
schoolboy, was left to the mercies of 'my protestant friends and
kindred' (who ignored him) and 'my day-master', who thankfully
made over the boy to his mother's brother, who turned up at the
school. This uncle, it so happened, was really a secular priest. 'He
sent me into Wales where I was converted and then in the year
1642 he sent me into Flanders to Antwerp where he then lived and
where I heard my humanity; whence, about four years after, he
sent me to Douay . . .'

There were model Catholic families, whose sons never came
under Protestant masters, but passed from the tuition of missioners
or some impeccably Catholic private school straight to St Omer or
Douai. But they were in a minority amongst the Papist gentry. Even
apparently solidly Catholic families could send their sons to local
grammar schools or private schools of no very definitely Catholic
character, and then to Oxford or Cambridge and an Inn of Court.
Then there was the host of Papist families containing mixed marriages, Protestant members, Church-papist heads and elder sons.
Such people might send their younger sons abroad to Douai, as did
a completely conformist north Yorkshire JP. More often the children's education was a strange mixture of Catholic and Protestant.

The Scropes of Danby in north Yorkshire were not untypical of such Papists. Old Francis Scrope, who died in 1626, was a complete conformist living apart from his devotedly Catholic recusant wife. His heir and successor, his brother Christopher, was a recusant until 1630 when he conformed to avoid an increased recusancy fine. Christopher had five sons. Henry, the eldest, was a Church-papist who made a Catholic marriage and then used its illegality to secure an annulment in an Anglican church court so that he could marry a Protestant. Francis, the second son, was educated in a grammar school and at the very Puritan Sidney Sussex College, Cambridge. Even this ultra-Protestant seminary contained, perhaps by reaction, an anti-Puritan movement. Some of the tutors used Jesuit textbooks. The undergraduates included Lord Goring, later the Queen's special friend. Francis Scrope made a Catholic marriage the year he left College and became a recusant. The third son, John entered the English College, Douai around the time that his brother went to Cambridge. The fourth and fifth sons were educated locally; one became a conformist, the other a recusant. Of their sisters, one married a Catholic, and the rest probably lapsed from their religion. In the West Riding of Yorkshire the Papist Sir Thomas Reresby had been strictly educated at home by a Catholic tutor and allowed no further schooling. He was so impressed by the inadequacy of this system and doubtful about College schooling abroad that he sent his eldest son to a secular priest, then to a grammar school, and lastly to Cambridge and an Inn of Court. The 1st Lord Dunbar, in his childhood, long before his family came within reach of a peerage, had been sent by his Church-papist father and devoutly Catholic mother to a fashionable Anglican private school run by a parson. He later presented the parson, who had become Dean of Ripon, with a Catholic book in appreciation of his excellent grounding in the humanities.

The professions were barred to Papists but passage across the barriers was possible, if difficult. The legal profession was prestigious, lucrative and, by tradition, favoured by the gentry. It was at the heart of the Protestant Establishment. As private individuals lawyers had their own religious opinions, and many in this age were rigid Protestants. Nevertheless the profession had a curious inbuilt bias which profited Catholics, a tendency to interpret the law mildly, a pride in succouring hard cases, and a traditionalism which cherished medieval legal principles. Three of the greatest lawyers of the age helped Catholics. The great Sir Edward Coke was a resolute Protestant, but he interpreted some laws in unrestrictive ways which helped recusants (and he had a convert daughter and Catholic relatives). John Rushworth attacked Catholicism in print but specialised in collusive actions and trusts to help recusants. Sir Henry Swinburne wrote a textbook on the Anglican law of marriage which incorporated medieval Catholic principles and so incidentally helped Catholics; his son was a convert.

Without the help of the legal profession, the Catholic gentry could not have survived. Entry into the profession and practice involved some degree of religious conformism: the holding of legal offices involved complete conformism. Economic necessity and, in some cases, family tradition, pushed a surprisingly large number of Papists into at least the outer edges of the profession. A considerable number of them read law in chambers without being called to the Bar, and then acted as men-of-affairs and legal advisers to their Catholic neighbours. Every district contained several men of this sort. A relatively small number of Papists, usually moved by long family tradition (for instance the Plowdens of Shropshire, Pudseys and Withams of Durham and Yorkshire and the Walmesleys of Lancashire) were called to the Bar, practised in the courts, and even, very occasionally, became judges. Old Sir Thomas Walmesley, a Church-papist, was a Justice of the Court of Common Pleas at Westminster: his eldest son was a practising barrister and MP. Both men had recusant wives and younger children. There were even a few Protestant lawyers who, like William Drury, became Catholics and yet retained their offices. Drury was master of the Archbishop of Canterbury's Prerogative Court. His Catholicism was long-suspected but never open until his death-bed. His son attended the Jesuit school at St Omer. Such conformist practices by Papist lawyers were frowned on by strict Catholics, who nevertheless (even the Jesuit Provincials) used their expert services with profit.

The English medical profession was still small and without prestige and hence attracted few recruits from the major gentry. Physicians were forbidden to practise if they were convicted recusants and needed a licence from an Anglican bishop. By periodical conformism and evasive practices a few Catholic doctors existed in 1640. The 'mystery' tended to run in families like the Vodkas of York and the Shorts of Bury St Edmunds and Norwich. By the 1650s physicians, Protestant and Catholic, were increasing in numbers markedly as the fashionable cult of science grew. The profession came to have a peculiar attraction for the younger sons of Catholic gentry.

On the other hand schoolteaching was, at this period and long afterwards, an occupation with little appeal for Catholic gentry. It was still mostly a clerical preserve reserved for priests, ordinands, spoiled priests and lay auxiliaries of the clergy. This was so strong a tradition amongst both Protestants and Catholics that teachers were subjected to a closer official control than even lawyers. A convicted recusant might not teach children, and the penalty for disobedience might easily be years in gaol and ruin. Schools, school-teachers and even private tutors required, with increasing strictness after the Laudian bishops gained power, episcopal licence and were subject to episcopal inspection. As we have seen, many Papist gentry sent their sons to Protestant schools. Catholic lay school-masters were few. Very probably because their academic standards were low, they did not attract many Catholic pupils. In 1625 at Knaresborough and Helmsley in Yorkshire, and in 1640 at York, the Anglican authorities unearthed and closed small schools run by Church-papists. They were in no sense fully Catholic schools and only a minority of the pupils were Papists. At Helmsley the master had always a dozen sons of recusants, but he took all his pupils regularly to services at the parish church as the law directed. At York twenty-six of the fifty-six pupils were Papists. A substantial and increasing number of Catholic gentry were sending their child-ren overseas to English Colleges and convents by 1640. It is unlikely that most of these parents were motivated solely by religion. They generally detested losing sight of their children for years. With reason they were uneasy about the real risks of the operation. Send-ing children abroad for Catholic schooling was a serious legal offence. Those educated abroad could lose their inheritances to the next Protestant heirs. In fact the children passed overseas in clerically-conducted groups without much difficulty, bearing expen-sive official licences to travel for their health and sightseeing. But every now and then the customs officials arrested pupils returning home, with awkward consequences. Parents also usually disliked foreign influences, were anxious about war-conditions on the Con-tinent, and fearful of the epidemics which struck the Colleges all too frequently. The average Catholic parent was not persuaded that education in the cloistered atmosphere of a College or convent was a strict religious duty or academically good. What perhaps did per-suade him to send abroad one or two of his children was a growing conviction that Catholic ecclesiastical life now offered the young who could face it a fairly safe, eminently respectable and gentle-manly billet in life. It was even a career open to the talents, offering archdeaconries, places on the Clergy Chapter, College professor-ships, snug missioners' places in good families, Priorships, posts as Prioresses. As for the Colleges and convents, they were now a little anxious about manning their much expanded establishments, and were offering bursaries, reduced fees, and (at least in the case of the Jesuits) an assurance that fees would not rise even in time of inflation.

The profession of arms had a greater attraction for the younger sons of the Papist gentry than their registered pedigrees reveal. It was true that by law military commissions in England and commands of fortresses and arsenals might not be entrusted to recusants. But it was difficult to enforce the law strictly. There were Papists who were quite prepared to make gestures of outward conformism; others were dispensed by court influence. The military profession (more even than the law or the civil service) seemed to foster a certain indifference to religious niceties. It was full of mercenaries of all nationalities about whose private religious allegiances employers found it wise not to enquire too closely. The mercenaries themselves were brothers in arms regardless of religious divisions. Protestant gentry's sons were generally despatched to learn their trade in safely Protestant armies in the United Provinces or Sweden. Once away from home they sometimes drifted unblushingly to spells of service in officially Catholic armies in Flanders or France. Catholics went first to the Spanish or French forces, but just as easily might drift into Protestant armies. Sir Arthur Aston, a firm Papist, had a long record of service in the Spanish, Polish, Dutch and Russian armies. A surprising number of sprigs of the Papist gentry took commissions in Strafford's Irish Protestant army (along with many Irish Catholics).

To belong to the major gentry and *not* to have a place in government was to be excluded from what the Earl of Strafford called 'the public weal' or 'the State'. Public office brought trouble and small stipends or expense accounts, but it did bring worship, influence and perquisites in patronage and bribes. Unfortunately the number of available offices never kept pace with gentry demand and Papists' shares were severely rationed. In theory recusants and those with recusant wives could not hold office. The Oaths of Supremacy and Allegiance, like lions, guarded the portals of the most desirable and profitable offices. In practice a small quota of Papists, if 'quiet', was allowed into office. This was especially true in areas like Wales and Yorkshire where recusant gentry were thick enough on the ground to be of electoral importance. But it was only in the area of Wales under Raglan Castle's patronage that Papist gentry strutted about in local offices as if they had *droit de cité*. Elsewhere such people existed in driblets and conducted themselves discreetly.

A romantic observer of surviving Catholic major gentry portraits of the early seventeenth century could easily claim to detect in their stiff, hieratic poses, their air of classical aristocratic grandeur, the splendour of their stiff, expensive clothes, an essential aristocratic Catholicism, aloof, other-worldly, medieval. The impression would be false, though just the one that the sitters and painters hoped to convey. In real life the portraits, the new classical façades to homely Elizabethan mansions, the silver plate, courtesy and best clothes, were for appearance. The day-to-day reality behind it, revealed in household accounts, house inventories, wills, private notebooks was, even for the hundred Catholic baronets and knights, homespun and bourgeois. Like the rest of their class, the Catholic major gentry had middle-class preoccupations, even if they were of the minority whose religion was narrowly intense and monastic. Like pious Puritans, pious Catholics tended to be shrewd men of business and their womenfolk efficient managers. The Mallorys of Studley in Nidderdale had a country house in a sylvan, remote paradise. The menfolk patronised the most austere of English monastic Orders, the Carthusians; two of them, including a widower head of the family, had become Carthusians. Yet the family roots were in City of London big business. Sir John Mallory was a director of the Virginia Company. His wealth came from intensive sheep-farming and lead-mining; his estate management was keen and competitive. The most intensely Catholic gentry family of the period was the Gascoignes of Barnbow in Yorkshire. They produced rows of Benedictines, were the main support of the Benedictine Congregation and the rescuers of Mary Ward's shattered little Institute. Yet in business matters the family had a Quaker power of application; they marled their arable, enclosed wasteland, exploited coal seams. Sir Thomas Gascoigne's private notebooks contain a lot of narrow piety: 'Intentions: those that have fewest or noe friends to praye for em, in particular Application of all Plenary Indulgences pro defunctis positively granted . . .' In his small, neat writing such passages stand cheek-by-jowl with business notes, for instance on the engineering of coal pits:

> I did sinke the Ginn pitt deeper and added another Pumpe and did lenthen the Pumpe 4 yeardes and drew the water 4 yeards more . . . the Soughes, watercourses, Stanks and Damms must be carefully attended to . . . from Parlington Hollins there is two rowes of bottom cole and one rowe of hardband to be gotten . . .

In the contemporary iron trade, the most successful syndicate consisted of two Protestants and three Catholics, Sir John Winter, Sir Basil Brooke and Benedict Hall. Winter was a Glamorgan iron-master and coal owner, director of the Royal Fisheries Company and an adviser of the Queen. He was a pious practising Catholic and the author of two books, *On Ironworks* and *Observations on the Oath of Supremacy* (justifying the Catholic practice of taking the Oath with mental reservations). Brooke was an ironmaster at Coalbrookdale in Shropshire from his nearby mansion at Madeley. He was a director of the Royal Mineral and Battery Company and a close friend and host of Bishop Richard Smith. He also was an author, in this case of *Entertainments for Lent* (the translation of a devotional treatise by a French Jesuit), dedicated to the Queen. Hall was a Gloucester ironmaster and the father of a nun at Cambrai. His widow took her private chaplain with her to take up residence beside her daughter in the convent guesthouse for the rest of her life. The profits of the iron business beautified the convent chapel.

Sir Richard Weston of Sutton in Surrey was a practising Catholic and England's best-known progressive agriculturalist. His *Discours of Husbandrie,* his schemes to use turnips and enclosures for arable, his drainage schemes and agricultural canals were the talk of go-ahead gentry. He and his family, with City of London backing (which they were accustomed to courting), projected and built a canal in Surrey. Humphrey Weld of Surrey and his new medieval folly in Dorset, Lulworth Castle, was a strict, quiet Papist whose family were great in the City and its magistracies. In Lancashire the Papist Towneley and Walmesley families studied the chemistry of the soil and ran a salon of mainly Protestant scientists in touch with Gresham College. In Northamptonshire, the most hotly progressive and competitive of all counties, the Brudenells and Treshams, stout Papists, had a name for keen practice in business. Up on the Derbyshire moorland, the practising Catholic Eyres of Hassop spent £10,000 on buying more land between 1600 and 1642, fought innumerable lawsuits and made money from intensive lead-mining. In the background to all this gentry piety and business endeavour stood Endymion Porter, the Hispaniolised Papist courtier and master-fixer of contracts and government licences, and Augustine Baker, the monk, mystic and legal man-of-affairs employed by Catholic gentry.

But for every Brooke, Winter, Gascoigne or Weld there were thirty or forty families of Catholics of middling gentry status. There was a social and income gulf between the upper gentry (between £5000 and £1500 a year) and the middling gentry (£700 to £500). The former were within measurable reach of the court and peerages, the latter struggling to maintain themselves above the plebeians. The Yorkshire Meynells were fairly typical of these people. They claimed relationship with a late medieval baronial family of the same name. In fact their arrival in the ranks of landowning county gentry was due to the investment of an early Tudor Judge, their ancestor, in ex-monastic lands with which he endowed, rather slenderly, his three sons. From them derived three allied but separate Meynell families, all of whom moved over to Catholicism. The Catholic strand in the lives of the three families was persistent. At one time or another it produced a few secular priests, a Jesuit, and two nuns. But the families also had an equally persistent strand of Church-papists and apostates. Thomas Meynell of North Kilvington, a hamlet perched on the Hambleton Hills above the Great North Road in country even then famed for bloodstock and horse-racing, lived from 1560 to 1650 and kept a revealing commonplace book. In it he recorded, in a bold, thick hand, the mercies of God and the Mother of God to his family and their social and economic struggles, with no distinction between the two. A page or two of fanciful Meynell genealogy was followed by the minute details of land-purchases and lawsuits, a doggerel poem celebrating a wedding and the coat-armours it brought into the family, a note on the religious profession of a relative ('pleadged her Virginitie to pure Divinitie'). Here, in miniature and more crudely, is the same mixture of hard-headed business practicality, snobbery and Catholic piety we found in the great Sir Thomas Gascoigne. Thomas Meynell wrote:

> Md. Anno domini 1628. I did sell unto my Brother George Meynell those lands wch. I had in Denton wch. I purchased of my Aunt, the wch. I could never lett for more than £8 per annum for £130 videlicet xvj yeres purchase and more. I praye God Blesse him and all his for I am truely paide herefore . . .

With some local scandal the Meynells had totally enclosed the lands of their hamlet, ousting most of the tenants and turning all into a home-farm. They lacked money and influence to acquire Anglican rectories, prebends and tithe-farms. Even if Thomas had not been a Papist, he would have been far back in the queue waiting for local government office. The manor house at North Kilvington had no new classical façade, and was equipped as a working farm. The older men of the family had been educated at Northallerton Grammar School and they were slow to join the fashion of sending a few children overseas to school. Thomas had a rather rusty ability with Latin, but his life and tastes were plain and bucolic:

> I bequeath to Richard Meynell eight Oxen or stotts,wth.waine

and plowes and other Implements thereunto belonginge and one hundred weathers [sheep] . . . Md. 1621. We wonn hitherto to Kilvington from Gaterley [horse races] the Gould bell, and from Hambleton the Silver bell, from Bagby Moor a Silver cupp for ever . . .

For every middling gentry family like the Meynells there were several of Catholic mere or poor gentry, with incomes of under £200 a year. They were especially numerous in Wales and the west and in the north, the more backward parts of the country. They were pathetically anxious to assert their gentility. But in practice it was hard for an outsider to their narrow, hierarchical county societies to distinguish them from freeholding yeomen or respectable tenant farmers. There were a good many successful yeomen and farmers with no pretensions to gentle blood who had larger incomes, and lived better, than a good many poor gentry. On the other hand, some 'mere gentry' were successful yeomen climbing the social ladder. They had either illegally assumed a coat of arms or recently bought one from the Heralds. Most mere gentry by 1640 had all the appearances of decay, economic and social. They were usually the victims of mismanagement and debt, or of the system of gentry primogeniture, which condemned younger sons to exist on exiguous child's portions, annuities or rent-charges.

It is certain that numerically the majority of early seventeenth-century Catholics must have belonged to this inextricably intertwined mass of mere gentry and better-off yeomen and tenant farmers. A good deal of English talent (including Oliver Cromwell and Isaac Newton) came originally from this social background, about which there was nothing aristocratic. Amongst the Catholics, some had vain pretensions, were overspending, and lived in an atmosphere of genteel indigence. Others were strictly dependent for their daily bread on well-off Catholic gentry or peers: the Marquis of Worcester had a big trail of such Papist gentry followers in Monmouth and Glamorgan. Others, owning all or most of their land freehold, had an air of independence. They lived frugally, without pretensions, made money and could provide rent-charges for sons who became mission priests. This independence was made possible where landlords had chosen to auction off blocks of small farms or even whole villages, and sell to sitting tenants or local farmers. Charles I sold off a considerable number of large moorland manors of a type which could not be easily improved by any great landlord. The City of London or financiers who bought the properties usually broke them up into smaller parcels for local resale. Large landowners in serious debt sometimes raised capital by offering the tenant farmers on the less productive parts of their estates 1000-year leases in return for sizable lump sum fines. For all these reasons there had come to be a line of division between village communities subjected tightly to great landowners' wills and others which were free, even if still technically owned by magnates. The latter places breathed a spirit of independence or even defiance of landlord-power. Quite often such communities were relatively free also of Anglican clerical control. On the wilder parts of the country few people had settled in earlier ages, so parishes were vast and parish churches far apart. Such parishes could contain a multiplicity of isolated hamlets and farms. Before the Protestant Reformation these churches were poorly endowed and their scattered chapels-of-ease badly served by the clergy. Since the Reformation the Anglican authorities had tried to remedy the situation, made worse by an increase in population in such areas. They found the task daunting. The landlords were unwilling to put their hands into their pockets, and the free hamlet communities either lapsed into stony religious indifference and near-paganism or went over readily to religious nonconformity, Protestant or Catholic. This was true of wide areas of Yorkshire (for instance Nidderdale and the Whitby moors) and Lancashire. In Nidderdale the few Anglican parish clergymen made little impact on moorland communities of sheep-farming poor gentry, miners and labourers. The upper and middling gentry of the dale were almost all Papist with their tenants and exercised a sort of feudal protection (social and religious, not economic) over Catholic mere gentry in the free hamlets. But there was not, in Nidderdale or elsewhere, anything peculiarly Catholic about these arrangements. In Nidderdale the wealthy and Puritan Proctor family of Fountains Abbey exercised a similar strait control over their estate tenants, and a loose protection over the many more or less nonconformist Protestant freemen in the dale.

As we have seen, the Catholic peerage suffered far more from Establishment ostracism than from outright legal persecution. The major Papist gentry, because of their wealth and involvement with the Establishment, shared the peers' relative immunity from persecution. Families like the Westons, Gascoignes, Winters and Brookes bought royal letters of protection from conviction for their recusancy. But the middling and mere Catholic gentry were largely unprotected. Since 1603 the rather haphazard penal laws had been shaped into a large, coherent body of law. JPs and Catholic gentry now found it advisable to possess convenient little handbooks to the penal laws. Firstly there were the capital offences. A person convicted of being a Catholic priest ordained abroad and come into England was liable to the penalty for treason: being hanged, cut down while still alive, and then butchered into quarters. The laity convicted of giving aid of any kind or shelter to such a priest faced the same capital sentence and the confiscation of all their property to the State. Moreover in times of national stress—war or even economic depression or famine and plague—Protestant mob-frenzy could blow up suddenly and viciously against all known or suspected Papists. Their property could be wrecked and themselves molested or even arrested on denunciations for plotting against the State. In such heated circumstances there was a real likelihood not of mass-murder, but of the sacrifice of a few Catholics' lives to appease public feeling. At such times judges and juries could convict of plain treason on merely fanciful or circumstantial evidence. For these reasons, quite apart from any others, sensible Papists practised their religion with exaggerated caution.

Secondly there were the recusancy fining laws, which had become more and more complex with the years. JPs were bound to put parish authorities on oath regularly to list all wilful absentees from Anglican church services for at least four successive Sundays. The absentees were summoned to court. If they did not appear at all, or did not hand in certificates of church-attendance, they were automatically convicted of the crime of Catholic recusancy. The Clerk of the Peace certified all recusants to the Westminster Exchequer, which charged them with fines at the rate of £260 a year per person, if over the age of thirteen. For a family of five adult recusants the fine would be £1300 a year. The practical difficulties of collection, exacerbated by mass evasion or accumulating indebtedness to the Exchequer very soon produced cumbersome and ingenious administrative schemes. Their purpose was frankly to extract the maximum possible from as many Papists of property as possible with least trouble and expense to the State and the local authorities. The wage-earning poor were usually completely ignored. The cost of pursuing them and distraining on their few chattels bore no proportion to the money they could pay. The great majority of well-to-do Papists, peers and major gentry, were exempted from fining by letters of protection or were able to escape by the use of good lawyers. The main weight of the fining system therefore fell on the middling and mere gentry and farmers. The delicate business of outwitting their (often clumsy) efforts at evasion and deciding the practical maximum proportion of the legal fine they could pay without being totally ruined was entrusted to two official bodies of Recusancy Commissioners, one for the north and one for the south. Although the original purpose of the huge fines was to terrify Catholics wholesale into apostasy, by the 1630s the Recusancy Commissioners behaved and talked as if their task was to conserve the Catholic gentry community in a healthy condition so as to extract from it a good revenue for the State. The State had come to regard Catholics as medieval kings had the Jews: as cows to be cherished and milked. From 1627 the Commissioners drove bargains with Catholics: if they would accept recusancy conviction and a very moderate blanket fine for themselves and all their families, the Catholic compounders would be given letters of protection against all other legal charges or molestations for their Catholicism.

Thirdly there were the molesting laws, remarkably numerous and draconic. The local authorities had power to exact on the spot an extra fine of one shilling per person for every single wilful absence from the parish church on a Sunday or weekday holiday of obligation (by law the English were required to attend church some seventy-five times a year). A persistent absentee or a persistent non-communicant could be subjected to a bond of hundreds of pounds, forfeited if he did not certify conformity within a fixed time. There was no limit to the number of times a recusant could be caught by such bonds. The authorities had power also to demand that any recusant or suspect should take the anti-Catholic Oath of Allegiance. Persistent refusal to take it was a felony punishable with life-imprisonment and confiscation of all property. Catholics caught at a Roman Mass, or found guilty of using Catholic rites, had to pay £100 fine for each offence. It was an offence, punishable by substantial fines, to make the sign of the cross, use a rosary, a blessed medal or any Catholic object or book of devotion. It was a grave offence to bequeath property 'to superstitious uses' (for Masses, prayers for the dead, to endow priests and missions, support seminaries or religious houses) or act as trustee for such bequests. On conviction the property was confiscated and the offender fined. A Catholic recusant might not travel over five miles from home or come within ten miles of Westminster or the court without a current written permit from the JPs for local journeys or the King's Council for longer ones. A Council permit was required by recusants for visits abroad, and the recipient could be barred (if necessary by bonds) from visiting Catholic establishments. The sending of children abroad for Catholic schooling was rigorously penalised. The mere inheritance of property of consequence by Catholics was barred by the requirement of the Oath of Supremacy before livery (legal registration) of ownership. The Protestant husband of a recusant wife was heavily penalised: he was normally liable for her recusancy fines and unable to hold office of State.

This tremendous accumulation of penal laws included still more provisions. From 1629 recusants were charged double rates, hitherto reserved for aliens, whenever Parliamentary subsidies (property taxes) were imposed. Gentry Papists were charged especially high contributions to the county militia, on the grounds that national defence was mostly required to counter the threat of Catholic revolution. As we have already seen, the system of royal Wardship was used to impose Protestant instruction on Catholic wards and marry them off compulsorily to Protestants. The Anglican Church courts operated an independent course of harassment of Papists. They issued repeated summonses to face reprimands, prosecutions for Catholic baptisms, weddings and funerals, and legal fees. In the areas where Catholics were most numerous, the ordinary episcopal courts were reinforced by Courts of High Commission which duplicated these molestations and could impose gaol sentences, bonds and fines.

If these penal laws had been consistently executed the practice of Catholicism would have become impossible for all except a very few landless and hunted fugitives. In practice the impact of the laws was greatly cushioned by a good many factors. The government and high society had long ago decided that English Catholicism was a threat best contained by the threat of punishment and a practical policy of ostracism and discrimination. A kind of practical *modus vivendi* had been arrived at by both Protestants and Catholics, excluding an extremist minority on both sides. In the society of each county, in business circles, at court, in the professions, and in literary and artistic circles 'quiet' Catholics were admitted to a strictly subordinate place provided they accepted their position. The Recusancy Commissioners expedited their business with polite recusants with courtesy and gave free dinners to the socially more acceptable amongst them. Indulgent Protestant grandees put in a good word for 'quiet' Papist relations, acquaintances or dependants. Indulgent Anglican clergymen said nothing when a Catholic squire's body was brought to burial in the family vault in the parish church chancel, provided the Papist relations and bearers played the game: they must deposit the coffin in the choir silently and depart before the parson conducted the Anglican burial service. (Occasionally fanatical Papists broke into parish churches by night and conducted burials there with Catholic rites in the light of tapers.) Sometimes unsolicited, parsons on good terms with Papist squires would voluntarily enter the births of their children in the church registers.

These amenities however often did not stretch down the nicely-graduated social scale to Papist mere gentry and farmers. Their lot, and sometimes that even of the Papist middling gentry, was often hard. There were freelance informers who made a living out of harassing and blackmailing Catholics whose social influence was slight. Thomas Meynell, on one occasion, had the great satisfaction of securing the arrest and punishment of one such informer who terrified his old widowed aunt and carted her off to gaol in a wheelbarrow. Some years later Thomas himself, along with several members of his family, was summarily arrested by an informer and hustled off to York Castle. In York there were unscrupulous minor officials who made a good living out of blackmail extorted from respectable Catholics. In Lancashire and county Durham extreme Puritans made it their business to delate Papists to the Church officials. These officials had a fine sense of social distinctions: they conveniently lost accusations against wealthy Catholic gentry or accepted from them the most scanty of excuses for non-attendance at court. But middling and mere gentry were rarely treated so leniently. The poorer Catholic gentry could ill afford the frequent summonses to court, the legal fees and tips to sergeants, apparitors, constables and clerks. In times of persecution it was they, not the upper gentry, who landed in gaol. Double subsidies and militia money were flea-bites to the wealthy Papists, but a serious drain on the resources of many of the poorer gentry. Recusancy compositions fell just as unfairly: most peers and wealthy gentry Papists were exempted; yeomen paid mere token sums, and the main weight fell on the middling and mere gentry.

Catholic tradition treasured the memory of the sufferings of these people. Their recusancy papers (recusancy compositions, summonses, prison bills, licences to travel) were often carefully preserved or even bound into a volume. Tradition exaggerated the weight of the sufferings and passed over the factors which often largely offset them. Protestant writers were quick to list these factors. They pointed out that most of the penal laws were barely executed. It was almost unheard of for a gentry Papist to be arrested and tried for sheltering a priest. The houses of Catholics were very rarely searched. Catholic books were sold openly in Protestant bookshops and kept in Protestant gentry's libraries. The Oath of Allegiance was only very fitfully administered and normally taken by the great majority of Papists confronted with it. After 1629 the new composition system greatly reduced the incidence of summonses and legal molestations of the many compounders. Protestants, with good reason, doubted whether, by the 1630s, any Papist gentry were really reduced to indigence by recusancy fines. In these years a large number of lesser gentry, Protestant and Catholic, became steadily poorer or even had to sell up and move. But in most cases the cause was fecklessness an ordinary misfortune. Catholics in this state found fines and molestation for their recusancy by no means major causes of their troubles. Protestants remarked, on the contrary, that middling gentry recusants were commonly remarkably prosperous. It was suspected that charges for recusancy provided a spur to economic effort. The Yorkshire Protestants could not fail to notice that, at the very time that Mr Meynell of Kilvington and Mr Middleton of Stockeld were in gaol in York Castle (in private rooms with servants and meals sent in), both were buying land extensively. All the middling and upper gentry of the day were well-practised in legal subterfuges to escape government charges on their estates. Elaborate trusts and collusive lawsuits were common. Catholic recusants had a deserved reputation for a special skill in this business of evasion. The commonplace book of Thomas Meynell casts light on the realities of his sufferings for the faith. In 1631 his grandson, on entry into the English College, Douai, reported 'my grandfather has been imprisoned fifteen times for the Catholic Faith, and my father once: between them they have paid to the King £4000 sterling for the same cause'. Up to 1627 Thomas Meynell certainly had to endure plenty of worry and molestation, including a dozen short periods in gaol, charges of £450 for forfeited bonds, a prosecution for his Catholic marriage, the tendering to him of the Oath of Allegiance, two attacks by blackmailing informers, and steady recusancy fining from 1596. But there was another side to the coin. By 1631 he had actually paid into the Exchequer in fines £618 in thirty-four years (not £4000), mainly because of collusive trusts which put most of his property into the hands of Protestants or Church-papist relations. During these years, although his gross income can rarely have exceeded £600 a year, he expended over £800 on the purchase of land. He enclosed the common fields and waste of North Kilvington with such thoroughness, ousting tenants, that in 1617 a Royal Commission added his name to the list of notoriously oppressive landlords. By good luck, influence, legal evasion and bribery he repeatedly had forfeited bonds cancelled and so evaded almost completely debts to the Crown of well over £1000. By luck and good legal advice he got his Catholic marriage registered in the episcopal court. In an area famous for bloodstock and horseracing, at one time or another he won most of the local gold and silver bell racing prizes.

Meynell made no secret of two facts: his resolute Catholicism and his complete dependence for survival on a series of easy compromises with the Protestant Establishment. Apart from two brief acts of conformity (taking the Oaths of Supremacy and Allegiance) he stuck to recusancy throughout his adult life. His Catholic piety was solid, antique and given much to trust in our Lady, the holy angels and patron saints. The deed of his recusancy fine composition of 1627 has written on the back in his big hand: 'Sancte Michaell ora pro me: 1627.' His religious faith was inextricably mixed up with his sense of family, gentry and estate:

> As it pleased god in all ages to whose blessed name be all honour and glory and I poore wretch humbly beseech his blessed mother to thank his maiestie in my behalfe, to upholde our name, Familie and Armorye: soe he always furnished me with meanes to maintain our Gentry . . .

In an area where Catholic gentry were thick on the ground, Meynell had a sense of belonging to a Papist local community and to a family which exercised a leadership amongst it. In 1654 a Catholic neighbour wrote to his wife of the Meynells:

> . . . in regard of the great respect I doe him and the obligacion I have to that family, and the gratitude for that good which wee and a great many moe have received from them . . . it is gods goodnesse to that house for the great good they have done . . .

Thomas Meynell also felt that he and his kind, the Papist gentry, stood for and were defending an ancient and essential order of religion and society in a world of flux which had turned against it. The Papists, facing the big battalions, must rely on God, our Lady and their own native wit.

But this sense of Dissenting opposition amongst men like Meynell, as amongst contemporary Puritan gentry, was tempered by an acknowledgment of dependence on the Establishment. Meynell was no fanatic. He contributed to a fund for the maintenance of travelling missioners. He was friendly with two of them, 'a vertuous Catholicke Queen Mary Preiste' (he clearly did not find all these aged clergy respectable) who married him and who was housed in a cottage by a neighbour, and 'a religious Gent.', a Benedictine relation who claimed to have found a 'Saint Menelaus (Meynell)' in the Kalendar of saints. But until Meynell's extreme old age, when a priest grandson returned from Douai, he maintained no resident chaplain at North Kilvington. He admitted that the family's estate and Catholicism owed their survival to his own gestures of conformism and the Church-papistry of his grandfather, father and brothers. He had 'very good Protestant' friends (some of them Puritans). He had business dealings with the Protestant Earl of Salisbury who owned lands marching with his own. He had friendly business dealings with John Bramhall, a great Laudian divine, rector

F

of a nearby parish and given to public debates with Catholic missioners.

Indeed, in these years the astonishing allegiance to Catholicism of so many compromisers, conformists and Church-papists, or even nominal Protestants seems a more striking evidence for the strength of English Catholicism than the straightforward, heroic recusancy of the relatively few. It was the Church-papists who saved the Catholic community.

The politicians and amateur statisticians were then uninterested in Catholic numbers amongst the people or plebeians. Contemporary guesses at the overall numbers of Catholics most probably related only to gentry. A Spanish ambassador, Sarmiento, thought that fifty per cent were really Protestant (thirty-three per cent ordinary Anglicans, seventeen per cent Puritans), twenty-five per cent 'atheists' (that is non-church-goers or people who merely went to church for social and economic reasons) and twenty-five per cent Catholics (eight per cent recusants, seventeen per cent Church-papists). Padre Alessandro, an Italian Capuchin visitor to England, reported to Rome that most of the English were (even by Italian standards) easy-going in religious matters, and a third of them quite willing to become Catholics. Protestant observers fought shy of detailed statistics and their judgments reflected their personal preoccupations. Administrators and Anglican bishops stressed how few the total numbers of Catholic recusants were. Puritans tended to detect Papists lurking under every bush. In general the upper classes in the seventeenth century felt very unsure of the loyalty to the Establishment or, indeed, to any gentry cause, Protestant or Catholic, of the people. There was something concealed, incalculable, violent about them. Dissent, likely to have religious overtones even if it had little religious inspiration, was to be expected of them, if only to demonstrate their resentment against their betters.

Plebeian Catholicism was a small and amorphous thing. A good deal of it existed under the wing of the Papist gentry amongst their household servants and farm tenants. But it would be unwise to imagine that such gentry were always the centre of a solidly Catholic clientele. Church-papist gentry commonly had mostly Protestant servants and tenants. Many recusant gentry employed some Protestants. There were moorland areas of free villages where there was a scattering of small farmers, weavers and miners who were Catholics and not under the protection of any Papist gentry. With the exception of London and Westminster—a rabbit-warren hiding a very shifting population of country immigrants who sometimes brought their Catholicism with them—the towns contained very little working-class Catholicism: the relatively few urban poor Catholics were usually dependent on Papist gentry who frequently had town-houses in which they only resided during the winter season.

7. The Civil War and the Republic, 1642–60

In Englefield parish church in Berkshire there is, on the nave wall facing the door, a large and tastefully simple monument to commemorate the Catholic faith and royalist loyalty of the Marquis of Winchester:

> He who in impious times untainted stood,
> And mid'st Rebellion durst be just and good;
> Whose Armes asserted, and whose sufferings more
> Confirm'd the cause for which he fought before,
> Rests here, rewarded by an Heavenly Prince
> For what his Earthly could not recompence.
> Pray (Reader) that sutch times no more appeare,
> Or, if they happen, learn true Honour here.
>
> Ark of thy Age's faith and Loyalty,
> Which (to preserve them) Heav'n confin'd in thee,
> Few Subjects could a King like thine deserve,
> And fewer such a King so well could serve.
> Blest King, blest Subject, whose exalted state
> By suffrings rose, and gave the law to fate.
> Such Soules are rare but mighty patterns given
> To Earth were meant for ornaments to Heaven.
>
> *By John Dryden, Poet Laureate.*

After 1660 Catholic peers and gentry all maintained loudly that they had been strong royalists during the late troubles. Few of their family pedigrees (meant for official registration) do not incorporate the legend in notes: 'killed at Marston Moore'; 'killed at Honiton fight'; 'served K.Charles I in the warres'; 'spent £1000 in k.Charles cause'. The Marquis of Winchester's memorial asserted a common notion that Catholicism stood for an antique view of the monarchy and the religious duty of loyalty even to a King who treated Catholics as second-class citizens and failed to reward them for their sufferings on his behalf. By the nineteenth century even Protestant history books assumed without question that in the seventeenth century all Catholics were Tories. But the truth is not so simple.

The great political crisis of 1638–42 produced a typical, violent anti-Catholic panic. The Parliamentary Opposition—which included, at that stage in the crisis, many who were, by 1642, destined to move over more or less reluctantly to the King's side—claimed that Charles I was drifting fast towards a Catholic despotism. The King assented to a full execution of the penal laws: a few priests were arrested and executed. There were anti-Catholic riots in a dozen counties and the Queen's chapels and a few houses of Catholics were damaged by mobs. In 1638 the Queen attempted to raise money for the King from the Pope and leading Catholics. Thomas Meynell's eldest son was one of the collectors for the North Riding of Yorkshire. The sums collected were small. The Catholic peers and gentry shared the doubt and bewilderment of most people about the issues at stake. The great majority of the population, not only the illiterate poor, but many farmers, tradesmen, and mere gentry did not understand the complex issues or had no desire to understand them; they remained cautiously neutral. The peers, upper and middling gentry were often disposed to think the same way, but they found neutrality difficult. Their estates, offices and multiple links of dependence on the court were put in peril. They would suffer badly if they took sides, but almost as badly if they did not, only to become the prey of the warring factions.

The Catholic members of these classes had additional reasons for finding the decision hard. To start with, it was then no part of Catholic belief that armed resistance to a King was always sinful. Indeed, Catholic moral theology was confused on this matter and certainly offered no easy solution to the narrow points disputed between King and Parliament. Until 1648–9 both sides in the civil wars accepted monarchy and assumed that its powers needed some degree of Parliamentary control. So much for principle. When an educated Catholic turned to the weighing of advantages and to prudence, it was far from evident that a Parliamentary victory would be disastrous for Catholics, or even more damaging than a victory for the King. The King stood for a contemptuous quasi-toleration and ostracism of Catholics and discrimination against them, with increasingly realistic fining. When cornered politically he was ready at one moment to promise almost anything to Catholics, and at another to allow priests to be executed. In England, as

The Handle and the Axe

even more evidently in Ireland, he doled out to Catholics minor graces which could at any time be abridged or set aside. In return he demanded, as of right, that they should contribute extra to his funds and commit themselves to his policies. In Ireland in 1641 such treatment precipitated a general Catholic rebellion, though, typically, some Irish Catholic peers and gentry held doubtfully aloof from the rebels. At the outset of the King's 'Bishops' War' against the Scots in 1638, the King issued commissions of array to leading northern Catholics, requiring them to raise forces for national defence, ostensibly at their own expense. The King's Scottish policy was unpopular in England, and the northern Catholics were mostly subjected to stiff recusancy compositions. Many of them showed no desire to court unpopularity amongst their Protestant neighbours or face the great expense. The Papist 2nd Lord Fairfax, who received a commission of array and did little to execute it, was paying £260 a year in recusancy fines and threatened by the Court of Wards with legal proceedings to take away his eldest son and educate him as a Protestant. In Yorkshire and Lancashire a few Church-papists (and in Lancashire two or three recusants) had recently faced imprisonment for refusing to pay to the King a forced loan.

It was therefore not surprising that Catholics reacted to the greater crisis of civil war in 1642 much as their Protestant neighbours did. Some Catholic families, like Protestant ones, were divided: one adventurous brother went to war for the King, while his father and brothers preferred neutrality. Perhaps (though there seems to be no evidence for this) the parting of ways was deliberate family policy of provision for the future. A sizable minority of Catholic peers and gentry decided on complete, militant royalism. Sometimes this was spontaneous monarchism. Often it was, at least in part, forced on a family. When the Protestant Marquis of Newcastle, an immensely wealthy coalowner and power in the north-east, declared for militant royalism and proceeded to raise an army for the King largely at his own expense, north-eastern Catholic gentry were caught in a dilemma. To reject the Marquis's request for aid was, for the Catholic gentry community of the area, to invite royalist attentions of an unpleasant kind in an area mostly under their control. The list of northern Catholics granted officers' commissions in Newcastle's army was no real indication of strong local royalist sentiment amongst Catholics. The Papist Marquis of Worcester became a leading royalist commander, but he did not do so easily and naturally. His disposition was to make his country neutral. But his local power depended largely on offices granted to himself, his son and his followers, offices which were graces that would have been withdrawn if he had refused to help the King substantially. Worcester's iron-making syndicate was vital to the King's war-effort: if the Marquis had not used it for the King, the royalists would have appropriated it. The Marquis several times complained bitterly of the looting of his and his Catholic followers' resources by the King's Commissioners during the war. On one occasion he actually used a simple trick to frighten them out of Raglan Castle. The Marquis of Winchester, 'the Great Loyalist', was, in spite of the statements made on his memorial stone, also a reluctant royalist fighter. His wealth and the extraordinary graces he had received made it impossible for him to refuse the King's demands from 1638 for large interest-free 'loans' (which would never be repaid, even if the King were victorious) and then that Basing House should be converted into a royalist stronghold at the Marquis's expense. The house unfortunately occupied a highly strategic position by the main road from London to the west. The Marquis was eventually compelled to exclude some hostile Protestant royalist officers from his house because they behaved so badly and treated his possessions as fair game.

The commitments to the Queen and court and great industrial enterprises of Sir John Winter made it practically impossible for him to avoid declaring for the King, though he did his best to avoid too complete a sacrifice and kept open throughout the war secret connections with his business associates in London. Sir Basil Brooke the ironmaster tried to escape the net of commitment by staying in London throughout the war, posing as a secret royalist agent, but really trying to be neutral and to conserve his business interests. In Lancashire the civil war divisions largely reflected a pre-war faction-fight between the Earl of Derby's clients and his gentry opponents. When Derby declared for the King, his prominent Catholic upper gentry supporters (such as Sir Thomas Tyldesley and Thomas Clifton) were compelled to back him.

Once Catholics appeared in arms in the King's forces they faced a good deal of Protestant prejudice. The royalist Lord Chancellor, Edward Hyde, strenuously opposed the grant of commissions to them as illegal and politically damaging to the cause. He lost no opportunity to suggest that they must be untrustworthy or, if they were successful commanders, that they were not really Papists. He picked on Sir Arthur Aston, the only Papist, he wrote with satisfaction, to be made a full general: Aston was not really a Catholic ('whom the Papists notwithstanding would not acknowledge for a Papist'), he was untrustworthy (had he not hesitated whether to serve King or Parliament?), a rank coward and a great lecher. The appointment of a Catholic, Sir Henry Gage, to the command of a fortress, roused Protestant royalist jealousy, only appeased by his gallant death in action.

Some, but apparently few, Catholics supported the Parliament. Its manifestos were blood-thirstily anti-Catholic, and habitually equated popery with royalism. Its Commissioners, in areas held by Parliament troops, began with draconic measures of fining Catholics and standing aside when soldiers, mobs and informers got into action against their property. But, at any rate during the confusion of war to 1646, a good many Catholic peers and gentry lived under the Parliament's rule and found its bark worse than its bite. At least it was not certain that they would have been better-off in royalist territory. Both sides attempted intermittently to collect recusancy fines, both levied heavy monthly assessments and excises, both forcibly billeted troops on civilians and requisitioned their crops and livestock. Thomas Stitch, a Papist civil servant at Westminster, refused to follow the royalist Exchequer officials to the King's shadow government at Oxford. He remained in the Parliament's Exchequer throughout the war and subscribed to its public loans. William Salvin, a Yorkshire gentleman ordinand at the English College, Lisbon, returned to England in 1644, enlisted in the King's forces, was taken prisoner at Naseby, and promptly enlisted in the Parliament's New Model Army. Two young Catholics, Charles Howard (later 1st Earl of Carlisle and brought up by his uncle, the Catholic 2nd Lord Fairfax) and Thomas Bellasis (later 2nd Lord Fauconberg), by the end of the war had taken commissions in the New Model Army. Admittedly by then their perseverance in the Catholic religion was in doubt. The Parliamentary armies contained a number of officers and administrators who showed a measure of tolerance of Catholics. In Yorkshire alone there were four or five Parliamentary officers who had recusant wives or who were themselves to end up as Catholics. Dr John Troutbeck, Surgeon-General to the New Model Army, was never openly a Catholic, but had many Catholic friends to whom he acted frequently as trustee. William Petty, Surveyor-General and a pioneer of statistics and political economy, was educated by the Jesuits in France. His early Catholic training (it is not certain that he ever practised as a Catholic) left traces. He had Catholic friends and was famous for his brilliant imitations of Jesuit and Capuchin preaching styles. John Rushworth, Oliver Cromwell's legal secretary, ran a thriving business in protecting Catholic gentlemen's property from fines.

The majority of Catholic peers and gentry remained neutral during the war. Some, like the Church-papist Richard Sherburne of Stonyhurst in Lancashire, endured uneasily the buffets of both sides and then tried to take refuge in the wilds of the Lake District. The King's Commissioners had forced him to enter into a bond of £1000 'for the advance of Ready Monies to buye Armes and do other Publique service for the King'. After the war his Catholic recusant wife told Parliamentary Commissioners that the family had subscribed to the King's funds only under duress and had similarly been forced, on their way to Cumberland, to stay a short time in the King's fortress of York. Richard himself carefully subscribed to a series of anti-Catholic oaths. After 1660 and the triumph of royalism, Mrs Sherburne told a different story: they had been consistently, if secretly, royalist. Sir Philip Constable of Everingham, Yorkshire, was captured at the fall of Newark Castle to the Scottish Army in 1646. He swore to Parliamentary Commissioners (most probably truly) that he was a neutral but on bond by the royalists and fled as a civilian refugee to Newark. Other neutral Papists spent the war years in voluntary exile abroad, Lord Baltimore partly in America, Lords Lumley and Teynham in Flanders, Lords Arundell and Somerset in Italy, Lord Montague in France. After the war close scrutiny by Parliamentary Commissioners failed to make charges of royalism stick against Lords Abergavenny, Arundell the younger, Brudenell, Stourton, Stafford, Vaux, Mordaunt, Rivers, Mounteagle and the Earl of Portland. The Earl of Shrewsbury and young Lord Petre were convicted on only slender evidence. The Commissioners' records tell the same story for the Papist gentry, county by county. The tale of royalist delinquents and neutrals is: London fourteen and forty-six; Suffolk three and sixty; Northampton six and eighteen; Somerset ten and twenty-six; Buckingham one and nineteen; Monmouthshire nineteen and sixty; Lancashire seventy-six and 240; Yorkshire fifty-four and 130.

The predominance of hard-headed, unheroic Catholic neutralism stands in strange contrast to the true, and often described strand of heroic Catholic royalism. The New Model Army took Basing House by storm and sacked it. A good many of its mainly Catholic garrison were killed in the fight or as prisoners, as were several priests and civilians. Old Inigo Jones and Wenceslas Hollar were spared though roughly handled. The Marquis of Winchester, no soldier, was given quarter and hustled off to live under house-arrest in London. He had spent £600,000 in the King's cause: he now had his entire vast estate confiscated and he lived on the Parliament's charity in London. Wardour Castle, another Catholic fortress, was stormed in spite of the heroism of old Lady Arundell. Richard Prater held Nunney Castle in Somerset against several assaults and then, or so he later insisted, in surrendering offered to transfer his sword and allegiance to the Parliament. Sir Jordan Crosland, a

Church-papist, commanded the royalist garrison of Helmsley Castle in Yorkshire: he only yielded it on condition that it was 'slighted' (ruined) and that he, his garrison and civilian followers marched out freely. The Catholic royalists had their casualty lists: the 1st Lord Dunbar died of wounds at Scarborough, Sir Henry Gage in the midlands, the 1st Lord Widdrington in Lancashire, Sir Thomas Metham at Marston Moor, Sir Arthur Aston 'knocked on the head' after the surrender of Drogheda, the Earl of Carnarvon near Oxford. Two wartime Catholic converts, Lords Bellasis and Langdale, commanded royalist brigades with distinction. There were even clerical royalist soldiers: William Salvin, student of Lisbon College, captured at Naseby; George Metham, an ex-Jesuit novice in Langdale's brigade, captured near Newark; and John Huddleston, a secular priest missioner in Lancashire who temporarily exchanged the duties of a chaplain in the Earl of Derby's army for those of a gentleman volunteer.

The years after the first civil war (1646–60) provided most English Catholics with a strange mixture of freedom and repression. On the whole, for the majority, the freedom was probably greater and the repression more severe than in the life of Catholics under the Crown before the war. During the first war the Parliament laid down the principles of its policy of repression of Catholicism. Its County Committees were to investigate and list delinquents (persons who had, during the war, supported, or who were still secretly aiding, the royalist cause by military action or money) and Papists. Delinquents were to be classified by the gravity of their offences into traitors and mere delinquents. Traitors, if caught in armed insurrection, were liable to the death penalty or transportation to forced labour in the West Indies; if not now in arms they might or might not be gaoled, depending on how dangerous they were to the State, but they were all to suffer confiscation of all their goods and real estate. At the discretion of the authorities, one fifth might be allowed for the maintenance of the traitor's wife and children. Mere delinquents were offered a choice. If they took oaths to obey the Republic and disowned the King, they could be allowed to recover all their property on payment of a lump sum fine or composition, which usually amounted to a year or two's income.

Papists were originally defined harshly to include not only recusants convicted in the usual way, but non-recusants who had ever been present at Mass since 1642 (even if only once), or who kept in their house a person (even if only one) brought up as a Papist. In practice this severe regulation was soon replaced by a single test

to decide popery: the rejection of a long and exceedingly offensive
and explicitly anti-Catholic Oath of Abjuration. It went beyond the
old Oaths of Supremacy and Allegiance in clarity. A convicted
Papist was subject to confiscation of two-thirds of all his property.
A person found guilty on both counts, delinquency and popery was
hard-hit indeed. If he refused to swear to obey the Republic, he
suffered the four-fifths loss, and a hundred per cent loss if he would
not agree to the Protestant education of his children. If he took the
Oath of Allegiance and paid his composition fine for delinquency,
he was next subjected to two-thirds seizure for popery. Moreover
the pre-war principle of double-taxation of Papists was retained, and
ordinary taxation rates were now far harder and the money far
more efficiently exacted.

But how did these savage regulations work out in practice? As
we have seen, only a relatively small number of Catholics qualified
as traitors, and they were ruined. The two Catholic Marquises fell
into this category, as did Lord Langdale and Lord Bellasis. The
Catholic mere delinquents—a minority of the Papist gentry—often
took the Oath of Allegiance and a good many of them avoided the
charge of popery by taking the Oath of Abjuration. After all, very
many Catholics were long practised in taking directly anti-Catholic
oaths with private mental reservations. They had long ago settled
this moral issue with their consciences. Those who insisted on
remaining royalists before the world still had one (very hard)
method of escape from ruin. They could procure a lawyer and a
body of non-Catholic trustees who would buy up the auctioned
property and advance the cash; the buyers would then lease it at a
peppercorn rent to the victim. He would be landed with a great
weight of debt and its interest, which he would have to hope that
he could pay off gradually out of the profits of intensive farming
and exploitation of industrial resources, if he had any.

The family papers of determined Catholic mere delinquent persons show repeatedly that this method of collusive buying and
leasing was carried out successfully, if painfully, on a large scale.
John Rushworth and Gilbert Crouch were lawyers, with personal
Catholic connections, who specialised in this service. They borrowed
the money in the City. In some cases it was probably raised through
the good offices of a Papist City merchant and landowner, Humphrey Weld, whose name occurs quite often in the deeds of
Yorkshire Catholic trusts. Sometimes it was necessary to have
Parliamentary friends at court.

Sir Philip Constable of Everingham, Yorkshire and Drax Abbey,
Lincolnshire was a Catholic delinquent who had been a convicted
recusant for some years before 1642. His war record was disputed.

The Commissioners at first believed his story that he had merely subscribed to royalist funds under pressure: four-fifths of his estate were seized. By strenuous efforts and the intercession of friends and relations who were Parliamentarians, he secured a lease of the seized four-fifths in the name of his grandson. But by 1652 the authorities judged that he was deceiving them and was really a royalist activist: he was reclassified, this time as a traitor. In a panic he approached John Rushworth. Rushworth, with some help from Sir William Constable of Flamborough, a cousin of Sir Philip's but a rigid Parliamentarian and a regicide who had signed the death-warrant of Charles I, raised £15,880 in the City and bought the estate. Sir William wrote to Sir Philip to explain that he could not see the family ruined when it was of his own blood. (Sir William was also a strong Puritan.) The estate was then leased to three Catholic trustees, really for the benefit of Sir Philip. In the course of the transaction Rushworth cheerfully took an oath that he was not buying the estate as an agent for Sir Philip. The State's purchase price, probably due to Sir William, was relatively low. Sir Philip now could expect an income from rents of £1600 a year, from which he had to find interest charges of almost £1000 and means to repay the capital debt. By violent exertions directed at improving his estate and raising rents, he pushed his income up to £2118 by 1656; but his total debt then amounted to £19,000.

Thomas Fairfax, Lord Fairfax of Cameron, was a devoted Presbyterian who had been the commander of the Parliament's New Model Army in both civil wars. By 1649 he had voluntarily retired from the Army and active politics, making no secret of his distaste for the extremist Independents who now controlled the Republic. In his retirement he used his still considerable prestige and influence to protect two Catholic families. Up to this time relations between him and his distant cousins, the mainly Catholic Viscounts Fairfax of Gilling Castle, had been strained. Early in the first war the General had taken part in the forcible removal by the Parliament's Court of Wards of the Catholic eldest son of the 2nd Viscount Fairfax. The boy was sent to board with the Puritan headmaster of Felsted School. He grew up a Protestant and made a teenage runaway match with a Protestant girl; on his father's death he became 3rd Viscount. The General went out of his way to defend Gilling Castle from molestation by troops and the young Viscount's Catholic brothers from charges of popery and (though these charges had no basis in fact) delinquency. In rapid succession, after the General's retirement, the 3rd Viscount and his small son died and the title and estate passed to a Catholic 5th Viscount. The General now engaged in a pull of influences in which he achieved the dropping by the Parliamentary Commissioners of all charges of popery against the openly practising Catholic 5th Viscount and his family. At one point in the battle the Commissioners put bailiffs into the General's house to distrain for sums they demanded for the Viscount's popery. Relations between the two Fairfax families, if never warm, became courteous and the General seems to have had some hand in the Catholic marriage of the Viscount's sister to George Metham of Howden. George was another Catholic cousin under his protection. George's grandfather, Sir Thomas Metham, had been a prominent Yorkshire politician, a firm Anglican, and a royalist officer killed in action at Marston Moor. George, the heir, was a Catholic and former Jesuit novice, who, more by accident and folly than design, was technically a royalist delinquent taken in arms. The General intervened to save him and his family from ruin; the delinquency charge was quashed. George refused the Oath of Abjuration and endured a two-thirds seizure for his popery. He was too feckless or unlucky to secure the services of Rushworth or Crouch. The family became irretrievably poorer. But the Fairfax marriage guaranteed them some continuing status and help.

General Fairfax had had other, wider dealings with the Catholic community. In 1647, during the uneasy period after the first civil war, constant secret negotiations were in train between the King, then a prisoner of war, the Parliament, the New Model Army and the Scots government. The political situation was extremely uncertain and delicate. Quite unexpectedly Fairfax and the generals of the New Model Army entered into highly secret talks with Catholic leaders. Prominent in all this was the Papist Lord Brudenell. Fairfax wanted Charles I restored to the throne, but solely by the Army and on terms dictated by it. He was seeking to bring over to this scheme any and every group with influence, and he clearly thought that the Catholic peers and gentry were worth courting. He knew that most of them were neutrals, and he hoped to detach the minority who were adherents of official royalism from a cause which had treated them badly. Fairfax was extraordinarily successful. He obtained the signatures of all the Catholic clerical superiors—including even the Jesuit Provincial—and of a small but quite representative Catholic lay group—Lords Brudenell, Teynham, Petre, Powis and the Marquis of Winchester, and twenty-seven gentry. Fairfax promised, as part of his projected settlement with the King, the repeal of all the penal and fining laws with certain important exceptions: Catholics were to have no churches, hold no offices and bear no arms; it was to be a capital offence to teach or write that the Pope had power to issue binding political directives.

The King rejected the Army's terms and found time in 1648 to make overtures to Lord Brudenell, seeking to win him and as many Catholic neutrals as possible over to official royalism. For this and other reasons the Catholic agreement with the Army came to nothing. The Pope condemned it. The Catholic royalist faction attacked it furiously.

But Brudenell was not discouraged. After the second civil war and the execution of the King, he seems to have organised a Catholic lobby at Westminster to seek yet another agreement, this time with the Independent Republic. The Catholic royalist minority remained bitterly opposed to any such agreement. Some of their leaders were hanging about the courts in exile of Charles II or the widowed Queen Mother Henrietta Maria. These Catholic courtiers were not only strong adherents to a cause for which they had suffered ruin. They pinned their hopes of an eventual toleration for Catholics in England on Charles II's known but secret interest in Catholicism. After his abortive bid to recover the throne and his defeat at the battle of Worcester, he had escaped across England sheltered and guided by royalists. His first protectors in Worcestershire and Staffordshire were Catholic priests and gentry. Prominent amongst them was John Huddleston, the secular priest who had put aside his cassock and served as a royalist soldier in the first civil war. Charles II was deeply impressed by his adventures and grateful to his Catholic helpers.

Other ruined Catholic royalists had found shelter in the guesthouses of English monasteries. The convert Lord Langdale was fretting at the Benedictine monastery of Lambspring in Hanover, showering Charles II and royalist friends in England with suggestions for a royalist insurrection. Other Catholic royalists lived uncomfortably in England on the fragments of their estates or on the charity of friends and relations. A few of them were prominent in royalist undercover organisations. Lord Bellasis was a committeeman of the official secret organisation, 'The Sealed Knot'. John Weston of Sutton, Surrey sat on the committee of an extremist action group. Some ruined Papist gentry, like Sir William Blackiston of Gibside, Northumberland and Lawrence Sayer of Worsall, north Yorkshire, lurked as self-appointed resistance fighters or highwaymen on the north-eastern moorlands. There were ardent royalists in every Catholic clerical group and John Leyburne, the rector of the English College, Douai, had an ever open door for poor royalist exiles, Protestant or Catholic.

But the confidence of the Catholic royalists that their sufferings for the cause would win the Catholic gentry offices and toleration when Charles II's ship came home often wore thin. Hyde, the King's chief adviser, in public spoke warmly of Catholic devotion and charity to exiled royalists. In private he used his considerable influence and that of the great mass of Anglican royalism to destroy all idea of concessions, now or hereafter, to Catholics. He detached the King's court from close contact with that of Henrietta Maria. He ostracised Lord Langdale because of his conversion. He fought to check a wave of conversions amongst High Church Anglican clergy exiles in France. The official coldness of the royalist shadow government towards Catholics became icy. In 'The Sealed Knot' Lord Bellasis felt impotent and cold-shouldered by his Protestant colleagues—at least one of whom was a Republican double-agent. John Weston felt himself tolerated by the action group because of his City connections but was otherwise excluded from their plotting.

Above all, the Catholic royalists felt bitterly their isolation from most of their Catholic fellows whose neutralism was steadily moving towards acceptance of the Republic and rejection of the King. Lord Brudenell and his friends seemed to be making headway. The Republic appeared to be moving towards a practical toleration of friendly Catholics. The authorities, as a small military junta, knew they had no future unless they could win over to their side groups who, like most Catholics, were basically opposed to a restoration of the pre-war Establishment. The junta was ideologically strongly anti-Catholic. As we have seen, with great efficiency and method, it had dealt a heavy financial blow at Catholics.

On the other hand the junta's officialdom was a strange mixture of types. Some of its leaders were extremist Dissenting Protestants of a Quaker kind, who hated priesthoods and Established Churches, yet were totally averse to denying freedom of worship to any Christian. Others were a rag-tag and bobtail collection of highly able men of very diverse origins, some formerly Anglicans or Catholics, who had thrown in their lot with the Republic partly out of ambition and partly because they were fascinated by the unique opportunities for political and social power and engineering offered by an all-powerful revolutionary government. The careerists could see little point in persecuting Catholics. Little by little therefore, the authorities proved indulgent to them. Though they were heavily mulcted financially, they were now largely free of molestation. The Church courts no longer existed. The Parliamentary Commissioners hunted Catholics to drag them into the fining system, but recusancy proceedings ended. There were Army road-blocks and visitors to London had to register with the troops, but Catholic gentry could move about more freely than in pre-war days. The Republic's police-chief, Thurloe, had dossiers on everyone of importance, but these, and Army watches on race-meetings, public houses and theatres, were counter-insurrectionary measures not especially concerned with Catholics. The old, oppressive weight of the Anglican clerical Establishment was being dissolved.

The old parish churches had parsons and Sunday services of a nonconformist type: tithe payments were enforced but church-attendance was not. Protestant nonconformity, in churches, chapels or private houses, mushroomed. This was its great formative age, the age of George Fox, John Bunyan, the early Quakers, Seekers and Baptists, a charismatic age. Catholic congregations functioned quietly and almost unnoticed in the midst of this burst of religious freedom of expression. The freedom broke down iron barriers of denomination and tradition. There was a small but significant flow of conversions to Catholicism from ardent Protestant nonconformity: Captain John Saltmarsh, retired from the New Model Army and married to Thomas Meynell's Catholic granddaughter; Major John Graunt of the London Trained Bands; Captain Arthur Beckwith; serving officers at Army Headquarters. General Lord Fairfax was not the only nonconformist who suddenly conceived a stiff fondness for Catholic friends and relations. The Lord Protector himself, Oliver Cromwell, invited to dine at his own royal table the Catholic Lords Arundell and Brudenell and that well-known royalist Catholic scientist and philosopher, Sir Kenelm Digby. Meanwhile, in a palace back-room, his secretary, John Rushworth, was immersed in protecting the estates of Catholic gentry at a price. In the counties, now that most of the old Establishment clique was out of office, new men of humbler origins held power and were quite often friendly and helpful to Catholics. In Yorkshire that fanatical nonconformist committeeman, Ralph Rymer, was the 'dear friend' and trustee of several Catholic gentry. William Metham, a Catholic, was Cromwell's unofficial agent at Rome. A Jesuit was invited to debate with cavalry officers and troopers in their quarters at Putney.

The traffic across the denominational barriers also flowed the other way. The heavy popery compositions drove an increasing number of hitherto recusant gentry to take the Oath of Abjuration, revert to Church-papistry, and eventually start to move finally right out of the Catholic community. Looking back, older Catholics maintained that the numbers of Catholic gentry had reached their peak in the 1620s: the King's severer fining policy of the 1630s had begun a falling-away, and the Republic's harshness had speeded up the process of decline. Moreover the strange open-mindedness of the times brought questioning of all institutions and principles. The younger generation of Catholics, dragged up during the confusion of war and revolution, had contracted a strange rootlessness deeply disturbing to their elders. The most respectable of Catholic families now had their apostates. Lord Bellasis's nephew, the 2nd Lord Fauconberg, was a Republican officer of the Protector's Guard and married to his daughter. The young and raffish 2nd Duke of Buckingham, the son of the Catholic Countess of Antrim, had deserted Charles II's court, risked imprisonment in England, and married the daughter of General Lord Fairfax. The heirs of the Catholic Marquises of Winchester and Worcester had both turned nonconformists and were officers in the Army. Sir Charles Howard of Naworth, in spite of a model Catholic upbringing, had followed suit. A Catholic priest, brother of the royalist Catholic hero, Sir Henry Gage, had turned Protestant and a Republican informer. One of Endymion Porter's sons deserted the royalist forces for the New Model Army; the other abducted a Protestant girl and became London's best-known duellist.

Backed by the pamphlets and encouragement of Blacklow and a group of priest intellectuals, Lords Brudenell and Arundell lobbied the Protector. The Meynell family were the lucky recipients of the first fruits of the *détente*. Although they escaped fining for delinquency (because they had been strictly neutral), in 1644 they endured a two-thirds seizure for popery which reduced their net income to £140 a year. Pleas to the County Committee produced no result until 1648 when the seized parts of the estate were leased back to the family. But the terms of the lease were so steep that their financial position was still desperate. In 1650 the Parliamentary Commissioners announced their intention of distraining on Papists' property for payment of the instalments of recusancy compositions fixed before the wars but not actually collected between 1641 and the end of the first war. By 1654 the Meynells, like most of the resolutely Papist gentry in the country, faced ruin. The Catholic Lords' Westminster lobby summoned a meeting of delegates of the gentry at which the Meynells were represented by a Catholic barrister friend. In the name of this meeting, Lords Brudenell, Arundell and Montague approached the Protector. The result was a compromise. The fining regulations were unaltered. But the demand for arrears was dropped, and the gentry told privately that the Republic's Attorney-General would in future accept pleas on family or compassionate grounds for the reduction of the portions of Papists' estates seized. The Meynells' counsel promptly put into court pleas of entails on the estate and of mistakes in the wording of the composition deeds, pleas which had previously been rejected by the State as manifest subterfuges. The Attorney-General now accepted all their pleas without demur. The State relinquished to the family ownership of all the estate except two-thirds of the manor house and its garden, which were regarded as unentailed.

The lease of this amounted to £5 a year. The Meynell's income returned to £650 a year. Presumably many other Catholic gentry families took advantage similarly of the immense relaxation in the Republic's policy. Lord Baltimore, so much of whose fortune was tied up in Maryland (annexed by the State) and Irish lands (threatened by the Cromwellian Settlement), now applied to Cromwell and was granted back his proprietary rights in Maryland and assurances about his Irish property.

In September 1658, when this sun was shining on non-royalist Catholics but a full agreement with the State was still unsigned, Oliver Cromwell died. Between now and May 1660, when Charles II landed peacefully in England, the palmy days of the Republic were over and the future very uncertain. Another civil war appeared inevitable. Timid Catholics fled abroad or went to ground in remote places. The Catholic lobby broke up. It and the Catholic royalists were perforce largely spectators of the quarrels of the Army generals and the miraculous—or so it seemed—intervention of General Monck and the invitation of a Convention Parliament to Charles II. Here and there Catholic gentry who had particular links with local politics played a very minor part. In Yorkshire General Lord Fairfax was active, and probably allowed his young Catholic client and cousin, Viscount Fairfax of Gilling, to hold a secret meeting of Catholics and Protestants at Gilling Castle to plan aid for Monck's troops. The Convention Parliament contained some Catholics, like the Earl of Portland, and Church-papists, like Solomon Swale, who proposed the motion that the King be invited to return.

As Charles II stepped cheerfully ashore on the quay at Dover the most thoughtful Catholics could not make head or tail of the wildly contradictory features of their situation. Numbers of gentry recusants had slithered down from the level of the 1630s. The political world was sprinkled with ex-Catholics. The colleges and religious houses were heavily in debt, since before 1654–5 the gentry had for years been unable to keep up their contributions. The clergy were infected by the general wave of scepticism and restlessness, as were younger Catholics. It seemed that, with the restoration of the King, there would be a scramble for Establishment jobs and Catholic royalists and neutrals alike would be elbowed aside: the royalist minority were too few and already too much on the shelf to make good claims to compensation for their sufferings; the neutral Catholic majority would be victimised for their support of the Republic. Meanwhile Catholics noted sourly that ex-Catholic nonconformist servants of the Republic like Lord Fauconberg and Sir Charles Howard were turning their coats, posing as royalist Anglicans, and winning seats on Charles II's Council. There were pious or pessi-mistic Jesuits and old Catholic gentlemen who foresaw a long bleak age for the Catholic community and counselled a return to the ghetto.

Yet there were other Catholics, lay and clerical—including Jesuits—who saw the restoration of the Stuart monarchy as a second wind for the community, a golden chance to achieve through court Catholicism real freedom and even real power which they had reached at but failed to get in the 1630s and again in 1654–8. Catholicism was still strong in the royal family and at court. Past experience showed that apostates and Church-papists (now so often in important posts) retained links with Catholicism. Even during the most difficult days of the 1650s Catholicism had enough life in it to make converts amongst courtiers, seasoned royalist and New Model Army soldiers and Laudian clergymen. The weary quietists—like the old Marquis of Winchester who retired to his exquisite rose-gardens at his Berkshire house, Englefield, to remember sadly the glories of Basing House and the fortune he had poured out for Charles I and for which he knew he would get no recompense—expected nothing and feared the 1660s. They mistrusted the violent and sceptical temper of the young. Winchester's memorial regards the future gloomily: 'sutch times' as the 'troubles' may well return.

8. The Restoration Catholics, 1660–78

Before the civil wars court Catholicism had been an alien, minor, contemptuously tolerated influence in a confidently Anglican court. After its return to Westminster in 1660 its ramifications and influence rapidly grew so much that court Anglicanism was put on the defensive. The number of practising or latent Catholics at court did not actually increase greatly, and the Protestant Establishment still controlled most of the main seats of power. Nevertheless Anglicans became convinced by the 1670s that Catholicism, in a very hidden and insidious way, was close to capturing power.

Charles II ostentatiously, if carelessly, practised as an Anglican. He showed little sign of religious devotion to Anglicanism at any stage in his life, but was very aware of the political importance of adherence to it. He most probably had no Anglican confessor and his almost constant acts of adultery naturally made Communion a difficulty and provided a convenient excuse for an abstention which he might well have chosen in any case and which might easily have been interpreted as Catholicism. He made little secret of his acquaintance with Catholic beliefs and practices or of his idea that Catholicism was the proper religion for gentlemen. But, again conveniently for him, all of this could be innocently explained as due to his Catholic nurses, mother, residence abroad, and foreign mistresses. Charles inherited his family's policies of drawing the sting of Catholicism by receiving Catholics at court, marrying Catholic princesses, and forming alliances with Catholic powers. He could therefore, again conveniently, carry these policies quite far without arousing too much suspicion about the sincerity of his adherence to Anglicanism. He did, in fact, keep his Protestant subjects guessing about his real religious opinions all his life. Few people who really knew them had ever been in serious doubt about the sincerity of James I's and Charles I's Protestantism. Charles II thus was a true Church-papist. Church-papistry had long been a familiar, if mysterious and disliked English phenomenon.

The Queen-Mother, Henrietta Maria, was allowed an official Catholic Household and palace (St James's) in London to her death in 1669. She had a chapel and priests. In one way this was of little consequence. She was often absent in France, had little chance to resume her pre-civil war political and social ties in England, and was by now rather discredited by her mysteriously close association with Harry Jermyn, the old *roué* who had danced attendance on her since the 1630s, and who was now a Catholic and Earl of Dover. Yet Henrietta Maria's presence and chapel helped in the accumulation of royal Catholic influences. The King's favourite sister and confidante, Henriette, Duchess of Orleans, spent long periods in London at St James's Palace. She was a devout Catholic. Charles II's choice as a bride was another devout Catholic, Catherine of Braganza, whose large and mostly Catholic household at Somerset House included a chapel of Portuguese, Irish and English priests (including an Englishman who was a diocesan bishop in Portugal), and two small monasteries, of Portuguese friars and English Benedictine monks. At her favourite villa at Hammersmith, the Queen protected a convent of Mary Ward's Institute running a fashionable school. The King had no issue by Catherine, but an almost oriental train of mistresses and illegitimate children. This train was far from wholly Catholic, but it had a distinctly Catholic flavour. The eldest bastard was a Catholic priest (though his birth was not acknowledged); the eldest acknowledged son, the Duke of Monmouth, was carefully educated in France as a Catholic by a convert Oratorian priest, though his mother was a Protestant. Monmouth later gradually moved over to Protestantism.

The King's next brother and the heir to the throne was James, Duke of York. Unlike the King, York went through a period of genuine Anglicanism and married—somewhat discreditably and morganatically—an Englishwoman who was a strict High Anglican with a confessor. York and his wife went through a very long and painful process of conversion to Catholicism. In his case it was a covert and smudged affair. By 1670 he seems to have been canonically a Catholic who attended Mass behind locked doors. But for years to come he went on parading Sunday by Sunday at Anglican Mattins at court or on his flagship when he was at sea with the Fleet. In any case he was so continuously entangled with mistresses, usually Protestant ones, that he could rarely communicate as a Catholic. His Duchess's conversion was even more secret. It only became evident on her deathbed and then her Anglican confessor was enraged and confounded. Their two daughters, the Princesses Mary and Anne, were born during their parents' Anglican period and the King insisted that they should be brought up as Protestants. The Duke's bastards were mostly brought up as Catholics.

To many Protestants this increasing grip of Catholicism on the royal family was a puzzle. There were reasons which long inclined some to think it very offensive but harmless: a family vice like wenching. The King and York seemed utterly determined Church-papists unwilling to break with the Establishment. Both had numerous, if not close, Protestant friends who were devoted to them. The Duke was a bull-headed sailor, respected for his courage in action.

In the government Ministries of the Restoration Catholic influences seemed to be more covert and yet more widespread than in pre-war years. The Earl of Arlington, ostensibly a Protestant, went along with the King's policies and is credibly reported to have sent for a Catholic priest on his deathbed. The Earl of Danby was a solid Anglican but had a devoutly Catholic mother and relations. The raffish 2nd Duke of Buckingham had an indiscreetly Catholic mother, the Countess of Antrim: he purposely veiled his religious opinions in a cloud of cynicism. When he died suddenly in Yorkshire, his friends hastily sent for the local vicar, while the Papist Viscount Fairfax brought his Catholic chaplain. Lord Clifford, the Treasurer, went through agonies of conscience before finally declaring his conversion to Catholicism in 1672 and resigning his offices. The feeble 2nd Earl of Portland, now a Church-papist, was a royal Councillor to his death in 1663. The Earl of Carlisle was a former Catholic who remained very friendly with, and helpful to, his many northern Papist clients and relations. He acted as their trustee and provided a good many of their sons with commissions in his regiment. The Earl of Scarborough (the Lord Lumley who had spent the war years in voluntary exile in Flanders) was another ex-Catholic with Papist connections and sympathies. The Earl of Fauconberg, Oliver Cromwell's son-in-law, had Catholic origins, a Papist brother and heir, and an enigmatic attitude towards religion.

In Westminster and Whitehall amongst the civil servants the rules excluding Catholic recusants were apparently carried out more strictly than before the wars. But, concealed (or half-concealed) behind this Anglican façade and behind the undoubted current of religious scepticism amongst civil servants, Catholic influences seemed to lurk more widely than ever. There was a practising Catholic secular priest serving as an advocate in Doctors' Commons. The Church-papist Sherburne family had returned to the Tower of

London and the Ordnance Office. Samuel Pepys, secretary at the Admiralty, had a French Huguenot wife who was in the secret processes of conversion to Catholicism. Sir Wiliam Petty, the government's adviser on political economy, was a sceptic with some sort of Catholic past. The Duke of York ran the Admiralty. His secretary, Edward Coleman, was a practising Catholic convert. The Navy recruited, at least as gentlemen volunteers, Church-papists like Roger Strickland (a future Admiral) and the Earl of Portland's son and heir. The Army was, according to the House of Commons, so stuffed with Papists (400 with commissions, sixty of them in the 1st Regiment of Foot Guards) that the long queue of Catholic gentry applicants had to be accommodated by the Duchess of Orleans in a specially-created English Regiment in the French service.

The incidence of Catholicism in the fashionable London world amongst artists, musicians, writers and—after 1660 as tastes changed —mathematicians and scientists was, in the opinion of good judges, as muted and yet as covertly diffused as elsewhere at court. One of the two leading actor-managers, Sir William Davenant, had close past associations with the Queen-Mother's circle and was reputed perhaps rashly, to be a secret Catholic. There were four known Catholics amongst the two dozen London playwrights, the Earl of Bristol, Sir Samuel Tuke (an immensely popular writer), John Lacy (also a comic actor) and William Wycherley (one of the genuine talents of the Restoration stage). All four were converts. Tuke's Catholicism was solid; the others practised fitfully. Amongst poets old Sir Edward Sherburne still ran his salon at the Tower and Richard Flecknoe, a secular priest friend of Andrew Marvell, was much in society. Marvell's Catholic and Puritan pasts rubbed shoulders uneasily in his verse. Anglicans dominated the Chapel Royal and cathedral music. But the Catholic composer Matthew Locke drew crowds to the Queen's chapel. An increasing host of French and Italian artists, often negligent Catholics, were employed in England. Old Wenceslas Hollar, become a Catholic, was in business as court engraver to his death in 1677. In the field of science and mathematics the Royal Society had replaced Gresham College. It was very fashionable and the King and Duke of York had their own private laboratories. The Papist Lords Norwich and Stafford were Fellows of the Royal Society. John Evelyn visited Lord Norwich's laboratory and returned in his coach with 'a very ingenious young gent.', a Mr White, who turned out to be a mathematician and nephew of Thomas White *alias* Blacklow, the great radical Catholic priest. Blacklow himself made visits to London where he lived in intimacy with the King's favourite philosopher, the Protestant arch-radical Thomas Hobbes. The

Papist Earl of Castlemaine was a noted mathematician. The new Marquis of Worcester, a Catholic like his father, lived usually at Vauxhall, where his laboratory specialised in coke-smelting projects. On the edge of the scientific world were earnest Papists like Major Graunt, the statistician, Charles Towneley and Edward Sheldon.

The number of Catholic peers had actually increased to about forty-five: six Dukes and Duchesses, two Marquises, eleven Earls; six Viscounts, and over twenty Barons. As before the wars, their Catholicism was, for the most part, fragile and unimpressive. The 1st Duke of Norfolk was a lunatic confined in an Italian asylum. The restoration of this Dukedom to the great Howard family in 1661 was their reward for many years of lobbying and a peculiar piece of political jobbery: it was supposed to recompense their doubtful services to the royal cause during the wars. The family had a strongly, if sometimes thin, Catholic atmosphere, and was headed by the Duke, the Earls of Norwich and Berkshire, Viscount Stafford and the apparently Protestant Earl of Suffolk. The fertility, ambition, snobbishness and intrigue of this clan were notorious. The revival of the Duchy brought back to them the ducal estates and control of its Parliamentary boroughs and the hereditary office of Earl Marshal of the court. The young Duke of Monmouth was in the process of abandoning his Catholicism. The French Duchess of Portsmouth and the convert Duchess of Lennox and Richmond were former mistresses of the King. The old dowager Duchess of Buckingham was in Ireland with her husband. Carlo Dudley, 'Duke of Northumberland', was the son of a bastard of Queen Elizabeth's Earl of Leicester. His title was recognised by the Emperor and the Grand Duke of Florence, where he resided. For all his pretensions and Italian manners, he was pure English and an old student of the English College at Douai. English Catholics paid him much respect.

After the Howards in political importance came the convert Earl of Bristol, an eccentric who protested his Catholicism in the House of Lords but periodically attended Anglican services. Then there was a group of Catholic peers who had deserved well of the royalists. Lord Bellasis, formerly of 'The Sealed Knot', was rewarded rather scantily with the governorship of Hull, the Captaincy of the Gentleman Pensioners, an honorary Colonelcy of Foot Guards and governorship of the colony of Tangier. His marital affairs were in some disarray. The Earl of Castlehaven, once a royalist general officer in Ireland, received very minor military posts. He lived with a mistress, apart from his wife—a Catholic—who was, according to Pepys, 'an impudent jade' and wildly promiscuous. Lord Widdrington, in reward for his father's death in action, was an honorary Colonel of Horse Guards and governor of Berwick on Tweed. He practised his religion with such carelessness or ultra-caution that he was rated a Church-papist. Lord Molyneux, the governor of Liverpool Castle, was a grandee with much the same reputation. The Earl of Norwich was living with a plebeian mistress whom he later insisted on marrying, though Howard respectability and family pride then banished the couple abroad. The old Lord Vaux, now decently married to Lady Banbury, his mistress, was an almost penniless recluse. His brother and heir, an officer in the Spanish army, could never afford to live in England or to take his seat in the House of Lords. The 3rd Earl of Portland, a naval officer, was killed in action, leaving an estate so burdened with debt that his heir, the 4th Earl, sold the remnants, never married or took his seat in the Lords, and died in the guesthouse of an English monastery in Flanders, where he had lived for years on charity.

Earl Rivers and Lord Mounteagle had not been seen at Mass within living memory, though they still considered themselves Catholics. Rivers was twice warned by the House of Lords for fraudulent use of his legal privileges as a peer to baulk his many creditors. During the Republic he had seen the inside of a debtors' gaol. Mounteagle was gaoled by the House of Lords for persistently terrifying London citizens by night with his gang of ruffians. The 4th Lord Petre, a very rich man with estates in five counties, had a stormy life. As a boy he endured a State wardship and a determined effort to make him a Protestant. By 1652, as a result of a loss of over £14,000 to the Court of Wards and a heavy composition for popery under the Republic, he was in desperate straits and took the Oath of Abjuration. Meanwhile he had contracted a disastrous Catholic marriage to a lady who was violent, absurdly extravagant, and promiscuous. Pepys followed the scandals of her career: her imprisonments for debt, her separation from her husband and her boon companionship with that other Catholic 'impudent jade', the Countess of Castlehaven. Her death in 1665 relieved Lord Petre of an incubus. The 3rd Lord Dunbar, a practising Catholic, received a royal pardon for homicide in a duel. His Catholic wife had a bad reputation: the talk of the town was that she had a child by her confessor. She was Lord Bellasis's daughter. The Catholic Earl of Shrewsbury was killed in a duel in 1668 by his wife's lover, the Duke of Buckingham. The Countess, a daughter of the Catholic Earl of Cardigan, was said to have attended the duel disguised as Buckingham's horse-holder. Shrewsbury's son and successor, a mercenary soldier in Flanders, was soon to abandon Catholicism. The 1st Lord Carrington, a Papist, was murdered in France. The

Catholic Earl of Castlemaine owed his peerage to his willingness to marry one of the King's Protestant mistresses. The Earl was the court's most notorious cuckold. The eldest son of the pious old Marquis of Winchester was an MP and well on his way towards complete apostasy. The scientist Marquis of Worcester's eldest son had abandoned Catholicism for Republicanism and Protestant non-conformity in 1650 and then for Anglicanism in 1660.

There were some small islands of Catholic piety and solid worth amongst the Papist peers. The Englefield monument to the Marquis of Winchester records his happy marriage to his third wife, a Howard: 'The Lady Marchionesse Dowager (in testimony of her love and sorrow) gave this Monument to the memory of a most affectionate tender Husband.' To his death the Marquis practised his antique integrity and his complicated French devotions. At Gilling Castle in Yorkshire, Abigail, Viscountess Fairfax practised contemplation by Augustine Baker's methods and was deeply admired by her Protestant neighbours for her unaffected charity. The children of a good many Catholic peers now (in spite of their parents' vagaries) went abroad to be educated in English Colleges and convents, though they rarely became priests or nuns. The Marquis of Worcester's family was exceptional: around 1660 three of them, including Lord Thomas Somerset, were ordained. At least two, and probably all three, stayed abroad as canons of French cathedrals. The Duke of Norfolk's family produced one Dominican, Philip Howard, and one novice nun, who died before profession. Philip Howard's entry into a friary in Italy during his family's self-imposed wartime exile had been vigorously opposed by them. There was never any danger that the close relation of a Duke (and also a Howard) would ever become a simple friar in a Roman convent. Philip came to the Queen's Household at Somerset House as her Almoner, was much in society, and was destined to be a Cardinal in spite of his modest abilities. The Queen's Household included an odd collection of aristocratic and mildly eccentric priests. There was Louis Stuart, Sieur d'Aubigny, a cousin of the King and a relation of the Duke of Lennox and Richmond. If he had lived, he also would have become a Cardinal. There was 'Lord Digby'—John Digby, younger brother of the eccentric Earl of Bristol, and, like him, a wartime convert. He was a strange, effeminate creature who had been an officer of cavalry in Charles I's Western Army, and who was ordained abroad privately after a short, informal course of studies. There was the old Abbé Wat Montague, who had his name added to the list of Catholic peers in the secret Agreement of 1647 with the New Model Army.

The number of outright conversions to Catholicism amongst the peerage was now small. The defensive mechanism of the Protestant Establishment was working hard to prevent any repetition of the pre-war stream of conversions. Lord Clifford's was painful and condemned him to ostracism. Lord Arlington kept his very dark. The Duchess of York took immense pains to conceal her moves into Catholicism. Her family, the Hydes, were almost clerically Anglican and officially coldly anti-Catholic. It was unknown to polite society that John Sergeant, the Catholic community's best priest-apologist, was paying regular visits to Finchampstead in Berkshire, ostensibly to confer with the Papist Lord Henry Howard, but also to call on his close neighbour, the Earl of Rochester, the Duchess of York's Anglican brother. A daughter of the stuffily Anglican Earl of Salisbury fell in love with a Papist Scots peer: she had to make a runaway match with him in a London Catholic chapel. A younger son of the Anglican Earl of Rutland was converted by a Jesuit. The Society expressed surprise and pleasure. The Duchess of Lennox and Richmond's conversion, on the other hand, roused little Protestant anger or concern because of her moral reputation, the many Catholic connections of her husband's family, and her decency in going to France to be converted.

Protestants looked at the odd array of Papist peers with the same puzzlement they felt about Catholicism in the royal family. On the one hand, in a period when the English aristocracy showed all the symptoms of post-war demoralisation, it was reassuring for Protestants to see that Papist aristocrats were at least as immoral as their Protestant fellows. It was also reassuring to see how furtive and evanescent their Catholicism was. Yet on the other hand there was no disguising the uncomfortable fact that, feeble or not, the Catholic peerage was slowly increasing in numbers and weight. Republican persecution, royalist ostracism, apostasies—nothing seemed to be able to halt their progress. The financial blows of the war years should have prostrated them for many years. Yet most of them survived and had recovered by 1670. The Marquis of Winchester lost over £750,000 in the wars, yet his son was soon to be the very wealthy 1st Duke of Bolton. Lord Petre, in spite of staggering losses, was as rich as ever by 1670. Even the Papist Lord Stourton, out at elbow and down to his last penny before the wars, was just solvent in 1670. The devil appeared to look after his own.

Country Catholicism in the Restoration period regarded the fortunes of court Catholicism with just as mixed feelings. Some Catholic gentry ostentatiously supported the court Catholics by word and action. They were impressed by their growth in numbers and their potential influence and inclined to excuse their moral vagaries and covert Catholicism as part passing weakness, part political realism. Before the wars there had been a gulf between court and country Catholics. Now an increasing number of squires pushed forward to get their sons and daughters into posts in the Catholic royal households and commissions in the forces. Up and down the country and in London there were frequent meetings where Papist squires respectfully met Papist peers and toasted the Duke of York. In Lancashire the Papist Walmesleys, Prestons, Towneleys, Cliftons, Andertons, Blundells and Bellasises met, first at one of their houses, then at another, with Lords Molyneux and Carrington. Their devotion to, and hopes in, the convert Duke of York were expressed not only in their toasts but in old-fashioned gestures. Richard Walmesley of Dunkenhalgh bequeathed '. . . to his Royal Highness the Duke of Yorke one blacke horse lately bought of my Cozen Towneley . . .'

In Yorkshire, county Durham and Northumberland similar meetings centred on Lords Fairfax and Widdrington. Their large families, after 1660, were bound together in a broad net of marriage alliances connecting them with the Howards, Lord Carrington, Lord Castlemaine and leading Catholic major gentry in Lancashire, the far north, Lincolnshire, Berkshire and Dorset. They were on friendly terms with even the Duke of Buckingham, a neighbour (at Helmsley Castle) of Lord Fairfax and the husband of a Protestant Fairfax. The ex-Catholic Earl of Carlisle was a close associate through his Catholic brothers and their multiple marriage connections with the Papist Fairfaxes, Walmesleys and Lawsons of Brough. Even so modest a Yorkshire Papist family as the Hungates of Saxton had, through the Fairfax network, links with the peerage and the court. Sir Francis Hungate was married to Lord Carrington's daughter; his brother, Colonel William Hungate, was of Lord Douglas's Regiment in the French Army. The brothers were closely related to Lord Fairfax, to Lady Southcott of the Duke of York's household and her mother, Mrs Catharine Elliott, who had been the Duke of York's Catholic wet-nurse. Sir Francis Hungate's son Philip was married to Lord Castlemaine's daughter.

These activist Catholic country gentry must have been spurred on by a sense that a victory of court and royal Catholicism was now their only hope of breaking into an Establishment which was, in their own counties, resolutely excluding them from office. The ban on the employment in local government of recusants or even notorious Church-papists was now executed much more strictly than before the wars. Here and there an odd Church-papist clung to office as a JP, county Sheriff or Deputy-Lieutenant. Three or four particularly brazen, unscrupulous or lucky Church-papists sat in the first Parliament of Charles II. In remote Cornwall the practising Catholic Sir John Arundell of Lanherne played a very marginal part in county affairs as a militia captain, commissioner for the tin mines, and patron of MPs for his privately-owned borough constituencies. But most major Catholic gentry, even baronets, held no local office at all.

The situation was made more acute and urgent because overall Papist gentry numbers were sharply declining and yet the major Papist gentry were getting richer. In every way they felt their position becoming more intolerable. The decline in gentry numbers was obvious. The aura of Church-papists, a great feature of the expansive Catholic days of the 1620s, had been much pared away by 1670. Wartime inflation, recusancy compositions, bad husbandry and sheer loss of nerve and male heirs had taken a heavy toll in every county. Faced with these pressures, the Papist gentry seem to have taken one or other of three different courses: the passive defence gambit, the activist reaction, and the retreat into piety.

Passive gentry families seemed to spend all their energies on the mere preservation intact of their property and Catholicism. They did not usually manage to afford a family chaplain. They only occasionally sent a child abroad to school. Very few of such families became priests or nuns, or, for that matter, launched out into the professions or trade. A large proportion of their younger children remained unmarried and stayed at home. Probably, as with some Irish farming families today, this cult of celibacy partly reflected a narrow Catholic piety, and partly an ancient gentry and peasant device to prevent subdivision of the property. The Waterton family of Walton Hall, Yorkshire, passed through a severe phase of passivity between 1660 and the 1720s, trying to recuperate from the financial damage they had suffered under the Republic. In the first post-1660 generation of four living children, two remained at home unmarried and a daughter brought her husband to live and die in Walton Hall. In the next generation Charles Waterton had three wives and seven surviving children of whom only one married. One became a Jesuit, and another failed the Jesuit noviciate and became a bachelor physician. At Naburn Hall outside York the same pattern of life was reproduced by the Palmes family. William Palmes had six children of whom only two married; three died unmarried in their twenties, and another son lived at home, a bachelor, to a ripe old age. In the next generation the elder son produced five children, of whom three remained bachelors or spinsters. The younger son produced four children, of whom two remained spinsters living with their widowed mother.

The activist families seemed to take the poverty of the 1650s and the load of debt as an inducement to extraordinary exertions. Piety often reinforced family temperament. Active families managed their properties skilfully, bought land, exploited mineral and industrial resources, and sent their younger children out from home into profitable occupations. They expended care and money on their children's education as a good investment. If they had a vein of piety, their priests, and even their nuns, tended often to rise high in their profession. They paid off their large wartime debts surprisingly quickly and prospered. The Salvins of Croxdale, county Durham, in spite of a heavy composition and long occupation by Scots troops, were sufficiently recovered by 1658–9 to begin a major rebuilding of their Elizabethan mansion. The Sherburnes of Stonyhurst, Lancashire, protested they were ruined in 1650, but were solidly prosperous by 1670. The Constables of Everingham, Yorkshire, had paid off their £19,000 debt by 1672. A fine example of an activist family was the Withams of Yorkshire and county Durham. George Witham, a middling gentry landowner, farmed intensively, bought land, mined coal and owned saltpans in Sunderland. He had an uncle and brother who were undistinguished Benedictine missioners, the brother serving economically as the family chaplain. But George's children, carefully educated abroad, were almost all good investments. Of the nine who lived, three became distinguished secular priests (a bishop, a Vicar-General and a President of Douai College), one a successful lawyer, one a popular physician in Durham, and two Augustinian Canonesses of Paris. One daughter married well and, as a widow, proved a better estate-manager than her husband. The only bad investment was the youngest daughter, who failed a convent noviciate and ended her life as a spinster. In the next generation there were eight children. One became a Benedictine Prior, one Prioress of the Paris Canonesses, two married well and two became physicians in Durham. Out of the nine there were only two passive failures: a spinster and a daughter who married a ne'er-do-well. It was much the same story with the Jerninghams of Costessy, Norfolk, the Sheldons of Beoley, Warwickshire (lawyers and soldiers), the Carrs of Hexham, Northumberland (three successive heads of the family town-bailiffs of Hexham), the Maires of Hardwick, Durham (agricultural improvers, lawyers and coal-owners), the Westons of Sutton, Surrey, and the Fermors of Tusmore, Oxfordshire.

The most entertaining example of activism was Sir Solomon Swale, baronet of Grinton in the Yorkshire dales. He had been left an orphan in the 1620s with an estate saddled with debt, but also with the help of numerous Catholic gentry relations. He qualified as a barrister and was in practice in London, now a Church-papist, in 1642. That year he was convicted as a recusant. But he weaved and ducked through the years of war and the Republic, serving both sides and dodging composition as a Papist. In 1659 he actually married the widow of a Presbyterian Parliamentary general and sat as an MP in the Convention Parliament of 1660. Political calculation now made him an early convert to loud royalism and a baronet for his pains. When most other Catholics were denied government posts or reduced to abject conformism to keep them, Sir Solomon stuck to his seat in the House of Commons down to 1674, though he was quite openly a practising Catholic. He maintained a chaplain in his London and Yorkshire residences, and saw to it that his two sons (lapsed into Protestantism) should be reclaimed to Catholicism. His will, written in 1675, breathes his buoyant spirit:

> I blesse God by his grace for making me a member of his Roman Catholique Church and that my selfe and ancient family have been constantly loyall to the Crowne although I have suffered much therefore in the last rebellious tymes & I charge my children that they continewe loyall as they expecte Gods blessinge, & that I have impaired my healthe & my estate by waiving my good practice in the lawe & serving constantly the Crowne and my country in Parliament, being the first that moved the then House of Commons the 7th of Maye 1660 to proclaime his Matie. Kinge. I charge my son Henry Swale esq. that he spare not his purse in the good education of my grandsonne but that he will breede him abroad at school to be a good scholar by Gods blessing and about his age of 21 yeares to admitt him to the Inner Temple to study the Common lawe . . .

In spite of his baronetcy, Sir Solomon was not quite accepted into the inner circle of activist Catholic peers and gentry. But he certainly tried hard. He bequeathed his best horse to the Duke of York. He became, rather inexpensively, known as a patron of both secular clergy and Benedictines and invited the monks' Northern Province to hold a Chapter in his house.

The 'retreat into piety' pattern of Catholic gentry life meant a household chaplain, usually a Jesuit, daily Mass for the whole household with prayers (vespers and readings aloud from books of devotion), frequent Confession, the strict keeping of the Church's traditional fasts and feasts, and the cultivation of favourite devotions of a complex kind. There was much room for differences of practice amongst Catholics about fasting, abstinence from meat, and the keeping of religious holidays from work. The medieval Catholic Kalendar and rules had been very full and strict, so much so that rural and urban communities had to shape their timetables of life and labour round them. After 1570 it became practically impossible for English Catholics to observe this round without leading a secluded and well-provided life, rather like the Amish in modern America. Strict observance would certainly arouse notice amongst Protestant neighbours. The rules included frequent holidays of obligation, for hearing Mass and abstaining from work, and severe fasting (throughout Lent and on every Friday; the Eves of a good many feastdays; and abstinence from meat, eggs and lard every Saturday). Moreover, in communities of mixed religion, observant Catholics were severely penalised financially by the holidays.

In the 1580s some bold Jesuits sensibly proposed relaxations but without success. By the 1670s a pious minority and most clergy were keeping the rules to the letter, while the majority sat light to a good many of them. Thus an observant, pious household inevitably had some of the characteristics we associate today with Orthodox Jewish families. This intensely clerical religiosity, then equalled only by a few High Church Laudian Anglicans and the more devout Protestant Dissenters, in the judgment of cooler Catholics and educated Protestants stamped the pious with a distinctively foreign cast of mind. Sir John Reresby, a Yorkshire Protestant politician head of a gentry family fast declining from its pre-war Catholicism, wrote that the strong Catholics were 'educated another way' from their fellow-countrymen. Sir Christopher Wyvill, the product of a similar background, wrote two small handbooks in the 1670s designed to speed the conversion to Protestantism of lax or sceptical Catholics. He admitted, from his personal experience as a Catholic child, the great strength of 'all those little Sophisms which laid hold on me, when I was a Child (or thought as a Child) . . . I am not unwilling to communicate what Antidotes I found most effectual . . .'

The impact, indeed, of a severe religious training in a pious home, followed by a foreign College education by clergy or religious, in which lay schoolchildren were equated with ordinands and novices, was powerful. Frequent Confession to scrupulous clergy who abominated modern life, and a diet of austerely monastic devotional manuals completed the mental conditioning. Pious families were expected to eschew worldly ambition. All, even married couples, had to consider regularly whether they had a call to the 'one necessary thing', a monastic vocation. If they had not, or not yet, they must at least share in the spirit of the cloister. Marital relations must be kept strictly for propagation, and otherwise avoided: there must be marital abstinence on fast days and Saturdays. Thomas Kempis's *Imitation of Christ* was better-known to the pious and clergy than the Bible. All Benedictine missioners carried a copy, made by hand during their noviciate. The child Alexander Pope, under the influence of a priest and his pious convert tradesman father made paraphrases of the *Imitation* as his first essays in verse. Celibacy was highly prized. 'A good death' was a burning preoccupation from childhood. Perfectly naturally an old secular priest, Nicholas Postgate, on being visited by two pious ladies who were pregnant, blessed them and observed: 'Be of good heart, children, your fruit will be saved', meaning that the babies would die in infancy.

The Jesuits produced the most advanced piety in the households they directed. In 1664 a Jesuit converted a Suffolk baronet, Sir John Warner, and his entire family. Almost immediately the household moved to the Continent. Sir John, by Papal permission, separated from his wife and became a Jesuit (later Provincial). His wife and her sister became Poor Clare nuns. Sir John's brother was drowned on his way to Nieuport to become a Carthusian. The Warners' children entered Jesuit and convent schools. In Lancashire in the 1660s two wealthy Papist landowners, Sir Thomas Preston and Laurence Ireland, both widowers, became Jesuits. The Tempest family of Broughton Hall, Yorkshire, began to come under Jesuit direction in the 1670s. Of Stephen Tempest's seven children, two became Jesuits, two nuns, and a third daughter failed her noviciate and remained unmarried. Of the four children in the next generation of the family, three became nuns.

The majority of Catholic peers and gentry preferred Catholic marriages, everything else being equal, but mixed marriages with Protestants were not uncommon amongst them. The pious minority absolutely required not only marriage to practising Catholics but to partners of approved piety. The majority sought partners in the usual ways, social gatherings, race-meetings, 'the season' in London or county towns, or by enquiry to lawyers. The pious generally leaned in these matters on the skill of priest marriage brokers. One such, with a big practice in the north and an encyclopaedic knowledge of the spiritual and financial state of the main Papist gentry in most counties, was the Benedictine Procurator, Dunstan of St Marie Pettinger *alias* 'Captain Bolde'. Pettinger was a bluff ex-officer of much gallantry, piety and shrewdness. He died of the plague, ministering as a priest volunteer in London in 1665.

G

The busy political activists contributed greatly to the survival of the Papist gentry. The influence of the King and Duke of York and the lobbying 'by the fireside' in the House of Lords of the Howard clan and the Earl of Bristol produced, with the tacit consent of the Protestant peers, a temporary cessation of prosecutions of Catholics. The machinery of recusancy fining at Quarter Sessions and in the Exchequer ground almost to a halt. Between 1660 and 1672 Protestant Dissenters equalled Papists in the short lists of recusants convicted. The Exchequer proved so lenient with the few Papists convicted that it collected only £157 in fines from them in twelve years. Priests were left unmolested. The Anglican Church courts made only the most formal of efforts to list and summons Catholics. Where JPs and other local officials questioned this policy, the local Catholic gentry activists confidently, boldly and successfully defied them.

This peace of the Church, so financially beneficial to Catholic gentry restoring their battered fortunes, was ostensibly based on an understanding between court and country Catholic activists and the moderate majority of Protestant peers and gentry. These latter were primarily afraid of an unholy alliance between their own extremists, Protestant Dissenters and secret Republicans ready to launch an insurrection. The Catholic activists were sure that they had persuaded the moderates that they were no danger to the Establishment but sought only a modest, subordinate place within its fringes. Persistent efforts by the Earl of Bristol and others to cement the understanding by Acts of Parliament repealing the penal laws in return for the taking of some new Oath of Allegiance by Catholics foundered. The scheme went beyond the limits of tolerance for the Protestant moderates. The very words 'Oath of Allegiance' touched off amongst pious Catholics and priests a storm of indignation and bitter controversy in which the scheme went to ground. The Pope flatly pronounced against such an implied toleration of Protestantism. Bristol sulked. But most Catholic activists were content with the unwritten agreement and its fruits and were willing to bide their time.

In 1672–4 there blew up mysteriously, and subsided just as mysteriously, a political storm against the agreement. Rumours of the Duke of York's conversion brought a gale of anti-Catholic feeling. Simultaneously the King was engaged in highly secret negotiations with Louis XIV of France. No real details were leaked except the fact of a military alliance. But many Protestants suspected and feared that the King had signed private clauses securing French military and financial help for the forcible imposition of Catholicism on England. The King resolutely denied any such intention and protested his Anglicanism. York nervously frequented Anglican Mattins each Sunday. Protestant opinion was shaken.

In 1673 Parliament forced on the King (and on some of the Protestant moderates) a Test Act designed to flush out of government all Catholics and real Church-papists. Office-holders now had to sign a declaration flatly rejecting the main Catholic beliefs, produce a certificate of Anglican Communion, and take the old Oaths of Supremacy and Allegiance. The Duke of York, like a partridge, was flushed out of his Church-papist covert and resigned all his offices, as did Lord Clifford, the Lord Treasurer. Old Sir Edward Sherburne and his eldest son had to quit the Ordnance. Catholic peers quit their governorships. Here and there an odd Catholic took the Test with private reservations (for instance Lord Widdrington, the prime activist). Sir Solomon Swale battened on loopholes in the Act few others could see. In the counties JPs and Archdeacons began to list and summons Catholics as in the old pre-war days.

But then the storm rapidly died away. A second Test Act extended to peers, intended to drive Catholics from the House of Lords, was repeatedly defeated. It ultimately passed into law narrowly in 1678. After the vote the moderate Protestant peers banded together to wring the hands of the Papist peers departing from the House, assuring them that soon the Act was bound to be repealed. In the counties JPs and Archdeacons relapsed into their usual tolerance of Catholics. In those early months of 1678 many landowners thought they could clearly discern the future course of England. To the Protestants it seemed that Catholicism and wenching were Stuart weaknesses. Both were equally without deep significance. The royal bastards would never take the throne. Catholicism would never rule England. A Church-papist Charles II would be succeeded by a Church-papist (or nearly) James II. Neither had any intention of subverting the Protestant Establishment. Sooner or later the Test Acts would be quietly repealed without danger. Catholic priests would continue to haunt Whitehall, awesome but really insignificant. Popery amongst landowners would remain a minority eccentricity, harmless and slowly decaying. After James II the throne would pass to the High Church Anglican Princess Mary. Political Catholicism was a Utopia which, like Catholic textbook spirituality, had long attracted the drop-outs of Protestant society, rebellious sons of peers and parsons, student rebels and English eccentrics. It would continue to attract them fruitlessly. Meanwhile the solid Protestant Establishment would soldier on. The self-confident cynicism of these intelligent Protestants comes out well in the note made by John Aubrey in 1676, when he was a bankrupt:

> I am stormed by my chiefest freinds afresh, vizt. Baron Bertie, Sir William Petty, Sir John Hoskyns, the Bishop of Sarum, etc. to turn Ecclesiastique; but the King of France growes stronger and stronger, and what if the Roman Religion should come-in againe? Why then, say they, cannot you turne too? You, I saye, knowe well that I am no puritan, nor an enemy to the old Gentleman on the other side of the Alpes . . .

To Anglicans who had recently swallowed Italian Papist music and Anglicised it into cathedral anthems, and who had Anglicised St Peter's, Rome into the new St Paul's cathedral in London, Anglicanism could easily triumph in even a formal reunion with the Pope. The history of English Romanism showed how English it was, how Protestant even.

But where did the Catholic clergy come in all these developments? For the most part secular clergy and religious spent these years of the Restoration recovering from the grave dislocations of their organisation inflicted during the troubles of 1642–60. Most of the able minds amongst them had their energies engrossed in rebuilding the shaky finances of the Colleges and monasteries, and recruiting young men and women to fill their depleted ranks. Inevitably these clerical leaders needed the sympathy and active support of the Catholic peers and gentry. They were unwilling to offend them by any revival of pre-war idealistic clericalism. They were basically prepared to go along with, or acquiesce tacitly in, the unwritten agreement between the laity and the Protestant Establishment. The spirit of the secular clergy leaders was expressed vividly by George Leyburne, head of the English College, Douai. Reporting on the state of the College in 1668, he wrote of his Vice-President, one of the very 'middling' gentry Meynell family:

> . . . a priest of great probity, descended from the ancient baronial family of the Meynells, and so, because of the authority this would fittingly give him amongst the English Catholics, a worthy successor to the Presidency . . .

Surveying the College students, Leyburne wrote:

> Note: of the convictors 10 are of the highest nobility, vizt: Godfrey Dudley, son of the Duke of Northumberland, Robert and William Smith sons of Viscount Dunbar; Edward, Francis

and Thomas Gray, sons of the Baronet Radcliffe, who is descended from the ancient Earls of Suffolk; Edward Witherington, son of the Baronet Witherington; Charles and William Fairfax, relations of Lord Fairfax; William Blount, a relation of Lord Windsor. The remainder are all of the lesser nobility, except for Mr. Sutfield, Edward Smith, John Lodge and John Griffith, who, however, are of honest and catholic families.

Leyburne could not dream of clerical authority *over* the lay aristocracy and gentry, but he strove for an adequate clerical authority *amongst* them based on an effort to recruit clergy more from the sons of peers and upper gentry. In spite of his claims, the effort was hardly a success. As before the wars, the majority of secular priests seems to have been drawn from the lesser gentry, mere gentry and farming stock. This fact alone doomed them to acceptance of the status of hireling chaplains, not the social equals of their patrons. The secular clergy would therefore remain outside the centres of real power and policy-making of the Catholic community, and continue, as in pre-war days, to turn in on themselves, band together in self-defence and immerse themselves in the minutiae of clerical gossip and politics. Leyburne was also letting his aspirations outrun reality in another way. His suggestion that his students were from solidly Catholic stock was a wild exaggeration. He himself came of a mixed marriage and had a Protestant brother. In 1668 there was a minority of complete converts in the College, an ex-Anglican rector of Southampton, two middle-aged men from completely Protestant families, and two youths recently converted by Catholic relatives. The English College, Rome student body from 1622 to 1683 had a steady proportion of one convert to two 'born Catholics'. As in pre-war days a high proportion of the best minds amongst the clergy were converts: the two best apologists, John Sergeant and John Gother; three of the four original theologians—Sergeant and the Dominicans Lionel Anderson and Raymund Greene; Blacklow was a 'cradle-Catholic; the one Cardinal, Philip Howard, had a very mixed religious upbringing and was really a teenage convert from Church-papistry.

The spirit of most secular priest missioners in England is probably well conveyed by the memoirs of Mr Augustine Smithson:

> I came to England in the year 1660, the happy year of King Charles the second his Restoration to his crown; much also overjoyed that God was pleased to blesse my first arrival with the conversion of Sir Henry Swales and his brother Dr. Robert Swales. Upon wch. (the times favouring) Sir Solomon Swales,

their Father, was pleased to invite me to live with him. Being thus settled at Stainley, that favourable precinct lying under the protection and encouragement of three of the most ancient Priests of the North: to wit, my cousin, Geo. Cattherick of Kilvington, Mr. John Young of Sir Thomas Tankreds of Brampton: and Mr. Thomas Gooderick of Mr. Bartons of Whenby, by this happy station, I wanted no assistance that could animate the tolerable diligence and endeavours of a young missioner; and they were often pleased to tell me that I deserved a cherishing hand; and both by counsel and manifest encouragement and their edifying example, were always ready to promote Gods service in me. And they accordingly employed me in preaching at Kilvington, Brampton, Whenby, Sir John Savilles and elsewhere; so did they plentifully reward my poor labours . . .

Smithson, like almost all secular priests, belonged to a county Brotherhood that met occasionally in a Catholic inn in the county town. He and his brethren acknowledged the canonical authority of the English Secular Clergy Chapter, a self-perpetuating body of senior priests originally founded by Bishop Richard Smith. The Chapter was in theory a caretaker for the empty episcopal throne. Rome did not recognise that it had any authority and asserted that the Roman department for Foreign Missions ruled the English clergy. Yet the secular priest missioners periodically renewed their sacramental authority and sought permissions and dispensations for themselves and their congregations from Rome through the Chapter without trouble. But, for all except a few pious, clericalised gentry families, these clerical minutiae were of little interest or, indeed, importance. In reality it was the peer and gentry lay patrons who appointed, paid and dismissed at will the majority of priests. The chaplains for the most part tried to please their patrons and fit in with their prejudices and wishes.

It is noticeable also that Mr Smithson, for all his undoubted (but unstated) sense of spiritual vocation and acceptance of the Catholic Faith and Papal authority, speaks remarkably like any Anglican vicar of the period. He is concerned about his place, his living, his status, is proud of the patrons he pleases. It is preaching which interests him, and which gains him credit. He wants to have status in his local clerical company. In it, in spite of Pope, Chapter, Archdeacons and Rural Dean, real power lies with Mr John Young, who has most credit with all the local patrons. A word from Mr Young gains a young missioner a good place in that country. Mr Young has in his hands control of most of the local Catholic clerical trust funds, the final support of indigent or aged missioners. When Mr Young died, Smithson hoped, in vain, to succeed to Mr Young's power and trusts.

What about the separate little world of the Catholic religious? They and the secular priests still inhabited separate planets divided by deep mutual suspicions. Each tiny group of religious, Jesuits, Benedictines, Franciscans, Dominicans, Carmelites, spent its energies during the Restoration years repairing the ravages of war. The Jesuits had lost twenty-five per cent of their manpower, the Benedictines twenty per cent. The Carthusians had now only eight or nine monks. The male side of the Bridgettine Order died out. The convents of nuns were still founding new houses, no longer to accommodate an overflow of subjects or get rid of dissidents, but to find either some new site on the Continent less subject to the ravages of war and taxation, or a place more in the eye of the Catholic gentry so as to attract more of their daughters. Most of the men's Orders strove to increase their acceptance with gentry patrons and so their hold on places. This was the surest source of gentry pupils for their schools and thence of novices for their Orders and so of lay benefactions. Inevitably therefore the collision course between seculars and regulars for places, so sharp before the wars, continued. Since the numbers of Catholic gentry, and so of places, had decreased, the competition grew stiffer.

These were the realities of Restoration clerical life. Through the earthiness ran a broad strand of solid, genuine spirituality. Smithson and Young were conscientious pastors. Within fifty miles of them laboured for forty years on the moors Nicholas Postgate, serving first old Lady Dunbar, and then, without complaint, some hundreds of poor Catholics in free hamlets and farmsteads. His poor parishioners were often lax, often married to Protestants. In forty years he formally reconciled over 1800 persons to the Catholic Church. Undoubtedly many were real converts, but many were apostates and the lapsed. He was a poor farmer's son of the locality, educated at Douai on a bursary. He was shabbily dressed and travelled on foot incessantly over foul moorland tracks amongst Catholics or ex-Catholics who often insulted him and were finally to betray him to his death.

The flame of Catholic clerical radicalism was distinctly weaker than before the civil wars. But it still burned amongst a small minority of seculars and religious. That horrific secular priest radical, Thomas White *alias* Blacklow, lived on to 1676. Throughout the years of war and the Republic he had chosen to live in Holland. After thirty years abroad, he slipped back into England in about 1667 and lived in retirement in lodgings in Drury Lane to his death. Pious Catholics had never ceased to regard Blacklow as practically an atheist and the secret source of all scepticism and unrest amongst the younger generation of clergy and laity. Any Catholic who expressed the most mildly critical notions was called 'a Blacklowist'. During the secret negotiations with the New Model Army in 1647 and with Oliver Cromwell in the 1650s, Blacklow had certainly urged the clergy Chapter by letter to press on to a legal agreement in spite of all Papal, Jesuit and Catholic royalist opposition. In a stream of books, published in Holland or Paris, he simultaneously appeared to be constructing a revolutionary new system of Catholic theology, at least as novel as the new philosophy of that shocking French Catholic radical, René Descartes. When the Chaptermen scrupulously objected that, as Catholics, they must abide by Roman decisions, Blacklow had answered sharply: 'Rome is not the proper place to treat of such business, which importeth the circumcising of Papal authority . . .' In Paris Henry Holden, Blacklow's chief secular priest supporter, backed up his master. He wrote bluntly to Blacklow: 'Our Clergy is not worth the paines you take for them: nor will ever dare to goe to the close stool [lavatory] without a Breve from Rome.' To their disgust their old ally, Bishop Richard Smith, living in his dotage in Paris, became orthodox and declared against the proposed agreement. At the time of Blacklow's return to England in 1667 a similar agreement was being discussed and promoted by the activist Catholic peers and gentry. To Blacklow's annoyance, the Chapter and clergy again withheld support, retreating into furious internal arguments. Blacklow was represented at Chapter meetings by a brilliant new supporter, John Sergeant.

Sergeant was a man after Blacklow's heart, and was to carry on the apostolic succession of Catholic clerical radicalism to his death in 1707. He came to Catholicism from the very core of Laudian Anglican royalism. Before the civil war he had been lay secretary to the Bishop of Durham. Then he fought in the war as a royalist gentleman volunteer, was wounded in action and persuaded to become a Catholic by a priest whom he met in Sussex, probably during his convalescence. He came back to England after his ordination, after the Restoration, and was quickly in the centre of clerical affairs as secretary to the Chapter and the ablest literary apologist for Catholicism of the period. As always with Catholic clerical radicals, a veil of mystery hangs over his activities and, to some extent, over the exact purport of his arguments. Like Blacklow (a relation of the Earl of Portland, the Shropshire Plowdens, the Howards and a good many other Papist activist peers and gentry), Sergeant was friendly with the lay activists and visited them in their country houses. Both priests, very unusually for Catholic clergy, had friendships far outside the Catholic camp: Blacklow with Thomas Hobbes and his circle and Sergeant with the Anglican Earl of Rochester. In 1673 Sergeant abruptly left England. He later explained that his flight was caused by a violent attack on Blacklowists by Papist conservatives of every hue. The Jesuits, he said, urged the authorities to imprison him. George Leyburne, the President of Douai, had certainly waged a private war on Blacklowism for years. Leyburne, a rigid conservative, saw the serpent of Blacklowism lurking under every bush. He expelled, as infected with the heresy, every Douai professor or student who showed the mildest signs of unrest or even those who secretly smoked tobacco. That vile weed was, to conservatives, what 'pot' is today. Leyburne wrote of that 'Indian herb, smelling vilely and scandalous; its use has always been prohibited by me and my predecessors to such an extent that College rules absolutely bar the ordination of tobacco-addicts . . .' The conservatives had long memories. The Catholic student riots in the seminaries from 1598 had been associated with tobacco pipes and card-playing. Religious superiors had waged war since the 1620s on these vices amongst missioners. In their eyes they were invariably associated with scepticism and unrest and the highroad to apostasy. The day had not yet come, but was soon to be, when a Catholic priest martyr would enjoy a pipeful of tobacco on his way to the scaffold.

But what exactly was the aim of Blacklow, Holden and Sergeant? On one interpretation, perfectly consonant with the letter of their books and correspondence, they were clerical idealists, successors of the late Elizabethan Appellants, concerned to create an episcopally- and clerically-controlled Catholic community. This would call the peers and gentry patrons and the religious Orders to heel and impose peace and apple-pie order on the community. The bishops would then negotiate with the government an Oath of Allegiance and the legal toleration of obedient Catholics as a subordinate but loyal part of English Protestant society. An omelette cannot be made without breaking eggs. The price of this achievement would inevitably be a considerable loosening of relations between the core of English Catholicism and Rome and the expulsion from England of such Jesuits and other recalcitrants as would not toe the line. As Holden once wrote, such a scheme would achieve the apparently impossible (and so clearly was an inspiration of the Holy Ghost): it would give the Catholic lay activists most of what they wanted and yet achieve the dream of the clericalists also. But does this interpretation of the radical dream really fit the minds of Blacklow, Holden and Sergeant . . . ? Perhaps they were not sure themselves. Just as Augustine Baker and Mary Ward, Catholics in some ways very traditionalistic, had propounded principles the full and proper consequences of which would be an immensely radical reconstruction of Catholicism, so Blacklow, Holden and Sergeant were far greater radicals than they themselves realised. Leyburne and the Jesuits were probably justified, on their grounds, in accusing them of Protestant heresy. For their part the three radicals sincerely believed that they were being loyal to the Papacy, rightly conceived.

They had no monopoly of clerical radicalism. Up in the north of England, as chaplain to the 2nd Lord Langdale, was the Lisbon priest Edward Booth, a dedicated experimental scientist and inventor, and a man who mingled a disconcerting originality of mind with a shell of deeply conventional piety. He ended his days as a humdrum ecclesiastical administrator. Across at Dunkenhalgh in Lancashire, the chaplain to the Walmesley family was Francis Line, a Jesuit mathematician. Line, and his Jesuit disciple, Anthony Lucas, engaged in a pamphlet-war with Isaac Newton and Robert Boyle. The controversy was no simple one between Catholic traditionalist Aristotelians and progressively modern Protestants. The four protagonists fenced across a largely common ground in which hypotheses of a startling modernity stood cheek-by-jowl with medieval superstitions and Biblical literalism. In the English Franciscan house at Douai Anthony Le Grand, a popular spiritual director, was writing books which made him famous amongst Protestant younger dons at Oxford and Cambridge as a master of the new philosophy of Descartes and the avowed enemy of medievalism. The superiors of English seminaries and religious houses regarded him as a Blacklowist.

Meanwhile, across in France and Flanders, Jansenism was the issue of the hour. Jansenism, like all sixteenth- and seventeenth-century Catholic radical movements, was so mystified by its supporters and opponents that modern historians have often been tempted to wildly opposite interpretations of its significance. Some have seen it (like Blacklowism) as a mere aberration of clericalist Catholic conservatism. Others have seen in it a covert effort to Protestantise Catholicism. Whatever the truth, it was a Dutch and French equivalent of English Blacklowism, and it attracted a considerable amount of English and Irish Catholic support. From the remote origins of the Jansenist movement in the 1630s in Paris and Louvain and Holland, English and Irish secular clergy and religious associated themselves enthusiastically with its leaders. Bishop Richard Smith was so close to them that his name figured in Jansenist lists of sufferers for the cause. In the 1660s the Jansenist convent of Port-Royal, near Paris, had English Benedictine chaplains and the direction of the English Capuchin, Archange de Pembroke. The community of male lay solitaries in the grounds of the convent included Englishmen.

9. 'The Popish Plot' 1678–85

In the summer of 1678, while taking his usual early morning exercise, Charles II was handed by his laboratory assistant an information. This purported to offer detailed evidence of a plot by the Catholic activists to murder the King and usher in the reign of James II with a Papist military takeover of the Establishment. Catholics would seize arsenals and fortresses and Whitehall; Protestant leaders would be dismissed from office and imprisoned or exiled. Then, by propaganda, the threat of dismissal from office, and 'dragonnades' Protestants would be converted wholesale to Catholicism. After some hesitation the King and his moderate Protestant ministers decided to go through the forms of an official investigation of the evidence. It would be politically unwise to ignore or suppress it. They summoned the author of the information, a certain Titus Oates.

In spite of oddities in his character and career, Oates belonged to a broad and well-known strand in contemporary Catholicism, so broad and often so respectable that it would be unjust to dub it the Catholic underworld. It included, first, Church-papists (such as the King, the Duke of York and Lord Arlington), and then numerous people who, for a wide variety of reasons (for instance rampant radicalism, marital troubles, mental illness, bankruptcy, criminal tendencies, laziness) were lapsed from the practice of their religion or looked at askance by the Catholic Church authorities. There were, as we have seen, adulterous, drunken or ruffianly Papist peers like Lord Mounteagle. There were Papist whores, English and French, some of them of good birth and culture. There were hunted but pious radical priests (like Blacklow and Sergeant) who might often find it advisable to take refuge in Protestant Amsterdam. There were priests living more or less under a cloud. Some passed rapidly from place to place and were often hanging about in London unemployed. Richard Flecknoe, the priest-poet, was the subject of a special enquiry by the Department of Propaganda in Rome, which remained deeply suspicious of his wanderings, Bohemian way of life in London garrets or even in Constantinople, and Protestant literary friendships. There were priests illicitly married, and fugitive Irish and foreign clergy. A secular priest, Alexander Bowker, was hanged for coining at Tyburn in 1618. There were priests who had joined the Church of England and who later made constant overtures to the Catholic authorities for reconciliation. There were spoiled priests, men who had (sometimes repeatedly) failed noviciates and left seminaries: some of these lapsed and lived on their wits. There were Papist army officers without employment—a good many such had been dismissed from the Army during the anti-Catholic stirrings in 1673-4—desperate for money and employment and ready to serve any enterprise. There were Irish footpads, thieves and coiners (sometimes Protestants, but more often nominal Catholics) who infested London. There was a host of actors, writers and artists, English and foreign, amongst whom were many more or less Papist in background. They included respectable lapsed Catholics like William Wycherley. Lastly there were the sullenly dissenting Papist smallholders in free villages who gave so much anxiety to poor missioners by their lapses and anticlericalism, and who were increasingly migrating to London and the larger towns. Against this Catholic background, many of Titus Oates's attitudes and characteristics must have seemed almost normal.

He was a convert clergyman with a wide, if superficial, education, brains, wit, daring and a real charm mixed with striking facial ugliness. He had been expelled from three eminent public schools in turn but each time readily befriended by new patrons. He had been rusticated from Cambridge but ordained as an Anglican without difficulty. He had troubles in each of his Anglican cures, a parish, a naval chaplaincy, and ministering to the Catholic Earl of Norwich's Protestant servants. But each time he fell on his feet. Once converted to Catholicism, he was befriended by the Jesuit Provincial who found him a place as an ordinand at Valladolid. Moved on from there as incapable of sustaining seminary discipline, he was placed by the Provincial in the Jesuit pre-noviciate establishment attached to their school at St Omer. A new Provincial dismissed him, and Oates was cast into the pool of spoiled priests in London, knocking vainly on the doors of religious superiors and incapable of any job but schoolmastering or return to the Anglican ministry.

The reasons why he became an informer against Catholics on a grand scale have often been analysed. In 1678-83 devout

Protestants attributed his action to the light of grace and true Protestant fervour shocked by clear evidence of Catholic treason. Catholics, and most Protestant historians in later ages, dismissed him as a criminal mind, devoid of religious sincerity and plain honesty. It has recently been suggested that his actions, and the favour shown to him repeatedly by patrons and even a Jesuit Provincial, can only be explained by supposing that he was a practising homosexual able to charm or blackmail respectable persons with the same concealed tendencies. The seventeenth century abounds with strange characters, with fanatics and sceptics, and with apparently respectable, normal people in whose make-up orthodoxy collided with streaks of superstition and fanaticism. James I, Augustine Baker, Benet Fitch, Mary Ward, Guy Fawkes and the Gunpowder Plot Catholic conspirators, Oliver Cromwell and Isaac Newton are famous examples. But there were many more, whose mental underworld was revealed by the memoirs of John Aubrey: John Milton, Thomas Hobbes, William Prynne, Sir Edward Coke, Ezrel Tonge.

Even very cool, moderate Protestants could have a dark, fanatical underside to their minds. Samuel Pepys was ostensibly a sensible, tolerant, rational man, even a cynic. He served the Papist Duke of York at the Admiralty with affectionate loyalty; he put up with Mrs Pepys's conversion to Catholicism; he was fond of his foreign Catholic music teacher. But under the modernity in Pepys's mind lay depths formed by the strict, idealistic Puritan nonconformity of the wartime years. He could not repress feelings of panic and almost of apocalyptic horror at the rise of court Catholicism. He confessed that he really believed the rumour that the Great Fire of London in 1666 was caused by Catholic plotters. Modern Ulster Protestants, even if they are liberal, personally friendly with Catholic associates, and not members of Loyalist organisations, cannot avoid feeling that all Ulster Catholics, however close to themselves in outlook, are fundamentally untrustworthy, that the mere profession of Catholicism involves commitment to Irish Republican principles and Catholic clericalism. In the same way, Protestants like Pepys and John Evelyn felt a deep suspicion of the mildest of Catholics. They hated the idea of executing the old, bloody penal laws or of beggaring families with effective recusancy fining but they regarded firmly discriminatory legislation like the Test Acts as utterly justified and necessary. They never doubted that the Catholic community contained political and military revolutionaries who would, like Guy Fawkes, stick at nothing.

The general disposition of modern historians, Catholic and non-Catholic alike, has been to regard this seventeenth-century

Protestant outlook as mistaken, and to exonerate the Catholics from any serious intention of revolutionary action or conspiracy. The real fanaticism of Guy Fawkes and his associates (all eminently respectable Catholic gentry) has usually been explained away or, more often, ignored. Similarly, it has been taken for granted that in 1678 there can have been no real 'Popish Plot'. In fact mid-seventeenth-century English Catholics lived in the same religious atmosphere as Protestants. They might often have been mildly conformist in temper of mind and strongly critical of Rome and the clergy, but their very commitment to Catholicism compelled them to accept, however tacitly, a fundamentally internationalist, clericalist and absolutist religion and to be at odds with an Anglicanism which was, in its own way, just as absolutist. Seen objectively, there was no real difference between Protestants and Catholics over moral principles. In both camps the standard moral teaching was the same and notably austere, even Puritan. Rebellion against legal authority was strongly condemned and tyrannicide detested. Oaths and vows were treated with immense respect. Punishments and penances were severe. Moral or religious laxity was heavily condemned. But precisely because of the perfectionism of this official morality and antique virtue in a society daily becoming more complex and sophisticated, amongst both Protestants and Catholics, popular morality paid lip-service to traditional respectability while quietly accepting modifications, for instance concerning honour, feuds, duelling and many points of commercial practice; also, the officially monastic morality had long ago ceased to square with the popular morality of marriage and sexual relations. Popular morality and the acute practical difficulties of Catholic life under discriminatory laws had long ago opened the way for most Catholics to practise multiple nonconformities to orthodox morality, State law and Catholic canon law. Protestants therefore had some justification for thinking that Catholics were dangerous because they could not be trusted to be loyal citizens or to tell the truth. What could one make of people who, for instance, like old Lady Falkland, concealed her conversion to Catholicism from her Protestant husband for fourteen years, or of Catholics who sat on the Anglican Court of High Commission's bench, or (like the 2nd Earl of Portland) swore in the House of Lords that they had never been Catholics?

In 1678 *some* conspiring certainly was afoot within the Catholic community. Charles II, albeit without any serious intention of carrying it out, in 1672 had very secretly assured Louis XIV that someday he would announce his conversion to Catholicism, an event which would then have inevitably meant some political power for Catholics. Edward Coleman, a Catholic convert layman employed in the Duke of York's household, had for years been writing to Louis XIV's Jesuit confessor about a 'grand design' of a Catholic takeover of the Establishment, presumably when his master became King. A number of leading activist Papist peers had lately been meeting more frequently and travelling backwards and forwards to France. They were associated with numbers of unemployed Catholic English and Irish army officers. In Catholic activist circles in the provinces by 1678 there were signs of almost apocalyptic expectation of the Catholic religion coming in again. In Yorkshire several priests bequeathed money in secret clauses to found chantry chapels in Anglican parish churches 'if the Catholic religion comes in'. Others bequeathed Mass vestments and chalices in the same way. In the summer of 1678 the JPs of the North Riding of Yorkshire had informations that some wilder spirits amongst the Papist gentry were talking rebellion. One had said in an inn: 'I have forty men ready to rise up at the holding upp of my finger and when I come on the field I will give no quarter.' Another, a respectable Papist farmer's wife on the Gilling estate of Viscount Fairfax, had said:

> The King of France is our Kinge: I praye God he may get the victory this battle, and then I hope in God he will be here ere it be longe, and the Protestant Ministers be putt forth of the churches and ours be putt in, and except all Protestants will turne they must all be killed, and the Kinge also must be killed except he will turne. The Kinge is nothing to us, the Queene is; the Kinge is a Protestant in outwarde showe and a Catholike in his heart ...

Before the year was out the Bench had two more reports of Catholics saying that Charles II would be killed if he did not soon announce his conversion openly.

Oates must have been well aware of this ferment of activist Catholic expectation, impatience and frustration. It was a similar mood which had touched off the Catholic plots of 1604–5 and the Papist stirrings of those years in Wales. The Jesuit Provincial who dismissed Oates from St Omer wrote of 'his seditious language and treasonable words too horrible to be repeated'. It seems that Catholics in the Colleges had been affected by the ferment, and that Oates had proposed revolutionary action, even the killing of the King. Oates was a strange mixture of sincerity and insincerity. In 1675 the old Marquis of Winchester and his wife (witness his memorial stone at Englefield) had feared the imminence of an ultra-Protestant rebellion, another civil war like that of 1642–6: 'Pray (Reader) that sutch times no more appeare, Or, if they happen, learn true Honour here.' And, even for such a peace-loving Catholic, the memorial implies, there is a duty in Honour to resort again to 'Armes'. That same year John Aubrey's distinguished Anglican friends had taken it as a real possibility that Catholicism would come in and that they must turn. It is likely that Oates's conversion owed something to the same calculation, and that he left St Omer disillusioned not only by the Jesuits' rejection of his person but by their flat rejection of a revolutionary course of action which he thought to be required by the nature of Catholicism and the circumstances it was in.

In London Oates secretly returned to Anglicanism and took up residence with an incumbent there, Ezrel Tonge. Historians have generally dismissed Tonge as an absurd anti-Catholic fanatic. He was certainly full of an apocalyptic sense of doom and the need to rouse Protestants to the Papist threat. He shared this preoccupation with many of his contemporaries. His books were no more superstitious or vicious than hundreds by other Anglican authors of unimpeachable respectability and orthodoxy. Tonge was well-thought-of in the City and generously supported by patrons. He may well be the Ezrel Tonge whom John Aubrey knew as an educationalist willing to make use of Jesuit academic methods.

Whatever we may think of Oates's motives for becoming an informer, it is clear that he was risking his neck. He had sufficient evidence to indicate some sort of treasonable talk and activity by some Catholics, but none to prove it, or to show its exact degree of seriousness. It is quite unlikely that the 'plot' had got beyond the stage of discussions. The King might easily have ignored the information. If matters had come to charges and trials for treason, the outcome would depend on government instructions to the Judges and the temper of the juries. Both these factors varied with the political situation of the time. At one time and place apparently clear accusations could be quietly disregarded, as were the North Riding informations. At other times and during a popular drive against Catholics, slight evidence or none was needed to get conviction for treason. When Oates started informing there was no tumult against Catholics and the authorities seemed determined to do nothing to provoke one. Informing against wealthy or aristocratic Catholics in times of peace could be fatal for the informer.

In fact Oates was incredibly lucky. The King accepted the informations, and they were investigated by the Council and Parliament. Almost at once two strokes of luck turned Oates into a public hero. The first was Coleman's failure to hide or burn his correspondence. He was arrested and his whole correspondence taken. At a blow Oates's trustworthiness seemed vindicated. Simultaneously the London JP before whom Oates had sworn his information originally, Sir Edmund Berry Godfrey, was found murdered in a ditch in the London suburbs. He had not been robbed, and it seemed that the murder had been committed with ferocity. The combination of Coleman's letters and the murder created a panic in London and a swiftly-mounting outcry against Catholics. It was inevitably presumed that Godfrey had been murdered by Catholic activists anxious to snuff out the informer and his associates. Rumour soon credited the Duke of York's servants with the deed.

The 'Popish Plot' scare now assumed a life of its own. The most sensible and balanced Protestants, especially in London and Westminster, were either swept willy-nilly into the prosecution of investigations and charges by public hysteria and their own inner fears, or cynically climbed on to the band-wagon. It was obviously politically dangerous to oppose it or, indeed, ostentatiously to stand apart from the clamour. The King himself, with reservations, was compelled to go far along the same path, or at least appear to do so. Oates was not reluctant to go along with the plot investigations, and he was soon receiving a government pension as informer and investigator. But now he could not have avoided further revelations: the government, Parliament and London opinion demanded them of him. He supplied lists of Catholic activists. As the arrests, interrogations and trials of Catholics grew, Oates was inevitably called in as the great expert to add extra informations on the cases, and he frequently did so. It was not surprising in such circumstances that he went far past the limits of his original knowledge and suppositions to wilder guesses which he passed off as knowledge. He certainly became a great perjurer and thereby contributed to the deaths of Catholics. But Catholic tradition was wrong in regarding him as the sole creator of the plot and its scare (they called it 'Oates's Plot'). The plot had a slender basis in fact. The scare was mostly accidental and not of Oates's making. Once the scare was going, a good many different people contributed to give it force and direction. The Earl of Shaftesbury and his political associates made use of the plot to launch a movement to exclude the Duke of York by law from succession to the throne and to discredit the moderate Protestant ministers. Informers appeared like mushrooms, uninvited by Oates or Shaftesbury, mostly from the Catholic underworld.

In Yorkshire the informers were Lawrence Mowbray and Robert Bolron, converts who had been, until their recent dismissal, the legal clerk and colliery manager of the wealthy Catholic Sir Thomas

Gascoigne. The two men used the scare to enable them to get their revenge on Gascoigne and his friends. In Staffordshire a former estate agent to the Catholic Lord Aston, Stephen Dugdale (himself a Catholic), behaved in the same way. In county Durham Robert Jenison, a lapsed Catholic failure member of an otherwise pious, Jesuit-directed gentry family, took out his animus against the priests of the district. In Wales the tightly-organised rural Catholic communities protected by the Marquis of Worcester and the Jesuit mission-centre of the Cwm were ravaged by Edward Turberville and jealous Protestant relations and neighbours. Turberville, like Jenison was a genteel Catholic remittance man, who had passed into the London Catholic underworld by way of Dominican and Benedictine noviciates and military service in France. In London the new informers were William Bedloe and Miles Prance. Bedloe was a professional criminal, who claimed to have been a Catholic for the last two years. He invented fantastically detailed information about a military Catholic plot and the murder of Godfrey by the Duke of York's servants. Prance, a respectable London Catholic goldsmith, faced with conviction for treason on account of careless words said before witnesses, in terror turned King's Evidence and wildly fabricated any evidence needed to corroborate Bedloe's stories.

Then there were other Catholic informers. John Sergeant and David Morris, both Blacklowist Chaptermen secular priests, had already for some years been well-known to the King's moderate Protestant ministers and had negotiated abortively with them on the Chapter's behalf. Both were in receipt of small pensions from the Secret Service Fund. In 1679 both volunteered information about the plot before the Council. They produced a wealth of highly academic theological evidence attempting to establish that the English Jesuits did not see any moral objections to a Catholic revolution and even to tyrannicide. The informers also gave it as their opinion that Edward Coleman (already dead) had been a genuine conspirator, and that Jesuit machinations lay behind all the plotting. These informations apparently did no harm to any Catholics. Sergeant lived on to 1707 as a Chapterman of good standing and the most distinguished apologist for Catholicism. He never ceased to say and write that there were Catholic militants who seriously intended revolution in 1678, and that the Jesuits were morally responsible and deserved what they suffered. In Jesuit tradition Sergeant became the arch-traitor renegade, worse even than the Elizabethan William Gifford.

Lionel Anderson, a convert Dominican priest and an aggressively liberal individualist, was arrested and questioned by the Council.

It is unlikely that he remained silent about the plot in general terms. The Council was unable to save him from trial and conviction for his priesthood, but the King reprieved him. Banished from England, he travelled to Palestine, returned to London in 1686 and died there at a great age in 1710, unrepentant. He is recorded honourably on his Province's death-roll. John Portman *alias* Smith was a convert Ignatian secular priest, trained by the Jesuits in Rome and serving on a Jesuit mission in county Durham. Shortly before 1678 he had turned against the Jesuits and all their works and persuaded his patrons to follow suit. The Jesuits were cut to the quick by his defection and accused him of having written against them and informed to the authorities on Jesuits in the county. Father Travers *alias* Savage had been dismissed from the Society of Jesus before 1678 for breach of its rules. In 1679 the Jesuits accused him of informing against one of them.

There were a few Catholic informers within the camp of the plotters. Richard Langhorne was a London Catholic attorney. Oates knew that he was the Jesuits' solicitor and procured his arrest. When condemned to death for treason solely on the basis of Oates's guesses, Langhorne was tortured by scruples. He eventually revealed to the authorities the whereabouts of the deeds of the English Province of the Society's property and mission funds. He also asked to see an Anglican prison chaplain. His behaviour (though he eventually faced execution bravely as a Catholic) embarrassed the Jesuits and played havoc with their property and funds. He tried to justify his behaviour by arguing that telling the truth about the deeds ought to convince the authorities and the world that his denials that he or the Jesuits were plotters must be genuine.

Lord Stafford, a Catholic activist, was a tactless and stupid man at odds with his fellow Catholic peers and even with the other members of the Howard family clan. It is hard to avoid having the impression that, in his case, as in those of some other Catholics executed during these years, the King and the moderate Protestant peers decided the sacrifice of one man's life might appease the crowd and so spare the lives of many others, or that the Catholic peers still in England accepted the sacrifice gracefully. The Protestant members of the Howard family certainly voted for his death. So did most of the Catholic Howard peers. In an effort to save his life, Stafford volunteered information about secret Catholic intrigues in 1671–2. Again, to the intense annoyance of the Jesuit Provincial, his local superior in Staffordshire, Peter Giffard, on being arrested voluntarily handed over to the authorities the deeds and papers of Jesuit missions in his care.

Even this does not complete the list of Catholic contributions to feed the fuel of the plot scare. Although, as we shall see, many of the wealthier Catholics went to ground or fled abroad, most could not. Amongst them remained activists of the sort whose intemperate remarks in public about 'the Catholic religion coming in again' had contributed to build up Protestant alarm before 1678. The leopard does not change its spots. These people tended to react to the plot scare with open indignation. They were anxious to assert to all and sundry that Oates and the other Catholic informers were cheats and liars. They had strong words to say about Shaftesbury and the opposition Protestant politicians exploiting the plot. They defended the Duke of York with loyal vigour. The boldest, when carried away by passion, did not stick at declaring that the day of the Catholics would come. All this Catholic panache fed oil into the fire of the plot and helped to bring the Catholic speakers to gaol (and sometimes death) and to convince doubting Thomases amongst Protestants that there really had been a Catholic plot. But it is hard to avoid sympathy for some poor London Catholics who ended in gaol for brave words: a scissors-maker, an ironmonger, a yeoman; there was even a salesman who pursued a prominent informer until he took refuge in a house of easement and then hammered on the door, shouting abuse.

The oddest revelation to Protestants of what Catholic activists were capable of, even when under persecution, was the 'Meal-Tub Plot'. In the spring of 1680 a strangely assorted group of Papists decided to go over to the offensive and try to discredit the persecutors by using their informing methods against them. The group included two ardent and indiscreet women both devoted to the Jesuits, the Countess of Powis and Mrs Cellier, a convert midwife with a practice in fashionable society. There was also Henry Nevill who, according to John Aubrey, was 'an ingeniose and well-bred Gentleman, an excellent (but Concealed) Poet', and two gentlemen named Tasborough and Price. Mrs Cellier bribed Dangerfield, a minor informer hitherto against Catholics, to forge and plant evidence that Shaftesbury and his associates were plotting to kill the King. Henry Nevill's contribution was the publication of anonymous verses in defence of his executed friend, Edward Coleman. Meanwhile Tasborough and Price raked together and published anonymously evidence of immoral behaviour by Oates and the other chief informers. The effort misfired. Dangerfield betrayed the ladies, who were arrested and put on trial for treason. The forged papers were discovered in a meal tub in Mrs Cellier's kitchen. By this stage the plot scare was running out of steam and public interest, so the ladies were acquitted. But Mrs Cellier promptly began to publish wild lampoons on the persecutors. She was found guilty of libel and sentenced to a fine and time standing in the pillory. Only the mercy of the magistrates rescued her, still alive but severely injured, from the dead cats and brickbats of the London mob while she stood locked by the neck in the pillory. Tasborough and Price also endured ruin.

The Catholic resistance played into the hands of the persecutors immediately. But, in the long run, it helped to repair the tacit alliance between Catholics and moderate Protestants, an alliance which had been shaken by the plot scare. The moderate Protestants, at first driven into disarray and retreat by the sheer virulence and accumulation of evidence against Catholics, soon recovered their balance and came up fighting to defend the Duke of York and his right to succeed to the throne. Moderate Protestants everywhere by 1679–80 were themselves lampooning Oates and Shaftesbury. In York, for instance, an Anglican squire named his dogs 'Oates' and 'Bedloe': he was a practical farmer who treated his dogs with severity.

When estimating the extent of the damage done to the Catholic community by the plot scare and persecution, it is important to realise how popular and legal persecution then worked. There was no police network of a modern kind. The execution or non-execution of penal laws depended on a combination of factors. At law the principal executive was the benches of JPs, who were expected to pass on major offenders to the King's Judges coming periodically to county towns to hold Assize Courts; in London such major cases tended to go to the main government courts in Westminster Hall. The degree of active execution of the laws by JPs depended on the political, social and religious climate of opinion. Before the civil wars there were multiple ways in which the government could spur the JPs on to action: orders circulated by the Council and Assize Judges, strong pressure by the local central government agencies, the Councils of the north and Wales, pressures by eminent peers who were both royal Councillors and powerful in the counties. After 1660 the agencies no longer existed and in general Westminster had fewer means of disciplining recalcitrant JPs. Partly because of deliberate calculation by the government, and partly because of JPs' tenderness for gentry neighbours even if they were Papists, the bloody penal laws against Catholics never had been executed to the letter. More often than not, even in times of public panic, they were only very partially enforced. Since 1603 Stuart government policy and the growth of the tacit agreement between Protestant and Papist peers and gentry had largely put the penal laws into a state of desuetude. They remained on the Statute Book and could, in theory, and to some degree in practice. be activated, like delayed-action bombs. Every now and then they were slightly activated by unusual local circumstances, JPs with a special animus against some Catholics or priests, or professional informers at work.

The scare of 1678 brought royal proclamations ordering the literal execution of the penal laws. The extent to which they were obeyed by JPs depended on their estimate of how serious the government's intention was and how serious the national situation and the plot; it also depended on gentry public opinion. Cutting across all this came the wave of informers and the setting up by the King's Council and Parliament of committees empowered to order searches and arrests on evidence suggested by the informers. Thus the benches of JPs were jerked, willy-nilly, into action and found other executive action being taken over their heads by government agencies. On the whole action was taken most thoroughly, and the persecution was most severe, in and around London. Persecution operated only patchily and fitfully in the provinces. There were no areas in which the laws were unenforced, but in some counties action was sluggish and perfunctory, while it could be sharp and thorough in counties where major informers were at work.

The Catholic clergy suffered a staggering blow. In a real sense they were regarded as expendable, and the Jesuits, because of their popular reputation (even amongst a good many Catholics), could hardly expect mercy. Of the 600–700 missioners, about one hundred were arrested. Of these seventeen were executed—occasionally for plotting, more usually under the Elizabethan statute making ordination abroad a treasonable offence. Another twenty-three died in gaol or later, as a result of imprisonment. The Jesuits suffered heavy casualties. Of their ninety missioners (they were now much under their pre-war strength), forty were arrested, nine were executed and eighteen died of imprisonment. The physical blow was sorely felt by the clergy for a number of reasons. As a body, a half-century of almost complete immunity from major bloody persecution had not prepared them for the sudden resumption of such barbaric treatment. The seventeenth century was an age of contrasts. On the one hand a modernity of outlook and of living standards was coming in amongst educated people. On the other hand their minds and their daily lives still contained a solid residuum of medievalism. The executions of Catholics with the butcher's cleaver and apron, halter, quartering block, fire and tar were as crowded as ever and part of a social scene where hangings were frequent. The priests who were executed generally had a stolid attitude to the scaffold. They were accustomed to death in unpleasant forms and to acute physical discomfort and pain. Yet both the priests and the educated Catholics and Protestants watching executions felt a new, modern sense of repulsion; this was, they felt, a medieval barbarism remote from the concerns of religion. The priests, for all their Puritan solidity, felt the physical penalties with a new shrinking. For one thing they were conscious that they often lacked the physical toughness of their Elizabethan predecessors. For another they were often in poor health. The seventeenth century was not a healthy century. The Plague was endemic, epidemics were unusually frequent and devastating, and it was climatically a cold century. Catholic priests and religious suffered greatly from consumption and fevers contracted in damp, cold Colleges, monasteries and mission stations. The average age of missioners was now abnormally high. Hence a spell in gaol meant danger of death to a good many priests.

The mission organisation received shattering blows. The backbone of the Society of Jesus in England was broken swiftly in 1678-9. The Provincial was arrested and executed and his files seized. In key areas in London and the south, in Nottinghamshire and Staffordshire and the Cwm in Wales, Jesuit local mission headquarters were raided and closed with a great haul for the searchers of papers, books and Mass gear. Probably two-thirds of the Jesuit missions ceased to operate because the missioners were arrested, or fled overseas, or the patrons were removed. John Warner, the new Provincial, was forced to remain abroad until 1683, almost completely out of touch with his men in England. The few reinforcements he sent were mostly arrested on landing. Many of the Carmelite and Franciscan missions were raided and shut. The Benedictines escaped more lightly. Their one formed monastery in London had been disbanded long before 1678, and their papers and libraries were prudently stored in remote places like Netherwitton in Northumberland. The secular clergy Chapter fled from its rooms in Gray's Inn in London in 1678, hiding its papers. Most of its officials were overseas or dead of old age by 1683. For almost six years the Catholic clergy went unshepherded.

The sufferings of the Catholic laity were never exactly recorded. It was an age in which the pious few of all religious denominations took care to collect and publish volumes of 'Sufferings' of their martyrs and confessors. The Quaker meetings' secretaries collected accounts of imprisonments, speeches before magistrates, and dying meditations of the tortured saints. Calamy collected accounts of the tribulations of Dissenting ministers. Walker published the sufferings of loyalist Anglican clergy in 1642-60. The Catholics were surprisingly backward in this matter. Here and there pious persons retained copies of martyrs' dying speeches. Bits of hangman's rope, fragments of martyrs' hair, bones and bloodstained clothing were treasured privately by a few. The pious attributed this lack of general Catholic devotion to the martyrs and confessors to the 'Protestantisation' of so many Catholics' religion and to the increasingly rationalistic spirit of the age. If John Aubrey lamented the death of witchcraft and fairies, the Catholic pious felt the same about neglect of exorcism, the disappearance of the cult of priests as 'wonderworkers' and lack of interest in holy relics. Also the lack of interest in the Catholic sufferers had other reasons. There was a strong division of opinion amongst Catholics about the plot, and many felt that the storm was deserved. The community was so sharply divided into factions by clerical allegiance and locality that sufferings tended to have a merely local interest. Certainly the Catholic chroniclers were mostly priests whose interest rarely looked outside the ranks of 'ours'. Class-divisions were as clear as ever. George Leyburne averted his eyes from clergy who were not noble by birth. Lord Castlemaine explained that Catholicism had nothing to do with the plebeians:

> . . . the Catholicks that have bin from their Infancy bred so, are of the chiefest Ranck in England . . . our Converts were and are still of Persons of Eminency both in their Parts and Quality. And whereas heretical seducers ever prey upon the meanest and simplest of the Land, on the contrary our Missioners had rather deale in universities than in shops . . . when they chance to make Converts, 'tis tenn to one but they are Persons of prime note either for their Families or Accomplishments . . .

The damage done to the laity must have been quite severe. Of the forty Catholic peers, eleven were arrested on treason charges. One (Lord Stafford) was executed and one (Lord Petre) died in the Tower of London. Three were not released until 1685. Eighteen others went to ground in ways which must have been expensive to their pockets, their pride, and, sometimes to their consciences. Two of the eighteen fully and finally conformed to Anglicanism (the Earl of Shrewsbury and the Duke of Norfolk's heir). Two more camouflaged themselves: the Earl of St Albans by taking the Anglican Communion a few times, Lord Arlington by his membership of the Council Committee investigating the plot. The other fourteen, usually with expensive trains of coaches, relations, chaplains and servants, hurried into indefinite voluntary exile abroad (Lord Baltimore to Maryland). The surviving dozen Catholic peers who stayed at home relatively unmolested formed an inactive and unimpressive group. They included the notorious and impecunious rakes, Lord Rivers, Mounteagle and Gerard. The arrests, the mass flight, and the action of the Howard clan in voting for Stafford's guilt seemed to put paid once and for all to the prestige of the Catholic peerage.

The Catholic gentry suffered also, but in rather different ways. Relatively few of them were arrested (perhaps fifty) or prosecuted for treason (six), and none were executed. Relatively few seem to have fled overseas. On the other hand the gentry had to suffer direct harassments much more than stay-at-home peers. Their houses were often rudely searched, their offensive weapons confiscated—a serious matter in so unpoliced an age—their chapels looted or shut, their priests driven away and their servants, Catholics as well as Protestants, transformed into potential enemies and informers. All journeys were hampered by the resumption of licensing and the gentry's usual lodgings in London and provincial towns were no longer approachable safely. The seizure of so many papers and deeds of missions caused anxiety about prosecution for superstitious uses. The JPs' machinery for convicting recusants ground rustily into action again. In itself it was theoretical, slow, antiquated, but it was time-consuming for the victims and opened the way, after conviction, for more dangerous legal proceedings. The government ordered the tendering of the old Oath of Allegiance to recusants. Many took it, but possibly 400 of the gentry and their relations were gaoled indefinitely for refusing it. Once gaoled, these people suffered confiscation of all property they had not previously conveyed away into the hands of Protestant trustees. In 1685 some 300 were still in gaol and sympathetic lawyers found it hard to suggest any legal means by which even a Catholic James II could pardon them. The unfortunates in gaol included a group of Mary Ward 'Jesuitesses' arrested in Yorkshire. The recusancy fining machinery was even rustier, but now its resumed workings gave many Catholic gentry a severe fright and put some to considerable expense.

On the whole the Papist gentry felt aggrieved. The activists amongst them felt let down by Charles II (the Duke of York had, early in the scare, been sent by the King into temporary exile in Scotland). All of them felt their class had had to bear more than its fair share of persecution. Some, probably many, tended to blame it all on hotheads and Jesuits. An old Staffordshire Papist squire observed bluntly to the Council, when cross-questioned about one Jesuit: '. . . if Jesuits can be honest men, Evers may be so also . . .' A Yorkshire Papist gentleman, perhaps brought up in pious

principles or just cynical and bewildered, wrote sourly to friends:
'A Preist att ye head of 40 people swore the Oath att Winchester
Sessions; if soe my opinion is Sir Tho: Moore and B. Fisher dyed
much mistaken . . .' Divisions amongst priests did not help. In
1679, according to the informer Bolron, he went to Confession in
the chaplain's room in Sir Thomas Gascoigne's house in Yorkshire
to one Rushton, who said it was a mortal sin to take the Oath of
Allegiance. When Bolron remarked that a neighbouring priest
thought differently, Rushton said it was nonsense and the priest a
fool.

It was the Catholic middle class who supplied much of the
drama and action, the arch-villains and saints, during the crisis.
There were relatively few 'gentlemen born' amongst the clergy
sufferers. Amongst the main Catholic informers only two, Dugdale
and Turberville, were gentlemen. The key figures in the most
publicised treason trials were mostly *bourgeois*: Coleman, the
parson's son; Langhorne, the attorney; Wakeman and Fogarty,
physicians; Elizabeth Cellier, midwife; Miles Prance, goldsmith;
Matthew Medburne; a Drury Lane Theatre comedian; William
Staley, son of a Catholic goldsmith; James Corker, convert Benedictine son of a parson. In London there was a tightly-packed
community of perhaps some 3000 Catholics, gentry and middle
class, respectable and raffish. The London middle-class Catholics
provided some twenty martyrs (a few executed, the rest, including
Dr Fogarty and Medburne, dead in gaol) and another hundred
arrested. Amongst these were printers and booksellers (David
Mallet, Langley Curtis, Richard Tonson, Randolph Taylor) who
dared to publish Catholic apologias. There were aggressive tradesmen who spoke out of turn. There was one small group of London
citizens who refused the Oath of Allegiance; the group included a
distiller, a jeweller, a glover, a woolwinder, several merchants and
women, including the wife of a barber-surgeon. Another sixty
were released on bond as dangerous Papists, for instance one of
the King's doctors, John Betts; three hop merchants, two innkeepers, a dancing-master, a barber, several glassmakers and booksellers. Convicted recusants were drawn into the fining machine.
However the London Catholics betrayed little sign of being cowed.
Most disobeyed with impunity Council orders to quit the City.
Papists crowded to the funeral of the executed William Staley. They
thronged the spectators' benches at treason trials to the disgust of
Counsel for the prosecution. In the provincial towns middle-class
Papists were still few, but they behaved as doggedly and spiritedly
as the Londoners.

By 1684-5 the plot scare had faded away and the Catholic

community could surface to lick its wounds and count the cost. The
storm-damage was heavy enough. Contemporary Catholics would
probably not have included in the damage the new war of books
beginning between John Warner, the Jesuit Provincial, and John
Sergeant. Sergeant roundly blamed the whole affair on to the Jesuits.
Warner, in a Latin treatise, exonerated the Society and put the
blame squarely on 'false brethren' including Sergeant. He gloomily
recounted 'the deaths of the persecutors', with particular stress on
an informer who died raving and swallowing his tongue, and on
an informing Ignatian priest who was doomed to spend the rest of
his life as an unqualified physician in Ireland. Nor would most
contemporary Catholics have placed as damage the revelation that
only 300 of them had firmly rejected the Oath of Allegiance. The
quarrel between Jesuits and others, and the practice of taking anti-
Catholic Oaths were well-established long before 1678.

But the credit balance of the Catholic account was surprisingly
heartening. First of all the tacit alliance between Catholics and
moderate Protestants was restored. The moderate Protestants had
sheltered some Catholic gentry from harm: their testimony acquitted
Sir Thomas Gascoigne at his treason trial. They had fought like
tigers to save the Duke of York's right to succeed to the throne.
The Duke was back in England and, in the last months of Charles
II's reign, Protestants rallied round him. Secondly the recovery of
the Catholic clergy was assured. When the dust created by the plot
cleared, it became evident that in wide areas of the country
missioners had gone to ground but stayed in place, undisturbed.
The superiors and organisations were practised in survival and rose
again. They all, with surprising unanimity, reported a distinct
upsurge in vocations from 1681–2. Due to the length of training
required numbers of missioners would not begin to increase
markedly before 1685–7 and, in the case of the Jesuits, whose
training was long, before 1693–5. But, especially if the upward trend
in vocations continued, as it was to do, the clergy could fill the
gaps in their ranks felt since 1660 and perhaps even return to the
numbers of the 1630s. The Jesuits could feel that the plot had been
Providential for them. It relieved them of embarrassing surpluses
of money and obligations in the south-east and midlands without
vitally impoverishing their other areas. Lastly missioners reported
an upsurge in conversions from 1681–2 (in some places from 1679).
Cynics had little doubt that the conversions and vocations had very
natural explanations: the conversions due to the imminence of the
succession of a Catholic King; the vocations to the establishment
of a string of clerical schools in England from 1679 and an influx
into the Colleges and convents abroad of the children of voluntary

exiles during the plot scare. Idealists were unconvinced. Prospective converts sharp enough to calculate political advantages must also have realised that the Duke of York had no son: he was in indifferent health and his heir was the Protestant Princess Mary. The Catholic monarchy was unlikely to last for more than a few years. Its political stay, the moderate Protestants, showed not the slightest disposition to yield any but insignificant offices to Catholics. The upsurges of vocations seemed mysterious indeed. The new schools in England—at Holywell in Lancashire, Osmotherley and Quosque in Yorkshire, at Twyford and Silkstead in Hampshire, at Wolverhampton, York and Hammersmith—really dated from the 1660s and had produced no significant increase in vocations before 1681–2.

Thus in 1685, as in 1660, the wisest of Catholics could not discern the future of the community. Meanwhile Charles II was dying. The Duke of York conferred with him. When the King was sure there was no hope, he consented to receive a Catholic priest. As the Anglican clergy were ushered out of the bedchamber, a toothless, shabby old man, John Huddleston, carrying a stole and an oil-bottle, was hurried in through a side-door from the antechamber in which he had long been kept waiting. He was a Benedictine who, many years before when a secular priest missioner in Staffordshire, had helped to shelter the King fleeing after the battle of Worcester. Huddleston was probably the best-known priest in England, since, by special royal orders, his name (and those of a few of his parishioners who had helped the fugitive King) had figured in every Act of Parliament or royal Proclamation concerning Catholics: they had been protected from all prosecutions and awarded pensions for life. Huddleston now received the King into the Catholic Church. The following morning the King died.

10. A Catholic King, 1685–88

On February 6th, 1685 the Catholic Duke of York was proclaimed as King James II. He enjoyed the goodwill of probably the majority of his Protestant subjects, who had recently battled and even suffered to preserve his rights of succession to the throne. The Catholic community greeted his accession with joy and expectation. During the last difficult years the thought of this day had sustained their courage. Yet just under four years later, on December 23rd, 1688, James II, a sick and shattered man muffled for disguise in a thick boat-cloak, was assisted ashore from a trawler at Ambleteuse in France as a fugitive who had been deprived of his throne.

His short reign was so packed with rapid changes of royal policy and extraordinary, even mad, royal decisions and appointments that ordinary citizens found it impossible to keep abreast of developments or to understand what was happening. For most Catholics it seems to have been an experience in which bewilderment, fear and exhilaration were mixed in equal proportions.

The reign began deceptively quietly. By slow, gentle stages, Catholics had restored to them the limited practical toleration they had enjoyed between 1660 and 1678. Court Catholicism was reconstituted and reassumed the subordinate position on the fringes of the Establishment allowed to it before 1678. The offices of State and of the King's Household remained solidly in the hands of Tory Protestants. The Anglican Chapel Royal functioned as usual as the spiritual centre of the government. This was all strikingly manifested by the Anglican coronation in Westminster Abbey, when James II and his devoutly Catholic second wife, Mary of Modena, submitted themselves to the Anglican service, Holy Communion excluded. Two anthems by the great Anglican composer, Henry Purcell, were sung. The coronation was only the first, and most obvious, of many small ways in which the Catholic King by protocol had to sit through Anglican prayers. It was typical also of the new order that some forty Catholic peers and peeresses were present at the coronation. The whole ceremony was organised, by hereditary right, by the Duke of Norfolk, an ex-Catholic. A few Catholic peers carried out minor duties in the service, Lord Montague as assistant Cupbearer, Lord Abergavenny as chief Laderer. There was no handout of titles and offices to Catholics. The King awarded military commissions to a small number, mostly in Ireland. Here and there a Papist civil servant, excluded in 1673, returned to minor office under letters of protection.

Queen Mary of Modena had her own Household and Catholic chapel in Whitehall, much like Catherine of Braganza, whose chapel was now transferred to Somerset House, though she was rarely there and it hardly functioned. The Queen's Household, by protocol, contained many Protestant officials, but, as before 1678, found room now for the Widdringtons, Carylls, Fairfaxes, Southcotts and Sheldons, Catholics who had served her when she was Duchess of York. On Sundays and holidays of obligation the King went in some state to Mass in the Queen's chapel. He did not communicate, since he was having a liaison with a Protestant mistress. Meanwhile, well after the coronation and with embarrassing difficulty and red tape, recusancy fining was quietly stopped and the 300 Catholic prisoners pardoned on the thin pretence that they had served Charles I during the civil wars. The King, not sure of the temper of the mostly Tory JPs, issued royal pardons and letters of protection wholesale to Catholic gentry. Unofficially, and not through the Establishment's ambassadorial service, the King accepted the appointment by Rome of John Leyburne, President of the English College, Douai (and a strong royalist Tory), as Vicar-Apostolic in England with powers which fell far short of Bishop Richard Smith's. Leyburne could be reasonably sure of royal subsidies and protection so long as he behaved circumspectly: he did not expect, or receive, any court position.

All of this was hardly the coming again of the Catholic religion which had figured since 1672 in the prayers of so many Catholics. In the summer of 1686 James II began to change his religious policy radically and head into a direct confrontation with the Protestant Establishment. The steps of this new policy were taken jerkily and piecemeal, as by a man very unsure of his ground but steeling himself for action. The King was indeed treading on thin ice. By his first wife he had had only two surviving children, the Princesses Mary and Anne, who were both devout Protestants and the heiresses to the throne, since Mary of Modena had no children, had last been pregnant in 1681, and seemed unlikely ever to conceive again. Hence any Catholic revolution which James could carry out had no chance of permanence. Also the King owed his throne to the Anglican Tories who controlled the government and who had exacted from him the severe limitations of tolerance of Catholics. They refused utterly to allow a repeal of the penal laws or even the Test Acts. The King had it in his power to dismiss from office all Tories and formally dispense Catholics from obedience to the Test Acts. In order to be effective these two actions would have to be very extensive indeed. Even if every Catholic peer and gentleman took one of the vacant offices, many would remain unfilled. Moreover this violent action and the wholesale use of the royal power of dispensation would precipitate a political and constitutional crisis so grave that it might issue in civil war. The Catholic community was so small that without many Protestant allies and much forbearance by the Tories the new policy had no hope whatever of success. There was little sign that Protestants in any numbers would go along with the King. His elder brother, Charles II, had been over all this ground thoroughly in the 1670s. He had been a far more able politician than James, and he had judged a Catholic revolution impossible.

Why therefore did James now attempt the impossible? A Protestant politician had said, in 1683, that he was 'more Catholic than the Pope'. In fact James was then a political Catholic. He was sincere about his adhesion to Catholicism, but his limited mentality appreciated only some aspects of it and was quite insensitive to its spiritual depths. By 1686 he was like an enraged bull. His simple, military mind appreciated stern discipline and a clear chain of command. He had abandoned Anglicanism for Catholicism because, as he gathered solely from simple Catholic catechisms and works of apologetic, Catholicism was a religion of authority with an impressive chain of command. He was never close enough to the realities of English Catholic life to grasp that its practice diverged remarkably from its theory. He also appreciated Catholic penitential discipline, compared with which Anglicanism seemed idealistically woolly. Now a year of experience as a Catholic King convinced him that his position was utterly intolerable. He was the prisoner of the Protestant Establishment, and his Catholicism gave him far less room for manoeuvre than did his brother's Church-popery. He could not really be a King until the Protestant Establishment was deprived of its power to check him: it would only lose that power when it became Catholic, or at least largely Catholic. He did not foresee that passing from a Protestant to a Catholic Establishment would merely be a change of his masters. His long experience in France (he had received his first military training under Turenne in the French Army) had taught him that a contemporary Catholic sovereign of a Catholic State could be, if strong-willed, more the master of the national Church than could an Anglican King. His French experience had also taught him that a weak or clericalist Catholic King could be mastered and led by the nose by clerics and religious parties. So James meant to stand no nonsense from English clericalists or Rome.

About the time of his decision to change his religious policy he went through a domestic crisis. The Queen remonstrated loudly with him about his mistress. With the help of Edward Petre, the Jesuit tutor of his illegitimate sons and a personal friend, James extricated himself. He did the decent thing and returned to the Catholic Sacraments, insisting on a dramatic break with his mistress, reconciliation with the Queen and physical penances. The royal conversion was merely formal: he now cohabited with the Queen, periodically fled to his Protestant mistress for solace and went immediately to Confession, and so was able to demonstrate to the sharp eyes of the courtiers a Catholic King who regularly communicated. He was pathetically grateful to Petre, almost the only priest with whom he felt any meeting of minds. The King began to press the Pope to make Petre a Cardinal and promoted him to the Royal Council. The Jesuit was later to be regarded by both Catholics and Protestants as James's evil genius and the promoter of his 'Popish Plot'. In fact Petre was a very run-of-the-mill Jesuit, innocent of any ambitious political schemings. The plot was the King's own idea. Petre's fault lay in his obtuseness, almost as great as James's, his conventionality, and complete failure to touch any real spiritual nerve in the King. James's real evil genius was the Earl of Sunderland, a sceptic and renegade Protestant Whig politician of great ambition, who gained his confidence and practical headship of the Council. Sunderland's mind did not move on a religious plane at all. He now went through a merely political conversion to Catholicism and assured the King that the new religious policy was bound to succeed, if only because many Protestants felt exactly as Sunderland did. He guaranteed that he would produce a long list of renegade Protestants, Anglican and Dissenting, ready to become Catholics in return for office.

James's *blitzkrieg* on the Protestant Establishment was spectacular. A Catholic Chapel Royal (the King's) was set up in Whitehall. The Anglican Chapel Royal was not closed, but it was starved of funds and encouragement. It wilted, and the Catholic Chapel flourished, with a larger choir—by no means all Catholic—more showy singing men (including a Jesuit of German origin and an Italian eunuch, Siface) and the Protestant violin-players attracted away from the Anglican Chapel. When the King was in residence

at Windsor Castle the Catholic Chapel went with him and similarly
reduced St George's Chapel there to insignificance. The one
Catholic Vicar-Apostolic gave way to four, and an Italian Papal
Nuncio was established in London and consecrated bishop in the
Chapel Royal. The King proposed to the Pope that he should have
no less than three Cardinals to dance attendance on him, d'Este
(the Queen's uncle, as Cardinal-Protector of England in Rome),
Philip Howard (as Royal Almoner in England) and Edward Petre.
James was furiously angry when the Pope rejected this plan.

The King appointed thirteen Catholics to his Council. Here, and
elsewhere in the government, it was simply impossible to find
enough Catholics to outnumber Protestants: there were still thirty
Protestant Councillors. The whole Council transacted formal business while policy was confined to a secret inner cabal of the
Catholic Councillors. Catholic Councillors of metal for the headship of departments of State hardly existed. Lord Arundell became
Lord Privy Seal and Lords Bellasis and Dover Treasury Commissioners, but these offices required little administrative skill (the
Lords had none). By the beginning of 1688 the main structures of
government in Whitehall remained Protestant, while the King
strove, through informal, amateur committees of Catholics, to
appropriate the making of policy. A secret committee of Catholic
lawyers devised all manner of highly ingenious ways of by-passing
government departments and the letter of the law. It was they who
devised a collusive lawsuit whereby the King drew a cover of
legality over his wholesale dispensations to Catholics to take offices
without subscribing to Oaths. It was they who invented a body of
royal Ecclesiastical Commissioners, entirely Anglican, which could
be used as a cover for introducing Catholics into posts hitherto
regarded as vital parts of the Anglican Establishment. A policy of
general religious toleration was proclaimed. To give it an appearance of reality, and to win the support of Dissenters, Protestant
Dissenters were freely dispensed from discriminatory laws. In the
name of the same policy, Anglican clergy were forbidden to preach
anti-Catholic sermons and even bishops were suspended and
prosecuted for disobedience. The Anglican monopoly of publishing
was breached. A Catholic Press was set up, with royal licence, in
Oxford. The King's printers in London and York, who both became
Catholic converts, started to publish Catholic books. A test-case
was launched to open the way for Catholics to matriculate and
graduate at the universities without submitting to Anglican formularies. A Catholic was made dean of Christ Church, Oxford;
another (a convert) was made head of University College, Oxford;
another became Master of Sidney Sussex College, Cambridge. But

the King planned a far bolder invasion of the Anglican preserves of Oxford. He found reasons to eject most of the Fellows of Magdalen College and replace them with Catholics, Jesuits, secular priests and ordinands imported from Douai. An Anglican see was kept vacant so that its income could provide a fund to aid the flood of convert clergymen the King expected. One convert parson was allowed to retain his Anglican benefice, though not to perform its duties.

In the realm of foreign policy similarly: the government's completely Protestant foreign service (apart from one career ambassador lately become a convert) stood idle while the King conducted his secret and bumbling foreign policy through special Catholic agents.

It was a matter of urgency that Catholics should be intruded in as large numbers as possible into the armed forces. Commissions were granted freely to the sons of Catholic peers and gentry. Catholic officers, English and Irish, in foreign armies were summoned home to get field rank. The Papist Lords Dover, Stafford, Bellasis, Carlingford, Hunsdon and Herbert became Colonels of regiments; the Irish Earl of Tyrconnel became a general. Catholic Army chaplains and military chapels appeared, quite in the French fashion, at Hounslow Heath, York and Portsmouth. The two main Army generals, the Earls of Feversham and Marlborough, were thought, with reason, to be open to persuasion to become Catholics. Feversham was a French Huguenot with Catholic connections and willing to appear at Catholic services. John Churchill, Earl of Marlborough, was ambitious, unscrupulous and very close to the King. His sister had been the King's favourite mistress, and the King's Catholic bastards were Marlborough's nephews. Even his formidably Protestant wife had a Catholic convert sister, Tyrconnel's wife. Hence by 1688 the Army had a Catholic tinge, though seven out of every eight of the officers and men were Protestants.

The legal profession was, for all its traditionally Catholic leanings, slow to yield to the King's persuasions. By 1688 only three, or perhaps four, judges were Catholics. When their Protestant fellows went in state to Anglican cathedrals on Assize days, the Catholic judges and trumpeters marched to Catholic chapels.

The assault on local government was, like a military operation, brutal and hasty. The King's secret committees prepared lists, county by county, of Catholics able to take office, of Protestants already in office and thought to be indulgent towards the King's proceedings, and of recalcitrant Protestant officials. The latter were generally dismissed from office; the first two classes were promoted. Catholic peers became the Lords-Lieutenant of a dozen counties. Catholic gentry filled up about a third of most county benches of JPs. Catholic gentry filtered into Recorderships, customerships, stewardships, sheriffdoms. In the corporate towns by 1688 it was common for a quarter or even a third of the Aldermen to be Catholics. Three or four cities had Catholic Mayors.

The sharply political eyes of the King and Lord Sunderland were fixed, not on the Catholics, but on the supposedly fellow-traveller Protestants. Some ways must be found of speeding their conversion to Catholicism. Both took a cynical view of the operation. They knew, like John Aubrey and any courtier, how many respectable, office-holding Anglicans had, of late years, spoken complacently of 'turning' if the Catholic religion came in. Even the Earl of Rochester, the model High Anglican layman, had received John Sergeant in his country house at Swallowfield in Berkshire. The Bishop of Salisbury, Aubrey's friend, spoke carelessly of turning. The Bishop of Chester was ready to offer hospitality to the Catholic Bishop Leyburne and his chaplains. The King therefore, through the inevitable committees, lavished money and influence to push the Catholic missioners into founding Catholic chapels and schools in as many strategic places as possible, as soon as possible.

Catholicism had originally been very thin on the ground in towns. Since the 1660s small congregations had begun to coalesce, particularly in county towns. They owed their existence to two factors: the financial losses and decline suffered by the poorer Catholic gentry, who now often took refuge in the professions or trade, and the growing fashion of the higher Catholic gentry for spending the winter-season in London or provincial capitals. The age of real urban industrialism had not yet come, but the seventeenth century saw the beginnings of semi-urban industrial areas connecting a market town and a good many adjacent villages, all filled increasingly with workshops and forges. Small Catholic congregations with chapels appeared before 1685 in such areas, around Newcastle and Hexham in Northumberland, round Sheffield in Yorkshire, and round Wolverhampton in Staffordshire. Catholic chapels—as distinct from temporary Mass-centres located in the garrets of country houses of gentry or farmers—appeared modestly from the 1660s, usually in the upstairs rooms of houses rented by missioners. The King now encouraged the superiors of the clergy, secular and regular, to speed on the process of establishing chapels more adventurously. As the local authorities became in part Catholic, it was safe to move existing chapels into more strategic places. Gentry were encouraged to build chapels beside their mansions, even separating them from the missioner's house and making them one-storey buildings with a larger seating space. In cities and towns royal ingenuity procured the use of quite prominent houses or halls which could be easily converted into Catholic chapels. The King clearly wanted Catholics to drop the appearance of back-street Dissenters and boldly, in stone, bricks and mortar, challenge Anglican worship face to face. Since the 1670s country Catholics had, as we have seen, dreamed of ousting their parsons from the old churches and intruding 'our priests'. The King also, for political and prestige reasons, wanted wherever possible to recover to Catholic use medieval chapels and churches.

All over the country, in Hexham and Newcastle on Tyne, in York and Pontefract, in Durham, in Preston, in Wolverhampton, Birmingham, Edgbaston, Tamworth and Brewood, in Abergavenny, Monmouth and Hereford, in Worcester, in Bath and Gloucester, in St Albans, Bury St Edmunds and Norwich, in Oxford and Cambridge, in Lincoln, in Warwick and Leominster, in Manchester, in Winchester and Windsor, Catholics set up open chapels. So, for instance, in Newcastle on Tyne the seculars, Jesuits and Dominicans had long maintained tiny upstairs chapels, often changing location to avoid notice. In 1686 they all hired larger premises with down-stairs chapels, organs and a Jesuit day school. The Benedictines joined them, hastily improvising premises, priest and fittings as impressive as they could afford. In York well before 1685 there had been various tiny, hidden chapels and a girls' school run with a convent in a heavily camouflaged private house by the Mary Ward Institute. By 1686 the seculars had leased a large house in the Liberty of St Peter, the close beside York Minster, and established there a chapel big enough to cause remark. The Franciscans moved from their cramped quarters in a backstreet to a large friary and school in a main street. The Mary Ward sisters bought a bigger house strategically placed just outside one of the city 'Bars' and in the country gentry's main residential area. A Jesuit missioner arrived in the city bearing a royal lease of the Crown property of the King's Manor, then incomparably the finest public building in the city and once the headquarters of the Council of the North. There the Jesuit fitted up the great hall as a Catholic chapel with organ, and opened a boys' school. In London from 1660 Catholic chapels had proliferated, though few were more than single bedchambers in rented houses, and most changed location frequently. From 1686, with the pace set by the King's and Queen's splendid Chapels in Whitehall, the ambassadors of the Catholic rulers were urged to enlarge their chapels, take on English-speaking priests, and throw open their doors to Londoners. In the Savoy, in Clerkenwell, in Lincoln's Inn Fields, Gray's Inn and even the Tower of London (a military chapel) Jesuits, Dominicans, Franciscans (all with boys' schools), Benedictines and seculars moved into more imposing premises. The King's urgings

persuaded the Jesuits (and perhaps the Franciscans) to advertise
their schools amongst Protestants and to take in Protestant
pupils.

In spite of James II's obtuseness and Sunderland's cynicism, this
hasty and often shakily improvised Catholic effort would have
achieved a fair success if the King's reign had lasted another ten
years. Anglican Protestantism had, indeed, a rock-like solidity.
The majority of educated English people would never have accepted
Catholicism. But there was a very substantial minority of Protestants who were vulnerable to attack. During the Popish plot crisis
there had begun a small wave of conversions to Catholicism,
drawn from every band in the spectrum of English Protestantism,
from amongst High Church Anglicans, former Whig zealots, former
Dissenters, and very nominal Anglicans. After 1686 the wave
increased in size. It included political converts (Lord Sunderland,
the Earl of Yarmouth, Sir Thomas Stradling, Sir Nicholas Butler,
Sir Thomas Wright) who smartly reverted to Anglicanism after
1688. But most of the converts of 1686–8 were sincere and stood
to their new religion bravely in the face of imprisonment, ostracism
or even ruin.

John Dryden was the most able and vocal of Jacobean converts.
He had been brought up a Puritan, and, as a Dissenter newly down
from Cambridge, took a post in Oliver Cromwell's civil service.
During the 1660s and 1670s he became a highly fashionable playwright and poet. He moved in a London society where people of all
faiths and sceptics rubbed shoulders familiarly. His aristocratic
wife's relations were mostly Catholics. He knew William Wycherley, probably a lapsed Catholic, while Dryden's best friend, John
Oldham, had written a verse *Satires upon the Jesuits*. Dryden's
successful plays were mostly bawdy. He attended meetings of the
Royal Society. He was fascinated and influenced for life by the
new philosophy of that arch-freethinker, Thomas Hobbes. By 1682
Dryden was caught up into the mood of his Tory Anglican friends.
His *Religio Laici* was an elegant and sincere, if light-weight,
defence of their rejection of the infallibilist absolutisms of both
Papists and rigid Protestants. In 1684 his rejection of orthodox
Protestantism was sealed by his reading of the Biblical criticism of
Richard Simon, a French Oratorian priest. In 1685 he put himself under the instruction of James Corker, a convert Benedictine
missioner in Clerkenwell, and became a Catholic. *The Hind and
the Panther* tried to expound his reasons. He retained for good his
total inability to base his faith on mystical experience. He was no
Pascal, George Fox or Bunyan. He had no illusions about the
actualities of Rome and English Catholicism. He did not share the

belief in a Catholic revolution of James II or militant Catholics. 'The Hind' (the Catholic Church) is the prey of 'the Panther' (the Church of England) and is: 'doomed to death, though fated not to die...'

Dryden was already Poet Laureate and he gained little or nothing materially from his conversion. At the Revolution of 1688 he lost the Laureateship and his pension. His wife became insane. His Catholic sons were exiles abroad. Yet he stuck to his Catholicism to the end. *The Hind and the Panther* gives one glimpse of his positive motive:

> One in herself, not rent by schism, but sound,
> Entire, one solid shining diamond:
> Not sparkles shattered into sects like you;
> One is the church, and must be to be true,
> One central principle of unity.

The tone is sincere, but the sentiments are hackneyed and second-hand. Though so capable of expression in other ways, he was deserted by his genius when he faced the most ultimate realities.

A conversion which caused even more stir in society was that of Lady Theophila Nelson, a daughter of the Earl of Berkeley, and wife of Robert Nelson, a devout High Anglican layman and the author of devotional manuals. Lady Theophila remained firm in her new Catholicism after 1688. Perhaps her husband followed her lead. They both certainly lived by choice in Italy in their old age. Henry Hills, the King's London printer, faced loss of his royal warrant and business after 1688 with equanimity. His son became a secular priest. Stephen Bulkeley, the convert York printer, persevered in business after 1688. Amongst convert Oxford dons, Matthew Tindal (Fellow of All Souls) later fell away into rampant secularism, but Obadiah Walker (head of University College, ejected in 1689 and became a private tutor), John Massey and Robert Charnock persevered in Catholicism. Joshua Basset, the convert Master of Sidney Sussex College, Cambridge, lost all in 1688 and died a Catholic in obscurity and poverty. There were convert clergymen or clergymen's sons who were equally resolute: John Bromley of Shropshire married and became a printer and schoolmaster; 'Mr Butler' of Northamptonshire was the father of a secular priest; Edward Burgis became a Dominican, Nathaniel Cook subscribed £10 to the Yorkshire secular clergy Fund.

There were resolute convert aristocrats. The oddest of these was James Cecil, 4th Earl of Salisbury. His grandfather had been a Parliamentarian during the civil wars and Republic; his father was

rampantly Whig during the Popish plot crisis. The 4th Earl was
notoriously eccentric. He was very fat, totally incapable of manag-
ing his large properties, and married without issue to a London
tradesman's daughter. He left his young wife in the broken-down
splendour of Hatfield House, Hertfordshire while he travelled the
Continent and became a Catholic in Rome. After 1688 he endured
every kind of privation—huge financial losses, imprisonment in
the Tower, public scorn, a murderous affray between two of his
brothers—firmly without abandoning his faith. Of the other aristocratic converts, the Countess of Tyrconnel, a reigning court beauty
from a stiffly Anglican family, founded a convent in Dublin in her
old age; the 2nd Earl of Peterborough, a gouty old soldier of a
family with Catholic antecedents, was imprisoned and taunted after
1688; the Earls of Melfort and Perth were Anglicised Scots who
went into exile with James II; Charles Carteret came of a solidly
Anglican Guernsey family. There were convert country squires
from a Tory background turned stubborn Catholics (Sir Edward
Hales and Sir John Curson) and middle-class officials who faced
ruin in 1688 (Sir Christopher Milton, a Judge, John Hill, Mayor
of Gloucester, Jonathan Moone, a Scarborough customs officer).

If the types of person converted were various, so were the
processes of conversion. Some, for instance the Duke of Richmond
and the Earl of Salisbury, became Catholics abroad. Some, like
Obadiah Walker, had been hovering on the brink of conversion for
years. Some, like Lady Tyrconnel, were affected by marriage to a
Catholic; others, for instance the Earl of Salisbury and perhaps
Lady Nelson were happily married to spouses who did not share
their attraction to Catholicism. Some converted themselves; others
fell to direct attacks by Catholic priests and friends. The Catholics,
both missioners and laity, were so often themselves converts or the
products of families of mixed religion that they were usually well-
informed about the psychology and beliefs of Protestants. Official
Catholic teaching on evangelism was complex. The Jesuits had a
reputation for thoroughgoing proselytism. But a widely-used Jesuit
set of instruction notes on the subject issued in the 1650s says firmly
that a missioner has 'no grave obligation' to attend the sick and
dying in England if they are not known certainly to be practising
Catholics: '. . . priests are easily excused the obligation in England
because commonly there is almost no hope of converting heretics.'
Yet the author presumes that missioners have a constant grave
obligation to attend to the reconciliation of persons who were
lapsed Catholics, had some Catholic family background, or who,
though practising Anglicans, had shown signs of interest in Catholicism:

Are heretics and schismatics not yet reconciled to be admitted to attend Mass? Answer: Schismatics of a Catholic mind and others who are believed never to have been anti-Catholic (and of this sort I think there are many in England) can be admitted to Mass as prudence directs.

Before 1685 conversion work amongst such persons was carried on everywhere. The 'obit' lists of priests contain numerous references to missioners who were especially successful. Thus amongst Franciscans, old Francis Davenport, who died in London in 1680, was a great maker of conversions, Francis Osbaldeston (died 1686) was 'very zealous in the conversion of souls', and Martin Grimston (died 1729) converted many, especially in Westmorland and Cumberland. Amongst the Benedictines Edward Llewellyn, a convert Headmaster of Pocklington Grammar School, Yorkshire, and James Corker, Dryden's priest, were successful proselytisers. The Benedictine Richard Huddleston (uncle of Charles II's priest, John Huddleston), who died in 1655, converted a string of a dozen Yorkshire and Lancashire gentry families. In 1688 his nephew published Richard's *A Short and Plain Way to the Faith and Church* which had been circulating in manuscript copies for many years with great effect, especially on Charles II. The Franciscan mission in Birmingham never had more than a dozen practising Catholic families, yet the average rate of reconciliations of the lapsed and conversions from 1660 to 1700 was between thirty and forty a year.

The Catholic clergy were thus prepared for James II's drive for conversions. They were, however, embarrassed by his demands for speed and boldness. Boldness could often, as they knew from long experience, be counter-productive. England was littered with lapsed converts. In 1686 an over-zealous Catholic physician in York lost almost all his Protestant patients because he systematically urged them to receive the visit of a missioner. James II positively repelled some of his Anglican courtiers by sending priests to visit them. Speed of conversions was difficult when there was still a shortage of clergy: vocations were increasing, but the full seminaries would begin to affect the missions only in the 1690s. The Jesuits, decimated by the plot crisis, were particularly short of men. All clerical groups tried to make do by hurrying to England Irish or foreign priests (the Franciscans imported a dozen Belgians) and ordinands to be used as school teachers. The clergy directed their main effort, as tradition required, to the lapsed and to schismatics of a Catholic mind. As a result, by 1688, they could report a real, if modest, degree of success and the hope of a few thousand conversions by the 1690s. Their new, more open chapels and schools were certainly crowded, and the adults and children coming in were often nominal Protestants.

The early stages of the drive come to light in the records of Bishop Leyburne's Confirmation tour of 1687. Since 1558 most English Catholics had died without the sacrament of Confirmation. An episcopal Confirmation tour was an immense novelty. It could hardly be a secret operation. The bishop, his chaplains and servants, travelled in a clumsy, springless coach with wide wheels. He took fourteen weeks to cover sixty Confirmations, passing from London through Northamptonshire and Lincolnshire into York-shire, on through county Durham and Northumberland and over into Cumberland and Westmorland, then down through Cheshire, Lancashire, Staffordshire and Warwickshire back to London. Catholics and their families moved across country for miles to crowd the small chapels or camp beside them. Some missed the bishop at one place and pursued him. The Confirmations must have been conducted on a shift-system in chapels in towns. In the country, where chapels were tiny and patrons unwilling to have their houses and grounds entered and trampled by crowds of strangers, the Confirmations must have been conducted in a medieval fashion out of doors. In Chester Leyburne was housed amicably in the Anglican episcopal palace. In Lancashire he conducted five Con-firmations each of over 1000 persons and another, equally large, in Durham. He confirmed 21,000 persons outside London and possibly some 30,000 in all, though he had no time to visit wide areas, for instance Wales and the west, the southern counties and East Anglia. His lists are stuffed with familiar surnames of practising Catholics. But they also contain a great many names either unidentified as previously Catholic. or of families known to have been Protestant or formerly Catholic. This was particularly true of the confirmees at chapels attached to the new town schools. In York Sir John Reresby, an Anglican Tory administrator, observed the events of these years closely. He was especially vulnerable to the drive. His family was in the process of throwing off the Catholicism it had embraced before the civil wars. He had Catholic relations and a brother who had become a Catholic in Spain. Sir John's attitude was an odd mixture of unwilling interest and disgust. He professed to know of only three Catholic converts in York by 1688. He commented sourly that it was absurd to have six Catholic chapels in a city which only had sixty fully-resident Catholics. There were at least fifteen priests and a dozen Mary Ward sisters. But he was quite foxed by the crowds of Catholic or part-Catholic country gentry lodging in the city and the unknown, but apparently large, numbers of schoolchildren arriving from all quarters to fill the new Jesuit and Franciscan schools.

The reactions of Catholics to the King's new religious policy were inevitably mixed. Here and there a few Catholic gentry refused appointments as JPs; a few, deliberately or by chance, stayed overseas. There was a disposition amongst at least some of the Catholic leaders (Lords Bellasis, Arundell and Dover and Bishop Leyburne) to protest more or less bluntly against the reckless speed and aggressiveness of the King's actions. Up to November 1687 it appeared certain that James II would be succeeded on the throne by his elder daughter, the Princess Mary. She and her husband, William, Prince of Orange, were Protestants. A precipitate Catholic drive would only invite an equally strong Protestant backlash when James II died. Leyburne counselled discretion. The Pope urged caution. Moreover the mental attitude of priests and instructed Catholic laity during these years was almost Calvinist in its pessimism and starkness. This spirit is well conveyed by the spiritual motto written by a Winchester secular priest, John Churcher, on the flyleaves of his books: *Nemo nisi post obitum felix*. (No one is happy until he is dead.) Or there is the ruling agreed on by the Hampshire secular clergy at a meeting in 1686: 'Agreed that eating Harts-horn jelly on fasting days be not allowed.' Or there is the minute of a discussion of the clergy at a meeting of the Yorkshire Brethren in 1686:

> At the Talbot at Yorke 22 Sept: 1686. Tho' this summer has bin god be thanked indifferent seasonable for weather, yet I dare say many of the more conscientious sort have suffered much for not working on some holydayes, when their corne has bin shaking, their haye layd at losse &c. Other less conscientious have fallen to it I fear in bad fayth. Nor is it only losse in their haye or corne people suffer, but in their workfolke whom to the number of 3, 4 or 5, a poore farmer must keepe in meat, drinke & wages to sitt still; or else they will goe to others and come no more at him ...

There was no easy triumphalism here. Yet, on the other hand, especially after the announcement in November 1687 that the Queen, after a royal pilgrimage to the Holy Well of St Winefride in Wales, was pregnant, and the birth of a healthy son in June 1688, most Catholics accepted a part in the King's operations. Many could not resist a strong feeling that Providence was overruling the King's folly and opening a way to a great Catholic triumph. Protestants complained that in many places Catholics were behaving with a new confident sense of *droit de cité*. Amongst both Catholics and Protestants, by the spring of 1688, there was an atmosphere of acute tension. On both sides the prudent were terrified that something awful, perhaps civil war, must be the outcome. This seventeenth century, with its constant political 'revolutions' (the term was born at this time) and alternations of physical disaster (plague, war, climatic disturbances, gales, catastrophic fires) and untold comfort was enervating and disturbing.

The tension probably helped to account for the renewal of strife amongst the clergy. Leyburne's appointment was bitterly resented by the Clergy Chapter. The four Vicars-Apostolic of 1688 were not received easily by Catholics. The bishops had difficulty in getting acceptance and houseroom. James Smith (once President of Douai), Vicar-Apostolic of the northern district, needed all his considerable private means to house himself and the Yorkshire, Lancashire and northern Brethren did not take kindly to his suggestion that they should hand over mission funds to him. Michael Ellis, the highly sophisticated convert Benedictine western Vicar-Apostolic, was a favoured preacher at Whitehall, but unacceptable to the western clergy. Bonaventure Gifford of the midland district was also James II's choice as President of Magdalen College, Oxford. Leyburne, now of the London district, where his northern bluntness was not understood, disliked Gifford and the Magdalen College project. The lay patrons regarded the Vicars-Apostolic with wary alarm remembering Bishop Richard Smith. The opening of chapels and schools provided abundant material for a renewal of the old clerical quarrels. The Jesuit chapel and school in the Savoy in London was previously an Embassy chapel served by secular priests who resented their ejection. The seculars accused the Jesuits of seizing two other chapels, one by force and guile. The Benedictines had long nursed ambitions of annexing back the medieval monastic sites. Ever since the 1620s, against that day, they had granted senior monks such honorary titles as Abbot of Westminster, Abbott of St Albans, Prior of Durham, Cathedral-Prior of Norwich. It was an ambition which others shared. Before 1685 the Franciscans had acquired the sites of medieval friaries in York and elsewhere, shrines at Osmotherley, Yorkshire, and Holy Well in Wales, and claims to the Holy Mountain near Abergavenny and St Michael's Mount in Cornwall. Northern secular priests had their eyes on York Minster and the old parish churches. Here and there, between 1686 and 1688, medieval manorial chapels, practically abandoned by the Anglicans, were taken over and fitted up for worship by Catholics. By 1686 the Benedictines became convinced that the Jesuits intended to annex St Albans Abbey and other medieval monastic sites and protested. Bishop Ellis's attempt to pour oil on the troubled waters by publicly disavowing any Catholic attempt to take over Anglican property was not kindly received by his brethren.

For their part, the Catholic peers and gentry had little time to adjust their often slow-moving minds to their new situation. Little has been recorded of their feelings. Some of them were, however hesitantly, kept very busy at administrative duties: Lord Arundell at the Council chamber and Privy Seal Office; Powis (now elevated to a Marquisate) as a Councilor and Lord-Lieutenant of Cheshire; Fairfax as chief government manager in Yorkshire; Bellasis in the Council and Treasury and the Army; Waldegrave as Comptroller of the Royal Household, Lord-Lieutenant of Somerset and Recorder of Taunton; Molyneux as Lord-Lieutenant and Custos Rotulorum of Lancashire; Dover as a Councillor, Lord-Lieutenant of Cambridgeshire and Colonel of Horse Guards; Melfort as Scottish Secretary; Tyrconnel as Lord-Lieutenant of Ireland; Castlemaine, d'Albeville (an Irishman who was a French Marquis) and Lord Thomas Howard as diplomatic envoys; Hunsdon, Herbert and Stafford as regimental Colonels. But a surprisingly large number of Catholic peers were left virtually unemployed: the Duke of Richmond, the Earls of Cardigan, Portland (in Flanders, bankrupt), Rivers, Salisbury, Lords Dunbar, Langdale, Gerard, Abergavenny, Baltimore, Derwentwater, Castlehaven, Widdrington, Stourton and Clifford. In some cases this unemployment was due to their youth or obvious incapacity of wits or fortune. It was not often due to any feeling of opposition to the King's policies. Indeed Salisbury, Derwentwater and Widdrington were hearty supporters of them.

The Papist country gentry of consequence were employed in government service almost to a man. In each county the unemployed amongst them appear to have been all minors, notorious fools (though some of those found employment) or lunatics. The adult children of the Papist gentry had never been so abundantly employed as they were now, as Army officers, barristers, court officials, diplomatic envoys, customs or town officials, ladies-in-waiting. The letters and diaries of men like Edward Dicconson and William Blundell of Lancashire and Sir Miles Stapleton of Yorkshire show that, whether they were, by inclination, confirmed countrymen or courtiers, they took the astonishing developments of 1686–8 in their stride. They were too busily occupied with county administration, estate business, seeking offices for their family, to have time to feel either alarmed or elated about the future.

11. The Glorious Revolution, 1688–1714

'The Glorious Revolution' of 1688 and the complete overthrow of James II, the Catholic monarchy and James's religious policies stemmed from the birth in Whitehall on June 10th, 1688, of a healthy son, James Francis Edward, to the King and Queen. Shortly after the birth the new Prince of Wales was baptised by Catholic rites. This was the first Catholic royal baptism in England (if we except the secret Catholic baptism of Charles I's daughter, the Princess Henrietta, at Exeter during the first civil war, without her father's knowledge) since the early sixteenth century. It signified the indefinite continuation of the Catholic monarchy and destroyed the certainty of Protestants that James's policies would automatically be reversed at his death.

The birth did not take place in the usual full glare of publicity simply because the Queen had been modestly secretive about the progress and timing of her pregnancy, and many Protestant courtiers were absent from the palace, expecting the birth some weeks later. In these circumstances, it was not surprising that a legend swiftly grew up that the birth was a fraud. The most widely believed rumour was that a foundling child had been smuggled into the palace hidden inside a copper warming-pan. Few Protestants really believed the legend or the rumour. But the birth came as a severe shock to them and they naturally sought any means of escaping from the unpleasant truth.

Ever since 1660 the Protestant Establishment had rebuilt itself on the twin principles of the sacredness of hereditary succession to the throne and the mortal sinfulness of armed rebellion. Those principles had been challenged in 1678–83 by Shaftesbury and the Whigs, seeking to exclude the Duke of York from succession to the throne because he was a Catholic. Even so, the Whigs had used every possible argument to prove that they were only modifying, not upsetting, the sacred principles. Charles II and the Tories, by far the majority of the peers and gentry, had successfully beaten off this challenge and reasserted even more strongly the two sacred principles. It seemed therefore that the birth of the Prince of Wales in 1688 had tied the hands of Protestant opponents of James II's policies. Neither he nor the Prince could possibly be excluded from the throne, and resistance which could be construed as rebellion was immoral. Moreover the King was a trained soldier and had a regular army which he was in process of increasing from 20,000 to 30,000 men.

The more militant Protestant politicians decided to use armed rebellion, disguised as a political demonstration. On June 30th seven Whig and Tory leaders signed an invitation to the Prince of Orange to assume control of the kingdom, promising him every assistance. It was natural that, amongst the signatories and their unseen supporters, there should have been ex-Catholics or Protestants with some Catholic background. The aristocracy was closely intermarried and few of their families had escaped some Catholic infiltration since 1600. Of the signatories Lord Shrewsbury and Lord Lumley had once been Catholics, and Danby and Bishop Compton had Catholic relatives. Among the supporters, the Duke of Beaufort had been a Catholic. Meanwhile a form of General Strike was organised. Grand Juries were set up to challenge the legality of the orders of all Catholic officials. Protestant JPs were encouraged to refuse to work alongside Catholics. Mass demonstrations were launched, especially in London.

By October 1688 James II, with military decision, sharply reversed his policies. Catholics were dismissed wholesale from all but military and private court offices. They were cleared out of the universities and Anglican offices. There was a superb military decisiveness about this action. But its results were disastrous. Catholics were demoralised, since their hopes had so recently been built up to a peak by the royal birth. They were not soldiers, and could not but feel betrayed by the King. Protestants were not reassured by the reversal of policy, since the King did not assemble a Parliament or disband his forces. In October the Prince of Orange sailed with an army for England while, in the north and west, Protestant militant leaders secretly organised for war and to engineer desertions from the Army. The King received, and, indeed, sought, few offers of service from Catholics other than his devoted court officials. The great majority of Protestants were also determined to be nervous spectators of the coming struggle. They hoped against hope that by some miracle, without fighting the King would collapse or flee the country.

In November the Prince landed. Ironically, his forces probably

contained at least as many Catholics (mainly Dutch) as those of
James II. Ironically also, the Prince was the political ally of the
Pope. There was no fighting, apart from one minor skirmish
between cavalry outposts in the suburbs of Reading. The King's
Army began to dissolve as its Protestant generals deserted to
Orange and the Irish regiments ran into great popular hostility.
James II collapsed in a fit of nervous prostration and heavy nose-
bleeding. He was outraged by the desertion of his younger daughter,
the Princess Anne, and of some of his most trusted aides. Most of
all he felt the hostility of his elder daughter, Mary, the wife of the
Prince of Orange. The King's simple, conventional mind regarded
all rebellion with an intense moral detestation: the rebellion of his
children was an ultimate in evil. Strangely enough his daughters
were sufficiently the products of his breeding to feel the same way.
They turned against their father after agonising scruples of conscience, convinced that their Protestant duty came before their duty
as children and subjects. But though the decision was made and
acted on, both women suffered agonies of guilt for the rest of their
lives. In varying degrees educated English people shared the feeling.
Later generations talked lightly of 'the Glorious Revolution of
1688'. The generation which took part in or lived during the
revolution felt so guilty about it that they had a compulsive need to
justify to themselves and the world their part in it. The easiest and
commonest type of justification was to argue that James II voluntarily abdicated and was insane, so there was really no revolution
at all.

When Orange's forces entered London, the King was put under
house arrest. He was then provoked into flight abroad. Mob
violence against Catholics had already begun. In London and most
other towns Catholic chapels and schools were looted or burned.
Some country chapels were attacked. Here and there mobs and
informers hunted for priests and a few unlucky Catholics, especially
Irish soldiers attempting to escape back to Ireland, were beaten up.
With a skill born of practice, Catholic peers, gentry and missioners
went to ground. Warrants were issued by Orange's provisional
government for the arrest of the four Vicars-Apostolic. Leyburne
was taken and sent to the Tower of London, Gifford and Ellis went
to Newgate gaol. James Smith, Vicar-Apostolic of the northern
district, escaped arrest by going to ground smartly at Wycliffe
Hall amongst friends. Wycliffe was strategically placed in a legal
no-man's-land between county Durham and Yorkshire and so
peculiarly free of molestation by local authorities. In 1690 the three
imprisoned bishops were released on bail, without being brought to
trial. Ellis was so shattered by his experiences that he withdrew

abroad, though he did not resign his Vicariate until 1705. Relatively
few missioners were gaoled. In London there were a dozen arrested,
of whom one, the Jesuit superior of the Savoy chapel, died in
prison. In York five missioners spent a year or two in the Castle
gaol. Almost all these priests were released on bail without trial,
some after a few weeks. A few dozen clergy hastily left England.
Some had particular reasons (for instance Edward Petre and
James Corker) for fearing reprisals. Others were especially strong
Jacobites—supporters of James II's rights to rule. Others were
foreigners or seminarists posted temporarily to the mission during
James II's drive. The Benedictines were caught napping by the
sudden dispersal of their two communities in London at Somerset
House and Clerkenwell. The thirty monks hastily shipped to
France were temporarily accommodated in their Congregation's
Paris monastery, while its community was uncomfortably boarded
out. The Jesuits and Franciscans shipped overseas were more easily
settled, some in foreign houses of their Orders at St-Germain-en-
Laye in France, beside the château loaned by Louis XIV to the
exiled James II. The Franciscan obituary of Nicholas of the Holy
Cross of Derbyshire explains:

> After 43 years of labour in the Mission, after many imprison-
> ments, after exile in Scotland and Brabant, at last, as a result
> of that bloody and fatal persecution which destroyed the Lord's
> vineyard, he accompanied the most Serene Queen Mary (to
> whom he was chaplain and most dear) into France in 1688 and
> resided in the Court of St. Germain en Laye.

The writer of the obituary was carried away by his rhetoric. The
Catholic clerical alarums and excursions of 1688 were minor compared with those of the Popish plot crisis. After a few months of
Protestant fury proceedings against missioners ended. They emerged
from their hiding-places and resumed work. Town and country
chapels, whether wrecked or not, were quickly re-established,
usually in less conspicuous premises. The large schools for Protestant sympathisers were naturally discontinued. The older, smaller
Catholic schools, and a few begun in 1686–8, restarted in quieter
places. Most significantly the Chapters and assemblies of missioners
took place as usual in 1689. The temporary break in episcopal rule
passed almost unnoticed. The Vicars-Apostolic had not been in
their places long enough to make their presence felt or their absence
missed.

It was otherwise with the Catholic laity. The peers and major
gentry clearly expected big trouble. So many of them fled overseas

(more than in 1678–83) that they had trouble in finding accommodation abroad. The novices and junior nuns of the English Benedictine convent at Pontoise in France complained of the inordinate length of time they had to spend in the attics while lady refugees from England occupied their cells. Half of the Catholic peers went overseas. Some, who were directly in James II's service, gravitated to St-Germain-en-Laye, where, apart from the excitements of the King's unfortunate military expedition to Ireland in 1690, they lived in discomfort and acute boredom. The King, now a sick man, decided on another 'decent thing'. He underwent a very formal conversion to penitential devotion. The château was organised like a religious house. Attendance at frequent services, including prolonged Expositions of the Sacrament and of relics (especially those of St Macarius of Egypt, thought to preserve the Prince of Wales from the family ailment, convulsions) was compulsory. Ladies were dragooned and veiled. Here were assembled a dozen peers. If we add James II's two illegitimate sons, the Dukes of Berwick and Albemarle—the one a distinguished soldier, the other living on French Church benefices though a layman—and a dozen Catholic and Protestant gentry ennobled by James II at St Germain we get a glimpse of the Jacobite Court in its early years of splendour. The King was still regarded by Louis XIV as a valuable political asset. Though Jacobitism was officially taboo in England and the country was at war with France, a Jacobitism compounded of religious principle, sentiment and guilt-feelings was strong even in the highest quarters. English Protestant politicians, in or out of office, mostly took care to maintain secret links with St Germain. Half a dozen other Catholic peers and peeresses resided elsewhere on the Continent, partly because they had no offices at St Germain and partly because they detested its rigours. Some of these, like the Duchess of Richmond, who was doing penance intermittently for her lurid past, resident in Paris, and the Earl of Carlingford (killed in action at the battle of the Boyne) were strongly Jacobite. Others, like Lord Teynham, settled with his family for years in Belgium, or Lord Widdrington, moving in a coach round France pretending to be a tourist, were successfully avoiding the Acts of Attainder (convictions *in absentia* of treason, with confiscation of all property in England) which the London government inflicted now on Jacobites who were political or military activists.

The ranks of the exiles included quite numerous Catholic gentry. Some hundreds, if we count their wives and children, lived at St Germain or manned James II's embassies in foreign capitals. They included people drawn from every shire and mourning the loss, by Attainder, of their manor houses and estates: Sheldons of

Warwickshire, Dormers of Oxfordshire, Phelipses of Hampshire, Carterets of Jersey and Guernsey, Hales of Kent, Stricklands of Westmorland and Yorkshire, Widdringtons of Northumberland, Coxes of Kent, Carylls of Sussex, Jerninghams of Norfolk. Living elsewhere on the Continent were Catholic Army officers thrown out of work by the collapse of James II's forces—Fermors, Dormers, Sheldons, Fairfaxes, Widdringtons, Lawsons, Flemings, Constables —and Catholic university graduates, like John Dryden's three sons living in Rome in the service of Cardinal Howard, equally shut out of preferment in England. The war in Ireland took some of these young men; Edward Widdrington killed at the Boyne, Sir James Phelips dead of fever in Cork. Others joined the French or Spanish or Austrian armies (the new Earl of Carlingford was eventually a Field Marshal in the Emperor's service), depending on the strength of their Jacobite convictions. At least one, Charles Lawson of Brough, Yorkshire, returned to England, gained a commission in the British Army in the Earl of Monmouth's Regiment and died in action in Germany fighting for William III. The English Catholic exiles often had large families and problems in finding them careers. Mary of Modena busied herself particularly in this matter. In 1706 she wrote to the French Bishop of Valence thanking him for his backing of her request that the bearer, 'a young English Lady, the daughter of Sir Carteret, a servant of the King with a numerous family' should be received as a nun into the convent of the Visitation at Valence. Of Sir Charles Carteret's other children, two became Jesuits, one a Benedictine, and one a secular priest and canon of Lille, by Mary of Modena's patronage. The Jacobites had greater difficulties in finding marriage-partners. Their restricted circle offered little choice and some parents, expecting return to England in triumph, disapproved of marriage to French or Irish suitors.

The flavour of this early Jacobitism in exile defies analysis. It is a long-lost cause whose records are buried in foreign, mostly French, archives, military and ecclesiastical, where the awkward English surnames and titles are mutilated by French clerks. It was a cause which, in spite of the rampant Catholicism of its royal family, still had adherents who were in the majority solid Anglicans. The ideology of Jacobitism was, for all its associations with Catholicism in the minds of James II and his Catholic supporters, not specifically Catholic. From 1688 there were pious Catholics who seem to have identified Jacobitism with militant Catholic revolution. As the Jacobite cause decayed in failure, they, with their almost Calvinist pessimism, readily identified Jacobite sufferings and crucifixion with, as they thought, the progressive agony of traditional Catholic-

ism being smothered by the tide of modern rationalism and science.
In the homes of pious families who thought this way holy medals
touched by James II (and so a certain cure for 'the King's Evil',
scrofula) and fragments of rope which hanged Jacobite plotters
occupied a place of honour beside crucifixes and relics of saints.
There were Catholics, on the other hand, who felt themselves
bound in conscience and moral principle to support James II, while
criticising official Jacobitism and rejecting pious Catholic Jacobitism. There were Catholics who went further and rejected every kind
of Jacobitism.

By 1698–1700 the band of Catholic exiles was thinning. Death
had removed most of its older generation. Some of their children
were much weaker Jacobites than their parents or rebels against
their principles. In Lord Widdrington's family the pattern of the
minds of three successive generations after 1688 was: mild Jacobite;
barely Jacobite at all; wildly militant Jacobite. Lord Waldegrave
died at St Germain, a pious Catholic Jacobite. His son, the 2nd
Lord, preferred England and gradually drifted from mild Jacobitism to Whig Protestantism. The Earl of Stafford's Jacobitism was
real but so moderate that in 1699 he sought and obtained a pardon
from William III in order to recover his estates. His son, the 2nd
Earl, resided in England but was secretly a militant, pious Jacobite
who asked that his heart should be buried in that shrine of pious
Jacobitism, the chapel of the English Blue Nuns' convent in Paris.
The Earl of Dover was a convert and reformed rake like James II
and reacted like his master. He directed that his heart should be
buried in the chapel of the Carmelite convent in Bruges. But in
1698 he begged for a pardon from William III and slipped quietly
back into England to take over his estate. Henceforward his
Jacobitism was merely a sentiment. The 4th Lord Montague did not
leave England in 1688. If he was a Jacobite, he did not manifest
his belief in action. His heir and younger brother, the 5th Lord,
alternated between bouts of profligacy and fits of superstitious piety
and penance. In 1691 he was at St Germain as James II's Secretary
of State. Yet later he threw up his job, left the King and shot dead
a priest who refused him absolution. He lived in hiding until his
death in 1717. The 1st Marquis of Powis was a pious Jacobite who
died at St Germain. His son, the 2nd Marquis, had not left England.
For years he was a leader of militant Jacobite resistance but then
threw up both Jacobitism and Catholicism.

That half of the Catholic peerage which remained in England
after 1688 had its pious militant Jacobites. In 1689 the Earls of
Peterborough and Salisbury were put in the Tower of London on
suspicion of plotting against William III. Peterborough was soon

released and left for St Germain practically a dying man without Catholic heirs. Salisbury endured three years in the Tower before he, also a sick man without Catholic heirs, was allowed to go home to his half-ruined mansion at Hatfield and his encumbered estate. In 1692 Lord Stourton was imprisoned in the Tower for plotting, and was joined there in 1694 by Lords Molyneux and Montgomery. There were Catholic peers who, like Viscount Fairfax, had numerous relatives at St Germain and who exchanged Jacobite messages in code and emblems. (Fairfax had wineglasses made with his crest and secret Jacobite signs engraved on them.) Yet, like Fairfax, such men were careful never to commit any real act of conspiracy and were left undisturbed by the government. Old Lord Arundell, one of this sort and James II's Lord Privy Seal to 1688, quietly gardened and raised a pack of foxhounds in the country. There were other Catholic peers who betrayed no trace of even sentimental Jacobitism.

In theory therefore, the Catholic peerage should have been destroyed by the Revolution. Half its members were exiles, and often attainted and so financially ruined. The rest were living under suspicion of treason and deprived of all government office. Of the thirty-eight Catholic peerages of 1688 only twenty-three survived in 1714. Fifteen had vanished from the list due to apostasy, or failure of male heirs, or succession by a Protestant. Moreover from 1692 Parliament used the Jacobite threat as a sufficient excuse for new anti-Catholic penal legislation. The new code was superimposed upon the often obsolescent older one and had about it a modern, scientific efficiency reminiscent of the Republic's penal laws. Propertied Catholics (defined as Catholics by refusal to take the Test Act Oaths) were subjected to paying a double rate of Land Tax. This tax was new and annual. Its rate fluctuated: during the years of the great French wars (1689–1714) it was high. The tax was levied on freehold real property and annuities derived from it. Every effort was made to render double Land Tax really effective and to defeat evasion, at which Papists were known to be experts. From 1714 they were required to register every detail of their freehold property and trusts with county authorities. Jacobite conspiracy was made a treasonable offence.

The exclusion of Papists from government office was made far more explicit, and holes in previous legislation of this kind stopped up. The profession of Catholicism now automatically deprived members of the royal family of their rights of succession to the throne: even marriage to a Catholic had the same effect. Catholics might not be employed in any rank in the forces. The new annual Mutiny Acts actually defined the Army as a national defence against militant popery. Catholics were now excluded from the Bar. They were declared legally incapable of purchasing land. Protestant next-of-kin might now, if they made application to the courts, exclude in their own favour rightful Catholic heirs to landed property. A Catholic undertaking a journey out of his district without licence, or visiting London even with a licence was automatically thereby taken as convicted of recusancy. Anyone so convicted, or convicted in the old-fashioned way at Quarter Sessions for monthly absences from the Anglican churches, was to be faced with the Test Act Oaths. The penalty for a first refusal of the Oaths was £2, for the second £10, and for the third subjection to bonds for 'good behaviour'. Papists were forbidden to keep offensive weapons or horses of over £5 value. Anglican rectories and advowsons in Catholic hands were to be confiscated without compensation and given to Oxford and Cambridge colleges. Common informers against Catholic missioners or against parents sending their children abroad to Catholic schools were promised a reward of £50 for each case proved in court. Priests arrested by such an information were to be given life-sentences in special, remote gaols to be set up as top-security places where the priests would have solitary confinement. As a wartime measure a special surveillance of Catholic letters was established at the General Post Office in St Martin's Lane, London. Catholics had long ago accustomed themselves to the use of government services. Their letters, instructions to missioners and even marriage dispensations from Rome travelled by the public postal service: mission funds were increasingly being invested in government loans bearing interest. Lastly the government established a body of Commissioners to investigate Catholic trusts established for superstitious uses. Informers would be rewarded, and superstitious trusts would be cancelled and the funds confiscated.

Similar legislation was, rather more slowly, being applied in Ireland, together with a systematic expropriation of Catholic gentry landowners convicted of rebellion or conspiracy. The results in Ireland were naturally frustrated by much evasion, but were still sufficiently effective to shatter the Irish Catholic landed gentry. Many of them emigrated to the Continent ('the Wild Geese') never to return. The protection and leadership of the Irish peasant Catholics passed largely to the Catholic middle class. It seemed likely that the new English penal code might have the same effect. If it did, English Catholicism would be left in a far worse case than Irish, because it had no peasant masses.

By 1714 it was clear that the code was biting the English Catholic peerage. In 1714 Lord Stourton, one of the poorest of peers, sold his main property, Stourton House and its estate, for £19,400. In 1709 the 3rd Earl of Cardigan renounced Catholicism and took his seat in the House of Lords. He was at once made Master of the Royal Buckhounds. By 1714 the profligate and murderous Lord Montague was known to be in grave financial straits. In 1713 the 4th Lord Baltimore (who had been deprived of his proprietorship of Maryland in 1689) renounced Catholicism: he was regranted the proprietorship. In 1714 Viscount Strangford renounced Catholicism; he mainly owned lands in Ireland.

Yet it seems that the Catholic peerage, though heavily damaged and threatened, was still not a sinking ship. By 1714 it had gained three peerages from Protestantism (the Duke of Norfolk, Earl Fauconberg and Lord Dormer). Three wives or widows of Protestant peers were now Catholics (the Countesses of Sussex and Lindsey and Lady Jersey). The fifteen lost Catholic peerages did not seem by any means all gone beyond recall. The heirs of three of them were firm Catholics. Several extinct Catholic peerages were still represented by practising Catholic dowagers or daughters. In 1706 an unknown but Jacobite writer listed Catholic patrons supporting missioners. His list of 'Persons of First Quality' totalled thirty-six. There were twenty-one peers, peeresses and courtesy Lords 'who depend upon the secular clergy', a further twelve 'who depend upon the Regulars', and another three whose ecclesiastical preferences varied from time to time. The list did not, of course, include the small group of Papist peers and peeresses resident abroad. The writer clearly thought it was an impressive list. He also considered that these people gave the Catholic community importance and status, though other features of his list show that he realised that the great majority of other Catholics did not depend economically or spiritually on the peers. Indeed the Revolution of 1688 had been a defeat for monarchy in England, and not just for James II: the victory lay with the major landowners, and especially the peers. It had been important for the Catholic community in the sixteenth and seventeenth centuries that it had penetrated so much into the landowning classes; after 1688, and even down to the 1870s, it was even more important that it should not lose this vital asset. In 1714 it was losing ground, but still not fatally.

Again, although the Catholic peers were now deprived of all office, they still had some electoral influence and connections with the inner circles of Protestant political groups. The Duke of Norfolk was, because of his property, especially strong in electoral influence, a fact increasingly appreciated by Parliamentary group leaders. This was one reason why, from now onwards the Dukedom became not merely a pawn of the chances of family succession for many years, but an asset the possession of which was clearly a major issue between the Catholic community and the Establishment. When the Duke was a Catholic, Catholics felt more secure: when he was a Protestant, they felt insecure with some good reason. William III employed foreign Catholics in his service in Holland and was conversant with Catholic politics in general. After all, in the great war he was the Pope's ally. Queen Mary, his wife, was a rigid Protestant and, for personal reasons, feared Catholicism. But she was, again for deeply personal reasons, always conscious of her father and half-brother at St Germain. Queen Anne, who succeeded to the throne in 1702, shared her sister's weaknesses. She kept in her private bureau a miniature of the Old Pretender, and, late in her life, increasingly took it out. Sarah, Duchess of Marlborough, the Queen's enemy but erstwhile bosom friend, had a dear sister who was the convert Jacobite Duchess of Tyrconnel. They corresponded. The Duke of Marlborough had numerous Catholic relatives in the Jacobite camp and kept in touch with them. Mrs Endymion Porter had been his great-aunt and the dubiously Catholic Porters and Lord Strangford were his cousins. Marlborough's first mistress had been the wife of the Catholic Earl of Castlemaine. Society generally agreed that Lady Castlemaine's youngest child, Barbara, was of Marlborough's begetting. The child, not without his cognisance, was educated by the English Blue Nuns in Paris and ended her life as a Benedictine Prioress at Pontoise. Marlborough was the uncle of his sister's bastards by James II, the Jacobite Dukes of Berwick and Albemarle, Lady Waldegrave and another daughter who became a nun in France. Marlborough's close friend and political ally, Earl Godolphin, had an elder brother who was a Catholic convert. The ranks of the Tory and Whig politicians were now stuffed with newly-created Dukes. The Duke of Leeds was of a part-Catholic family; the Duke of Richmond was a Catholic from 1685 to 1688; the Dukes of Shrewsbury, Beaufort and Bolton had all formerly been Catholics. In 1714 the eccentric young Whig Duke of Wharton had begun his wild gyrations between the opposite poles of Protestant Whiggery and Catholic Jacobitism. The ex-Catholic Dukes had close relations who were Papists and, if increasingly distantly, did something to protect the interests of the Catholic tenants who still lived on their estates.

The Protestant Establishment was now at least as virulently anti-Catholic in its pronouncements as it had been in the days of the Spanish Armada. In its propaganda Anglicanism was equated with political liberty, lay control of the clergy, plain truth-telling and all the other virtues of 'Englishry'. Catholicism was equated with political despotism, priestcraft, moral double-talk and all the other foreign vices. Anglicanism naturally went with a high national standard of living and economic progress: Catholicism went with 'wooden shoes' (poverty and economic stagnation). On her one and only foreign tour, Queen Anne had set foot shuddering within Papist churches in Flanders and was not disappointed: they were, she reported, full of infantile superstitions. Only a madman like the Duke of Wharton could embrace such a religion. But it was not only pious Protestants who felt like this. Rationalistic and progressive ones frankly regarded Rome as the bastion of medievalist obscurantism. Yet, in spite of this tall barrier of prejudice, there were, at the turn of the century, ways around its flanks. Educated Protestants and Catholics had much common ground. William Dicconson of Wrightington, Lancashire, a Catholic squire, kept a diary. In 1697–8 he made a long stay in London, dining out frequently in company which rarely was purely Catholic. A typical evening out was Monday, July 11th, 1698: '. . . din'd at the Duke of Ormonds head with the 2 Ld Fairfaxes (Charles, Viscount Fairfax, a Catholic, and Thomas, 5th Lord Fairfax, an Anglican, Colonel of Horse Guards), Brigadier Fairfax (Protestant), Mr. Scroop (Catholic) etc.'

What did they talk about? If it was politics and war, then they had plenty of common ground. The Protestant Establishment was, of course, anti-Jacobite. The English Catholic Establishment was equally solidly Jacobite. The Vicars-Apostolic constantly ordered all missioners to insert the name of James II (and later James III) in the liturgy. In the Colleges there were festal High Masses and bonfires on the saints' days of the St Germain family. St Germain, as of right, intervened in English Catholic clerical affairs. In the Colleges the successes of French arms were greeted with *Te Deums* and of Marlborough with the seven penitential psalms. In his diary, Edward Dicconson, a professor at the English College, Douai recorded that he led a deputation to St Germain in July 1704 to give birthday compliments to 'The King and Queen'. The victory of Marlborough at Blenheim had this reception from him: 'Wednesday, August 13th: This day that unfortunate battle was given where the Duke of Bavaria was beaten at Hockstet . . .' Yet this 'treason' actually commended Catholics to the Anglican Tories, who had a strong guilt-feeling about James II and a hatred of the 'Whig War'. On the other hand English pragmatism was already, by 1714, eroding away sentimental Jacobitism amongst both Catholics and Protestants. The steady procession to England to seek pardons of the exiled Catholic Jacobite peers and gentry manifested this. The radical Catholic tradition of Blacklow and John Sergeant did its

work. By 1714 younger Catholics, priests and gentry, were turning
against the Jacobitism of their fathers. Edward Dicconson's close
relation, William Dicconson of Wrightington, was dining in London
with Whig peers.

In the fields of learning and culture Catholics and Protestants
also had common ground. The contemporary division between
reactionary conservatism and progressive rationalism cut across
denominational boundaries and the minds of individuals. Amongst
Protestant gentry the reactionaries who applauded satires against
Whiggery and science had their parallels amongst Catholics. The
English College, Douai clung to the death to its outmoded classical
syllabus. The midland Vicar-Apostolic, Bonaventure Gifford, a
Tory Jacobite, wrote that he had never known such great openness
towards Catholicism amongst Protestants. Yet there were Whigs
and scientists who were friendly with Catholic scientists like the
Towneleys of Lancashire and who detected in these progressive
Catholics a plain, rational Christianity very like the best Protestantism and far removed from the idolatrous superstition of reactionary
pious Catholics. The two writers most shocking to Anglican Tories
had both, like Dryden, caught their sceptical temper from the
Blacklowist apologetic of John Sergeant. These were (both once
Catholics) Matthew Tindal (*Christianity as Old as Creation*, 1720)
and John Toland (*Christianity not Mysterious*, 1696).

Even sociology and economics served to bring together the
Protestant and Catholic gentry. The landed gentry had their golden
age between 1570 and 1642 when they were, as a class, greatly
inflated in numbers and political importance. The civil war crisis
struck many of them a grave financial blow from which their
weaker brethren never recovered. Then the heavy war taxation of
1697–1713 and a series of bad harvests in the 1690s turned the
decline of the country gentry into something like a rout. Between
1642 and 1714 many gentry estates changed hands. It was the end
of an ordering of country society. In fact what replaced it seems,
from a modern point of view, not so very different from the old
order. The peerage expanded greatly, receiving much new blood
and buying up much land from bankrupt old gentry. New gentry
bought their way into the system, using the profits of trade and the
professions. To our eye the new masters of the counties assumed
a manner of life very like that of their predecessors. Yet the old
gentry clearly bitterly resented the change as revolutionary and
sought every way they could to demonstrate a really quite mythical
total difference in ethos between themselves and their supplanters.
Perhaps there was—at least up to 1714 before the new men had
settled into power and grown fully conservative—some real differ-

ence, some marked new degree of rationalism and commercialism invisible to us moderns.

The Catholic list of country gentry patrons in 1706 still made a bravely defiant show. The conservative Jacobite author pushed to the end and into a vague obscurity the 'numerous catholicks of lower rank' who, he says, supported riding missioners corporately especially in Lancashire and the north. He omitted to point out that these people supported two-thirds of the 600 missioners. His attention was riveted on the peers and the gentry (210 'Persons of Lesser Quality' each keeping a private chaplain). Of the 210, forty-six were 'Barts: and Knights', fifty-one 'Gents: of Considerable Estates over £1000', and 101 'Gents: of Estates between £400 and £1000'; twelve had unknown incomes. He omitted from consideration some dozens of gentry families living on the Continent because of Jacobite conviction, piety or poverty, people like Mrs Brooke in a convent guesthouse with her chaplain and four maids or Lady Crosland in another guesthouse with servants and grandchildren.

The old Catholic gentry, for all their bravery (and, in some cases, as Mr Weld of Lulworth, Sir Henry Lawson 2nd baronet of Brough and Sir Philip Constable 2nd baronet of Everingham, their wealth) were suffering the common rout of their class. In Yorkshire in 1603 there were 386 families of Catholic gentry, in 1642 300, in 1680 under 200, by 1700 barely 150 and by 1714 barely one hundred. In those years scores of lesser gentry families had sold out and moved away to other counties or to towns. Even middling gentry often had a tough battle. The Scropes of Danby, Yorkshire were ruined by 1697 and yet by 1714 were back in their house, their estate mostly intact, because of rigid economy and lucky marriages. Here and there the conversion of Protestant gentry and the buying of Catholic estates by Papist tradesmen or lawyers also helped to put a brake on the decline. The Sayers of Worsall went resoundingly bankrupt. But Nicholas Mayes of Newcastle, merchant, the son of a poor Catholic tenant-farmer of the Sayers', bought the estate. His family needed some decades to win acceptance as real gentry. At Stokesley, high on the York moors, the Forsters sold out and a Catholic attorney from London, William Pierson, bought the estate and moved in. He and his family never did gain social acceptance from the county's old Catholic gentry. The gentry of the north and north midlands held their ground rather better than their fellows in the south, west and Wales. Before 1680 the south and west had the lion's share of missioners. By 1714 the balance had shifted significantly in favour of the northerners.

The declining Protestant Tory old gentry were vocal in their accusations that their ruin was contrived deliberately by Whig grandees and the trading interest. The declining Catholic old gentry shared their lament. It was, they wrote, the viciousness of double Land Tax and the penalisation of Jacobitism which did the damage. A Warwickshire squire grimly estimated that 'the iron age of double taxes' had cost him £10,000 in two decades. He was exaggerating, as his ancestors had exaggerated about recusancy fines, but he had a point. Jacobitism did ruin a few militants. But it is astonishing how often a Catholic family, sold up by Act of Attainder, some years later gained a pardon and the restitution of at least some of their properties.

In 1714 the Catholic prophets of doom foresaw the end of their community, dead with the last Catholic peer and old gentry. Rationalistic Protestants thought that by the 1720s pious Catholics would be gone into the same limbo as the fairies and the witches. The sane Catholic minority would then be Protestants. Bonaventure Gifford, for all his old gentry Toryism, begged to differ. He noted 'the large numbers of converts' who were mostly 'of the middling sort of people'.

12. The Death of Catholic Aristocracy, 1714–1830

Popular Catholic history told of two deaths of the English Catholic community, each followed by a miraculous resurrection or Spring. The first death lasted from 1534 to 1570 and the first Spring from 1570 to 1688. The second death lasted from 1688 to the 1830s and was the prelude to the second Spring in Victorian England. In the legend the nadir of the second death began in 1714. There followed a period of loss of faith and of degeneracy, relieved only by the heroism of the Jacobite martyrs and Bishop Richard Challoner.

In this picture the highlights were focussed on the near-extinction of the Catholic monarchy and aristocracy. Indeed the Stuart Catholic monarchy died out, but its last agonies were slow and humiliating. James II died (in the odour of sanctity in the eyes of pious Catholics; his corpse lay in the English Benedictine monastic chapel of St Edmund in Paris until the revolutionaries of 1789 tossed it out) in 1701. His son, James III, enjoyed an immensely long reign down to 1765. The family's titles and claims were carried on into the nineteenth century by his sons, Charles III and Henry IX. Attachment to the family and the Jacobite cause lingered on tenaciously amongst Protestant Tories and pious Catholics down to the 1770s. The fact that practising Catholics were not confronted during these years with the simple political choice of an Oath of Allegiance allowed many to lose their moral and religious adhesion to Jacobitism by a slow, almost unnoticed process of attrition. Scrupulous and pious Catholics, like Bishop Challoner, even in 1760 admitted that George III was rightfully King by English Law, but reserved a private allegiance to James III. At that time the presidents of the English, Irish and Scots Colleges in Rome willingly paid the price of loss of their posts rather than accept a Papal command not to address Charles III as their sovereign. In the 1770s the Mary Ward sisters at the Bar Convent in York used holy medals touched by Charles III to cure the poor of the city of the 'King's Evil'.

But in reality the credibility of the Catholic monarchy and the volume of English Catholic support for it was waning in 1719. That year a new Vicar-Apostolic, John Stonor, and his priest-friend, Thomas Strickland, openly provoked a controversy. They advocated an official, clean break between the Catholic community and the Stuarts and a firm declaration of loyalty to George I. By 1745, the year of the most impressive and dangerous Jacobite rising, there was glaring evidence that very few Catholics any longer had a real faith in the cause. Even the charismatic presence of Prince Charles Edward at the head of an army in the streets of Carlisle, Preston, Manchester and Derby brought only a small response from Catholics. At the English College, Douai the President ordered a votive High Mass to ask a blessing on the Prince's efforts. A good many missioners furtively offered Mass for the same intention. But the Prince gained only a few scores of Catholic recruits, and amongst them were none of the Catholic community's leaders. A fairly representative Yorkshire Catholic squire, Sir Edward Gascoigne, wrote of the Jacobite army as 'wild animals scampering on the hills'. In 1750 the Prince visited London secretly and was there formally received into the Anglican Church. He did not choose to publicise the fact until 1759, but then announced his apostasy bluntly: 'The Roman Catholick Religion . . . the artfull system of Roman Infallibility . . . has been the ruin of the Royal family.' At Avignon he dismissed from his service his few popish servants. For the Catholic Jacobite faithful the impact of this was veiled by the solid Catholicism of the Prince's father, James III. At his death in 1765 the Prince, now Charles III, came to reside in lodgings in Rome. But he came as a Protestant. The Pope was glad that this fact enabled him to escape at last from the embarrassing necessity of continuing to recognise the Stuarts as sovereigns of Britain. The English Vicars-Apostolic, whose private opinions about the matter varied, were equally glad to make the Pope's decision the occasion of a Pastoral Letter to the faithful to pray for George III at Mass.

After 1765 the affairs of the Stuarts were of little concern to most Catholics. Charles III died, a physical wreck, still in Rome, in 1788. Through the influence of his younger brother and male heir, Henry Benedict Stuart, Cardinal of York and the bishop of an Italian diocese, Charles eventually returned to Catholicism. The reconciliation was superficial. His illegitimate daughter, Charlotte,

Duchess of Albany, was unmarried and reputed to have children by a French bishop. Cardinal Stuart took little interest in his title 'Henry IX' and none in the faint remnants of the Jacobite cause. Ousted from his diocese by the armies of Napoleon, he gratefully lived the rest of his life on a large secret service pension from George III. When he died *The Times* newspaper ventured a leading-article in praise of his virtues. Meanwhile the Duchess of Albany's confessor, an English Benedictine, serving as a secret agent for the British government in Italy, smuggled to England 'the Stuart Papers' and traded them in to George III for a pension.

As Catholic allegiance to the Stuarts faded away, attachment to the House of Hanover slowly grew to replace it. The attachment was probably made easier by the fact that the Hanoverians proved to have Catholic connections. George I was a Continental-type Protestant prince of the stamp of William III. While solidly committed for political reasons to a Protestant Establishment, he and his family had had much experience of Catholicism. Their German principality was an accumulation of duchies and cities (Brunswick, Luneburg, Celle, Hanover) commonly nicknamed, for convenience, 'Hanover'. Its government was normally shared out between the brothers and uncles of each generation of the family. In George's father's generation the tide of Catholicism had been running fast in north Germany and the family had come very close to turning Catholic. Two of George's uncles had, albeit only temporarily, become Catholics, as had George's younger brother. George's first mistress was a Catholic. Moreover the family were enthusiastically loyal clients of the Emperor, a great Catholic power, and held hereditary offices—Elector, Grand Treasurer—in the Holy Roman Empire. Catholics were not numerous in Hanover, but family policy there, and in neighbouring Brandenburg-Prussia, made great use as civil officials, soldiers, artists and technicians of foreigners and Germans of other states, whether Protestants or Catholics. The English Benedictine Congregation had long ago established a monastery at Lambspring in Hanover, an enclave protected jointly by the Elector of Hanover and the Catholic Emperor. (The English Abbot of Lambspring was legally a princeling of the Empire with civil jurisdiction.) The sons of English Catholic gentry took officers' commissions in the Elector's army in Hanover long before, in 1778, they were first allowed to serve in some British Army formations. The first few pages of a late-eighteenth-century book of Catholic family pedigrees kept at Brough Hall in Yorkshire contain three such officers: Charles Langdale of Houghton Hall, Yorkshire (dead, unmarried, in 1776 'an officer in the Brunswick service'); Edward Sheldon of Beoley, Warwickshire (a family hitherto Jacobite; dead unmarried in 1780 'in the Hanover service'); and John Jones of Llanarth, Glamorganshire ('a Major in the Hanoverian Army, now in England on half-pay').

In 1749 George II's son-in-law, the Landgrave Frederick of Hesse-Cassel, became a Catholic convert. George II lived more than half of his reign in Hanover and his Hanoverian regiments, with some English Catholic officers, fought alongside British regiments at Dettingen. His blue-stocking wife, Queen Caroline of Anspach, was a friend of the Saxon philosopher Leibniz, and his pioneering ecumenical conference between Catholics and Protestants took place in Hanover. His son, Frederick, Prince of Wales, was constantly at odds with his parents. One of the Prince's refuges and meeting-places with opposition politicians was Norfolk House, the London residence of the Catholic Edward Howard, 5th Duke of Norfolk. Norfolk's great wealth made him, in spite of his Catholicism a man of electoral weight. The House of Hanover stood for a rigid legislative exclusion of Catholics from office, but its practice was less rigid than its theory. By 1760 it seemed unlikely that the King would object to the view of an increasingly large number of Protestant politicians that Catholics were now so few (at least in the upper ranks of society) and so detached from Jacobitism that it would be safe to grant them some very limited legal concessions. The accession in 1760 of Frederick's young son, George III, forwarded this policy. He went along with the slight legislative concessions of the Catholic Relief Acts of 1778 and 1791. He enjoyed tea-parties *en famille* with the devoutly Catholic Welds at Lulworth Castle during his sea-bathing holidays at Weymouth. He enjoyed granting secret service pensions for compassionate reasons to a few worthy Catholic aristocrats who had fallen on hard times. The sentimentally Jacobite Dr Samuel Johnson was quite conquered by a meeting with George III in the library at Windsor Castle. The sentimentally Jacobite Viscount Fairfax, a Yorkshire Catholic, pinned up in his library maps of Europe with red flags to follow the victories of the King's arms in the French wars and bought the court circulars.

The affair of George, Prince of Wales, and the Catholic Maria Anne Fitzherbert dropped like a bomb-shell into this scene of growing amity. In 1785 the Prince, self-indulgent and irresponsible to a high degree, became violently enamoured of Mrs Fitzherbert. She was already twice-widowed, though young, and a typical victim of the marital and family degeneration of the Catholic aristocracy, where the pious and conventional few desperately competed for even fewer suitable mates and proved all too often unable to beget heirs. It was out of the question that the lady should become another of the Prince's mistresses. Anyway he had a grand passion for her in the new romantic style with nose-bleeds, tears and protestations of fidelity to death. His secret marriage to her in a London drawing-room before a bribed Fleet clergyman was a folly on the grand scale of his other oddity, the Brighton Pavilion. Mrs Fitzherbert also acted with utmost folly, since she knew well that, by law, such a marriage was null and void because she was a Catholic and George III's permission had not been gained. The King was already alarmed by evidence that Whig politicians, who surrounded the Prince, were planning to win legal concessions for Catholics amounting to an almost total emancipation from penal laws. To his mind, and, indeed, to most conservative Protestants, such an emancipation would breach his Coronation Oath to preserve the Protestant Establishment. He was unmoved by prudential arguments. His simple Anglican conservatism and horror of politicians and modernity endeared him to pious conservative Catholics like the Welds of Lulworth (the greatest patrons of the Jesuits) and made him feel a sympathy with them. But now he had visions of a plot of James II proportions hatched between Liberal Whig politicians, godless Whig Liberal Catholics and the Irish. Even if this were not true, by law the marriage of the Prince would deprive him of succession to the throne. Hence the King firmly treated the marriage as null, and hastily married the Prince off, in spite of his romantic tantrums and threats of suicide to the Protestant Caroline of Brunswick. Eventually the Prince deserted Caroline and besought Mrs Fitzherbert to return to live with him. She and her Catholic confessor took the case to Rome. Rome declared the clandestine marriage reprehensible but undoubtedly valid in the eyes of the Catholic Church: Mrs Fitzherbert was instructed to cohabit with the Prince. They lived together for a number of years secretly. Then the Prince's gross selfishness and inconstancy combined with heavy political pressures finally separated them. George III's lengthening bouts of mental illness gave the Prince the office of Regent. To her death at Brighton in 1837 (the year of the accession of Queen Victoria) Mrs Fitzherbert remained a fascination for Catholics. The romantic and some of the pious saw her as a Henrietta Maria or Catherine of Braganza *manquée*. In a curious way the episode served both to harden the King's resolution never to submit to Catholic emancipation and to put a seal on growing popular Catholic devotion to the Hanoverians.

The withering-away of the Catholic peerage was also a reality and a very serious one in an Augustan Age when peers had an ever-

I

increasing prestige, seeming to be demi-gods. By 1791 there were only seven Catholic peers left: the Earls of Shrewsbury and Derwentwater-Newburgh, and Lords Arundell, Clifford, Dormer, Petre and Stourton. To Catholic legend the nine apostasies and eight natural extinctions since 1714 seemed abnormal and horrific. The stories of the disasters lost nothing in the telling. So, for instance, Benedict Calvert, 4th Lord Baltimore, conformed to the Church of England in 1713 and was rewarded with the restitution of his proprietorial rights over Maryland, taken away in 1689. The family was henceforward Anglican. But retribution came to the 6th Lord, an extravagant rake who was put on trial for rape in 1768, fled to Naples, and died there without male heirs three years later. There was the dramatic story of the lingering end of Catholicism in the family of the Ropers, Lords Teynham. The 8th Lord conformed to Anglicanism in 1716 and was rewarded with the office of Lord of the Royal Bedchamber. He committed suicide in London in 1723 and was succeeded in turn by his two elder and Catholic sons, who both died without male heirs. Their younger brother, the 11th Lord, apostatised and the family was henceforward Anglican. Down to 1786 the Dukes of Norfolk were Catholics. But in that year the succession passed to Charles Howard, an apostate. With gloomy satisfaction Catholics noted that he was almost illiterate, 'the dirtiest man in England', an alcoholic and a great rake. His wife became insane, and the Duke died in 1815 leaving no son. The 2nd Marquis of Powis had been a keen Catholic Jacobite. Then came the collapse, first into allegiance to the Hanoverians, and then, in 1722 his apostasy. By 1745 he was dead, leaving no male heirs.

These stories were surpassed in Gothic horror by that of the Viscounts Montague of Cowdray and Battle, Sussex. The 5th Viscount was a Catholic Jacobite whose gross profligacy led him to shoot dead his confessor for refusing him absolution: the Viscount became a lifelong fugitive from justice. His Catholic son, the 6th Viscount, had to sell off Battle. The 7th Viscount apostatised in 1786, but had to sell off all the other estates except Cowdray House. He moved to Brussels to live cheaply. There his deathbed repentance and reconciliation with the Catholic Church came too late to prevent the title passing to his Protestant son, the 8th Viscount, who was accidentally drowned in 1793. In that year fire consumed Cowdray House. The title, and little else, passed to a cousin who was a Franciscan friar at Douai. This new 9th Viscount was advanced in years but procured a Papal dispensation from his vows and married. He died childless.

Material gain was certainly one motive for these apostasies. After

1714 the Protestant Establishment had the key to offices vastly more financially rewarding than those of earlier ages: Paymasterships to the Forces, Treasury commissionerships, bishoprics, posts in India. The lucky Protestant grandees who commanded this patronage waxed immensely rich and raised the level of aristocratic living almost out of reach of all but the richest Catholic peers. Apostasy therefore became a great temptation. The insincerity of a good many of the Catholic peer apostates was evident. Lord Langdale, a devout but weak man, hastily apostatised in 1723 in an attempt to escape an especially heavy, once-for-all levy made on Catholics that year. He speedily repented, was reconciled, and became a great patron of the Franciscans. The 4th Viscount Dunbar apostatised in 1716. A jotting, in the hand of his practising Catholic heir, in the margin of the legal certificate of conformity seeks to excuse him: 'Memorandum: That my Ld. William Dunbar lived only two years after taking this unreasonable oath and it may be reasonably imagined that it contributed not a little to his end.'

This century's apostates repented much more frequently than those of the seventeenth century, though usually too late in the day to prevent their heirs being brought up as Protestants. In the cases of Earl Fauconberg, Earl Nugent, a disreputable Anglo-Irish political boss, the 7th Viscount Montague, whose wife turned Methodist, and Viscount Gage, that was the pattern. Fauconberg's ostensible reason for apostasy was a quarrel over property with priests. But the apostasy won him an inscribed Bible and warm friendship from George III, a Ministerial post and political control of the North Riding of Yorkshire. He clung to these gifts while letting his Catholic wife and daughters support missions and while maintaining close intimacy with his still Catholic friends and relations. Then, on his deathbed, he made his peace with the Catholic Church.

A second reason for apostasy lay in that slovenly mode of bringing up children which had always been a curse of the English aristocracy, Protestant and Catholic. Their households were so large and lavish and widely dispersed, their servants so unruly or corrupt and the heads of families so preoccupied that the children could easily become eccentric or debauched. Spasmodic efforts at imposing a strict nursery discipline (Anglican, Dissenting or Catholic) on this background not infrequently backfired. Mrs Fitzherbert's convent education did not enable her to cope with the aristocratic gambols of Regency Brighton. The apostate 9th Duke of Norfolk had little formal schooling other than that given by stable boys and under-maids. The Duke of Wharton's strict Dissenting upbringing did not prevent him from becoming the century's

greatest eccentric. Moreover hereditary succession to large respons-
ibilities often brought to peerages men like the 9th Lord Fairfax,
hitherto a penniless distant cousin living on the Continent.

It is not easy to account satisfactorily for the childlessness of so
many of the eighteenth-century Catholic peers. In some cases, for
instance Lord Dunbar, the ancient curses of mistresses and syphilis
applied. In general the causes were probably a mixture of narrow
Catholic pietism, late marriages, the old natural reaction of celibacy
in times of economic stress, and the baleful effects of epidemics of
smallpox and consumption. The last Lord Fairfax lost eight of his
nine children in five years by epidemics. The last Lord Widdrington
and both his brothers died childless. The last Lords Aston and
Langdale left only daughters and no nephews of their own name.
Lords Carlingford, Rivers, Gerard and Newburgh left no heirs
whatever, male or female. It was a sign of the times that heirs who
happened to be priests were not, as generally in earlier times, passed
over in the succession. There was now a phenomenal crop of titled
missioners: Jesuit Earl of Shrewsbury, Viscount Molyneux and
Lord Gerard, Franciscan Lord Montague, and secular priest Earl
Rivers and Lord Fauconberg. Perhaps also broken Catholic marriages accounted for some childlessness. Several Catholics had
resort to the rich Anglican's mode of divorce, a private Act of
Parliament. The 10th Duke of Norfolk, a Catholic third cousin of
his apostate predecessor, had divorced his Catholic wife for adultery
in 1794 in this fashion and so could not marry again in her lifetime.
They had been married for only four years. Some Catholics, in spite
of the strictures of the Common Law (severe after 1753) and
Catholic canon law against clandestine marriages resorted to them
and so cast much doubt on the validity of their unions. The widow
of the Catholic 6th Duke of Norfolk clandestinely married the
Hon. Peregrine Widdrington to the intense scandal of her Jesuit
confessor and the respectable. It was perhaps as a penance that she
spent a year or two as a parlour-boarder in the Bar Convent at
York.

Ostensibly during these years there was no great shortage of
aristocratic recruits to the Catholic peerage, though in almost every
case their advent had no lasting effect in stopping the decline. At
one time or another the list of Catholic peers had added to it the
names of the Duke and Duchess of Wharton, the 1st Marquis and
Marchioness of Buckingham, the Earl and Countess of Lindsey,
the 2nd Earl of Lichfield and his Countess, the Countess of
Abingdon, Viscountess Bolingbroke, Lady Farnham, the Countess
of Jersey, the Countess of Shaftesbury, Edward Wortley Montagu,
and—if he could be called aristocratic—Mr Shorter (brother-in-law

of the great Prime Minister, Sir Robert Walpole), and the Dowager Countess of Westmorland. There was very little real substance or new strength for the Catholic community in these people. Some of them were ridiculous eccentrics. Of the poor Duke of Wharton even the Catholic poet, Alexander Pope, wrote:

> *Wharton*, the scorn and wonder of our days,
> Whose ruling Passion was the Lust of Praise;
> Women and Fools must like him, or he dies,
> Wanting nothing but an honest heart.

Wharton twice fled London for St Germain, and the second time, in 1726, became a Catholic. He was attainted, lost his great wealth, and, with his childless Irish wife, wandered round Europe miserably for years until his death in a Spanish monastery. The Duchess in her old age lived in obscurity and poverty in London. Edward Wortley Montagu was fortune's darling, the brother of the traveller, Lady Mary Wortley Montague, and the brother-in-law of the Prime Minister Earl of Bute. After a disastrous career in the House of Commons, he travelled to the Near East, married a Nubian and became a Moslem, fell in with an Irish Catholic in Alexandria and himself became a Catholic in Jerusalem. London society followed, agog, the latest rumours of his crazy career, his applications in Rome for a nullity degree, his desertion of the Catholic girl, his death by choking on a bone. The other recruits were simply insignificant. The Marchioness of Buckingham was a born Catholic but so very discreet that people were never quite sure whether she had apostatised or not: her husband was called a Papist but there is no record of his conversion. Their heirs were Protestants. Lady Bolingbroke, a French widow educated in stiff Catholic piety by Madame de Maintenon, effortlessly became an Anglican when her husband's political career required it. The Lichfields, husband and wife, were definite enough Catholics to have their daughters educated in convents and married to Catholics, but their son was brought up a Protestant.

In a strange way the survival of the seven Catholic peerages was as much due to the extinction of their fellows as to their own firmness of religious conviction. Since they were now intermarried closely within the narrow circle, they inevitably inherited large properties from families that died out in the male line. Often these profits of doom transformed a bankrupt and declining peerage into a rich one. The Catholic Dukes of Norfolk in this way absorbed much of the great Sherburne inheritance in the north and that of the Savilles in Yorkshire. They had already, in an earlier generation reaped Sheffield from the Earldom of Shrewsbury. In 1791 Lord Petre was as rich as all but a half-dozen of the greatest Protestants. He owned 20,000 acres in Essex and, by inheritance, the Walmesley estates in the north. The Arundells of Wardour had stagnated in foxhunting and gaming down to the 1740s. Then marriage brought them the western estates of their Arundell cousins of Lanherne, Cornwall. Wardour Castle could now be extensively rebuilt.

The most startling reversal of fortune was that of the obscure Lords Clifford and Stourton, buried in the depths of the west country. In 1720 Lord Clifford was starting to sell land. In 1791 his successor was rich on a half share of the Warwickshire lands of the last Lord Aston and third of the estate of the last Lord Langdale. In 1714 Lord Stourton sold off Stourton House, Wiltshire. By 1791 his successor had inherited Walmesley lands in the north and Stonor lands in Oxfordshire, and was in easy circumstances.

The Catholic landed gentry of 1714–1830 never ceased to lament that they were a dying breed. They blamed it all on to their legendary royalism in the mid seventeenth century, their equally legendary militant Jacobitism, double taxes and the penal laws. The fact of their decline was obvious. By 1790–1830 the country-side in those counties, once well-stocked with Catholic gentry, was littered with their manor houses now empty or in Protestant hands. There were some areas in Cornwall where the desolation was striking. For instance in 1767 there were only two Catholic gentry estates left and able to sustain a missioner, and one of these had a non-resident landlord. In the whole county there were barely sixty practising Catholics. Also by the end of the century the school lists of fashionable Catholic convents and academies contain only a thin sprinkling of the old, familiar Catholic gentry names. Most sur-names in each class are unfamiliar English ones, Irish or foreign.

Yet the decline was slowed down and its effects masked by a number of factors. The Catholic legend represented apostasy, in the case of the gentry as of the peers, as a major and catastrophic cause of the decline. The most-quoted gentry apostasies were of the Gages and Shelleys of Sussex, the Giffords of Staffordshire, the Swinburnes and Brandlings of Northumberland, the Gascoignes, Tankreds and Smithsons of Yorkshire, the Chichesters of Devon-shire. These apostasies, and those of scores of more obscure families, certainly took place. But they were not unprecedented in either type or quantity: they were often not sudden or involving a whole family; they did not necessarily destroy Catholic com-munities and missions; and apostasy was far from being the chief cause of the gentry decline. As we have seen, apostasy on a large scale—permanent or temporary conformism—had always been a feature of the Catholic community's life. Statistically apostasy made deeper inroads in the ranks of the old Catholic gentry in 1660–1714 than after 1714. The eighteenth-century apostasies were of three types, all long familiar to Catholics. The first type was a very long-drawn-out slither from Catholic practice caused by bankruptcy, descent into genteel poverty or down the social scale, with the splitting up of the family, a loss of its cohesion and heirlooms, and a decline into near-illiteracy. Here and there in the country by the 1790s there were shopkeepers and labourers, bearing old Catholic gentry names, who were now Protestants. The city of York contained half a dozen such families of the Thwings, once the gentry owners of a big Catholic house in the outer suburbs and the protectors of the city's Catholic community. The Bar Convent sisters and their Jesuit chaplains laboured to try to shepherd the Thwings back into the Catholic fold, with little lasting success.

A second type of apostasy was frankly due to economic pressures. After 1750 the standard of living amongst the major gentry was so high and competition for government office so hot that only an already wealthy Catholic gentry family could hope to profit financially from apostasy. Moreover Treasury arrangements were such that conformity did not simply and immediately relieve the apostate of double Land Tax. The legal processes needed to gain exemption from it were so protracted and expensive that most apostates were compelled to continue paying double. Indeed the Treasury system fixed the double tax on the land so that Protestant purchasers of it were left in the same dilemma. Hence after 1714 apostasies for financial gain or to get offices were relatively few. The most-quoted examples dated in the early years of the century and concerned wealthy gentry. Thomas Gage of Sussex conformed in 1713, became a Whig MP and was awarded a peerage in 1720 for political services. As we have already seen, his conversion to Anglicanism was only skin-deep. Sir Hugh Smithson's case was dramatic. The first Sir Hugh was the son of a poor Yorkshire Catholic gentleman. He made a fortune in trade before 1660 in the City of London, acquired a baronetcy, retired from trade and bought himself the estate of a bankrupt Catholic family in his home area, Stanwick. There he set up as a new recruit to the Yorkshire major Catholic gentry, marrying the daughter of a Catholic peer, establishing a mission, and sending his daughters to convent schools. Through all the crisis of 1678–88 he stuck to his Catholicism gamely. Yet he had already decided to bring up his son as a Protestant, and the old baronet himself apostatised without fuss

in 1711. His wife and daughters and the Stanwick mission were
unaffected. Sir Hugh continued on good terms with his Catholic
friends and stood as trustee for them. When he died in 1733, an
old-fashioned Church-papist, his heir and grandson, the second
Sir Hugh, had left Eton and was entering the House of Commons.
He married the heiress to two Duchies, received an Earldom in
1760 and, in the right of his wife, the Dukedom of Northumberland
in 1766. In that year the new Duke's aunts and uncles were mostly
Catholics and his estate at Stanwick still housed sixty Catholics and
a missioner.

The third, and most usual, type of apostasy was by genuine
conversion to a Broad Church Anglicanism from an enlightened,
Liberal Catholicism. Pious, traditionalist Catholics regarded such
conversions with a peculiar horror as novel and the first-fruits of a
Jacobinism which would destroy English Catholicism. The three
legendary cases concerned William Constable of Burton Constable,
Yorkshire, Sir Thomas Gascoigne of Parlington, Yorkshire and
Peter Gifford of Chillington, Staffordshire. In the legend Constable
was a monster, the friend of that enlightened sceptic, Jean-Jacques
Rousseau, and a man who abandoned all religion and was buried
without ceremony in his front garden. Gascoigne became a Whig
Protestant, threw out his Catholic chaplain, and built a triumphal
arch on his estate to commemorate American Independence.
Gifford married a Protestant, attempted in vain to introduce
Protestant beliefs and practices into English Catholicism and then
apostatised, ejecting the midland Vicar-Apostolic from his residence on the Chillington estate. These men were casualties of a fierce
contemporary struggle to adapt the Catholic community to a
changing society. Some of their ideas were quite widely, if incoher-
ently, accepted by a good many gentry who remained Catholics.
The apostates' departure was not very dramatic or violent. Constable was a correspondent of Rousseau's. He was also the victim
of ostracism of a fierce and narrow kind by pious Catholics: in
earlier life he had even been jilted at the altar by the Honourable
Anne Fairfax, a person of that type, who ultimately rejected him
because he did not attend Mass daily. The mission at Burton
Constable was not disrupted, and Constable's heirs were steady
Catholics. Gascoigne was the product of Liberal Catholic schools
in Paris and Turin. He allowed a Benedictine missioner to stay on
the Parlington estate for the rest of his life, and built a chapel for
him nearby, at Aberford. Gifford was a prominent lay member of
a Liberal Catholic committee. It was his misfortune that his close
neighbour, the midland Vicar-Apostolic, John Milner, was the
greatest crusading champion of Catholic conservatism and a per-

secutor of Liberals. The Vicars-Apostolic owned the residence at Chillington and Milner's move away to Wolverhampton was his own idea.

The extinction of old Catholic gentry families by lack of male heirs or bankruptcy was a far larger cause of the decline than apostasy. This happened frequently, continuing a trend evident even before 1642 and common to both Protestant and Catholic gentry. Yet even in these cases, the decline was cushioned by a variety of moderating factors.

The thinning Catholic ranks were, to a small extent, reinforced by conversions of Protestant gentry and recruitment into the Catholic gentry of Papist lawyers and tradesmen who bought estates. Conversions were, admittedly, small in numbers and often produced no lasting effect. Nevertheless they occurred, especially in the earlier decades of the century. The Acton family of Aldenham, Shropshire, moved over from Anglicanism with a curious unanimity. The head of the family, Sir Richard Acton baronet, became a Catholic. His third cousins, brothers, moved from London trade to France and Italy and all became Catholics there independently. Sir Richard had no son, and the baronetcy passed, together with the estate, to the Catholic John Acton, former officer in the Navy of the Grand Duke of Tuscany and currently chief minister of the Bourbon King of Naples. In Lancashire there was a thin dribble of death-bed conversions of Protestant squires with Catholic wives, such as Mr Lomax of Dunkenhalgh and William Pugh of Brindle. In Yorkshire in the 1730s and 1740s there was a small rash of conversions of the heads of Anglican Tory gentry families, the Armitages of Kirklees, the Tempests of Tong, the Cutlers of Hayton, the Ferrands, David Winspear of Whitby (a merchant in Leghorn, converted there and the father of Count Antonio Winspear, general in the army of the King of Naples). By the 1790s conversions were at a low ebb, reduced to a few oddities like Emma, Lady Hamilton, Nelson's mistress. She died a pauper in Calais in 1814. As her daughter, Horatia Nelson, wrote: 'Lady H. had, ever since she had been in Calais, professed herself a Catholic.'

Yet Catholicism now aroused much interest amongst Protestants of fashion. The Prince of Wales's feeling that 'the Catholic religion is the religion for a gentleman' struck a chord amongst Whig Protestants romantically inclined and disgusted with high and dry Anglican formalism and Methodist enthusiasm. The Protestant gentry were at home in France and Italy as never before. One of George III's sons resided in Rome. Another took his French Catholic mistress with him on naval duty. The future Duke of Wellington became proficient in French and horsemanship in a

French Academy. The future Lord Palmerston went to school in France. The 3rd Lord Townshend's Anglican chaplain actually sent his son to school at the English Jesuit Academy at Liège. The boy, one of several non-Catholics in the school, remained a Protestant but had fragrant memories of Mass in the Academy chapel. In the 1770s Godfrey Wentworth, a Yorkshire Protestant MP, in process of divorcing his wife and remarrying, stayed in Rome and devoutly completed the formalities for obtaining a Papal Indulgence. The Whigs sent their daughters in Protestant convoys under duennas of approved religion to French convents to learn the language.

Recruitment of middle-class Catholics into the ranks of the landed gentry had once been common. During the eighteenth century very few such persons were able or willing to found a family of squires. Land was still socially desirable and a sound investment for money made in trade or the professions. But the economic situation was changing. Sensible landowners realised that it was perilous to rely only on rent-rolls. The Catholic middle class was anxious to move into landownership but only as an extra investment, economic and social. They bought farms and country villas or married their daughters to Catholic squires. Simultaneously Catholic squires, to a greater extent than in the past, were putting their younger sons into the professions and trade. Thus, one way or another, by 1790 the surviving Catholic squirearchy had been strengthened by transfusions of *bourgeois* spirit, capital and blood. Not infrequently the transfusion had a dramatic effect. The Tempests of Broughton Hall, Yorkshire, in the 1720s were in danger of sinking into a pious stagnation and extinction. The daughters moved wholesale into convents. Stephen Tempest wrote out for his son a gloomy, defensive statement of family policy. For him the greatest threat to their gentry and their Catholic spirit was plebeian commercialism. A Catholic squire must forbid his children to marry plebeians; he must be ready to buy dear and sell cheap; he had a quasi-priestly responsibility for his Catholic tenants. But though his three daughters obediently became nuns together in the English convent at Ghent, his two sons proved recalcitrant. The younger son became a physician, married (in spite of his father's fury and sanctions) a plebeian and departed for the French colony of Senegal. The elder son and heir, Stephen Walter Tempest, was so modern in his views that three of his sons went into business in Manchester. Of his four daughters three married and only one entered the Ghent convent.

The Fermors of Tusmore, Oxfordshire, were ostensibly leading lights amongst the pious or orthodox gentry. Dr Samuel Johnson held converse with 'an Abbess, Madam Fermor' at the English convent grill in Paris. Alexander Pope made a modest society beauty, Miss Arabella Fermor, the heroine of his poem *The Rape of the Lock*. It was a Fermor who was the only Catholic acquaintance of the Prime Minister, William Pitt. The family maintained its gentry by a steady policy of marriage with all the other leading Catholic families of its class. But it also received several substantial transfusions of middle-class blood and capital. There were two intermarriages with the Maires of Durham, wealthy lawyers and bankers, and in 1783 James Fermor captured one of the richest Catholic heiresses of the day, the only child of the plebeian solicitor, Nicholas Mayes.

The Lawsons of Brough, Yorkshire, had always hovered uneasily on a knife-edge between piety and commercialism. The struggle had begun in the early seventeenth century with the ultra-piety of old Mrs Dorothy Lawson, her monastic household planted on the family property of Byker in Northumberland amidst their coal-pits. The early eighteenth century was a period of Lawson pietism, of monks and Jesuits and nuns. In the middle of the century commercialism gained ground. There was an intermarriage with the heiress of the Durham Maires, as a result of which a Lawson younger son inherited the Maires' extensive legal, banking and coalmining businesses. By chance he later inherited Brough, which became the centre of his wide business operations. In this Sir Henry Lawson baronet, the family seemed to have reached a perfect equilibrium. He was a pious man, the generous patron of many convents and clerical institutions, and the brother of a nun at Bruges. He was impeccably genteel and patriarchal. As his manuscript collections of pedigrees of all the surviving Catholic gentry show, he was a firm believer in spoiling the Catholic middle-class Egyptians to conserve for ever the predominance of the old gentry over the Catholic community. Yet, as his business records—banking transactions, colliery accounts, factory accounts—show, he was a very shrewd man of affairs with an eye to every possible source of profit. He imported coffee from plantations he had bought in Jamaica; he opened a 'pott and pantile' factory at Byker; he made large advances to the Duke of Norfolk and Lord Arundell.

The decline of the Catholic gentry was also somewhat cushioned by a widening of the prospects of employment for their children. In their expansive days before 1688 it was the great shortage of jobs in administration which had, more than piety, driven so many of them into the priesthood, monasteries and convents. In the later seventeenth century Charles II and James II had opened up to Catholics commissions in the forces. Between 1688 and 1783, denied this opening, the sons of families which had acquired a military tradition sought and found places in Continental armies. Sir Henry Lawson's pedigree book shows the extent to which they trod this road into the Hessian, Brunswick, Imperial, Spanish, French, Neapolitan, Polish and even Russian armies. They were never so numerous as the Irish Catholics who are to be found everywhere in eighteenth-century Europe in whole regiments and even brigades. The Irish produced a bevy of general officers and a field marshal, Lord Carlingford in Austria. The English were too few to rival them, except with the Duke of Berwick and General Count Antonio Winspear. In one generation the Sheldons of Warwickshire produced four officers, scattered across the French, Austrian and Hanoverian armies. From 1778 successive Catholic Relief Acts very slowly and grudgingly admitted Catholics to serve in the British forces. The career of Henry Howard of Corby, Westmorland shows the process at work. After seven years of schooling with the English Benedictines and one year at the Sorbonne, Henry determined to be an officer. He did a three-year course in the Teresian Academy for officers in Vienna. But he did not find the prospect of prolonged garrison duties in an Austrian line regiment attractive and the British government's policy seemed to be changing. In 1778 a first Relief Act allowed Catholics to do non-commissioned service in the forces. In 1779 Henry applied to the Horse Guards for permission to serve as a gentleman-volunteer in a British line regiment in the American war. He was rejected, as a Catholic. In 1783 he applied again, this time for a commission in the King's German Legion. The War Office pointed out that he might as other Catholics had long been doing, serve in Hanoverian or Hessian regiments in British pay, but might not, by law, hold a commission in any established regiment under British command. Back at Corby he waited until 1791 when a further Relief Act allowed, in a limited way, commissioned service to Catholics in any regiment whose commander would take them. By 1793 and the outbreak of the great French wars Catholics, English, Irish and Scots, were flooding into all ranks of the forces. But poor Henry Howard was now too old for field service and he ended as a captain in the West Yorkshire Militia.

In the medical and legal professions Catholics figured, naturally, more numerously than the size of the Catholic community warranted. Entry into the medical profession was easy either by moving on from a Catholic college to the medical school at Montpellier, or by apprenticeship to one of the many Catholic doctors. The sons of Catholic gentry favoured general medical practice, in London or a provincial town (Durham, York and Winchester each never had less than six or eight Catholic doctors), or being apothecaries. They were so many and the Catholic gentry, their natural clients, so few and often so unwilling to entrust themselves to gentry-doctors whose faults they knew well and to whom they hesitated to reveal their private lives, that they were short of work. The foundation of municipal hospitals and dispensaries provided useful employment without denominational bars. In general Catholic gentry-doctors were not much respected. Dr John Lawson was a not unusual case. He was a gentleman and the grandson of a baronet. He was taken to court in York for bastardy cases, neglected his duties, and was dismissed from the post of Physician-Attendant to the York Dispensary for inefficiency. But there were exceptions, like Edward Jerningham, a specialist in cytology and Licentiate of the Royal College, though a cadet of a major gentry family of Costessey, Norfolk. In general also, better service was done by the middle-class Catholic physicians, barber-surgeons and male midwives.

A small number of Catholic gentry still read for the Bar in Inns of Court. (The Secular Clergy Chapter still had its headquarters in rooms in Gray's Inn, a tribute to the old link between Catholicism and the Bar.) But until the Relief Act of 1791 they could not be called to the Bar. Catholics therefore gravitated into conveyancing. According to Lord Eldon, who was trained in conveyancing by a Catholic, Catholics formed the cream of that branch of the profession. The Catholic gentry had always relied heavily on collusive trusts as a way of avoiding recusancy fines and double Land Tax. Since 1697 they also needed Protestant trustees to enable them to escape the laws forbidding them to buy land or pass it on to Catholic heirs. Throughout the eighteenth century few Catholic gentry ever fell foul of these laws, though they inherited and bought land freely. Some preferred to use Catholic conveyancers—though some Protestant trustees had to be found to connive in each transaction; others, even the Mary Ward sisters in York, habitually used Protestant lawyers. Provincial Catholic conveyancing was mostly in the hands of gentry practitioners; the London business (much bigger) was dominated by Irish and middle-class men.

The professions of literature, the arts and music had always been preserves of the lower orders of society: the gentry practised them only as amateurs, though, exceptionally, a few did become professionals. In the eighteenth century, as earlier, the taste of the Catholic gentry differed in no way from that of their Protestant social equals. A few of them actively patronised writers and a very few were admitted into the most exclusive literary circles. In the 1730s John Caryll of East Grinstead, Sussex, a Catholic squire and a particularly persistent literary amateur, was admitted to Lord

Burlington's circle. Through this connection Caryll and a group of provincial Catholic gentry amateurs (Blounts, Throckmortons, Fermors) launched the young middle-class Catholic poet, Alexander Pope, on his career in London. He afterwards deserted his early Catholic patrons. Late in the century Sir Henry Bedingfield of Oxburgh, Norfolk gained admittance to the most exclusive of all London literary circles, Dr Johnson's 'Club'. At Llangollen in the mountains of Wales two blue-stocking aristocratic spinsters ran for years a peculiar romantic salon visited by almost everyone of consequence. Sir Henry and Lady Bedingfield were received there. One of the two 'Ladies of Llangollen', Lady Eleanor Butler, an Irishwoman, had been brought up in Ireland and convents abroad as a Catholic, though her practice of her religion was eccentric. The strongly Evangelical Protestant poet William Cowper accidentally became acquainted with the same southern Catholic gentry circle of refined families which had helped Alexander Pope. Cowper's visits to them and his correspondence produced a great cult of his poetry throughout the Catholic gentry community. Between 1714 and 1830 there was only one Catholic gentry professional poet, John Dryden, but a host of amateurs. They were to be found writing verse in almost every Catholic country house, even amongst the pious circle living round the Bar Convent at York, where Edward Bedingfield exchanged verses and critical comments in his stilted friendship with William Mason, the fashionable Anglican parson poet.

The Catholic gentry were even more spectators of the scene in the fields of the other arts. Painting was dominated by foreign immigrants. The Catholic gentry produced two gifted amateurs, Giles Hussey and Edward Jerningham. The world of music was heavily dominated by foreigners. The contribution of the Catholic gentry was limited to employing them as teachers and avidly copying their techniques. The great days of English court and country-house music had passed. They had passed also in the Catholic colleges and religious houses. Before 1714, particularly at Nieuport, Paris and Brussels the English gentry entrants brought with them considerable skills as instrumentalists and composers. Now the national gift was fading. Convent organists were generally foreigners, musical taste foreign and florid and choirs indifferent. In Catholic chapels in England the musical tone was set by operatic Masses performed in London Embassy chapels by singers from the Italian Opera. The Catholic gentry in their house chapels attempted similar Masses on great feast-days if they could borrow professional singers; otherwise they had no liturgical music at all.

The Catholic gentry, like their Protestant fellows, were great amateurs of the theatre, London and provincial. Playwriting and acting were now much professionalised and plebeian. The few gentry in the theatrical world were entirely Protestant and often Irish. Architecture had followed the same path of standardisation and professionalisation. Although the fashionable style of building was Palladian, so that architects had to put in an apprenticeship in Italy and use Italian Catholic craftsmen for the finer decorative work, the profession was heavily Protestant. Of the host of provincial architects, almost all plebeian, exceedingly few were Catholics. William Carr, a minor member of an eminent York group of architects, happened to have a Catholic gentry wife. The only Catholic gentleman architect of the age, the great James Gibbs, was a Scot. In 1720 the Herald Warburton combined his official visitation with compiling a sketch-book of gentry mansions. He paid, for private, romantic reasons, particular attention to the houses of Catholics. He had to admit that, architecturally, they were almost all of no interest, ill-repaired jumbles of medieval, sixteenth-century and seventeenth-century pre-Palladian work. But that was a time of financial stringency for the Catholics. By 1830 the survivors of the gentry, twice as wealthy as their grandparents, lived mostly in much-modernised houses. Even in the 1740s, with the first dawn of better times, the Catholics had shown indecent haste to rebuild even if it strained their resources. Stuccoed Palladian fronts were fixed to old buildings, disguising their shambling antiquity. At Gilling Castle in Yorkshire Lord Fairfax pulled down his Elizabethan stables and clapped the new front on what had been the back of the house. Guests had formerly ridden the few yards from the village street to the ancient front of the house: now they must drive half a mile down a grand avenue towards the new front. Gardens were remodelled, with interesting mock ruins and 'Gothick' temples. The Catholic squire who carried the process furthest was Francis Cholmeley of Brandsby, Yorkshire. He not only modernised his Hall, but replanned the village, pulled down the medieval Anglican church and rebuilt it in the Palladian style too.

The English gentry tradition had never despised the higher grades of commerce. It was not that they *liked* commerce. Indeed they continued to regard it as fundamentally plebeian and lacking (to use Stephen Tempest's word) in 'honour', the sense of honour which was the core of real gentility. But long custom had largely appropriated the higher kinds of commerce—banking, import and export trade, wholesale dealing—to the use of the younger sons of peers and gentry and to foreigners. In the process, at any rate in theory, these realms of commerce had been rendered aristocratic in personnel and spirit. It was therefore natural that city and town government should be controlled by close olgarchies of gentry-merchants. This tradition and the eighteenth-century expansion of English trade made it inevitable that the sons of the surviving Catholic gentry should now have extended their involvement with trade. But in the course of the seventeenth century Catholics had, with steadily increasing efficiency, been shut out of civic office and so out of active membership of the official and unofficial rings of merchants. By 1714 Catholic gentry entering commerce preferred striking out into business abroad rather than enduring perpetually a limited and subordinate place in urban commerce in England. The only Catholic bank of any size in London was founded in the 1720s by the gentry family of Wright of Whealside, Essex, with offices in Convent Garden. 'Wrights the bankers' are mentioned often in Catholic correspondence. It was a tight family partnership and content to accept a very specialised and Catholic type of business. Its partners held the accounts of clerical institutions, visited the Continent to deal with convents and colleges, transferred money abroad to pay convent dowries and school bills, shipped in Catholic pictures and books. For mortgages and loans the Catholic gentry resorted mainly to Catholic 'private banks' in the provinces, such as that of Sir Henry Lawson of Brough and Newcastle.

There existed Catholic networks for placing gentry sons in trade on the Continent very like the late Victorian way of placing them in the colonies. The favoured areas were in Flanders (Dormer and Sons of Antwerp), Paris (Waters and Son, bankers), Bordeaux (Bellasis and Son), Naples and Leghorn (Jackson and Scrope, Gibbs, Falconet and Noble), Seville (Wiseman and Son), San Lucar (Henry Stonor), and Oporto. There was a special flavour about the way of life of these expatriates. They never forgot that they were gentry, and the plebeian side of the business was usually pushed on to middle-class partners and clerks. Their business was general dealing: they did banking services for English travellers; they paid Catholics' school and dowry bills; they shipped wine, statuary and pictures home. Wine was more and more their staple. Few of them grew rich. Periodically they branched out into consulate work for the London government, or took service in foreign administrations. They sent their children generally to English colleges and convents and tried (sometimes without success) to marry them to English gentry. They tended to drift home to England. Oddly enough their *diaspora* formed only a small part of two much larger ones, English Protestant and Irish. In the course of the century a large number of English Protestants settled in trade or as gentry residents all over the Continent, especially in Italy. The Irish 'Wild Geese' were to be found everywhere. The case of Henry Scrope is fairly typical. He was a younger son of Simon Scrope of Danby Hall, north York-shire. His father was in straitened circumstances in the 1720s. After schooling by the Jesuits at St Omer, Henry was taken on as a trainee partner by George Jackson, a convert merchant of Leghorn. He married Jackson's elder daughter and had one child, a daughter, educated in an Italian convent at Ancona. Late in life Henry grew weary of Leghorn and frightened of war scares. He sold out and retired to live with his daughter at Dunkirk. There she was jilted by Baron Brady, an Irish Catholic serving in the Coburg Army. After her father's death she returned home to Yorkshire and was ensconced comfortably in the little town of Richmond beside a Jesuit chapel. She did not forget her convent training in Italy. She bequeathed to her 'kind friend', Sir Henry Lawson, 'a large Holly Week book with Italian explications'. Typical also were the many English expatriates Admiral Lord Nelson met in Naples. There was the Catholic Sir John Acton baronet, married in his old age by Papal dispensation to his fourteen-year-old niece. There was the Catholic Count Joseph Gage, originally from Sussex and with a long and dubious history of financial juggling in Spain and Italy. As a stout, conventional Anglican, Nelson found these odd Catholics distasteful. He preferred the expatriate Protestants, Sir William Hamilton and his wife Emma, and, after later experience of her adaptability as a sailor's wife, the flighty Miss Wynne. She was the daughter of an impoverished Lincolnshire Protestant squire and his French Catholic wife. Miss Wynne married the Protestant Captain Freemantle, RN.

The Catholic gentry's sons penetrated increasingly, but with difficulty, into colonial fields of commerce and administration. The most lucrative field was India. The Honourable East India Com-pany ruled there, at Bombay, Madras and Calcutta, over a hetero-geneous native population which included many poor Catholics, ministered to by Portuguese and Spanish priests. The lower ranks of 'John Company's' European regiments and the domestic staffs of Company officers contained numerous plebeian Catholics, Portuguese, Swiss, Irish and English. But Company cadetships, civil and military, were denied to known Catholics down to 1791. Anyway the cadets were required to attend Anglican prayers twice a day and church on Sunday. Lapsed or apostate Catholic gentry certainly did sometimes penetrate even the top echelons of Com-pany service. In the 1750s Laurence Sullivan, the dictatorial Chair-man of the Directors, was pretty certainly once a Catholic. A few English gentry officers served in French India: Richard Fermor of Tusmore, Oxfordshire, died in a French military uniform in

Pondicherry. Late in the century the brilliant, handsome and dissolute Henry Crathorne of Ness, Yorkshire, passed through Calcutta on his way to China in company with his friend, Lord Macartney. But after 1791 Catholic gentry sons began to flow out to India as Company cadets or officers in 'King's regiments'. The Catholic chapel register of Tichbourne, Hampshire records John Tichbourne, dead at sea on his way home from India in 1812, and his brother, Benjamin, killed at the age of nineteen by mutineering sepoys at Vellore.

The next most profitable colonial areas were the West Indies and Spanish America. In the British West Indies there was a crazily heterogeneous European population of English, Irish, Scots, French and Spanish origin. The Catholics amongst them were cared for by Irish priests nominally under the authority of the Vicar-Apostolic of the London district. Even Sir Henry Lawson, who had business interests in Jamaica, failed to trace more than one English gentry settler, his agent 'Mr Winn', though there were family traditions of cadets long vanished and said to have 'died in the Indies', 'gone to Antigua', 'died in the Brazil Islands'. The English Catholic contingent in trade in France had connections with the French West Indies. The firm of Tuite and Sons (perhaps Anglo-Irish) was in the sugar trade out of Montserrat. The Tuites' main office was in London. They moved in Catholic gentry circles and, by intermarriage, their blood and money helped half a dozen families of squires in the north. The South American trade was best conducted under cover of nominal Spanish citizenship from offices in Seville, Malaga and Tenerife. In the 1760s Thomas Selby of Biddleston, Northumberland married 'Eleanor Tuite of Santa Cruz, Teneriffe and Ireland', and Barbara Strickland of Richmond, Yorkshire (by proxy), Nicholas White of Tenerife. In the second half of the eighteenth century the Catholic Anglo-Irish contingent at Malaga included Sir Sebastian Fabian Enrique Swale baronet and merchant, the poor and half-Spanish head of a long-ruined Yorkshire gentry family.

North America attracted few gentry Catholics. Maryland, because of its English Jesuit missioners, continued to attract a thin dribble, Knatchbulls, Jerninghams, Mores, Fenwicks, Withingtons. Even after 1783 a Yorkshire Tunstall sold up his merchant's business in Leeds and emigrated to Baltimore. The Carolinas had a few Catholic gentry settlers, descendants of Jacobite prisoners shipped out as indentured labour in 1716. The Canada Act of 1774 produced discreet enquiries from gentry parents through Lord Petre to Government. But prospects were doubtful and by 1830 the English gentry contingent in Canadian territory was limited to a few traders and one or two Army officers in the garrison at Halifax.

Few English gentry sons felt drawn voluntarily to a life at sea. Amongst the thin scattering of Catholic master-mariners occur an occasional gentry name or two: for instance 'Mr. Crathorne of Ness', mate of a ship of Whitby engaged in trade to Germany. Before 1791 commissioned service in the Navy was denied to Catholics. The exceptions were few. Sir Charles Hungate, 6th and last baronet of a decaying Yorkshire Catholic family, had originally, as the youngest son of a large family, taken service in the Royal Marines and been discharged insane with the rank of Captain. James Barrow, the son of a poor Catholic Lancashire gentleman, was pressed into the Navy while on his way to the English College, Rome. He served below decks for seven years before his honourable discharge set him back on his way to the priesthood. After 1791 commissions were granted quite freely to Catholics. Now Lord Dartmouth informed Lord Petre with compliments that he would recommend Francis Trapps of Nidd for the first vacant midshipman's berth. At least one Catholic midshipman served on HMS *Victory* at Trafalgar. Nelson's fleet contained one Catholic captain and two senior officers, Freemantle and Harvey, with Catholic gentry wives.

The eighteenth-century agrarian and industrial revolutions provided yet one more factor which slowed the decline of the gentry. Yet it was a factor which did not always and necessarily work in their favour. It produced a flood-tide of opportunity on which only the bold, energetic and fortunate could float; the timid and unlucky could easily be drowned in the flood.

The Catholic gentry in general had a good record for agrarian improvement in the past if only because it offered a way to cope with recusancy fining. They were, for such a small body, remarkably scientifically-minded. Philip Howard of Corby, Westmorland, Lord Petre of Essex, the Welds of Lulworth, Dorset, the Yorkshire Gascoignes and the Berkshire Eystons were all keen experimental agriculturalists. Sir Edward Gascoigne and Sir Marmaduke Constable were keen students of Flemish root-crops and rotation systems. The Lancashire Towneleys for generations had laboratories, contributed to learned journals, invented weather-recording, and collected coins and marbles. Marmaduke Tunstall of Wycliffe was a distinguished ornithologist, Charles Waterton of Walton an explorer of the Amazon, Richard Salusbery and Thomas Gage Fellows of the Linnaean Society, Charles Jerningham distinguished in medical research, Nathaniel and Edward Pigott astronomers with a European reputation. But the small, piecemeal agrarian improvements of the seventeenth century fell far short of the revolutionary changes in farming systems of the eighteenth century, and an academic interest in science or even the chemistry of the soil was no guarantee of possession of the business ability needed to carry out successfully a major enclosure.

In the agricultural heartland of central England in 1750 piecemeal modernisations had still left mostly intact the antique communal village farming system, with its vast common fields of ploughland divided into long strips and its common waste of rough pasture. The fashion now set in for total enclosure of the whole area of each village, destroying the common fields and waste and dividing up the land into individually-owned blocks. Such a change took away from the squire most of his medieval lordship rights over the tenants and his complex rights over the land. In return he gained a modern, freehold ownership of a third, or perhaps even a half, of the total area. So complete an extinction of legal rights required a special private Act of Parliament. The great expense of the Act, of the expert surveying, road-making, hedging of the new lands, and preparing them for more modern and productive use fell mostly on the squire. On the other hand, in an age of generally increasing food prices, he could, if he displayed vigour and prudence, hope ten years later to be well on his way to paying off his debt contracted, and twenty years later to have doubled his rent-roll income. Of course the timid and poorer squires could attempt to carry out the enclosure in two or more stages over a period of years. Often Catholic gentry property was not made up of whole villages but of a jumble of lordships, part-lordships (shared with other land-owners), and tenant-holdings in villages where others owned the lordships. In such cases policies of enclosure were often forced on the Catholics by the will of richer neighbours.

Traditional Catholic history paid almost no attention at all to these enclosures, though they undoubtedly preoccupied the Catholic gentry and their farm tenants for many years (1760–1830). A few case-histories will show the effects of the changes. In 1741 the Catholic Thomas Fitzherbert of Swynnerton, Staffordshire, began to take the plunge. The enclosure of the common waste of his main Staffordshire properties cost him so much that his income for years to come was reduced from £1500 a year to £400. He sold off inherited lands in Wales and took his family to live cheaply for some years in rented housing in York. Swynnerton Hall was temporarily leased to a Protestant. The Blundells of Crosby, Lancashire had hitherto been conservative landlords, hesitant about introducing annual leases and rent-increases. Now they carried out, in easy stages, a total enclosure with annual, economic rent-increases on their new farms. In the process they ousted their chaplain from Crosby Hall and planted him more economically on a small plot they made over for priest's house and chapel. By 1815 the Blundells' income had doubled. Lord Arundell, like most of the major Catholic landowners, was embarrassed by having a multiplicity of often inefficiently-managed inherited estates far from his main house at Wardour. Enclosure involved him in many years of worry and expense. By the 1790s he had already borrowed £8000 from Sir Henry Lawson of Brough.

On the other hand there were Catholic victims of enclosure. The Trapps family of Nidd, Yorkshire were heavily mortgaged by the 1760s. Their response to the stress of mid-seventeenth-century financial charges was to take refuge in cheese-paring economy and the cult of celibacy. As a result of this policy the family died out in the male line and the inheritance passed to a Trapps cousin with no experience in large estate-management. The expenses of an over-lavish rebuilding of Nidd Hall and of successive bouts of enclosure raised the family debt to over £20,000. Collapse was staved off during the Napoleonic wars by high food prices and plentiful jobs in the forces for the sons of the family. The great slump of 1815–22 brought retribution. The Hall and estate were auctioned off to a Protestant manufacturer. The head of the family retired to live cheaply in Boulogne and his children left Yorkshire to seek employment.

At Pocklington, in east Yorkshire, the Catholic Dolman family had long been sliding into genteel poverty. In the 1760s, as at Nidd, the extinction of the main line led to inheritance of the estate by a distant cousin: in this case a Dolman tradesman who had been living in Berkshire. He and his sons tried every way to pay the family debts. They sold land; they practised medicine; they opened a tanning business. Enclosure proved the last straw. By 1800 the family auctioned off the whole estate. The father retired to live in St Omer and his eldest son, a surgeon, settled in practice in York.

Traditional Catholic history has also paid little attention to the Catholic reaction to the first industrial revolution. The legendary picture of the typical Catholic eighteenth-century squire was of a Squire Western immersed in field-sports and as remote from the great wen of industry as were the characters in Jane Austen's novels. Indeed there were Catholic Squire Westerns. The eighteenth-century Catholic gentry did play a disproportionately large part in contemporary field-sports. The Meynells started the Quorn Hunt, the Vavasours the Bramham Hunt. The Scrope of Danby racehorses did well at most northern meetings in 1760–1820.

Catholics appear in cricketing history: John Nyren captained the Hambleden Club and later wrote the first guide to the game; Thomas Lord, a Thirsk Catholic, founded Lord's Cricket Ground. Neddy Haggerston of Ellingham, Northumberland was an almost illiterate squire-bumpkin who loved horses and dogs and hated trade and conversation. But in reality the seventeenth-century Catholic gentry had a solid tradition of industrial enterprise, in iron-forging, coal-mining, glass-making and soap-making. That great contemplative, Mrs Dorothy Lawson, had her monastic household beside her family's collieries at Byker, Newcastle. The pious Brookes of Madeley, Staffordshire began the first iron forges at Coalbrookdale. The new industries of the eighteenth century appeared mostly in midland and northern areas where the Catholic landowners were thickest on the ground. The big Catholic land-owners had, by chance, immense industrial potential. The Duke of Norfolk owned Sheffield (steel), Worksop (coal), Glossop (engineering, coal, textiles), and Lancashire properties (coal, textiles). The Earl of Shrewsbury, Lords Petre, Stourton and Clifford, the Welds, Lawsons and Haggerstons were all well-placed. Of all of these Catholic potentates, the earliest to react to the revolution were the Lords Molyneux, who energetically developed docks at Liverpool and soon apostatised. The Dukes of Norfolk reacted next. The Catholic 8th Duke started to develop Sheffield and Glossop. The work was carried on spasmodically by the Protestant rake 9th Duke (1786–1815) and his Catholic successors. By 1830 the Duke was an enormously rich man. The Earl of Shrewsbury was an intellectual and country recluse, 'addicted to music and mechanicks'. His successor (1827–54), 'the Builder', was devoted to expensive church-building in the new Gothic manner. The bills for this were paid out of the proceeds of enclosures and the unearned increments flowing in from the 'Black Country' industrial plant and housing springing up unbidden on the Earl's estates.

The northern Catholic gentry seized their industrial opportunities. By the 1830s it was a rare family which had not sons, uncles and nephews in business in Manchester, Liverpool, Newcastle, Leeds, Hull. The Brandlings of Newcastle and Middleton, Leeds pioneered the use of steam locomotives on their colliery railways. The Meynells of North Kilvington, Yorkshire inherited coal-bearing property in county Durham and Lancashire. From 1818 Thomas Meynell was a member of a consortium of Quakers and Catholics who established the Stockton and Darlington Railway Company; he was its first chairman. The Catholic Salvins of Croxdale, Durham were coalowners and associates of George and

Robert Stephenson, the Newcastle railway engineers. By the 1830s the Salvins had members who were architects in London, merchants in Manchester and administrators in India. We have already noted the banking and industrial enterprises of Sir Henry Lawson of Brough and Byker. By the 1830s an apparently stagnant Catholic gentry family in Lincolnshire, the Youngs of Market Rasen, were striking out into steelmaking in Sheffield. From 1780 the Catholics in the sprawl of industrial Sheffield were served by priests and chapels paid for by the Duke of Norfolk, Revells, Staniforths, Eyres and Broomheads—scions of country gentry branching out into steelmaking and general merchanting. In Lancashire scions of country Catholic gentry families had established the private banks of Greaves of Preston and Worswick of Lancaster, and the cotton milling firms of Anderton of Preston, Baron of Blackburn, Brettargh of Manchester and Marsh of Hindley.

A last factor which helped to moderate the decline of the gentry and perpetuate its influence was the legal device used to prevent the estates of extinct Catholic families from falling into Protestant ownership.

Anyone who has glanced through collections of gentry family papers will be familiar with the bundles of packets of folded parchment settlements, usually made on the occasion of a family marriage of an heir to the property. Successive settlements of this kind perpetuated elaborate entails and trusts. These endeavoured to protect the unity of the family property and insure it against the folly of individual heads of the family and government charges. They were also an insurance against lack of male heirs, and established in great detail a line of heirs. These trusts were common form in landowning families, Protestant and Catholic. They incidentally preserved Catholics from the worst charges of recusancy fines and largely defeated the purposes of the legislators who made the anti-Catholic penal legislation of the 1690s. Between 1697 and 1791 Catholic landowners bought land with impunity, in spite of the law to the contrary, and Protestant heirs very rarely indeed inherited Catholic land. All of this, of course, was made possible only by expert conveyancing and collusion by a host of respectable Protestant trustees acting for Catholics. Thus whenever a Catholic family ceased to have male heirs of its own name, long-established settlements carried their property into the hands of Catholic relations and heirs.

The decline of the Catholic gentry began well before 1660. From then onwards, at an increasing rate, the estates of extinct families accumulated more and more thickly in the possession of the

surviving few. Circumstances then determined which of several
different courses the new owners would pursue. Occasionally they
decided to auction off the inheritance and apply the purchase
money to paying off the debts on the estate. Alternatively they
might sell their own property in whole or part to pay their own
debts, and move into the new property. Thus in 1788 John Rowe of
Beaston, Devonshire inherited the much larger estate of the defunct
Husseys of Marnhull, Dorset. He sold Beaston, moved to Marnhull and changed his name to Hussey. Alternatively the heir might
decide to keep the property and either lease it to a tenant, Catholic
or Protestant, or put in an agent to manage it. In this way the Welds
of Lulworth, Dorset acquired by 1815 by inheritance no less than
five major Catholic estates of defunct families. Their experience
was not uncommon. The family papers of quite modest surviving
Catholic gentry often contain three, four or five bundles of deeds,
each inscribed on the outer wrapper with the name of an extinct
family whose land they had acquired.

This practice of accumulation had obvious disadvantages,
especially when total enclosure processes set in. The dying families
did their best to persuade their heirs to perpetuate the family name
and keep the house in use. It was often possible to ensure this, by
providing in a settlement that a younger son of the inheriting family
should take the defunct family's name and arms and reside in
their house to refound the family. This process of refoundation
by transfusion became popular by the 1780s and eventually
created immense complexities. Some examples will show what this
meant.

When the Constable family (Lords Dunbar) of Burton Constable,
east Yorkshire became extinct in the male line, the inheritance fell
to the Tunstalls of Scargill. The second son of that family changed
his name to Constable and took over Burton. By chance he also
died without male heirs, and so did his elder brother. The Scargill
and Burton estates now both passed to the next Catholic heirs, the
Sheldons of Winchester. They provided a second son to take
Burton, and the name Constable, and a third son to take Scargill,
and the name Tunstall. But then the Sheldons died out in the male
line. As they did so there was a great deal of hasty shuffling of
estates and surnames amongst the surviving heirs. Eventually
Burton Constable and the Constable name were inherited by a son
of Lord Clifford.

Sir Henry Lawson of Brough had himself been the victim of a
shuffle of this kind. He was a second son and a family settlement
had dictated that he should inherit the name and Durham properties
of the defunct Maires. Years later his elder brother died leaving no

son, so Henry Maire was translated back into Sir Henry Lawson. The Towneleys of Lancashire suffered an even more complicated shuffle. In one generation they were called upon to take over the names and estates of both the Yorkshire Stricklands and Lancashire Standishes. Luckily they had three available sons; the eldest inherited Towneley, the second (called Strickland) Catterick, and the third (called Standish) Standish. Then the third son died unmarried. So his next eldest brother was translated from Ralph Towneley Strickland into Ralph Towneley Standish and took both Catterick and Standish. The elaborate dance of inheritances was far from finished: Ralph died leaving no children.

There were even cases where a settlement enjoined that the husband of the sole heiress of a dying family should take his wife's surname. This happened twice in the history of the Nevils of Holt, Leicestershire. Early in the seventeenth century the husband of a Nevil heiress, Sir Thomas Smith, changed his name to Nevil. In 1740 history repeated itself and Count Pietro Migliorucci (a resourceful Florentine who had acquired his title in the service of the King of Poland) gracefully changed his name to Pietro Nevil.

By 1830 when the Catholic gentry met socially in London, Bath or Scarborough they needed agile wits to remember the current surnames of many of their clan. For instance was Michael Anne of Burghwallis an Anne or a Tasburgh? Charles Gregory Pigott was now calling himself Charles Fairfax. Was Mr Gandolphy really a Lancashire Hornyhold? How surprising that the gentleman announced by the butler as 'Mr Thomas Standish' turned out to be Tom Strickland of Sizergh! More surprising still, he tells us in confidence that, any day now, his brother-in-law, John Wright of Kelvedon, will change his name to Lawson of Brough and inherit that great property.

But many families of the lesser Catholic gentry did not manage to survive in this strange fashion. They became so enmeshed in debts and mortgages that outright sale of the whole property became inevitable. Entails and settlements to the contrary had to be broken. Such falls were intensely painful to the families concerned and to their Catholic neighbours. In most cases they soon sank out of their class and merged into the great anonymous herd of plebeians. But here and there, exceptionally, a fallen family was lucky and pertinacious enough to win back a place in the ranks of the gentry. This happened to the Trapps-Lomax family. After their bankruptcy and sale of Nidd Hall, Yorkshire, their young men made careers as solicitors, civil servants, Army officers and parish priests. In itself this upper-middle-class activism would never have kept them in

Burke's *Landed Gentry* or the Catholic gentry pedigree books. But they had luckily inherited the small Lancashire estate of the defunct family of Lomax. This fact, and continuing intermarriage with Catholic landed gentry assured them of retaining aristocratic status on through the nineteenth century.

The rearguard action fought by the retreating Catholic peerage and gentry down to 1830 was gallant and skilful. The 150 or so surviving families were generally well-off and self-assured. They still had, to the full, their traditional aristocratic eccentricity. The Charlton of Hesleyside memoirs are full of sharp comments on relations' oddities: Margaret Charlton's masculine vigour pulled family affairs together while her husband, William, rotted in alcoholism; her daughter-in-law, Katharine, was 'wholly devoid of common-sense'; the Cholmeleys of Brandsby were, as always, wildly eccentric; Lavinia Barnes 'up to the day of her death went on working irreparable harm. R.I.P.' Their social prestige in the Catholic community remained high.

After many years of argument and opposition, in 1829 a Conservative government, terrified by the threat of rebellion in Ireland, passed the Catholic Emancipation Act. Now, with a few humiliating exceptions, Catholics might hold any government post. The day for which the Catholic aristocrats had waited since 1688 had dawned, but it came far too late. A new Whig government and some Whig local authorities (for instance in York, which promptly elected a Petre as Lord Mayor) did their best to promote Catholics to office. The list of Catholic aristocrats not disqualified by residence abroad, old age, youth or eccentricity was small. Even inside the Catholic community, for all their social prestige, their real power was now small. They no longer dominated the clergy, the great majority of whom owed no allegiance to them. Yet, although they could not have guessed it in 1830 from the recent conversion of the Honourable George Spencer, they were soon to gain an unexpected new lease of life from two different sources. From the 1840s the Victorian agonies of doubt of Anglican Tractarians and other earnest Protestants were to bring into the Catholic community a rich harvest of aristocratic and middle-class converts. The numbers of the Catholic peerage were destined to climb up again from seven to over thirty. Meanwhile further advances of the British agrarian and industrial revolutions to 1880 were to bring the Catholic aristocrats an even larger unearned increment from farm-rents and coal royalties.

Yet in hard reality the day of the Catholic aristocracy had long passed even in 1830. They had themselves unconsciously admitted this by their adoption of upper-middle-class attitudes, professions and commercialism. They were now only an ornament and status-symbol of a changing Catholic community in which leadership had passed decisively to the middle classes.

13. The Revolt of the Plebeians, 1714–1830

In 1706 the author of the list of Catholic chaplaincies we have already noticed assumed the truth of the aristocratic view of society. To him there were ultimately, beneath all the innumerable distinctions between groups by income and occupation, only two classes of persons: those of Rank (qualified by their noble or gentry blood to command and have privilege) and the people (lacking that blood and so destined to be dependent and obey). In the 1720s Stephen Tempest's homily to his son endorsed the view bluntly. He flatly observed that there could not possibly be any exception to the rule that only those of noble or gentry blood could act with 'Honour' and 'Christianity'. Plebeians, the people, peasants must inevitably betray their origins and blood by 'base little Stratagems', by being thrusting, commercial, vulgar. The apparent exceptions really proved the rule since research would, he believed, always show that base gentry had plebeian blood and noble plebeians legitimate or illegitimate gentry blood.

The aristocratic view has had an immensely long innings. It remained strong, even amongst undoubted plebeians, throughout the nineteenth century. William Bernard Ullathorne, the most blunt and vigorous of early Victorian Catholic bishops, was, in some ways, unashamedly lower middle class. He dropped his 'h's, his tastes were plebeian. His father was a convert Catholic small-town shopkeeper and his father's family semi-itinerant village traders in Yorkshire. Yet secretly Ullathorne cherished the thought that his family had intermarried with impoverished gentry through whom he was descended from Sir Thomas More. It was the gentry blood which fascinated Ullathorne, not Catholic devotion to More. Like so many successful plebeian Catholics in the early nineteenth century he attributed the fall of his gentry ancestors (real or imagined) to plebeian status to Jacobitism and devotion to the Catholic religion. William Mawhood, a thriving wholesale draper in London at the end of the eighteenth century, cherished similar thoughts. A relation by marriage, a member of the College of Heralds, provided him with a rather speculative pedigree back to a family of seventeenth-century Yorkshire Protestant small gentry. This herald, Brooke, produced a volume of gentry pedigrees which displayed a marked interest in Catholic gentry marriages with plebeians and part-gentry families lurking in business life. Mawhood also, while suffering distastefully the demands for money of his feckless relations, cherished the knowledge that one of them had married a cousin of a Scots Jacobite peer. Even amongst the Victorian Catholic middle class who scorned such private snobbery and who rejected the right of the Catholic peers and gentry to a leading voice in the community's affairs, a version of the aristocratic view prevailed. They expected their children to marry into similar families of 'good stock' and thought poorly of the Catholic 'riff-raff' and Irish.

It was natural that, in every generation, the thrusting and successful should want to rise in the social scale, found a family and then fight to conserve it in a privileged status. The aristocratic theory voiced that feeling, but, as a theory, it defied the facts of history. The peers and landed gentry of 1714–1830 were, with a few exceptions, descended from plebeians who, luckier, more commercially-minded and politically skilful than their fellows, had thrust their way to privilege and titles. They had profited from modest upsurges of population, economic and governmental activity in pre-industrial England. In their rise to gentry and in their defence of that status under threat they had always either used 'base Stratagems' or had sunk, ruined, back into the plebeian mass. Up to 1760 the pace of English economic and social changes had remained slow and unrevolutionary. The political revolutions of 1642–60 and 1688–1714 were more violent and unsettling. But the aristocracy had had relatively great success in riding change and adapting to it so that they could remain in the saddle. Even with their special difficulties, the Catholic aristocracy had made a retreat in very good order. But after 1760 the pace of economic and social change, of industrialisation and urbanisation, grew hot and revolutionary. The old aristocracy, Protestant and Catholic, resorted once more to 'base Stratagems'. They married plebeian heiresses; they took government drainage and improvement grants to rationalise their estate management; they raked in coal royalties; they long dominated Cabinets. The Catholic gentry pulled every string to gain themselves peerages, often trying by ingenious genealogical charts to secure the revival in their favour of long-extinct ones. The Constables of Everingham (really Haggerstons) paid thousands of pounds in legal and research fees to win the extinct Scottish Barony of Herries. Miles Stapleton of Carlton (really Errington) did the same to win the Barony of Beaumont, which had been extinct since 1537. The Towneleys, the Welds, the Lawsons, the Scropes all competed in vain for the same glittering prizes.

But in society at large and amongst the Catholics the wealth and prestige of the old aristocracy veiled the fact that they were being pushed aside on to a shelf, displaced by a new, rising plebeian aristocracy. As early as 1678–85 educated Protestants and the Catholic gentry noticed, with a shock of surprise, that self-employed plebeian Catholics were becoming numerous in London. In 1724–6 the Protestant Dissenting journalist Daniel Defoe published his *A Tour through the Whole Island of Great Britain*, based on business journeys made mainly before 1714. He does not mention Catholics often and we have to make allowances for his journalism and his very *bourgeois* outlook. He seems to admit that Catholicism still contained a substantial element of aristocracy and superstition (see, for instance, his account of Holywell in Wales, then a 'little Lourdes', 'thronged' with Papists), but it had a solid, independent middle-class element evident in London and a few provincial towns like Durham. In London the popish chapels were numerous and respectable enough to be included in Defoe's list of public buildings. In Durham, 'a town full of Roman Catholics', he was struck by the sobriety and quietness of the way the Catholic citizens thronged to Mass, for all the world like the Dissenters going to their meeting-houses. In 1719 the Catholic Bishop Gifford had already observed that conversions were nowadays predominantly 'of the middling sort of people'.

From 1676 down to 1822 Parliament ordered fairly regular enquiries into Catholic numbers and property. From 1767 the questionnaire shifted its focus to business men, tradesmen and artisans. Manifestly now the traditional concentration on aristocrats and their dependents would leave out of account the majority of Catholics. Meanwhile the Vicars-Apostolic were attempting their own surveys. The two sets of reports tell the same story. Overall Catholic numbers were increasing fast, probably by fifty to sixty per cent between 1676 and 1804, though probably not nearly so fast as the contemporary population explosion. The Catholic rural population was slowly declining: the urban population was fast increasing, in some towns dramatically. The number of self-employed middle-class Catholics had increased greatly. By the 1780s there were upwards of 25,000 Catholics in London. Up to the 1780s a great many provincial market towns and some industrial ones (for instance Halifax, Huddersfield and Hull) had practically no Catholic inhabitants. Of those towns which had Catholic congregations, few had sizable numbers. These were either county towns popular as residences for Catholic gentry (like York, Winchester and Gloucester) or a few new industrial complexes like Sheffield and Wolverhampton. The sprawl of new Manchester in 1773 still contained only 500–600 Catholics, less than York. Of industrial towns Liverpool alone that year had over 1000 Catholics. By 1804 the picture was changing greatly. Congregations in the country towns were stationary. Those in industrial complexes and London were shooting up, and Catholics were beginning to make small but enduring settlements in hitherto hostile places like Huddersfield, Hull, Halifax, Newcastle, Bradford, Leeds. Manchester already had over 10,000 Catholics, Liverpool 6000, Preston 3000. 'Newcastle' (a great mission area then including outlying towns) had 4000.

Significantly also the lay-out of Catholic missions had greatly changed. In 1680–1700 there were more missioners in the south and west than in the north; perhaps over two-thirds of the missioners were employees of the aristocracy either as domestic chaplains or riding missioners serving outlying tenants. Under a third served congregational missions maintained by trust funds or collections. By the 1780s three-quarters of the missioners were independent of the aristocracy, mostly serving congregational missions which had increased sharply in numbers. Admittedly these missions in county towns (and even a few in the politer areas of London) had mainly gentry trustees and subscribers. But elsewhere the congregational missions owed their origins and continuance to the initiative and money of middle-class parishioners and priests.

Where did this new, large Catholic middle class come from? Some of them had been Catholic tradesmen, doctors or lawyers in towns for generations past. There were, for instance the Nappers and Behos who arrived in York in the 1680s from Oxford and London as established wholesale drapers. There were the Shorts, East Anglian doctors for generations and Catholics since at least the mid seventeenth century, settled in Norwich and Bury St Edmunds. There were the Brooks and Trescotts, merchants of Exeter. There were the Humbles (of Newcastle and Middleton, Leeds, colliers and colliery managers), the Hancocks (of Sheffield, 'small mesters' in the steel business and Catholics since at least the 1650s), the Haughtons (of Sedgeley, Staffordshire, iron manufacturers and Catholics since almost 1600), the Warburtons and Daniells (Staffordshire potters and Catholics since the mid seventeenth century).

Some of the new Catholic middle class had gentry origins. John

Couche, a small landowner in Fowey, Cornwall in 1767, was a Fowey man of minor gentry origins who had made good in London as a brewer and then retired. The vicar of Fowey reported that 'his predecessors have been Papists for many generations'. But the Couches now behaved in a very middle-class way; his sons (even the eldest) were in trade or doctors. In Sheffield in the 1780s most of the tiny Catholic chapels were kept going by the subscriptions of the Eyres, Revells, Broomheads and Staniforths who all had remote country gentry origins but were now immersed in the steel business and general dealing. In London in the 1750s Charles Tankred of Covent Garden was a bespoke tailor with a trade by post to the Yorkshire Catholic gentry. He was distantly related to the Tankred baronets of Brampton and used a signet ring with their arms. But he was married to a plebeian and plebeian in his tastes. From the 1770s to the 1830s the Langdales of Holborn were London's biggest gin-distillers. Thomas Langdale used the coat of arms of Lord Langdale by that family's leave, though no relationship could be proved. The Holborn family were steady Catholics and occasionally intermarried with the more indigent country gentry. In the 1760s there were several apothecaries' shops in Drury Lane run by tradesmen who sported aristocratic names or coats of arms: some, including Francis Bredall, were acknowledged poor relations of Catholic peers and gentry, though rarely received into their houses. At one time or another York sported a hat-shop belonging to a member of the Catholic gentry Palmes family of Naburn and a milliner's shop belonging to a female member of the Cholmeley of Brandsby family.

Another large slice of the new Catholic middle class was drawn from Catholic country immigrants. Some derived from families of tenant farmers on gentry estates. These were especially numerous in London, Lancashire and Yorkshire. Farming families in the remote north and west had a long tradition of seeking their fortunes in trade in the county town or in London. The Hodgsons, farmers of Ugthorpe, high on the north Yorkshire moors, in 1734 had two sons helping on the farm, another a perukemaker in Covent Garden, another a ship's chandler in Whitby, another a servant at Bell House in Essex, and a daughter who had married a Catholic tradesman in London. The Sturdy family, tenant-farmers of Lord Fairfax, had children in trade in London and York. Other Catholic urban tradesmen derived from the old free smallholding congregations of Papists, especially in Yorkshire and Lancashire. In Pennine Lancashire the growing number of Catholic handloom weavers derived naturally from local Catholic smallholders who had combined agriculture with home-weaving for many years. In

Tyneside the nucleus of the growing body of Catholic 'butties' and colliers in the new, deeper pits was drawn from families long experienced in combining smallholding with opencast mining. Few of these people bothered to record their pedigrees. An exception was Joseph Holdforth. His father was a self-employed joiner in the Protestant town of Helmsley, Yorkshire and had escaped from labouring work on the nearby estate of the Catholic Lord Fairfax. Joseph's parents were drowned accidentally. He was cared for by Lord Fairfax and apprenticed to trade in Hull. He moved to Leeds, prospered and opened his own woollen mill around 1800. In Leeds he was the founder of a Dominican mission and its sole support for years. Later the Holdforths bought a country estate, acquired a coat of arms and became minor gentry.

As Bishop Gifford had noted early in the eighteenth century, the Catholic middle class gained a substantial number of converts. A few of these were the result of spontaneous changes of heart. This was true in the cases of the Cave family of Winchester, John Floud an Exeter handloom weaver, the three Greenaway brothers of Tiverton (one a schoolmaster), Thomas Hearne the Berkshire antiquarian, John Walker the actor, George Fothergill a York draper. But most middle-class conversions to or from Catholicism owed a great deal to more mundane factors. In the contemporary setting of vigorous denominational differences, small town life and strong family pressures, a mixed marriage or service of a master of a different denomination could often change people's allegiances. Some Catholic congregations in towns had a tradition of aggressive expansion. Thus in Brindle, Lancashire by the 1740s quite half the small town's population was Catholic. Mixed marriages were surprisingly frequent, and the Protestant partners almost invariably became converts. From 1728 to 1800 there were never less than ten converts a year and sometimes fifteen. Other town congregations—for instance York and, at least to 1780, Birmingham—barely broke even; their loss-rate by apostasy almost cancelled their gains from marriage-converts and country immigrants. Then there were towns like Hull, Halifax and Doncaster which had a fearsome reputation amongst decent Catholic parents for being the ruin of almost all country immigrants. London was a case apart, containing every extreme of laxity and intense piety. Its sheer size made laxity easy and encouraged the 'English malady' of depression. On the other hand its size made natural the existence of almost self-contained villages and Catholic congregations which could have a high standard of pastoral and community care, preaching and liturgical music. The *Diary* of William Mawhood illustrates all sides of London Catholic life. He was the son of immigrants from Yorkshire

K

converted by such a congregation. William was brought up in an atmosphere of intense piety and at St Omer. Like so many lay boys returning from St Omer with a sense of having failed to take the one way in life possible he soon lapsed and married a Protestant. His first three children were baptised in Anglican City churches. Then he and his family were reconciled to Catholicism by Bishop Challoner. Henceforward he was a model parishioner of the Moor-fields chapel, a frequent Mass-goer and compulsive sermon-taster. The family pietism and growing wealth from Army contracts brought intense anxiety about his sons who proved irresponsible and unwilling Catholics.

The lists of middle-class converts includes a few of considerable distinction: Johann Christian Bach; Thomas Arne; Samuel Wesley; Susannah Cibber; Edward Gibbon; James Boswell; Thomas Atkinson; Thomas Hearne; Richard Challoner. We may include a number of persons who came under Catholic influence, mostly by marrying practising Catholics: David Garrick, Fanny Burney; Mrs Thrale; Christopher Smart; Edmund Burke (whose mother and sisters were Catholics in Ireland) and Henry Fielding (whose step-mother was a Catholic). With the exceptions of Challoner, Atkinson and Burke, these people were merely passing influences on the Catholic community and their association with it did it both good and damage. Johann Christian Bach had become a Catholic in Italy before he began his long residence in England. He was never a model Catholic. Thomas Arne was probably converted during a time he spent in Dublin. Back in England his fame as a composer delighted Catholics but his eccentricities increased. Dr Burney, who had been his pupil, reported frankly on his extreme selfishness, avarice and evil reputation with women. Mawhood's *Diary* contains a probably well-founded report that he apostatised on his death-bed. The young composer Samuel Wesley was an unexpected and prestigious recruit to the Catholic community. For a few years he was organist to a London Catholic chapel and composed several Masses. Then a bad accident and the 'English malady' brought on his return to Methodist Anglicanism. Susannah Cibber, a distinguished actress, was Arne's sister and acted as mother to his feckless children. She was a convert, most probably also in Dublin, though her religious practice was irregular. She was separated from her Protestant husband. Gibbon and Boswell were both converts on impulse and rebound from parental influence during their student days. Both speedily and finally abandoned Catholicism. Perhaps Gibbon's *Decline and Fall of the Roman Empire*, much admired by liberal Catholics, owed some of its Voltairean flavour to his early Catholicism. Although his friend,

Dr Samuel Johnson, had a persistent fellow-feeling for Catholics, Boswell never betrayed the faintest sympathy. Hearne, the Berkshire antiquary, was associated for years with Catholic gentry friends and so favourably disposed towards Catholicism that his deathbed conversion was taken for granted.

'The Club' had a distinctly Catholic atmosphere, though very few Catholic or convert members. Mrs Thrale, Dr Johnson's great friend, astonished the members by remarrying to an Italian Catholic singer, Gabriel Piozzi. Piozzi's simple pieties and visits to English convents abroad produced in Mrs Piozzi an uncritical, romantic enthusiasm for all things Catholic. Experience of Arne had given Dr Burney a distaste for Catholics which was increased by the impulsive marriage of his novelist daughter Fanny in middle age to a French refugee, General D'Arblay. D'Arblay rarely practised his religion and Fanny's comments on it were acid. Another member of 'The Club', the poet Christopher Smart, was a donnish man who married a Catholic Irishwoman. Smart died insane and his widow retired to edit a newspaper in Reading. Dr Burney had always regarded her as an exception to his anti-Catholicism and his letters contain a moving account of a visit to her in Reading in her old age. Henry Fielding's Catholic contacts were purely fortuitous and without any ascertainable influence on his life and opinions.

Challoner and Atkinson both came from that free, self-employed lower middle class: Challoner's forebears were smallholders and Dissenters; Atkinson's were master-craftsmen. Both owed their conversion to ardent Catholic proselytisers—Challoner to Lady Holman, in whose mansion he and his mother were Protestant servants, Atkinson to the York Bar Convent nuns, their Jesuit chaplain and gentry supporters who helped him when he was a struggling architect. Challoner, who became the eighteenth century's best-known missioner, significantly avoided gentry chaplaincies and was at his ease only amongst the urban middle class. Atkinson remained a Catholic but, as behoved a fashionable architect taking commissions from every quarter, sat lightly to the efforts of the Bar Convent pious clique to appropriate him. It is significant that his children by his first convert wife never became Catholics.

Edmund Burke was almost an honorary Catholic. He and his typically Irish 'cousinhood', all living together in the same suburban villa, belonged to that foreign Irish background in which Church-papistry was common form for the middle class. He had many Catholic friends, fought hard for Catholic emancipation, and was the hero of liberal Catholic gentry. The last Lord Fairfax was a devout Catholic who lived near Malton, the Yorkshire political

headquarters of Burke's Whig patron, the Marquis of Rockingham.
A mere rumour that the great Burke was coming to stay with the
Marquis at Malton brought from Fairfax a shower of invitations to
Gilling Castle and offers of game.

The growing Catholic middle class also recruited from 'foreigners' of many kinds, Irish, Scots, Americans, Italians, Belgians,
French, Austrians and Czechs. For the most part they formed a
regular but itinerant feature of London life, well-known in the
seventeenth century, but now attracted to England in far larger
numbers by her increasing wealth. Certain professions (music,
interior decoration, and the sleazier areas of politics) were crowded
thickly with them. A few succumbed to Anglicisation and settled
into the English scene; the majority remained stubbornly foreign
and so birds of passage. They certainly added colour and variety
to English society and the Catholic community. They reinforced
powerfully the vigour of the Catholic middle class. But the pious
English Catholics viewed them askance with some reason.

Burke was a representative Irish immigrant. Amongst the Irish,
Protestants and dubious Catholics much outnumbered sound
Catholics. There were Catholic Irish peers resident in provincial
capitals, Lords Cahir, Dillon, Fingall and Kingsland, all of
whom were Freemasons and uncomfortable parishioners in English
chapels. The Irish adventurers and politicians, Mr Kavanagh at
Winchester, Captain Miles McGrath in Essex, Laurence Sullivan
and the Burkes, were suspect. Mr Kavanagh's settlement with
the missioner in Winchester roused alarm amongst local Catholics.
The Irish Catholic merchant fraternity—Golightlys, Tuites—and
lawyers—Matthew Duane the great conveyancer—were more
acceptable and steadier Catholics. Nathaniel Hooke (author,
classicist, friend of Sarah, Duchess of Marlborough) was an oddly
alien figure, as was his secular priest son, Luke Hooke, a brilliant
theologian who chose to live in Paris and take French nationality.
The Italian Opera had its Irish stars and managers, irregular
Catholics all (Michael O'Kelly, O'Reilly, McSwiney, Mrs Cornely).
The theatre had many Irish, mostly Protestants, but including the
lonely figure of Mr Keregan, actor-manager of Norwich, York and
Scarborough, a sound Catholic though ostracised by the Catholic
gentry. London had rarely less than a dozen Irish missioners, some
foreign, some, like Challoner's friend, Richard Dillon sound and
Anglicised.

Scots Protestant immigrants were many but Catholic ones few.
James Gibbs, incomparably the greatest architect working in
England in the eighteenth century, was a discreetly Catholic Scot
who made little impact on English Catholic affairs. It was otherwise

with the handful of Scots priests, extremists in either radicalism (Alexander Geddes and Archibald Macdonald) or respectable orthodoxy (Mr Clinton and Mr Hamilton). American Catholics were rare poor relations in England. The middle-class Catholic aristocrats of Maryland and Pennsylvania persisted in sending their sons to St Omer, Liège and London for their education, and their daughters to English convents in Europe or the Bar, York. Charles, Daniel and Joseph Carroll reached St Omer in 1748. Charles was almost twenty-nine before he saw Annapolis again after St Omer, four French Academies and an Inn of Court in London. A small contingent of American Jesuits of the English Province served years in remote gentry missions like Lulworth in Dorset and Danby in north Yorkshire.

Amongst immigrants from Europe Italians and Imperialists predominated. The Italians were technicians of music, painting and sculpture, working by contract, often for months in provincial mansions of Protestant grandees. Some rarely, if ever, practised their religion in church in England. They were irregular attenders in Italy and detested English Catholic chapels, which were dark, small, had no music and endless English devotions. Some Italians were devout. John Bartholomasi of Siena converted his Protestant shopkeeper hosts while teaching in Winchester. Gabriel Piozzi nearly converted Mrs Thrale. Of the relatively few Italians who stayed in England for life, most founded thriving music-publishing houses (Corris, Clementis, Novellos) or concert halls. The Imperialists contained more talent: Mozart and Haydn (both briefly), Hummel, Gluck, Johann Christian Bach, Dussek, Hoppner, Zoffany, Angelica Kauffmann, Maria Teresa von Paradis, Scheemakers, the two Nollekens, Eva Violetti. Of the few of these (mostly German) who stayed in England permanently, Bach was barely a Catholic, the young Nollekens half-Protestant and fantastically mean, while Angelica Kauffmann and the old Nollekens were devout Catholics.

Before 1789 a French surname almost invariably meant a Huguenot Protestant. There were Catholic French language teachers in most county towns and London, and technicians of the glass and textile business in St Helens, Lancashire and round London. As we shall see later, it was only after 1792 that French and Irish immigration sharply increased and began to make a profound impression on the English Catholic community.

How did these new middle-class Catholics earn their living? We think immediately of industrial inventors, entrepreneurs and engineers, the technicians who pioneered the English industrial revolution. Traditional Catholic history painted a picture of an early Victorian community largely empty of such people. This view seemed to be confirmed by the standard economic histories. All the great names in the technological development of industry between 1760 and 1830 are Protestant, and many of them Quaker, Methodist or Presbyterian. In fact there was a contribution by Catholics. In the field of inventions it was very small. In the history of the pottery industry the Catholic Warburtons and Daniells of Cobridge and Burslem, John Sadler of the Herculaneum works at Liverpool, and Charles Gouyn of the Chelsea works have an honourable, if minor, place. In the history of English glass-making Robert Sherburne and his French team of workmen at the Ravenhead works, St Helen's, have a place. In the development of gin-distilling the large works of Langdale and Son in Holborn played a small role. In 1799 it seemed that English Catholicism would gain a major place in the history of engineering technology. That year a French refugee engineer, Marc Brunel, arrived at Falmouth from New York to start work for the Navy at Portsea dockyard. He was a Norman and had originally been destined for the Catholic priesthood. In 1830 Brunel and his son, Isambard Kingdom Brunel, were engaged in driving the Rotherhithe Tunnel under the Thames. Their firm was to prove the most brilliantly original one in English civil engineering before the 1860s. Yet father and son were intensely busy, practical men with sceptical minds. They cared little for Churches and dogmas, Catholic or Protestant. Marc married an English Protestant and allowed her to control the elementary education of his children. He insisted on sending Isambard to French academies in Caen and Paris, not interested in their Catholic teaching but in their tradition in mathematics, which was superior to anything then available in England.

Amongst industrial entrepreneurs Catholics occupied a bigger, but still modest, place. English industry in 1830 was still organised mostly in a great number of small workshops, amongst which the dozens of giant concerns stood thinly. There were some hundreds of Catholic-owned workshops in the textile, pottery, steel, iron and glassmaking industries. Catholics had a few works in each of the soap, furniture-making, distillery, decorated metalwork and flax-spinning industries. These Catholic firms played a significant part in the Catholic community's affairs. Their owners were, for instance, the chief subscribers maintaining the Catholic chapels and clergy in Leeds, Bradford, Halifax, Sheffield, Wigan, Bolton, Manchester. It was notable that Bishop Milner of the midland district transferred his residence from Chillington, on a gentry country estate, to industrial Wolverhampton. Bishop Ullathorne's family had a large flax-spinning manufactory with works in Barnard Castle, county Durham, London and France in the 1830s. When the English Catholic convents were bundled from France in 1793–4 accommodation and funds were offered generously by Lord Petre, Lord Stourton, the Welds of Lulworth and Robert Gillow, the wealthy Catholic furniture manufacturer. When the Earl of Shrewsbury and the architect Pugin started their campaign for Gothic church-building, they employed the ironworks at Birmingham of the Catholic John Hardman who made a fortune out of the movement. Between 1760 and 1830 a Catholic boys' school at Sedgeley Park, Staffordshire, in the midst of the Potteries, flourished. Its students were entirely middle class. Generations of ordinands destined for the secular clergy received there the Latinity needed for a seminary but lay boys had a separate course tailored for a career in commerce. If parents wished, boys could be prepared directly for apprenticeships in the iron and pottery industries. In 1793–4 when the English College, Douai was disbanded by the French Revolutionary government, some of the professors and ordinands found refuge in a house in county Durham. The house and grounds had been carefully chosen by the President, a local man. The coal seams under the grounds provided the transplanted College with a maintenance from royalties for many years.

For the most part nineteenth-century Catholic local historians took a clerical and aristocratic view of the chapels and congregations. They only occasionally mentioned parishioners' trades and business achievements. In fact, throughout the eighteenth and nineteenth centuries the Catholic middle class were engaged, exactly like their Protestant fellows, in every trade and with them seized every new commercial opportunity and suffered bankruptcy in every slump. In the early eighteenth century Catholic tradesmen still mostly sheltered under the protection of their aristocrats and based their goodwill on their custom. The traditional Catholic staples were wine and drapery. In the later eighteenth century the decline of the aristocrats and the multiplication of middle-class Catholic businesses created a temporary crisis. Thus in York old-fashioned Catholic businesses could not adapt and went bankrupt. The Hindleys, clock and instrument-makers, who had moved to York from a Manchester which then had only a small Catholic population in 1731, were feeling the decline of gentry business by 1774. Young Hindley decided to try a move to Hull but fared still worse and went out of business. In 1767 York, like Durham and Winchester, was full of Catholic drapers, hatters, saddlers, undertakers and milliners battening on the declining gentry trade. By 1830 most of these businesses had gone under or moved to Manchester, Preston, Newcastle or Hull. The future for Catholic business men lay increasingly in entering the tough world of Protestant competition and increasing their capital outlay. William Mawhood's turnover of £10,000 a year in the 1790s owed little to Catholic gentry custom. He clothed Protestant peers and made his main profits out of Army contracts. The Sharples of Brindle similarly moved out of local trading and into wholesale timber importing in Liverpool. Successful Catholic tradesmen had now to be adaptable. In Liverpool the Rossons began in wholesale merchanting, moved over to soap manufacture and then into the law. Joseph Holdforth started in Hull merchanting and moved successfully into woollen manufacture in Leeds. John Nyren, the son of a Hampshire Catholic publican, failed in trade in Portsea and then succeeded as a calico-printer at Bromley in Kent. Besides being an ardent cricketer, he was a model Catholic, educated at St Omer, and the father of an Abbess at Bruges.

Parliamentary enclosures and periodical rises in corn prices made large-scale cornmilling a profitable though speculative business. Of the two seminaries in England which grew out of the disbanded English College, Douai in the 1790s, Crook Hall was founded on coal royalties, and St Edmund's, Ware on a gift of £10,000 by Mr Soane, a wealthy Catholic miller of Bedhampton, Hampshire. From the 1740s great improvements in road-surfaces, by 'macadamising' and Turnpike Trusts, led to the rise of fast, regular coaching services and profit for the owners and managers of coaching inns. It was natural that Catholics should have participated in this development since inn-keeping had long been one of their staple occupations. Catholic innkeepers provided missioners and gentry with safe and discreet *poste restantes* and meeting-places. In York the part-Catholic Gibson family provided these services while modernising their Lendal inn. They put in stabling for 200 post-horses and contracted as caterers to the Committee of the Assembly Rooms. In Newcastle the Catholic Debord family long performed the same services and accommodated a Catholic chapel at the back of their inn-yard. In the 1770s the Jesuit superior's address-book was arranged not by houses but by Catholic posting-inns nearby: The Star, Holywell; The Star, Wolverhampton; The White Bull Post House, Preston; The Golden Lion, Warrington; The Globe, Leicester; The White Horse, Warwick; The Bell, Worcester; The Talbot, Bromsgrove; and The Bell Tree, Bath.

Then there were the more genteel professions. In 1760–1830 the number of Catholic lawyers and doctors, already relatively large, multiplied. The doyen of Catholic lawyers was Charles Butler, the son of a draper in business in Pall Mall. Outwardly the pattern of his career was all orthodoxy and success. Educated by the Mary Ward nuns at Hammersmith and the English College, Douai, he trained as a conveyancer under Duane and Maire in Lincoln's Inn. His immense practice and growing wealth secured him a gentry marriage with an Eyston of Berkshire. After the Relief Act of 1791 he was called to the Bar and died a Bencher of Lincoln's Inn. In private life Butler was cautiously liberal, letting prudence veil his inner scepticism about many features of Catholic life. Like so many successful Catholic business men he had close relations who were priests. By the 1740s the long dominance of higher clerical posts by scions of the gentry was coming to an end. The clerical state became a career open to middle-class talent. The old kind of Vicar-Apostolic had been a gentleman-born, a Stonor or Petre, ruling his district from a country mansion lent by his family or by gentry relations. The new kind was invariably the son of a middle-class tradesman, familiar with urban areas and business method and ill at ease in the company of gentry patrons. One of the earliest examples was William Walton of the northern district. In the 1770s he lived in modest but comfortable style in a large rented house in Trinity Street, York (not, like his predecessors, in a country mansion). He was near, but apart from, the Catholic gentry houses in Micklegate around the Bar Convent. He had a housekeeper, Mrs Scarsbrick, a manservant and three maids. His Lancashire family had deserted their farm for trade in Manchester. They acted as his bankers and trustees. In York he kept an avuncular eye on his relations, the Gibsons, innkeepers in Lendal. At his death in 1780 the Bishop left a private fortune of £3200 amassed by prudent investment of his inherited income. In 1774 the will of 'William Naylor of Brindle, Lancashire, gent., at present in Paris' was proved. Naylor was a Benedictine missioner of considerable shrewdness, the son of a tenant-farmer on a gentry estate in Lancashire. In 1722, as a young missioner, he took over the mission at Brindle, a normally vigorous parish but temporarily demoralised by the recent public apostasy of its gentleman-priest. By the time Naylor left Brindle in 1766 its congregation was doubled, and his business ability had provided a new, larger chapel in the Palladian style, a priest's house and a land endowment. He moved on to the Presidency of his Congregation. In his will he left 'to all such of my brothers and sisters' children as may be living one guinea each'. His successor at Brindle, Joseph Hadley, was a London tradesman's son and just as businesslike.

Letters as a profession did not attract the Catholic middle class. They could understand the printing business, where some of them made a moderate living by putting Anglican prayer books and Bibles and current secular literature in the front window of the shop and keeping Catholic books under the counter. In London the Hills family, in Norwich William Eusebius Andrews, in Liverpool John Sadler, and in York the Bollands practised trade in this way. Here and there (as in Reading where the widowed Mrs Smart inherited and ran as editress her stepfather's local newspaper) were a few Catholic journalists. Music-printing was a new (at least in England) and fairly lucrative business, but so technical that it was monopolised by Catholic Italian immigrants in London and New-castle. By 1830 the craft of novel-writing was well-established but rarely lucrative. The only Catholic who wrote a best-selling novel was Mrs Elizabeth Inchbald, the daughter of a Catholic tenant-farmer in Suffolk. She had married a Catholic actor. His feckless-ness and the need to provide for herself and her family made her, like Mrs Smart, a vigorous business woman. She became a success-ful actress, a fair playwright and the authoress of one good novel, *A Simple Story*.

Grub Street contained few Catholics. Charles Gildon, a poet, playwright and *enfant terrible* gone to seed, was an old student of St Omer and a lapsed Catholic. Dr Samuel Garth, a distinguished London physician and author, shared Dr Johnson's nostalgia for Catholicism and perhaps became a Catholic in his last days. The only undoubted Catholic who occupied a central place in the English literary scene after Dryden's death was Alexander Pope. Although Pope chose to adopt an aristocratic medium and prefer-red the company of aristocratic patrons to the professional, middle-class atmosphere of 'The Club', he was thoroughly middle class. His parents were London Protestant tradespeople in the linen business who had become Catholics while staying in Lisbon. Alexander was brought up in comfort. His father had made a fortune by middle life and retired to live on a Catholic gentry estate in Berkshire. He sent his son to middle-class Catholic schools. As an infant prodigy, he was launched in London literary society by Catholic gentry patrons. When he achieved acceptance there, he deserted his Catholic friends for much more influential Protestant ones, Harley, Lord Burlington, Lord Bolingbroke, Lord Harcourt and the Duke of Wharton. Like so many contemporary Catholic middle-class business men, he enjoyed the sensation of escaping from dependence on the Catholic gentry and succeeding in the wider world outside the Catholic community through the use of his own initiative and talents. Like them also, he enjoyed the sensation of talking to the Catholic gentry as their equal and even, through the power given him by his literary success and his Protestant friendships with the great, of doing them services. Also like the most successful Catholic business men he was strongly tempted to quit the narrow bounds of the Catholic community, but was held back from that course by a kind of family *pietas*.

At this period the theatre, London and provincial, was big business. The most successful managers and actors were received in aristocratic society. According to the political economist, Colquhoun, in 1803 the average income of the 500 'theatrical families' was £200 a year, as much as civil servants and well-to-do farmers. But the Catholic middle class fought shy of the profession, fearing its reputation for a Bohemian life, for leading Catholic actors into mixed marriages, and for periodical bouts of unemployment. The principal Catholic theatrical family was the Kembles and their history confirmed Catholic observers' views. Roger Kemble came to the provincial stage from respectable Welsh Catholic farming stock. He married a Protestant. Hence, in accordance with the custom of the time, the boys were brought up as Catholics at the English College, Douai while the girls were educated in their mother's religion. The sons were indifferent Catholics. The one considerable talent amongst the children was Sarah Kemble (Mrs Sarah Siddons), who was an Anglican. The London stage at the turn of the century contained two able Catholic actresses, Mrs Susannah Cibber and Mrs Elizabeth Inchbald. Both practised their religion by fits and starts. The only model Catholics in the theatrical world were the Keregans, whose daughter Mally became a nun in the genteel convent of the English Blue Nuns in Paris.

'The Lower Orders', or wage-earning poor labouring class, of Catholic society had always been a headache for their betters. Possibly before 1760, and certainly afterwards, their numbers appeared to be fast increasing. Few respectable Catholics, clergy or laity, gentry or middle class, could see in this any cause for rejoicing. Their traditional view was that the illiterate or semi-literate poor were infantile and barely capable of true religious conviction. In the 1760s a Benedictine missioner on a decaying gentry estate in east Yorkshire wrote out a very pessimistic report on his flock of poor Catholics. His Franciscan predecessor, now winning golden opinions from gentry and middle-class congregations in London, had tried in vain to instruct the country poor. Education (that is, drilling them in Catholic formulas from the Catechism, simple prayers and rituals, and using a 'Loaves and Fishes' policy to keep them on the estate and to their religious duties) produced at best a superficial regularity of religious practice. The exceptional clung pathetically to the rituals through thick and thin. Most slithered easily from Catholicism if they moved to the service of Protestants or to towns or even if they stayed on the estate but had idle patrons and pastors. The missioner noted that the Dissenting ministers and Anglican clergy had no more and no less success with the poor. At the same time an austere Jesuit chaplain at the Bar Convent, York admitted that he and the nuns had tried every possible method with poor parishioners and had failed. He was appalled by their ignorance and even more by the total ignorance of religion of prospective poor converts attracted to his classes by the nuns. In the 1740s the Franciscans had to endure a set-back in north York- shire. One of their missioners apostatised and became a Methodist. The mission, Osmotherley, had a free congregation not under gentry control. The apostate friar set out to win over his congregation to Methodism. It was noticeable that although the poor labourers lapsed from Catholicism or became Methodists, the three middle- class farming families were unaffected.

In the middle ages and much of the sixteenth century English Catholicism had a folk-religion character sustained by innumerable local holy sites, holy days, complex semi-official rituals, official liturgical rituals—such as 'creeping to the Cross' on Good Friday, ashes and palms, cribs and Easter Sepulchres, Easter blessings, Rogation blessings, exorcisms, St Brice's blessing, scapulars, relics, food regulations. This complex of observances and beliefs, often superstitious, had been partially conserved on into the seventeenth century on some gentry estates where patrons and priests were especially pious. But from the early eighteenth century the surviving rags and tatters wore thin and almost vanished. Some priests, particularly religious, attempted to reconstitute a folk-religion, using materials which had been devised, with some success, in attempts to re-Catholicise Protestant regions on the Continent. They became ardent campaigners for the wide use of things like the Camaldolese rosary, which was far more complex than the ordinary one, '*Bona Mors*', the Five First Fridays, solemn expositions of relics, Benediction and Exposition of the Blessed Sacrament, the Dominican Confraternity of the Rosary, the Francis- can scapular, Benedictine confratership, the Jesuit Sodality and 'Spiritual Exercises', and (a medievalist revival) the Jesus Psalter. But this movement had only a limited success because it was artificial, because it often required books and plant not easily obtainable in the remoter parts of the country, and, above all, because by the 1760s anything that smacked of superstition was unpopular amongst educated Catholics, both priests and laity.

Moreover just at the time (1760–1800) when the absence of

rituals capable of holding the illiterate poor to their religion was becoming most marked, there grew up as common form in most chapels English prayers suited only to the educated. These prayers grew up very naturally and for the best of reasons. On a good many missions that had to share a priest with their neighbours, the priest only appeared to say Mass once a fortnight or once in three weeks. On the Sunday mornings when there was no priest, the congregation assembled as usual and a layman read out Mass prayers from a standard, approved book of devotion. These prayers, partly English paraphrases of the Latin Mass prayers, partly devotions in English to be read by individuals to themselves at various points during Mass, became so well-known that the people could join in without books. On Sunday afternoons, when there was no priest, a reader would similarly go through an English version of Latin Vespers. It was a short step from this for the Mass and Vespers English prayers to be used congregationally when the priest was there and intoning the Latin prayers almost inaudibly at the altar. This whole system had become consecrated by long use and familiarity by 1830. But, powerful and evocative of domestic family prayers as it was to middle-class regular worshippers, it is doubtful whether it had much appeal for the feckless and near-illiterate poor.

Where did the increasing numbers of poor Catholics come from? Some of the increase was the natural result of the contemporary population explosion and the spread into most areas of the Speenhamland System of poor relief. This system subsidised poor families' incomes from the rates, and added extra amounts for each child. Moreover the rise of urban industrial areas attracted thither the surplus population of the countryside. The surviving Catholic gentry landowners often could not, even if they wanted to, arrest this drift. A considerable number of Catholic estates now had no resident landlords. The appearance of poor Catholic immigrants in increasing numbers in urban areas set a problem for the clergy and for middle-class Catholics resident in towns. They were compelled to improvise new missions and chapels in places where the need seemed most urgent. These places were often not those most convenient for the clergy and middle-class residents. The new urban areas were almost always sprawling, unplanned agglomerations of villages and small towns increasingly joined by ribbon development. Thus in 1804 the northern Vicar-Apostolic lamented that 'Manchester' now had over 10,000 Catholics and 'Newcastle' 4000. In fact Manchester really meant a complex covering many square miles and including Bolton, Rochdale, Stockport, Glossop and Macclesfield. There had never been more than one gentry chapel and estate in the area and it was extinct. Middle-class Catholic

residents in each of the six component places set up tiny House-
chapels and demanded regular Mass. The first missioner to be
posted to Manchester was that rare thing, a gentleman-priest. He
soon absconded, without episcopal leave, to the more congenial
atmosphere of a Yorkshire gentry mission. His successor, a middle-
class priest from a Sheffield tradesman's family, stuck to his task
with the help of his private income.

Newcastle in 1804 meant a similar string of Mass-houses at
Newcastle town, Blyth, Gateshead, North Shields and even Hexham. There began, in the industrial areas, a long struggle to build
up and man missions. In the process priests and middle-class
parishioners co-operated and quarrelled over sites and money and
times of Masses. The new chapels bore a strong resemblance
externally to Dissenters' meeting-houses. They were now placed
with little regard for secrecy, since the Catholic Relief Act of 1791
expressly legalised them. They were often structures which had
begun life as private houses, workshops or small factories. They
had little permanence. The surging growth of the new towns, successive slumps and booms and consequent changes of the patterns
of local employment soon made chapels obsolete as too small or
misplaced. They were then sold and new ones established in larger
premises or elsewhere. Hence in York and Newcastle abandoned
Catholic chapels were in use as Freemasons' Halls by 1830. Paying
for missioners and buildings became a drain on Catholic resources,
met by the introduction of proprietary pews, pew-rents and seat-
rents. Inevitably the middle-class parishioners acquired fitted box-
pews with lockable doors; the poor had to make do with hard, free
sittings on benches by the door or standing outside it. Thus, bit by
bit, and impelled by much the same reasons, Catholic chapels took
on the peculiar internal fittings of early Victorian Anglican churches.

How many poor Catholic immigrants from country missions
lapsed or apostatised in the new towns? The missioners had little
means of producing statistics. They were run off their feet by duties
round their multiplicity of Mass-houses, baptisms and sick-calls. In
Manchester in 1830 the average expectation of life was fourteen
years. The jerry-built housing of the urban poor lay in a warren
of courts and rows of back-to-back cottages. Several families
commonly shared one cottage. The missioners were sure that very
many lapsed. On the other hand a surprising number turned up,
if only occasionally, at the Mass-houses. The Dissenting chapels
and Catholic Mass-houses were often the only social-centres apart
from work-places and public houses. However long-winded and
incomprehensible the Catholic Prayers, at least they were a reminder
of the past and a link with relatives left behind in the country.

Another source of the poor Catholics in town congregations was converts. By 1830 even town missioners with little time or interest in evangelising non-Catholics were reporting the growing problem of non-Catholics brought to Mass by Catholics who lived or worked with them. It would be wrong to exaggerate this phenomenon. A great proportion of the working-class poor had never practised religion (that is, the religion of their betters) consistently in past centuries. In the industrial towns they sent their children to Sunday schools at the nearest church or chapel, but never dreamed of going themselves except on high feast days. The Catholic Mass-houses were very small and already uncomfortably crowded. In 1830 only a few, advanced missioners copied the Protestants and opened Sunday schools. Catholic parochial schools as yet existed only thinly. Nevertheless those missioners who had the time and space found that they had a never-ceasing supply of applicants for instruction. This, of course, brought up again, even more urgently, the need for new catechetical methods and the development of new techniques of ritual and devotion. Where missioners received into the Catholic Church scores of converts (poor ones) yearly, it remained to be seen whether they and the congregations could hold them to a religion which priests and middle-class parishioners saw primarily as a matter of duties, not of light entertainment.

Another source of the increase in poor Catholic numbers was the influx of immigrants, Irish and foreign. The problem of poor Irish and foreign immigrant workers was not new. Ever since the middle ages Irish hucksters and harvest-workers had descended on England in bands. In London and the seaports, even in the sixteenth century, Irish seamen, thieves and counterfeiters were a well-known scourge. In the eighteenth century, English people noticed that they were on the increase. In 1752 a Protestant writer went so far as to say that half the poor, and more than half the criminals hanged at Tyburn, London and Westminster were of Irish birth. He was probably not exaggerating. In that year at least one in ten of the paupers in Westminster was Irish. By the 1770s there were several Catholic Irish districts in Holborn, Wapping, Bermondsey, Whitechapel, Soho and Southwark. They had Irish priests, Mass-houses and public-houses with fiddling and Irish dancing and singing. The middle-class Irish congregated at St Patrick's, Soho, but those of them who prospered and became Anglicised moved out into suburban villas and joined English congregations. The working-class Irish naturally swarmed together in groups based on their home districts in Ireland. They filled courts and lodging-houses, exploited by Irish landlords. Few of them showed any desire to be Anglicised. They brought with them to England a religious folk-culture; this, baptisms, churchings, weddings, funerals and Mass-attendance on the great feast-days, sufficed most of them. They had never been susceptible to training in regular church-going as a duty. Only Irish priests could understand their minds and sympathise with their curious way of life. The Irish immigrants into London were so many and so foreign that English Cockney workpeople reacted against them violently. Early trade combinations almost invariably barred Irishmen. Fighting between the English and Irish was so common a feature of East End life as to cause no public comment. During the great anti-Catholic Gordon Riots of 1780, which terrorised much of London for five whole days, the rioters particularly attacked the Irish and burned all of their Mass-houses.

During the Napoleonic wars there was a further, increased flow of Irish soldiers, naval ratings, militiamen and dockers into London. Their families soon overflowed, seeking jobbing work in farms and market-gardens, into Kent, Essex, Middlesex and Surrey. At Thornden in Essex, a middle-class congregation on one of Lord Petre's estates, in 1807 there was a typical sudden irruption of a score of poor Irish families.

In the south and west of England by 1830, apart from regular invasions by Irish harvesting bands and tinkers and an occasional settled family, the only other solid Irish working-class enclave was in the Portsmouth–Portsea area. This originated during the Napoleonic wars in the usual irruption of Irish troops and dockers, together with some thousands of (mostly Irish rebel) convicts in 'hulks' moored offshore. For a time it seemed that Irish Mass-houses of the London type would grow up, and one or two Irish priests moved in from London. But after 1815 the congregations settled down uneasily as piebald, English, Irish and foreign mixed together.

In the new industrial areas of the midlands and north there was no similar wartime Irish influx, but a steady dribble of incomers. They accumulated wherever conditions were favourable for them: that is, in places where they found existing settlements of people from their own district at home, and where employers were willing or anxious to take them on in quantity. The Irish settlement by 1830 was distinctly patchy. Liverpool and Manchester already had Irish parishes larger even than those in London. Irish priests and Mass-houses had sprung up with the usual complex of lodging-houses, Irish public-houses and Saturday night riots. One whole quarter of Manchester was popularly known as 'Little Ireland'. The Irish had a harder job to make footholds in the other Lancashire agglomerations. They were fairly numerous in Wigan, but few in Preston. Up in Cumberland and Westmorland by 1830 coalmines and ironworks were being opened and contractors were going to Ireland to recruit labour. In the industrial midlands Irish settlement was patchy. They were accumulating fast in Birmingham and had an Irish quarter and Mass-house at St Chad's; elsewhere they were still thin on the ground. In the north-east they had not yet made any big lodgement. The slow growth of the South Wales coalfields and ironworks was still based on Welsh and immigrant English labour: the few Irish there had either succumbed to Protestantism or left.

By 1830 the English were aware that they had an Irish problem. In the 1830s Parliament was going to appoint a Select Committee to produce a report on *The State of the Irish Poor in Great Britain*. The Committee took evidence from Catholic missioners. Were the Irish dangerous? Their ranks contained many of the biggest agitators of the day: Daniel O'Connell, Catholic MP and socially conservative: John Doherty, Ulster Trade Unionist, Protestant; Feargus O'Connor and Bronterre O'Brien, Protestant Chartist leaders. The Committee and the missioners took a hopeful view: most of the Irish in the second generation lost their folk-culture and were readily Anglicised. But the Vicars-Apostolic and their middle-class English congregations were not so sure. The Irish were so alien. The uneducated ones, if they strayed into an English chapel, found its English prayers repulsive. The Irish mingled Catholicism and Protestantism so oddly. By English standards of duty over half the undoubtedly Catholic Irish poor were lapsed. Perhaps a third of the whole number of Irish immigrants were really Protestant, like the Reverend Patrick Brontë. Many came from mixed marriages. In 1767 the Anglican rector of Falmouth, Cornwall, noted the regular attendance at his church of one William Meagher, an Irish surgeon. Meagher said he had been for years in military service in France and French India; he was the product of a mixed marriage, had practised as a Catholic in France but was basically a Protestant. The rector wrote: 'I am still in doubt where to class him.'

Most English Catholics hoped the Irish would move out of England. They had no idea that they had come to stay and that, in the 1840s and 1850s, their immigration would rise to flood-proportions.

Compared with the Irish, European poor Catholic immigrants were hardly a problem at all. Seaport towns had long contained a thin sprinkling of seafaring foreigners, Portuguese, Spanish, French. In London and provincial towns there were scattered foreign domestic servants, craftsmen, even circus-performers (like Joseph Toscano, a trapeze artist who died suddenly in Yorkshire in the

1760s) and negro house-slaves said to be Catholics. William Mawhood for years had a French clerk and valet. Only during the
Napoleonic wars did their numbers become serious, but most of
the poor seamen, American, French, Spanish, Goanese, had gone
by 1815. Some, like the Audaers of York, Belgian gardeners and
linenweavers, adapted to English Catholicism. Most lapsed in
blank incomprehension of English prayers. If they became Anglicised, it was likely that they picked up a basic Protestantism with
the English language from their workmates.

In 1830 the aristocrats had lost their power over the Catholic
community. Who would fill the vacuum? The rising Catholic middle
class had strong claims. They supplied the clergy; their pew-rents
and subscriptions kept the chapels going; their fees and donations
supported the convents and schools. In many missions prominent
middle-class parishioners were leading mission-trustees or formed
unofficial committees with strong views on mission policy. The
Vicars-Apostolic were now almost totally drawn from the prosperous commercial middle class. In the United States in 1830 such
lay congregational committees dictated policy to the clergy. It
seemed natural that a similar Congregationalism should take over
in England. And what of the Catholic lower orders? They were
growing up unexpectedly as a great force in their own right. For the
most part they were not economically or socially dependent
on the Catholic middle class. In the new industrial areas and
London they often had their own Mass-houses and parishes. In
Catholic missions which were socially mixed, if the poor were
numerous there was tension between the middle-class pewholders
and the poor benchers. In 1830 the Irish already formed a clear
majority (in Liverpool and Manchester quite three-quarters) of the
Catholic poor. The Irish Catholics were far more volatile, gifted
and vocal than the stolid English Catholic poor. Did the English
Catholic poor have any future? Would the Irish poor multiply and
swallow them up? Would the Irish ever become Anglicised and
obedient to clerical and middle-class English standards? The
future was full of uncertainties.

14. The Clergy: Through Disaster to Victory, 1714–1830

In the late sixteenth and early seventeenth centuries the English clergy, secular and regular, had fought to win clerical control of the Catholic community. They had been soundly beaten. From the 1630s to the 1720s they were, much like their Anglican fellows, straitly subjected to aristocratic lay control. They and their superiors were almost exclusively recruited from the ranks of the aristocracy and their lay clients. Clerical appointments, even of Vicars-Apostolic, were largely dictated by lay patrons. Mission funds, College bursaries and recruitment, the support of monasteries and convents, all depended greatly on the aristocrats. But from the 1720s the grip of the aristocracy on the Catholic clergy loosened. The rising middle class showed clear signs of taking over their functions within the community. Were the clergy simply to change masters?

The situation offered them an opportunity to make a second effort to master the laity. Their chances of success appeared to be minimal. The history of Catholicism and of Protestantism showed that successive efforts to establish a clerical theocracy had, in spite of remarkable temporary successes, always ended in humiliating failure. The English Catholic clergy since 1570 had been greatly weakened by passionate quarrels between Jesuits and the rest, seculars and regulars, liberals and conservatives. There was no sign that eighteenth-century scepticism was abating these quarrels. More-over from the 1720s the English clergy suffered a long succession of major disasters which preoccupied and weakened them greatly, precisely when they needed to show a maximum strength and unity for their war on lay patrons. From 1720 to the 1780s they had to endure grave financial losses. Simultaneously recruitment to the priesthood dropped away sharply. From the 1770s there was a constant and worrying shortage of clerical manpower, just when Catholic lay numbers had doubled and the new industrial towns needed more missions and priests. Efforts to increase recruitment to the Colleges from the 1760s were completely nullified by both the financial crisis and the imposition on the English institutions abroad of restrictive, Liberal regulations by foreign Catholic governments. In 1773 the Society of Jesus was dissolved by the Pope. The ex-Jesuits formed over a third of the English clerical body and controlled a third of its missions. The effects of the dissolution were mixed: but it certainly gravely embarrassed the Vicars-Apostolic and further reduced the annual number of ordinations. In 1783 the American colonies became independent of Britain. As a result of this there was a small, but—especially in the straitened circumstances of the times—damaging loss of English priests moved to the new United States. The English Catholic community lost control of the American Mission. American priests could no longer be drafted into English missions. But these disasters were only the beginning of sorrows. In 1792-7 the French Revolutionary government acted radically. Some 6000 French Catholic bishops and clergy were expelled and dumped unceremoniously on English soil. Dealing with them strained the small resources of the English Catholics out of all proportion to the services rendered by a small minority of the French to the English Mission. Simultaneously all the surviving English Catholic institutions on the Continent were dissolved, usually violently, and their occupants—priests, lay-brothers, nuns, schoolchildren—expelled to England. The clergy and laity were faced with a rapid and extensive improvisation of Colleges and convents in England. In the process much was lost.

As these successive disasters mounted to a climax from the 1780s, there broke out in England a furious confrontation between Catholic liberals and conservatives. The party line cut right across the divide between clergy and laity.

It is astounding that the clergy, though gravely weakened and much battered by all these troubles, which dwarfed both the Elizabethan persecutions and the seventeenth-century crises, in 1830 were in sight of victory over the laity. The aristocracy were powerless; the middle class appeared tamed; and the Catholic working class, even the Irish, more tractable.

Outright Protestant persecution no longer bothered the clergy. Old-fashioned bloody persecution was practically obsolete. In 1729 an aged Franciscan missioner died after thirty years in solitary confinement in Hurst Castle in the Isle of Wight. He was almost the only victim of the savage-sounding Act of 1700, repealed in 1778. A few ordinands, and one or two priests, were convicted as Jacobite militants and transported to South Carolina in 1716. Down to the 1760s the London Vicars-Apostolic and missioners found it prudent to take secluded lodgings and change house periodically to avoid professional informers. In 1780 a Benedictine missioner in Yorkshire was put on trial at York Assizes for proselytising. The evidence provided by the informers was clear, but the judge instructed the jury to find the priest not guilty. Local anti-Catholic mob riots were a danger down to the 1850s. At Newcastle and in Reading missioners were murdered or frightened into heart attacks by mob action. Here and there in the 1720s and 1740s, sometimes incited by local committees of the Anglican Society for the Promotion of Christian Knowledge, mobs burned Mass-houses. From the 1770s England was very subject to mob action, which could sometimes be turned against Catholics. The Gordon Riots of 1780, which raged for five days and were suppressed by troops and artillery, grew out of many secular discontents but were turned by the insane Lord George Gordon into a protest against the Catholic Relief Act of 1778. A score of Mass-houses, chiefly in London, were destroyed.

Yet the Catholic clergy in the provinces rarely attempted to conceal their religion or whereabouts. In the 1770s the northern Vicar-Apostolic followed his usual practice when he alighted from a public coach in the market-place of Macclesfield and asked the first boy he met 'where the Catholics meet'. In the 1760s the Catholic Vavasours of Hazelwood Castle in Yorkshire had a sporting picture painted of baronet Vavasour at a meet; on one side of him is mounted his chaplain and on the other side a figure in unmistakably Anglican parsonical dress. In 1811, when he began residence on his remote northern mission, the priest-historian John Lingard was summoned by both the Protestant squire and the parson to join them at dinner and whist.

The personal safety of missioners and their acceptance in all but the most evangelical of Protestant households were guaranteed by a growing climate of tolerance. For their part, most missioners now slipped, consciously and unconsciously, into a style of religion, preaching and living which had much similarity to those of old Dissenting ministers and Anglican parsons. From 1660 the old-fashioned Catholic habit of worshipping secretly on the upper floors of private houses was abandoned. From 1680 purpose-built chapels appeared; by 1750 they were normal form. Outwardly they differed little from Dissenting meeting-houses. Inside, as we have already seen, they usually had most of the fittings common amongst Anglicans and old Dissenters—pulpits, small wooden altars, box-pews and benches for the poor, galleries. Reservation of the

Sacrament was practised only in a few private chapels in gentry houses. Statues were almost unknown, as were holy water stoups. Incense was used very sparingly indeed. Baptisms took place at portable basin-fonts. Weddings were furtive affairs in private houses after 1753. The Vicars-Apostolic grudgingly accepted Hardwicke's Marriage Act of that year which denied validity to all marriages not contracted in Anglican churches and with Anglican rites. Scrupulous Catholics went on from the Anglican wedding to exchange consents before a missioner, quite illegally. There were a few Catholic burial places (the most famous one was at Winchester), but normally all Catholics, even missioners, were buried by Anglican rites in vaults under the floors of Anglican churches or in their graveyards.

As we have also noticed, by the mid eighteenth century the English forms used at Mass and Sunday afternoon services in Mass-houses had a distinctly neutral or even Protestant character about them. The old *Manual of Devout Prayers,* derived from sixteenth-century Catholic *Primers,* became obsolete, and with it the old semi-monastic, superstitious devotional accompaniments of the Latin liturgy. The new-style clothing of the liturgy came from a series of devotional handbooks published by missioners from the 1720s. The most widely-used was Bishop Richard Challoner's *Garden of the Soul.* The English prayers in these books made only the slightest, almost apologetic, references to the Pope, the Sacrifice of the Mass, devotion to the Sacrament and the saints; the word Catholic was used sparingly. The accent was on solid, systematic Christian devotion of a pietistic and moralistic kind. With a comparatively small number of excisions, the prayers could have been used comfortably by any contemporary Anglican or old Dissenter. They even had the deliberate eschewing of enthusiasm characteristic of the age. Even in 1720 that Jesuit-educated traditionalist aristocrat, Stephen Tempest, had confided to his son that, in his experience, at any discussion of religion when Catholic and Protestant gentry met, they would find no real differences except on the authority of the Church.

There were Protestant and Catholic preachers who still delivered controversial sermons attacking other churches. But the most popular published collections of Catholic sermons of the century, by Robert Manning and James Archer, could have been read with pleasure by Protestants. Indeed, the barrister Charles Butler wrote: 'To almost every Protestant Library and to many a Protestant Toilet, Mr Archer's Sermons have found their way.' The stress of these sermons is on a solid Christian piety, which, the authors claim, is common to all Christians, to be carried out into the duties of daily life, the business office and the home. Sacraments and religious externals are commended, but put firmly in their place: it is a deep, individual piety and a charity shown in action that matter. The rest, monasticism, vows, rosaries, scapulars exist only to build up this piety and charity; they can all too often be used as a substitute for it.

By the 1770s the superiors of Colleges and religious houses were debating how to modernise their training courses. The Benedictines admitted that a too narrowly clerical and French education had rendered their men unfit to move in English society and communicate with the people, educated or uneducated. In fact, as the Benedictines' monastic library lists show, for many years they had been making a free use of books—sermons, devotion, Biblical studies—by Anglicans. From the 1770s young Benedictines were trained for preaching on books by the classical Anglican preachers.

By the 1720s missioners had finally abandoned the traditional Catholic practice of wearing secular clothes of upper- or middle-class quality and cut. Now they donned clerical costume of a Dissenting character: a brown coat and knee-breeches, a short white cravat and a dark-powdered sober wig. By 1830 some missioners had gone over to Anglican clerical garb: a black, tailed coat with breeches or tight trousers, a thin white cravat or tie, and a black top-hat; the wig was gone and the hair cut short.

It was not therefore surprising that in the 1840s Charlotte Brontë should have distinguished sharply between the Catholicism of England and that she met during her stay in Brussels. 'The mummeries' of Belgian Catholicism revolted her: 'I consider Methodism, Quakerism, and the extremes of High and Low Churchism foolish, but Roman Catholicism beats them all.' But she had to add: 'At the same time, allow me to tell you that there are some Catholics who are as good as any Christians can be to whom the Bible is a sealed book, and much better than many Protestants.'

The first, and, as we shall see, the least, of the Catholic clergy's disasters was financial. Catholic procurators had been quick to take advantage of the increasing eighteenth-century sophistication in banking and investment. By the 1720s they had abandoned the old practice of putting out their funds in driblets at interest to Catholic aristocrats. It was a practice which had led to many losses and quarrels. Now the funds were put into Consols, South Sea Company stock, or 'the Paris House' (the State-supported companies of the Scots financier, John Law, in Paris). But the collapse of the 'South Sea Bubble' and of Law's companies in 1720-1 seriously embarrassed the Benedictines and Franciscans and nearly caused the closure of the English College, Douai. No other single Catholic financial disaster before the bankruptcy of Wright's Bank in the 1840s caused so much heart-burning. In the 1740s and 1760s the Jesuits had their turn when their investments in French colonial companies were lost. Then, from the 1770s, taxes on religious establishments in Flanders and France were raised considerably. By the 1780s most English religious establishments abroad were in desperate financial trouble. St Gregory's College, Paris and the Benedictine convents at Boulogne and Pontoise had to be dispersed. In 1789 the Prior of the Benedictine house at Dieulouard was foolishly commissioning the King of France's organ-builder to create for him an expensive instrument while the monastic brewing-house (the source of much of the monastery's income) was losing money. Only the disasters caused by the French Revolution averted attention from the fact that, if there had been no Revolution, most English houses abroad would have been dispersed by bankruptcy by 1790.

Nevertheless it was the same sort of procurators who coped with the appalling financial problems of the flight of the Colleges and convents to England in 1793–7 and, later, with the foundation of fifty new Mass-houses in industrial areas by 1830. The new clergy of post-1720 contained a solid core of able financiers bred in their fathers' counting-houses and in middle-class families where the mysteries of investment were a part of daily conversation. In the 1790s the Newcastle Mission was lucky to have as its priest Mr Worswick, the son of a Lancaster banker and a mother from the Gillow family of furniture-manufacturers. At Newcastle he successfully built or rebuilt several Mass-houses and inspired trust in his more prosperous middle-class parishioners.

The second, and much worse, clerical disaster was the great decline in ordinations. At two peak-periods (1620–40 and 1680–1720) the number of Catholic missioners had soared to over 750: if we include priests retained on the Continent, the total number was possibly between 1000 and 1100. These numbers were far in excess of mission requirements. After 1720, with a brief respite in the 1760s, the numbers of missioners declined steeply, by 1740 to 500, by 1760 to 400 and by 1773 to 380 (with twenty-three missions untenanted). Thereafter the number remained stable: by 1830 it was probably 400 (all the priests then anywhere available). Yet during this catastrophic decline, the numbers of the Catholic laity had almost doubled and fifty extra missions were urgently required.

Why did ordinations decline so steeply in 1720–60? Vocations from the aristocracy were fading away and the rising middle-class families did not respond with sufficient alacrity to fill the gap. They had grown up in the years when it was notorious that there were too many priests. Middle-class youths, at least those not from families accustomed to being clients of the gentry, had noticed the boredom and servility of gentry chaplains. Moreover middle-class families were acutely conscious of the increasing number of secular professions and business jobs open to them. At the same time the modern teaching of liberal priests must have been having its effect. It now required a special kind of intense piety to drive a middle-class youth into a seminary or monastery and girl into a convent. To a youth at the Sedgeley Park School the contrast between the traditional humanities of the ordinands' course and the modernity of the lay students' course must have been glaring.

In the 1760s and early 1770s clerical superiors tried hard to modernise their courses to attract more recruits. Just as they were reporting some success, there came a further series of disasters which nullified their efforts and which seemed to be condemning the clergy to many more years of acute shortage of manpower.

In the mid 1760s the Imperial, Spanish, French and Portuguese governments embarked on legislation designed to speed the death of clerical obscurantism and superstition. In Austrian Flanders the brunt of the attack fell on contemplative religious houses; in France it fell on seminaries and religious houses of studies. The Imperial Government proceeded to try to tax the contemplatives out of existence. In 1786 the already much depleted English Carthusian monastery finally dispersed. Its ex-Prior, relieved of the obligations of his vows, was Minister of Public Instruction in Brussels. In 1792, when the invading French armies compelled the expulsion of all English institutions, most of them were on the verge of bankruptcy and dissolution. In France government regulations dictated ordinands' syllabuses, forbade their admission and profession before a mature age, and required them to do courses in central government seminaries. Even delaying action could not prevent these measures reducing still further the low numbers of English ordinands.

As a by-product of this governmental programme came the progressive shutting-down of the whole Society of Jesus. Between 1762 and 1767 the English Jesuit houses in France and Spain were compulsorily taken over by the State, the Jesuits expelled from the country, and the few English Jesuit missionaries in Brazil, Paraguay and Montserrat exiled to England. In 1773, cornered by political pressure, the Pope formally dissolved the Society. The English secular clergy and Dominicans were given first refusal of the Jesuit Colleges: they took over some, though they had neither the professors nor students to man them effectively. The secular clergy had for many years dreamed of such a total victory over the hated Jesuits. But the timing and consequences to the mission of the victory proved catastrophic for everyone. The secular clergy did not have the manpower to take over the 150 Jesuit missions or, indeed, any substantial part of them. For their part, the ex-Jesuits, as they were now known, with a few exceptions had no intention of letting themselves be peaceably absorbed into the secular priest body. The ex-Jesuits (about 150 of them) formed over a third of the entire body of missioners. They legally owned most of their mission properties. They had, much devoted to them and their ways, a small but influential group of lay supporters. The Welds of Lulworth, perhaps the richest Catholics in England, were strongly pro-Jesuit. Moreover the Society would not lie down and die, even on the orders of a Rome which, as the ex-Jesuits knew well, contained many officials who secretly wanted a resurrection of the Society. Some ex-Jesuits succumbed to the English malady of depression and sloth. Most clung together on their old missions, maintaining what they could of their discipline and observances, to await the day of resurrection. These devoted men began over forty years of a grim, unhappy rearguard action, part-sublime, part-absurd.

The Vicars-Apostolic made the best of a bad job by informally recognising facts and allowing the ex-Jesuits to continue as a separate body under their own superiors. By a political fluke and skilful action they retained control of one of their foreign Colleges, Liège. Realising that the day of resurrection might be far off and that death would thin ranks, the ex-Jesuits resorted to their traditional ploy of getting ordained Ignatians, secular priest associates closely bound to the Society. These young men could replace ex-Jesuits on the missions as they died and carry the standard on towards the day, when they, no doubt, would become Jesuits. Rome was persuaded to make the College at Liège a 'Pontifical Seminary' for this purpose.

The more militant ex-Jesuits had other plans. Some put their faith in founding new Congregations on Jesuit lines. Others hoped in Russia. There the Empress Catharine the Great had refused to allow the Papal Bull of Suppression to be published or executed. The small Russian Jesuit Province and its colleges survived, with Roman connivance. There were English ex-Jesuits who hoped to go to Russia and join that Province. One actually did reach St Petersburg, posing as a tutor in the English language.

The problem of the ex-Jesuits dragged on until 1814, when Pius VII formally reconstituted the Society. By then many of the original 150 English ex-Jesuits were dead and some had defaulted. Some of their missions had, perforce, to be given away to secular priests or Benedictines. The rest, and Stonyhurst College, Lancashire, which was Liège College transported into England in the 1790s, limped on painfully, manned by a few ageing ex-Jesuits and more Ignatians. The Vicars-Apostolic found it hard to calculate their profits and losses on the whole sad affair. It had undoubtedly lowered the level of English ordinations still further. Any hopes of the death of the Society had proved illusory. At a crisis time the ex-Jesuits had manned a great part of the crumbling defence line.

In the midst of these disasters, the clergy can have spared little attention for the revolt of the American colonies and the settling of the independence of the United States in 1783. Nevertheless these events did contribute a further, if small, burden. In 1773, of the 150,000 English-speaking Catholics some 60,000 were in England and Wales and over 30,000 in the American colonies. During the Revolutionary War control of the American Mission passed from the London district Vicar-Apostolic to John Carroll of Maryland, an ex-Jesuit of the English Province, now appointed Archpriest by Rome. The English connection meant something in America. The fifty missioners there in 1776 were mostly English ex-Jesuits, translated thither from Ghent, Liège, St Omer or missions in Liverpool, Lancaster or Lulworth. On the ex-Jesuit missions were a dozen or more Americans, most of whom had never seen America since they left it for St Omer at the age of fourteen or fifteen. John Carroll, a native Marylander, had spent a quarter of a century in English Jesuit houses and English country missions. He often and warmly corresponded with his many English friends. Perhaps some of them agreed with him that America should be independent. After all Benjamin Franklin would not have lodged in the English Benedictine monastery in Paris during the peace negotiations if the Prior and community had been hostile to his views. In 1790 Carroll crossed the Atlantic back to the Welds' mansion, Lulworth Castle in Dorset, a mission at which he had once served. There he was consecrated Bishop of Baltimore by the Vicars-Apostolic. The English ex-Jesuits still in the United States severed their connection with England. In 1790 the American prioress of the English Carmel of Hoogstraet in Flanders returned home to Maryland (leaving her community in some straits) to found an American Carmel. In 1804–5 a band of four English Dominicans (two of them American-born) left Carshalton in Surrey to join the United States Mission. They left their English Province at the point of collapse for lack of money and subjects. One of the Dominicans died Bishop of Cincinnati. Another founded an American Dominican Province in Kentucky.

The next disaster for the English clergy followed quickly. In 1792–3 there was a mass emigration of French royalists to England. Included amongst them were 6000 bishops, priests and religious. In 1794–7 the outbreak of war between England and Revolutionary France produced the closure of most English institutions on soil controlled by French arms. Hundreds of English Catholic refugees arrived in south coast ports—priests, laybrothers, nuns, school-children, lay residents in France. Once more, in theory these dramatic events fulfilled Catholic dreams. The Catholic liberals had long criticised English establishments abroad for their excessive traditionalism and foreignness: they must move to England and become part of the English scene. In England, for instance, Catholic lay students could not possibly be dressed any longer in cassocks, or convent schoolgirls be treated like novices; religious habits and strict conventual enclosure would have to go by the board. Latin Catholic devotions of a Belgian or French kind could not endure the English climate. Moreover the advent of the French clergy seemed Providential. Now, at last, the clerical manpower shortage would be ended. There would be priests galore. The French clergy had a reputation for advanced liberalism: their influence in England would be healthy.

First impressions seemed to bear out these dreams. There was a great wave of anti-Revolutionary feeling in England. The French clergy, thought of as sufferers victimised by the Revolutionaries, received an astonishingly warm welcome from the most Protestant of the English. Without batting an eyelid, the government set aside large sums to provide the French priests with pensions, and requisitioned large premises in Winchester, Reading, Somerstown (London), Thame and Barwick (Yorkshire) to house them. There was approbation for the establishment at public expense of Catholic chapels for the clergy. The English Catholic refugees received a less ecstatic, but still remarkably warm and friendly reception. Public funds were earmarked to provide the nuns with pensions, if they applied through a Protestant peer. Protestant grandees offered the nuns rent-free accommodation. George III (or so Catholic rumour believed) instructed the customs officials to set aside the law and admit all Catholic objects of devotion and funds brought by the refugees. The nuns themselves, who had arrived in England in ill-fitting second-hand lay clothes, soon found that they could wear full religious habits indoors without the least question or concern from Protestant neighbours, who usually thought they were French. The religious, in makeshift accommo-dation, on the other hand had to abandon enclosure rules, get used to travelling by public coach services, accepting hospitality in

Catholic family houses, and starting their schools again in the English manner. French clergy, bored with their monastic existence in hostels, began to offer to teach French to Protestants and were invited to replace English missioners on gentry missions. Some of the more zealous or proletarian undertook mission work dodged by Englishmen or found economically impossible. In a good many small country towns with tiny Catholic congregations, a French priest was willing to establish himself frugally and live on his government pension. In Cornwall, where English priests were few and Catholics thinly scattered, resident French priests from the Channel Islands appeared at Truro, St Columb, St Austell and Trelawney. In Portsmouth, Hull and other towns desperately short of clergy, French priests appeared in the nick of time.

Meanwhile, during the Napoleonic wars, the transplanted Colleges and convents took root. A new publication, *The Laity's Directory*, for all the world like a commercial catalogue, listed the array of new and old Catholic Colleges and schools. Catholics awoke, in reading the list and the school advertisements, to a sense of pride. They now had, at last, a real system of schools and all on English soil. There was something for every taste and pocket. The Jesuit faction had 'The gentlemen of Stonyhurst' and the College-Seminary. Liberal Catholic gentry and better-off middle-class people had a new Academy-Seminary at Oscott, near Birmingham, run by a lay committee in the modern way. The secular clergy body had Douai transplanted and rooted in two seminaries, at Crook Hall, Durham and Ware, Hertfordshire. They also had Sedgeley Park School. The Benedictine faction had St Gregory's School, Douai transplanted to Acton Burnell Hall, Shropshire; Dieulouard School was housed in a Temperance Inn in Tranmere, Lancashire. The Franciscans had their old school at Osmotherley, Yorkshire and another at Edgbaston, Birmingham. The Dominicans transplanted their school from Bornhem in Flanders to Carshalton in Surrey without even turning to a new page in their students' 'Entry Book'. There were scores of private Catholic schools for boys, offering every kind of education from modern to traditional. The two convent schools for girls—York and Hammersmith—had now multiplied to a dozen.

But all this had been achieved at a high price. By the 1840s English priests were thinking kindly and nostalgically of the services to the mission of the exiled French clergy. At Danby, Yorkshire, 'Monsr. La Londe' was fondly remembered as 'ingenious in patchwork, very steady in his clerical duties', holding the fort in a bankrupt English gentry mission whence even the Jesuits had fled, starved by the lack of stipend and driven to depression by the sheer loneliness. In 1843 'the Abbé Le Roux', toothless and with his huge old-fashioned French wig awry, was still tottering feebly round his parish at Burghwallis, Yorkshire, aged ninety-two. But in the 1790s the English clergy rarely felt much kindness for the French invaders. Most of them had no English and never acquired much. Of the 6000 barely a hundred were ever capable of being entrusted with full care of a mission. Most of the hundred were returned home to France or dead by 1805–10. For every French priest who founded a new mission in an area where one was really needed, there were scores who did nothing or actually did the English clergy and mission harm.

Some established Mass-centres briefly in areas which could never warrant the employment of an English missioner, roused lay expectations, and then vanished home to France. Others ousted English missioners from gentry missions (after all a Frenchman was cheaper and could teach French to the children of the house for nothing) and, worse, withdrew their patrons' financial support from neighbouring missions. For a few years during the French influx many an aspiring middle-class manufacturer with a suburban or country house imported a cheap French house-chaplain and so ceased to go to Mass at the struggling local mission. Since ordinations had to be adjusted to the supply of priests and places, the French flood upset the Vicars-Apostolic's calculations badly. Lastly the ranks of the Frenchmen included many odd fish. There were archbishops and bishops galore: numbers of them were aristocrats of no good moral reputation. On the other hand there were hosts of very plebeian *vicaires* and *obitiers* (jobbing curates, scraping a living in pre-Revolutionary France by singing Requiem Masses for stipends) whose freely expressed opinions were anti-episcopal and almost Jacobin. Some French clergy waxed rich from teaching French in high society or even from factory work. With some reason, many English Catholics were glad to see the backs of the Frenchmen. The lay royalist refugees also outlived their welcome. For every devout one there were a dozen of no determinate religion. There were English middle-class Catholic families who later had cause to rue the day their daughters married exotic French émigré 'Counts', 'Barons' and 'Chevaliers'.

The transplantation of the English from the Continent had its black side also. For the most part the operation was not performed speedily and cleanly. Most religious communities had to endure months or years of imprisonment in France and left behind them there a scattering of unfortunates. Some of these were foreign members or servants of communities. On the other hand two or three communities of nuns brought their foreigners with them to

England. Others left behind were invalids. A few were lost in the process of transplantation. At St Edmund's, Paris, a student-monk, quite carried away by the Messianism of the French Revolution, made off and joined a French Line regiment as a drummer. Other religious stayed behind, in some danger to their lives, to maintain their community's claim to the conventual property. In 1792–4 most communities had been understaffed, limping on with the help of foreign lay auxiliaries, and facing bankruptcy. Most of their capital was tied up in their property. Their conventual buildings had been their home for many years and still housed their dead and many cherished objects—altars, stained glass windows, portraits, relics. The religious rarely faced the move to England with hope. They felt it to be an exile from home and a final trial which might well destroy their communities. Most therefore were reluctant to put down strong roots in England and anxious to return home as soon as the war situation allowed. The Bridgettines of Lisbon, faced by a French invasion of Portugal, sent part of their community to safety in England and kept nine nuns behind Lord Wellington's Lines of Torres Vedras. As soon as the French troops retreated the nuns returned to their convent. The Bruges Canonesses returned home to Belgium in 1802 during a lull in the fighting and braved out the rest of the war. The Benedictine community of St Edmund's, Paris never settled in England. After 1814 they tried in vain to recover their monastery, and in 1818 were delighted to have first refusal of St Gregory's monastery in Douai: they were to be there for almost another century. When the Prussian government occupied Hanover in 1803 it suppressed the English Benedictine monastery at Lambspring. Half the community spent years dodging war operations, and finally homed back to lodge in farmhouses near the monastery in the hope of recovering it.

The religious Orders had been hit by the decline in vocations almost as badly as the secular clergy. For most of them the disturbance of their lives caused by the French Revolution, war and the move to England proved disastrous. By 1801 the English Dominican Province could muster only a handful, of whom two had remained at Bornhem in Flanders to protect the convent from looters and one at Bruges. In 1804–5 four left England for the United States. By 1815 the tiny band of survivors had actually taken over Bornhem again. By 1827 the Province ended with the death of the last Father. The Franciscan Province, moribund by 1815, lingered on until 1841. The English Benedictine Congregation came within inches of extinction. Of its four communities one (Lambspring) perished and the other three were much reduced. Even in 1830 their future was not assured and a determined effort was made to dissolve the

Congregation and transform its members into secular priests. As we have seen, the ex-Jesuits dwindled in numbers to a handful by the time of the official resurrection of their Society. In 1803 Charles Plowden opened a noviciate in Lancashire, though his novices could not be professed until 1815. He became the Provincial when the Society's organisation in England was recreated in 1817. But even by 1830 the number of Jesuit missioners was low.

The women's religious Orders suffered greatly and a number of communities—the Benedictines of Pontoise and Boulogne, the Paris Blue Nuns and the Mary Ward community at Hammersmith—foundered. But on the whole the nuns displayed more staying power and ingenuity than the male religious and recovered their feet faster. The contrast between the reactions to disaster of the Dieulouard Benedictines and the Nieuport Franciscan nuns was fairly typical. At Dieulouard the Prior and community coped badly with their ejection. The Prior eventually escaped by swimming the river Meuse; the community salvaged from the monastery only one heirloom, a tattered book of choir music. At Nieuport the Abbess, a member of the wealthy Weld family of Lulworth, began to prepare for evacuation as early as 1783. She transferred the invested funds to England, had the convent plate melted down, sold the pictures and valuables and mortgaged the buildings. Once in England, Thomas Weld took care of the community and its debts were all paid off by 1813. The nuns, with ferocious tenacity, recovered every removable scrap from their old convents whenever they had a chance. The Nieuport nuns had an agent recover 'Lady Teynham's embalmed heart'. As soon as funds and circumstances permitted, every tittle of tradition and observance was restored.

In principle the secular priest body rejoiced to see the number of religious who were missioners sharply declining. In 1773 the majority of missioners were religious. In 1830 the proportion had declined to thirty per cent. But in practice the victory seemed hollow. The removal of the English College, Douai to England (the only real seminary left to the secular clergy by 1792) had struck yet one more blow at the level of ordinations. On their arrival in England in driblets the professors and students of Douai were homeless and inevitably dispersed. The new beginnings at Crook Hall and Ware were modest and slow to take root. In the Crook Hall *Diary* the President (with only one professor and seven students) recorded the start of work in 1795 without much hope: 'After great, yes, daily sufferings, and the loss of all earthly hope, we have come together into this tranquil, secluded place to struggle to coax back into a flame the few dull embers of our sacred fire . . .' By 1830 there were four seminaries in operation, at Ushaw, Ware,

Oscott and, for Ignatians, Stonyhurst. But in spite of all this effort the total number of missioners only resumed an upward trend with painful slowness. In 1830 there were, counting religious and a sprinkling of Irishmen, Frenchmen and foreigners, still only 400. In 1840 it was 500, and in 1850, 700. Yet by 1850 the 80,000 Catholic laity of the 1780s had become at least 250,000.

Thus by 1830, after a very rough passage, the English Catholic clergy had at least preserved the bare essentials of their existence. Inevitably much of their energy had been expended on this struggle to survive in a fast-changing world where every decade brought new situations fraught simultaneously with promise and danger. Many priests regarded the survival of their body as enough victory. But in fact by 1830 they had gained a second and even more important victory, this time over the influential laity, aristocratic and middle class. The battle for survival had effects which all could see plainly for themselves. The battle to control the laity filled the air with pamphlets and noisy discussion, but its real course was hidden amongst administrative details and evident only to the few who were well informed. Yet even the wise ordinary priest and parishioner in 1830 could sense this victory: its symptoms were unmistakable. The average missioner had a new sense of assurance and command when he dealt with even his richest parishioners: those parishioners had a novel attitude of deference to their pastors. As for the Vicars-Apostolic, in 1780 they had been worried men, somehow insignificant and on the run. In 1830 they were still deeply worried, but occupied a new, commanding position in the Catholic community.

L

15. The Victory over the Laity, 1771–1830

In 1707 John Sergeant was buried in St Pancras churchyard, London. The Blacklowist priest rebel died at a great age, 'pen in hand'. His career and his ideas spanned the years back to the liberal Catholic radicals of the mid seventeenth century. One of his most acid clerical opponents, Sylvester Jenks, wrote: 'J.S. is dead. But I had rather write his faction had been dead . . .' The pious and orthodox Catholics, like Jenks and the Jesuit Francis Mannock of Swynnerton, Staffordshire, were sure that the faction (called by them Blacklowists, or now more often Jansenists) was as alive as a cancer rooted throughout the English Catholic body. In 1710 Mannock wrote to his Procurator that the cancer lurked even amongst Catholic gentry supposedly devoted to the Society. He had just had a furious row with his patrons, Mr and Mrs Fitzherbert. Mrs Fitzherbert flourished in his face a book entitled *The Imaginary Heresay*. She and her husband defended the Jansenists and condemned the orthodox as an intriguing, reactionary faction. When Mannock spoke of Roman decrees against Jansenism, he was shattered by the light way they were dismissed by the Fitzherberts. Mr Fitzherbert even said that the only final authority in the Catholic Church was a General Council, not the Pope.

Mannock and Jenks were right in detecting a wide Jansenist tendency, though they were wrong in thinking it a united conspiracy. In 1720 Stephen Tempest of Broughton, Yorkshire, educated at St Omer and the patron of the Jesuits, wrote secretly for his eldest son's instruction 'heresays' as clear as those of the Fitzherberts. He wrote that whenever Protestant and Catholic gentry met together and discussed religion they found no real differences between them 'except, of course, the authority of the church'. It was, he thought, the self-interest and lust for material gain of the clergy of both sides (he quoted Dryden aptly) which alone held Catholics and Protestants apart and exaggerated their differences. Tempest was no believer in Papal infallibility.

About this time the *Instructions* of John Gother were published. Gother had been a secular priest convert from Presbyterianism and a highly successful missioner. The solid and formally Catholic piety of the *Instructions* was beyond reproach. But the whole tone of them was subtly undenominational. Gother recognised devotion to the saints and relics, but gave it almost no place in his 'Christian devotion'. He sought peace with other Christians. His suggestions for congregational English prayers during Mass set Catholics on the road towards that curious middle-class order of service in the Mass-houses which we have already noticed flourishing in the later eighteenth century.

About this time also three students were expelled from the English College, Douai: Augustus Newdigate Poyntz, Thomas Strickland and John Stonor. Such expulsions happened in almost every generation of students. The College, along with its near neighbours, the English Benedictine and Franciscan schools, formed a community of some three hundred priest-professors, ordinands and schoolboys ranging in age from seventy down to eleven or twelve. A large proportion of the sons of educated English Catholics spent from four to seven years of their lives in Douai. The student community was mixed and turbulent. The great majority were lay boys who had only the vaguest of intentions, or none, of seeking ordination, though they were subject to a tough clerical discipline. The real ordinands were older and in a small minority. Amongst both lay boys and ordinands there was a marked distinction between plebeians, whose fees were paid for by bursaries and gentlemen, whose parents paid fees. The influence of the life was powerful, not least because there were no holidays at home and only the gentry had leave, and opportunities, to meet their relations and be taken out on excursions. For the plebeians, especially the ordinands (who might spend ten years in College), the College became their life. They came from homes without culture and often had a poor educational grounding. They developed a regimental community spirit marked by an intense schoolboy ritualism and traditionalism. The core of the training was ancient and based on dictated notes which had to be memorised and repeated back. Intellectualism was suspect, as were airs and graces, amongst the real College men. The plebeian Douai-trained missioner was destined for the poorer missions. He was hard-working, exact with his rubrics, uncultured, and ill at ease in polite society. Long experience of having to give place to the gentry had increased his roughness. He accepted having to dine with the servants in gentry houses (while a gentry priest dined *en famille*) and having to put up with the imperiousness of gentry patrons: but he resented it

increasingly and secretly. At Clergy Brotherhood assemblies in
county town inns, the formal business was rushed through before
the dinner. There the gentry priests sat apart, while the plebeians
bandied the old College nicknames—'Pickled Herring', 'Boots',
'Black Jack', 'Cockeye', 'Sticks'—and ended in schoolboy horse-
play. It was from this background that Richard Challoner came.

Naturally the gentry and upper-middle-class schoolboys and
ordinands often found this life difficult. At some periods it was
tolerable, because the President and some of the professors were,
openly or secretly, on their side. It was then possible for a group of
young professors to liberalise their courses to some degree, or at
least to give extra-curricular seminars to sympathetic pupils. Almost
invariably such novelties roused a backlash of conservatism, the
superannuation of the pupils and the sending of the professors to
England. Naturally also, the reverberations of these disputes had
an effect there.

Augustus Poyntz, a gentry ordinand, was a pious ultra-
conservative. He roundly accused most of the College professors of
Jansenist modernism. He was so well-connected, and probably
backed by Jesuit conservatives, that the local bishop intervened.
Poyntz was expelled, made off to the Jesuits in Rome, was ordained
there and spent the rest of his life, at his own expense, as a convent
chaplain in Flanders. In the eyes of the pious he was a martyr who
had exposed the modernism controlling the English College. Stonor
and Strickland were also gentry ordinands, but expelled for
precisely the opposite reason: they accused the professors of turning
pious superstitions into matters of faith. The two rebels took rooms
in St Gregory's College, Paris. Ever since the days of Bishop
Richard Smith, most of the English establishments in Paris had a
reputation amongst the orthodox for impiety and Jansenism. St
Edmund's, the English Benedictine house of studies for the Sorbonne, had considerable notoriety. An orthodox monk-student
there was soon to delate his superior for immorality and take off
for the French Cistercian monastery of La Trappe. A later Prior
of St Edmund's was the famous Cuthbert Wilkes, the 'dear friend'
of Dr Samuel Johnson and the extreme radical of the 1780s in
England. St Gregory's College had associations with Richard Smith,
Blacklow and Henry Holden. It normally housed a variety of
students, aristocratic ordinands who had escaped from (or never
entered) the English College, Douai, ambitious or intellectual
priests reading for higher degrees, and sprigs of the aristocracy using
the College as an accommodation address while they savoured the
delights of Paris.

Here Thomas Strickland went through with a brief course for

ordination, choosing his own teachers, was ordained, and went on a leisurely tour of Flanders, Vienna and Rome. John Stonor gave up the idea of the priesthood and returned to England to seek a wife. Seven years later, still unmarried, he returned to Paris. His ordination course and reading for a Paris doctorate were accomplished in a very short space of time. Both he and Strickland used all their considerable family influence to win bishoprics. Thwarted (because of his reputation for outspoken liberalism) of an English Vicariate, Strickland made do, first with a French abbacy, and then the bishopric of Namur. Stonor's friends were more powerful. Astonishingly quickly he procured from Rome Bulls creating him midland Vicar-Apostolic with the right to administer also, and succeed to, the London Vicariate, which was then held by a moribund bishop.

This was the curious start of the episcopal career (1716–56) of a man who proved the most effective Catholic clerical leader of the eighteenth century. Stonor was no textbook bishop. He was almost aggressively unecclesiastical in his manner of living. As a red-faced, bucolic country squire, residing habitually in his own or his family's mansions at Heythrop and Stonor Park in Oxfordshire, he shot and hunted with his Protestant neighbours, hob-nobbed with Protestant peers and experimented with enclosures and root crops. In his curious, pragmatic, lay fashion he had a genuine and perceptive interest in his pastoral duties. But he gave every outward appearance of bland disregard for ecclesiastical niceties. The contrast with most of his fellow Vicars-Apostolic was striking. Benjamin Petre was an even greater aristocrat. His course for ordination had been even briefer and less formal than Stonor's; unlike Stonor, he was genuinely ignorant of theology and clerical rules. A pious man, he was miserably aware of the anarchic state of the unreformed clergy and of his own unfitness for episcopal office. His reaction was to retire to his pieties on a family residence in Essex and provide suitably pious, well-trained suffragans to run his district for him. Witham and the Franciscan Prichard were pious, narrow middle-class practitioners. The Dominican Williams could get few clergy to approach him and few gentry to offer him house-room. The one plebeian bishop, Richard Challoner (whose appointment Stonor opposed) was traditionally pious and orthodox and cut out by nature to be a College President of the old school or an earnest London missioner. His style of episcopacy was monastic, conservative and immersed in London parochial affairs. All these bishops were devoted men in their various ways, but mere cogs in the antique, creaking machine of Catholic clerical life over which they had only a formal control. It was Stonor alone who devised a whole programme of reform and proposed methods by which it should be carried out.

In his eccentric, aristocratic way, using the 'pull' of his class on inferiors, equals and superiors alike, he laid the foundations of the reforms that were mostly achieved, or in train, in 1830. Without ever—for he was no intellectual—laying down radical theological principles like Barnes, Blacklow and Sergeant, he pragmatically urged courses of action which presupposed them. Through his two agents in Rome, one of whom was his priest-nephew, he devised ways of by-passing the Curia or pushing it into courses it distrusted. Though he never questioned the Papal primacy, he was clearly working towards the practical independence of English Catholics. Without ever laying down principles of episcopal authority, he much increased the prestige and weight in the community of the Vicars-Apostolic as a body. Without pontificating on lay participation, he accustomed the more responsible educated laity to working amicably with and for their clergy. He voiced no principles of doctrine, but cemented the already steady move of all but the most pious conservatives towards an almost Anglican approach. With good reason the pious feared and detested him as a heretic, but could rarely lay their finger on a definitely heretical statement.

The years after Stonor's death (1756–70) saw a period of bitter frustration for Catholic reformers. The Vicariates, Presidencies of Colleges and superiorships of the Orders were occupied by men who, even if they occasionally made reforming gestures, steadily blocked any real change. At the English College, Douai the Presidents made a gesture of introducing French into the Humanities course but simultaneously rooted out various modernisations of the theology and philosophy courses made in Stonor's days. The frustration and excitement of liberal-minded Catholics were greatly increased by the climate of opinion and the great events operating everywhere outside their narrow circle. These were the days when Continental Catholic governments were beginning their enlightened legislative assault on the Society of Jesus, pious superstition and Papalism. In England these were the days of 'Wilkes and Liberty', of an increasing agitation for Parliamentary reform. In Ireland Catholics and Nationalists were on the march. In America the demand for reform and self-government was mounting. It would have been strange if English Catholic liberals had stayed on quietly during the 1770s, contented with Richard Challoner's pious conservatism.

The early historians of the liberal Catholic explosion of the 1770s and 1780s dated its beginning in the 'Berington affair' at the English College, Douai, in 1771. Joseph Berington had begun a philosophy course of Logic and Psychology in 1769 as a newly-appointed professor. He came from a Herefordshire family of middling gentry hitherto noted only for their addiction to the Jesuits and piety. He had a sister who was a nun, and a cousin, Charles Berington, who was a priest studying for a doctorate at St Gregory's, Paris. Joseph had arrived at Douai in 1755, the year before Stonor died. He had endured, from the age of twelve to the age of twenty-eight, the rigours of a conservative régime. He now made his philosophy course not merely modern but a manifesto against the whole conservative ethos of the College and the ruling Catholic clergy. The result was a College broil. Alban Butler, a rigidly orthodox priest, President of the secular clergy's new College at St Omer (formerly Jesuit) and vicar-general to the Bishop of Arras, used episcopal sanctions to silence Berington. He was, in spite of his efforts to apologise, dismissed from the College. After a year as chaplain to his parents and an unhappy stint as a missioner in industrial Wolverhampton, he escaped thankfully to a chaplaincy at Carlton Hall in Yorkshire, provided by his friend Miles Stapleton.

Berrington's affair at Douai had brought him approving letters from a wide variety of Catholic liberals. In the 1770s he and Stapleton travelled round Catholic country houses and visited the Continent. Their acquaintance with liberals grew, as did their post-bag. It gradually became evident that there were liberals in almost every Catholic grouping, even the most unlikely ones. Of the Vicars-Apostolic three (Challoner, Matthew Gibson and Walmesley) were rigidly conservative and one (James Talbot) a cautious liberal. Liberals were widely distributed round the aristocracy, even amongst those with a Jesuit tradition: the Earl of Shrewsbury (Bishop Talbot's brother), Lords Petre, Stourton and Clifford, Throckmortons, Englefields, Fermors, Lawsons, Stapletons, Towne-leys, Howards, Jerninghams, Hornyholds. Their ranks even included an ardent recent convert from a family of arch-conservatives, the Plowdens. When the Society of Jesus was dissolved in 1773, Francis Plowden, one of its novices, not only returned to lay life but went up to Oxford and declared himself a convinced Whig. Even the Jesuits were divided. Their last Provincial, Thomas More, was a conservative, though hardly in the tradition of the famous Francis Mannock SJ, who, in the 1730s, had supplied the Vicars-Apostolic with 77 *Propositions* culled from liberal Catholic writings and designed to prove that heretical Jansenism had taken over English Catholicism completely. The leading young Jesuit, Charles Plowden, destined to survive to be the first Provincial of the restored Society in 1817, was an ardent conservative. His close Jesuit friend, the American John Carroll, was an equally ardent liberal. Amongst

the Benedictines Joseph Wilkes (soon to move from the Priorship
of St Edmund's, Paris to a chaplaincy of the Fitzherberts at
Swynnerton, Staffordshire, hitherto a Jesuit family), William
Gregson (chaplain to the Throckmortons) and Archibald Macdonald (in Liverpool) were all strong liberals whilst their superiors
were mostly rigid conservatives. The most distinguished Benedictine, Bishop Charles Walmesley, had been a liberal *enfant terrible*
and a mathematician with a European reputation : in middle age he
grew steadily more and more gloomily conservative, reading and
re-reading the Book of the Apocalypse to discover the number of
the Liberal Beast. The Dominicans included Matthew Norton, a
liberal with a passion for agricultural improvement and political
economy. When his fellows were shocked by the Imperial government's Enlightened legislation at Brussels, he warmly applauded
and was awarded prizes by the Imperial Academy for essays on
beekeeping, sheep-rearing and the use of oxen.

When Joseph Berington was expelled from Douai he received an
approving letter from an unexpected quarter, Theodore Augustus
Mann, Prior of the English Carthusians at Nieuport in Flanders.
Mann, a convert lawyer, had an amazing career. He became a
Catholic in Paris, a cavalry officer in an Irish Brigade in the Spanish
Army, and then a Carthusian. In 1777 he was to be secularised by
Rome at the request of the Imperial government and appointed
Minister of Public Instruction in Brussels. As the Abbé Mann he
rapidly became a European celebrity. He was awarded honorary
membership by the Royal Society and many Continental learned
societies. With great assurance, and an authority which came from
his governmental position, he compiled reports on a host of
projected reforms ranging from Church discipline to municipal fire-
brigades. His close friend and collaborator, John Turberville
Needham, rector of the Imperial Academy of Arts and Sciences
in Brussels, had had an equally remarkable career. He began life
as a middle-class clerical student at Douai, taught in a secular clergy
school and the English College, Lisbon and then spent twenty years
as tutor to Catholic noblemen being educated in Paris. Their fees
enabled him to devote his spare time to the study of physiology.
By the 1760s he was a fellow of the Royal Society and Académie
des Sciences and an acknowledged *savant*.

This enlightened liberalism was so bookish a thing that it could
hardly have much appeal for the bulk of educated Catholics in
England. A minority of them, missioners and business men of
middle-class origin and a College education, certainly did catch the
liberal virus. In the 1770s Charles Butler, a London law student and
and nephew of the rigidly conservative priest, Alban Butler, became

an enthusiastic convert to liberal ideas. In the London and midland districts most middle-class missioners were liberals: they included James Archer, the preacher, and Doctors Thomas Hussey and John Bew, the secular clergy's only real theologians. But the rest of the educated laity and clergy displayed a typical English mixture of stolid, instinctive conservatism and aggressive anti-Establishment-ism. The average secular priest defended tradition blindly, but automatically reacted against pressures by bishops and aristocrats. The average middle-class parishioner shrank from change in religion, but flatly refused to let bishops or clergy dictate to him how his Mass-house was to be run or where he should send his children to school.

The liberal movement began to jell amongst the aristocrats in 1765–8. Groups of them who enthusiastically supported Wilkes and the Parliamentary Reform movement became increasingly used to committee meetings, common action and consultation with Protestant politicians. The politicians were anxious to make a gesture of toleration for Catholics, especially since Yorkshire liberal Catholics had put their electoral influence behind Sir George Savile. Savile's Catholic Relief Act of 1778 was the result of this cooperation. Joseph Berington was, on the suggestion of the Stapletons, employed as the liberal Catholics' publicist. In 1780 he was asked to publish a party manifesto to demonstrate to Protestants that English Catholicism really was changing its character. The result was his *The State and Behaviour of the English Catholics from the Reformation to the year 1780*.

The thesis of this sensational little book was not new. It had all been said before by John Barnes, Thomas Blacklow, John Sergeant and Hugh Tootell (alias Charles Dodd). But their writings had, as Berington said, been rendered obscure by their technicality, and verbosity: he was writing briefly, bluntly and in language compre-hensible to plain Englishmen. Like the Catholic radicals before him, he assumes that basic Catholicism, stripped of its many gross superstitions and pagan accretions, of the Papal Monarchy and its politico-religious imperialism, is true, original Christianity. Both the Protestant Reformation and the Catholic Counter-Reformation were tragic aberrations. But how could English Protestants be blamed for persecuting a Catholicism temporarily controlled by clerical politicians and pious cranks? Yet now, in 1780, everything was changing marvellously. The Protestant English were fast losing interest in Protestant dogma: the Catholic English were fast dis-carding Counter-Reformation accretions. There was no longer any reason to have legal discrimination against Catholics.

The blunt Englishry and honesty of many phrases in the book are attractive: 'I am no Papist; nor is my religion Popery . . . The Pope is the first magistrate in a well-regulated State . . . he has no absolute jurisdiction over each bishop and pastor.' Berington's descriptions of the plebeian secular clergy as, for all their real virtues, narrow, bigoted, uncouth boors, and of the aristocratic patrons as far too often arrogant and imperious, are brave. He dismisses southern European Catholics as 'a motley crew' with a religion that is superstitious and superficial. Protestants had always believed that the Catholic clergy were a venal lot, polling their people. Amongst radical Catholics Dryden had admitted there was truth in this; so had Blacklow (the clergy had been infuriated by his attack on the accepted doctrine of Purgatory and on the cult of Masses for the dead with stipends) and so had Stephen Tempest. But Berington put it in blunt terms on which even Langland could not have improved. As for the religious Orders, they are parasites on the body politic: 'The earthly substance of families can be expended to better purpose than in maintaining men who have no return to make to their benefactors but a promise of a place in paradise . . .'

Conservative Catholics were outraged by the book. Bishops Challoner, Gibson and Walmesley would have condemned it publicly if they had dared. The President of Douai ordered the library copy to be placed in its 'Hell' alongside Protestant books and pornography. Liberal Catholics were enchanted with the book and wrote to tell its author so. John Carroll wrote enthusiastically from Maryland asking for further books and more explicit suggestions about reforms: what about having the Mass in English, much simplified? What about abolishing compulsory clerical celibacy? Berington replied strongly in favour of an English Mass; why should not Carroll use the opportunity of the establishment of American Catholic diocesan bishops for a declaration of independence from Papal absolutism? He was in favour of a married clergy and suggested joint Catholic-Protestant Sunday schools. There was a spate of published answers to Berington. Two caused both him and Carroll particular concern. They were written by personal friends of theirs, one formerly an American Jesuit, the other once a Benedictine, who had recently become Anglicans. These answers laid their finger on the crucial point: if English Catholicism was to be so drastically liberalised, why stop short at the claim to be the one true Church?

Catholic meetings now became common form both in London and in the main centres of Catholic population. The ostensible reason for them was to draft addresses to Parliament asking for further Relief Acts: the real purpose in the minds of the small Catholic Committees of liberals who called the meetings was to pass further addresses urging reforms. The first such reform was a threat to withdraw boys from the Colleges if they were not moved to England, put under lay committees and thoroughly modernised. The Catholic Committees were self-appointed, met in secret over the dinner table and were, in effect, party sessions. The Catholic meetings were open to all educated Catholics and drew large numbers of middle-class people and priests. In January 1780, for instance, Marmaduke Tunstall, a Yorkshire gentry conservative, complained bitterly that he had been invited to such a meeting in Beverley, where there were: 'many clergymen and few men of property . . .' and where foolish matters were discussed: 'there being scarce any extravagance or folly so absurd as has not its zealous votaries among our rising generations, at least in the south . . .' In London from 1782 William Mawhood was a regular attender at Catholic meetings, sometimes noting an attendance of hundreds. By that year, if not before, a central Catholic Committee was in existence in London. Bishop Talbot attended, and when he became moribund, was succeeded by Charles Berington, chosen by Rome as his coadjutant for the midland district. The other bishops were not exactly excluded: it was obvious that they objected violently to the whole movement, so they were politely ignored. Cuthbert Wilkes sat in on the Committee as the missioners' representative, and Joseph Berington was retained as usual as publicist.

His postbag continued to contain far more congratulatory letters than abusive ones. He was closely in touch with Carroll. To moderates who found his language sometimes too blunt, Berington explained that he was not writing ecclesiastical ('school terms') language but for Protestants and to remove their prejudices. When pressed to state, at least privately, in school terms his theological recasting of the faith, he pleaded for time. In fact, he suggested, perhaps the existing organisation of Catholic Committees and Meetings might serve as a permanent governmental structure for English Catholicism. To Carroll he wrote that the New Testament organisation of the Church was all that was essential: 'the rest is abuse and corruption'. In 1787 he published in Birmingham *A History of the Lives of Abellard and Heloisa.* This was light, skilfully devised, and a mixture of fashionable Gothic romance and sharp doctrine from a Catholic 'unshackled in his thought and free in his expressions'.

It seemed glorious to be alive in those exciting times. The Pope had abolished the Jesuits. America was free and Ireland nearly free,

In 1789 the French Monarchy was toppled by committees and meetings. Alexander Geddes, a liberal Scots priest now living in London as Lord Petre's chaplain, published *A Secular Ode on the French Revolution* cheerfully predicting a similar event in England. Sir John Throckmorton, a member of the central Catholic Committee was president of a branch of the radical *Friends of the People.* The strange fact was that the orthodox Catholics seemed powerless, even cowed. The Vicars-Apostolic now supported the Committee's aims by a vote of three to one. 240 missioners added their signatures, including majorities of the priests of the London and midland districts. The Staffordshire clergy were notoriously united behind liberalism as 'the Stafford Squadron'. The Vicars-Apostolic ordered the President of Douai to make gestures of reform. They themselves axed obsolete medieval fasts and feasts from the Church Kalendar. 1500 laymen (as Berrington wrote: 'almost all the laymen of eminence') subscribed to the Committee's aims. It was the London Committee, not the Vicars-Apostolic, which negotiated with the government the Relief Act of 1791. It was the Committee which interviewed William Pitt and secured his promise to abolish double Land Tax and his approval of the establishment of a part-lay-controlled school at Oscott near Birmingham. This school was to be the prototype of a gradual reform of the Catholic education system. The Committee employed as its President Dr John Bew, a radical secular priest.

The pace of liberal planning now increased. The central Committee enlarged its membership in 1791 and changed its name to *The Cisalpine Club* ('the Anti-Papalists'). Oscott became a *foyer* of reform. Joseph Berington now ensconced himself there with his cousin, Bishop Charles Berington, and a young priest-secretary, John Kirk. Nearby was Bew, organising his school and taking in ordinands. Kirk was a competent research historian. He and Joseph Berington divided their time between correspondence and the preparation of a vast *History of the Rise, Progress and Decline of the Papal Power.* The temptation was to try to out-Gibbon Gibbon. But the real purpose was to get behind the traditional Catholic view of the Church's history and dogma to fundamentals. Meanwhile, at their missions in Liverpool and Coughton, the Benedictines Archibald Macdonald and William Gregson were producing *A Book of Common Prayer and Administration of the Sacraments* to replace the Latin services, and perhaps eventually to be used also by Anglicans. In London Alexander Geddes was dividing his time between producing lampoons of orthodox religion and creating a new, Biblical theological system to replace Catholic scholastic theology. He hoped eventually to bring out a new English translation of the Bible to replace Challoner's version. (Challoner's version had doctrinal footnotes of an orthodox character; Geddes' version was, by its wording and notes, to teach a liberal view.) Joseph Berington and Geddes both insisted that the Bible was poetry and spiritual doctrine, not a quarry of proof-texts. Meanwhile the London Committee was trying to frame a new structure for English Catholicism. Missions would be run by lay committees, which would appoint missioners. Diocesan bishops, no longer Papal agents like the Vicars-Apostolic, would be freely elected by missioners, subject to powers of veto to be exercised by the government and Rome. Bishops would administer their dioceses in conjunction with frequent clerical synods and lay committtee meetings. The whole initiative in reform of the liturgy and clerical discipline would lie with the Synods and committees. It was therefore vital to press on the free election of liberal missioners as Vicars-Apostolic. If Rome disagreed, Rome could be pushed to consent or ignored. That would not be schism from Rome but the restoration of primitive Catholic freedom.

In 1791 the liberal movement was in full flood and meeting no real check. By 1801 it had practically collapsed. The reasons for the collapse are clear. From 1792 there swept through England a tremendous popular revulsion against liberal reformism of every kind, secular or ecclesiastical. The capture of power in France by extremist Jacobin revolutionaries, the Reign of Terror in Paris and the outbreak of war between England and France produced this revulsion. Liberalism became, almost overnight, Jacobin and unpatriotic. The war began disastrously for England and there were threats of invasion. William Pitt's government clamped down strongly on all radical meetings. His attitude to the Cisalpine Club became cool. He reported to them curtly that insurmountable administrative difficulties and the war situation prevented the abolition of double Land Tax. In 1798 came a dangerous rebellion in Ireland. From then to 1801 Pitt genuinely attempted to get George III's consent to a full Catholic Emancipation Act. This was in no real way a response by Pitt to the Cisalpine Club's overtures. He was simply trying conciliation to damp down Irish Catholic bitterness. George III refused the Act because he regarded it as a formal breach of his coronation oath to preserve the Protestant Establishment. His refusal put an end for a generation to any hope of obtaining Catholic Emancipation.

This was a severe setback for the Catholic liberal movement, which, meanwhile, had come under heavy pressure from the orthodox. Down to 1791 Catholic orthodoxy had appeared to be a dying thing. Even its strongest adherents habitually used the phraseology of enlightened liberalism. They had, except in the ex-Jesuit, Charles Plowden, little literary talent, positive ideology or organisation. The liberals seemed to have the cream of English Catholic ability and verve. The orthodox Vicars-Apostolic were at first very unsure of their authority. With the ghastly example before their eyes of the schism in the French Church between Constitutional liberals and royalist conservatives they were naturally fearful of provoking the English liberals into schism. But by 1793 the bishops felt surer of their ground. Edmund Burke, for so many years the idol of Catholics, had, in his *Reflections on the late Revolution in France*, provided a powerful apologia for complete conservatism. The swing against extreme liberalism was bound to draw some adherents of the Cisalpine Club over to orthodoxy. Hence the conservative Vicars-Apostolic began their counter-attack in 1793 by founding *The Roman Catholic Club*.

The purpose of this club was to demonstrate to the government and to Protestants that the liberals were only an insignificant, unofficial minority of the Catholic body. The Club carefully concealed its clerical inspiration: the bishops and priests were associate members who avoided turning up at meetings. The Club professed ardent loyalty to George III and the established order. Little open reference was made to the Pope. Yet the Club was not a success. It rallied only some fifty members, issued no statements, was increasingly ill-attended, and faded away in 1797. It won relatively few supporters of the liberals and gained no credence from the government, nor government measures against the Cisalpine Club. The truth of the matter was that the real strength of orthodoxy lay in the north, far from London. In any case many Catholics had had their fill of meetings by 1791. After its first meeting the Club performed no useful function to justify the expensive journey to London.

In sharp contrast with this failure, the orthodox achieved by 1803 complete control of the episcopate by a combination of good luck, lobbying in England, and pressure in Rome. Of the three liberal Vicars-Apostolic appointed, two (James Talbot and Gregory Stapleton) soon died. The third, William Gibson, was half-hearted and soon swung over to strong conservatism under pressure from his northern clergy. Bishop Charles Berington had a legal right of succession to the midland Vicariate. From 1796 to 1798 the post remained vacant while battle raged. Rome demanded that Berington should retract his liberal opinions. He hesitated, was persuaded by conservatives, but then died suddenly. Then pressure in Rome completed the orthodox victory. The entire bench, dominated by two bitter anti-liberals, John Douglass and John

Milner, was now unitedly conservative. In 1796–8 the liberals had seen clearly that their only chance of avoiding defeat was to reject Roman decisions and carry out free elections. That meant schism. All but a few of the most militant liberals shrank from a course they had hitherto accepted in theory.

Now the Vicars-Apostolic applied penal sanctions. Joseph Berington had already predicted a reign of terror which would 'reduce many learned and exemplary clergy to beggary'. The reality was less dramatic, but effectively silenced clerical dissent. Joseph was forced first out of the northern then out of the midland district. He took refuge with Sir John Throckmorton at Buckland House, Berkshire, on the edge of the western district. His writings and Sir John's, were publicly censured (declared unfit for reading by Catholics) and Berington was refused 'faculties' (authority to act as a missioner). He remained quietly at Buckland for the rest of his long life, charming and stimulating visitors, but saying Mass privately and keeping unpublished his vast *magnum opus* on Church History. Most of this and his papers survive. In the western district Cuthbert Wilkes was suspended, but he was lucky enough to find refuge in Shropshire with the liberal and powerful Earl of Shrewsbury. A group of laymen in Bath who protested against his suspension were actually excommunicated. William Gregson was forced out of Buckinghamshire. In the London district liberal priests were formally warned, and James Archer, for all his popularity, censured for laxity in his teaching. In the midland district there was a fairly systematic persecution. The 'Stafford Squadron' of thirteen liberal missioners was particularly attacked and each member ordered to make a public retraction on pain of suspension. Most of them eventually obeyed, but some, including John Wright, Bishop Berington's secretary, stoutly refused. He was lucky to find a refuge at Longford with the Earl of Shrewsbury for the rest of his life. Joseph Berington's secretary, the historian John Kirk, had a rough handling and survived by henceforward devoting himself to the innocuous pursuit of compiling a biographical dictionary of priests, though his comments are often allusive. Dr John Bew, declared a fugitive from the western district, held out stoutly at Oscott down to 1808, but then capitulated, handed over the school and seminary to Bishop Milner, and was allowed to retire to the mission at Brighton. Peter Gandolphi, an Ignatian priest trained at Stonyhurst and a convert to liberalism, was hunted out of his mission and his *Book of Common Prayer and Administration of the Sacraments for the Use of all the Christians of Great Britain* was censured and put on the Roman *Index of Prohibited Books.* Augustus Mann was never a clerical subject of the Vicars-Apostolic, and he died in Prague, far beyond their thunders. But Alexander Geddes was in London. He had reserved for him the fullest weight of episcopal reprobation. In 1792 he was suspended and his published works censured as Protestant or even non-Christian. When he died, still supported by Lord Petre and still studying in London, in 1802, no diocesan missioner attended him, though a French priest was there. Bishop Douglass would not allow Requiems for his soul. Lord Petre set over his grave in Paddington churchyard a stone inscribed with Geddes' own awkward verses:

> Christian is my name and Catholic my surname;
> I grant you are a Christian as well as I,
> And embrace you as a fellow disciple of Jesus;
> Still I would embrace you as my fellow man.

The Cisalpine Club quietly faded away. The Vicars-Apostolic hoped that it would never have a successor. But in 1808 the Whig politicians made it known that the cause of Catholic Emancipation could never be won unless they could deal with a lay Catholic committee. The Vicars-Apostolic were embarrassed. They were Tory in politics and detested the Whigs; they feared lay committees however hand-picked by themselves But there was no escape, and a Board of British Catholics came into being. It was intended to be no more than an agency controlled by the bishops and this, in spite of some tense moments, it proved to be.

During Bishop Stonor's time the bishops had used their powers of persuasion to get control of mission funds or, at least, have written into the deeds of trusteeship their ultimate right of veto. They had had a limited amount of success in secular priest missions. Then had come the age (1760–1800) of committees. In the establishment of new missions in the industrial north and midlands local lay committees often took the initiative, buying sites, building Mass-houses and schools and establishing permanent bodies of congregational trustees. If they so desired, and they sometimes clearly did, these lay bodies could practically dictate clerical appointments, fix clerical stipends, arrange services and repel episcopal intervention in no uncertain terms. In county town or country missions gentry trustees proved equally obdurate. What was particularly worrying to the bishops was that missioners could ally themselves with this lay power and use it to assert the right of the parochial clergy to a voice in Church government. All of this formed a practical liberalism analogous to, but separate from, ideological liberalism.

From 1793 the Vicars-Apostolic moved to crush this practical liberalism. They had many factors in their favour. The tide of ideological conservatism was rising. At the height of the Napoleonic wars the French assault on Pius VII turned him into a popular hero even amongst English Protestants. The religious Orders were sinking into decrepitude and unable to resist the bishops effectively. After 1814 the restored English Province of the once powerful Jesuits found itself excluded by the bishops from London and large areas of the country and had to wait, cap in hand, for their permission to work in them. The seminaries, once little Empires where the Presidents coopted their successors and pursued their way almost independently of the Vicars-Apostolic, were now struggling for funds and students and in England on their home ground. In 1811 the President of Ushaw College weakly capitulated to the demand of the northern Vicar-Apostolic that he should appoint future Presidents and be chief trustee of the College property. The battle of wills with the secular clergy missioners and congregational trustees was a more long-drawn-out affair. By 1830 the bishops had sustained checks here and there. There were missions and priests whom they still dared not touch. But in general they had won the campaign. The most dramatic battle took place in Liverpool and raged on for years with scuffles in the streets and Mass-houses, demonstrations, lawsuits, inflammatory pamphlets, noisy public meetings. In the end a legal compromise was found that saved the outward appearances of clerical and congregational control while giving the whiphand to the bishop. Meanwhile he and his fellows were tackling the liturgical arrangements in chapels. From 1803 they insisted that the old structure of English prayers and lay readers, varying widely from area to area, should be abolished. In its place they ordered a much truncated form of Prayers before and after Mass to be used everywhere without local variations. For a time there was much sullen resistance, but gradually episcopal insistence wore down the traditionalists.

Thus by 1830 the Catholic ecclesiastical structure was still distinctly untidy and full of anomalies and loose ends. But nevertheless a discernible order and the beginnings of uniformity had appeared miraculously for the first time since the 1570s.

Catholic liberalism had had its great chance in 1771–98 and had muffed it. Increasingly, in the years after 1820, its books, pamphlets and manifestos were lost to sight in the 'Hells' of Catholic institutional libraries. The official English Catholic line became so enthusiastically subservient to bishops and so anti-liberal that the whole liberal movement was formally condemned as a near-disaster. It was only in the 1960s, when a new English Catholic liberal movement began, that it became possible to view the movement of

1771–98 (and, indeed, the build-up before 1771 which created it) in perspective. It suffered for the naive wildness and romanticism of its idealism, the aggressive tactlessness of some of its main leaders, and their ultimate timidity. The official Catholic line after 1798 was that a victory of the liberals would have introduced Protestant heresy into Catholicism and, moreover, have reduced it to a complete anarchy. Bishop Milner's manifesto of the orthodox episcopal reaction, *The Divine Right of Episcopacy*, would not be acceptable to most Catholic theologians today. On the contrary they would accept the theology of Joseph Berington and Alexander Geddes as genuinely Catholic. It had its faults and limitations. Its mental climate is that of the later eighteenth century and foreign to us. But there is a considerable element of imperfection and historical relativity about Catholic theology in all ages. Alexander Geddes was dismissed by the orthodox reactionaries with a *frisson* of horror. Yet Charles Butler, a discerning man who knew Geddes well, insisted that although he was guilty of a perverse, donnish delight in shocking the *bourgeoisie*, he was always a devout Catholic.

It was also untrue to say that only strong episcopal rule could have coped with the immense pastoral problems set by the industrial revolution, urbanisation and Irish immigration. For many years before the rise of the episcopal 'Benevolent Despots' these emerging problems had been dealt with fairly successfully by local Catholic initiative. The episcopal contribution to the general effort (for instance of Stonor and Challoner) was vital but limited to clearing away administrative blocks and encouraging the workers in the pastoral field. After 1800 the real situation was unchanged. The main burden of initiating and planning, of founding new missions, building a system of parochial schools, creating the immense expansion of the work of religious communities throughout the nineteenth century was carried by individual priests, religious and lay people. More often than not Napoleonic episcopal efforts and programmes were abortive and their draconic regimentation stultifying. The official nineteenth-century history of English Catholicism gave most of the limelight and credit for the community's achievements to its hierarchs. This was about as untrue as that sort of medieval history which devotes most of its attention to the activities of kings.

The liberal movement, both ideological and practical, was driven underground by its defeat in 1798–1830. But, like its predecessors, the Catholic clerical radicals of the early seventeenth century and the Blacklowists of 1650–1700, it did not perish. It is true that there was little if any continuity of persons or institutions linking these successive Catholic rebel movements. Lord Acton, a leader of the new Liberal Catholic movement that grew up in the 1850s, confirmed this in a letter to Richard Simpson (editor of the Liberal Catholic review, *The Rambler*) in October 1862:

> The very old school of Berington, the 'Staffordshire clergy', long ago vanished. Something of its spirit survived in the Butlerites . . . Milner had almost succeeded in prevailing over these tendencies before Emancipation.

Acton distinguished three parties in his day:

> I believe you will find only 3 *parties*. 1o. The old school, not warmed up by the C. [Cardinal Manning] into devotion to Rome, and not intellectual or progressive—descendants of Milner, Lingard, and even Butler, so far as they all refuse, like chaos, to be converted. 2o. Ourselves. 3o. The zealous converts, and those of the old set who are under the C's influence, the Romanists, lovers of authority, fearing knowledge much, progress more, freedom most, and essentially unhistoric and unscientific. But the elements are very various and the leaven of different sorts.

He described his own party, the Liberal Catholics, as made up of: 'those converts who escaped the taint of Puseyism in one of several ways, and of those natives [born Catholics] who without losing the old English spirit of Milner and Lingard, are educated enough to follow the advance of knowledge . . .'

What sort of men were Milner and Lingard? By 1830 their party had triumphed over the Staffordshire clergy indeed. They were in reaction against ideological liberalism. But, as Acton perceived, they also were period pieces and their mentality was made up of very various elements.

John Milner was the son of a Catholic tailor who had left Lancashire for London. His background was lower middle class. Like most Church students of his day he received a very thorough institutional drilling: from the ages of nine to twelve at a Franciscan boarding school at Edgbaston, Birmingham, then a year at Sedgeley Park School, followed by eleven years at the English College, Douai. He was there at the time of Joseph Berington's rebellion. Milner was so ordinary and so devoid of intellectual spark that there was no question of offering him a professorship in the College. He was sent to London. Bishop Challoner's peculiar mission organisation included a number of jobbing clergy who were used by the bishop to supply vacancies or stand in for sick priests. Milner was kept at this for two years and then appointed missioner at Winchester, a plum post with a small but select congregation of gentry and trades-people. He stayed at Winchester for twenty-four years, the happiest time of his life. Winchester lay in Jane Austen country. Jane Austen's very Anglican, upper-class provincial world makes no reference to Catholicism or, for that matter, to the new industrial-ism. But she and Milner were mental products of the same culture: they were both tough, ruthless moralists with no sympathy whatever for the rising romantic movement with its enthusiasms and cult of emotion and sensibility. Milner did build a new, larger Mass-house in Winchester of brick and stucco in a faintly 'Gothick' manner. In its general appearance and interior fittings the chapel was ordinary late eighteenth century: the small Gothick features were not a concession to medievalist romanticism but a typically restrained hint that the Catholics might not possess the old English churches, but that the English past was theirs by right. Milner filled in his spare time at Winchester by writing and publishing history books. He was not a research historian, nor had he real historical talent: the books were works of apologetic. There was no romantic medievalism in them.

Meanwhile the liberal rebellion was running its course. Milner was not content merely to take the orthodox side: he published two very sharp pamphlets upholding the Catholic principles of episcopal authoritarianism as divine law and condemning the democracy of the liberals as mad and heterodox. Such vitriolic conservatism was common in the north but rare in the south: in Milner's own London district most clergy were liberals. Inevitably therefore Bishop Douglass relied on him for support. Milner began to travel frequently up to London. He displayed a flair for ecclesiastical tactics and lobbying. The orthodox bishops badly wanted him as a colleague. The fact that they did not get him until 1803 was largely due to both bitter liberal opposition and, after the liberal defeat in 1798, Milner's unpopularity amongst many moder-ate clergy. His tough language often caused offence. Of Charles Butler he wrote: 'his conduct through all this business . . . would petrify you with astonishment were I to unfold it to you, as perhaps I shall soon be obliged to unfold it to the world, *Hic niger est, hunc tu, Romane, caveto.* [He is all black. Romans, beware of him!]'

His promotion to the Vicariate of the midland district wrenched him away from Winchester and he took up residence in industrial Wolverhampton. Certainly one reason for his choice was his deter-mination to keep a close eye on the Staffordshire clergy, for so long the very standard-bearers of the liberal cause. During his episcopate (1803–26) his was the tough and uncompromising mind which dominated the bishops, completed the defeat of practical liberalism and carried on negotiations for Catholic Emancipation without strings or government controls.

He was aware of the necessity for making certain changes. He courted the Irish bishops and imported Irish priests to deal with the immigrants. He faced up to the new Catholic society of urban missions. He even, in spite of secular priest tradition, supported the revival of the Society of Jesus. He tried to curtail English players. But these were only tactical retreats for a man whose mind was eighteenth-century clerical-conservative. He was bitter about aristocratic patrons and told after-dinner stories of their arrogance towards chaplains: he detested their committees. But his manner towards them was automatically deferential. He had Jane Austen's sense of social hierarchy. He was one of the contemporary embodiments of middle-class business success. But, like Jane Austen, he could not take the industrial revolution and the new urbanism seriously. His spiritual home was pre-industrial Winchester and the mid-eighteenth-century small town and country missions. He dressed like a farmer in a many-caped greatcoat and beaver hat and drove about in a gig drawn at a spanking pace by his black horse. He was happy only amongst his Winchester lay cronies and his will breathes in every sentence his dislike for Wolverhampton and his love for Winchester. He was a great authoritarian. Although in pamphlets he had put together competently some sort of theological case for this, he was no thinker. The source of his authoritarianism was his College training; he reacted to liberal committees and congregational initiatives precisely as Douai Presidents did to student unrest. He relied considerably, perforce, on Roman decisions and visited Rome several times. His respect for Rome was genuine. It was based on his sense of due hierarchical order and tradition. He could no more have imagined a proper Christianity without a Pope at the top than he could have imagined English society without George III, the peers and gentry.

But his Romanism was not the result of intellectual conviction or, still less, of romantic enthusiasm. In his private letters he spoke of Rome with the traditional English Catholic contempt for southern Europeans and Curial corruption. Rome was a necessity. Rome was always dilatory and perverse and so must be humoured, cajoled and, if necessary, hoodwinked. Like a true child of English Catholic tradition Milner wanted Catholic Emancipation and yet did not want it. He wanted it chiefly as a tacit admission by Anglicanism of Roman claims. Yet he was no triumphalist. He cherished the subordinate, separated position of English Catholicism. He realised that most of its virtues and all of its peculiar ethos had come from acceptance of this position. He did not expect Catholics ever to be more than a quite small minority of the population. He had some acquaintances but no intimate friends amongst Protestants, and, as he wrote in 1811:

> I never persuade any person of a different religion to embrace mine; but I exhort all persons of my own and other communions with whom I have any relation or communication on the subject, seriously & impartially to examine the grounds of their respective codes of faith & to act agreeably to the dictates of their consciences, whatever these may be.

This was, indeed, the austere voice of traditional Catholicism.

John Lingard was of plebeian origin. His father was a carpenter and 'marriage convert' who had drifted from a Lincolnshire village to London and then on, in search of work, to settle finally in Winchester. John was born after the family's arrival there and Milner procured him a free education and bursary at Douai. He was a senior student there in 1794 when the College was dissolved and had an adventurous escape to England, bringing with him Lord Stourton's young heir. After a short time as a tutor in Stourton's mansion he joined the new seminary at Crook Hall in county Durham and stayed on there to be a professor and, briefly, Vice-President. This was the most exalted ecclesiastical post he ever occupied. He played no part in the affair of the liberal rebellion. His friend, Lord Stourton, was a mild liberal; the priests at Crook Hall were mostly orthodox; Lingard's clerical patron, now the orthodox leader, was Milner. In fact Lingard was a pure product of eighteenth-century clerical practical liberalism and remained so to his death in 1851.

He believed strongly in the old Trades Union rights of the secular clergy. No doubt in early-nineteenth-century circumstances Vicars-Apostolic should hold the reins more firmly. But Lingard stood up for clerical rights with great bluntness. In 1810 the old President of Ushaw College, to which the Crook Hall seminary had moved, was bullied by the northern Vicar-Apostolic into giving him effective control. Lingard resolutely refused to serve at Ushaw in the new régime. He refused also to accept from Milner the Presidency of Oscott or promotion in his own London district. His reason, as stated to the bishops, was: 'I have not sufficient nerve. Of a timid and indulgent disposition, always eager to please and abhorring the very idea of giving pain, I am not the person to preserve discipline.' Instead Lingard accepted the small free country mission at Hornby, ten miles from the industrial complex of

Lancaster, and remained there the rest of his life. Hornby contained no more than 300 inhabitants. The Catholics, who were for ever coming and going as the fortunes of farming changed, never numbered more than a hundred and were sometimes down to forty. Since it was a free mission, Lingard was not bothered with a Catholic squire. He was on intimate terms with his Protestant squire and *persona grata* (at least in his later years) with the Protestant villagers. The Anglican parish clerk escorted him to and from the squire's house when he dined and played whist there and wore one of Lingard's cast-off wigs on Sundays when he intoned the psalms and made the responses in church.

Lingard had already begun to use his bent for historical research and writing at Ushaw. His purpose, like Milner's, was the one traditional amongst English Catholic historians: apologetics. His methods were severely businesslike, though his research was done for him by relays of clerical friends in Paris, Rome and Salamanca. His *Antiquities of the Anglo-Saxon Church* (1806) and *History of England from the First Invasion of the Romans* (completed in 1830) are attractive and distinguished period-pieces. Catholics became proud of him, since he was the only scholar they had who had achieved any kind of recognition from Protestants. As apologetics his *History* probably helped a good many Tractarian converts into Catholicism, but Catholics exaggerated its historical value and its impact. Nevertheless it made him a person whom the bishops had to treat with care, and even, in his later years, with an appearance of deference to his opinions.

He constantly insisted that they should treat their priests with consideration and needed their consent for important decisions. He wrote of the clergy's rights in the matter of appointments to missions. He was very blunt about Ushaw College and insisted that it was no mere episcopal seminary subject to a bishop's whims, but the property of the secular clergy body. Powerful as the bishops now were, they were mostly ill-equipped intellectually and, as good College men, had a permanent inferiority complex when confronted by an ex-professor. He knew their weaknesses: one, he remarked, was subject to bouts of mental illness; another was a child where money was concerned; a third was a braggart. Little by little they came to rely on Lingard to compose their letters to Rome (their Latin was usually sketchy) and to government, and to deal with the Board (since he knew Lord Stourton its chairman) and with politicians. Lingard got on famously with unlikely friends: he was an intimate of Henry Brougham the Radical politician; he was on good terms with Liverpool Unitarians.

In every other way Lingard was, like Milner, a child of the

English Catholic past. He stuck doggedly, in spite of episcopal directives, to the old English prayers and even devised an English service of an Anglican kind for Sunday afternoon use at Hornby. He asked pointedly how else English Protestant country men and women could ever come to see what went on in the Catholic chapel as Christian worship, or how else he could train his occasional marriage converts. Late in life, using the excuse of ill-health, he actually increased his use of lay readers in the chapel, reading Epistles, Gospels and Passions, English prayers and psalms while he muttered the Latin service at the altar. When a new President of Ushaw hired Augustus Welby Pugin to build a great new medievalist chapel, Lingard was very rude: 'It is in my opinion most frightful . . .' We can leave him, in his old-fashioned Douai coat and discreet wig, with his dog, Ettie, his cat and his tortoise, writing affectionate scraps of doggerel verse for the birthday of the squire's daughter.

In 1830 the attention of educated Catholics was concentrated on the picturesque figure of Peter Augustine Baines, Vicar-Apostolic of the western district. He came of a tradesman's family and had about him much of the panache of his class in those frontier days of the industrial revolution. He was never satisfied with things as they were, but was always itching to improve them and fertile with daring, speculative plans. His career began as a young Benedictine teaching in a struggling house of his Congregation at Ampleforth Lodge in Yorkshire. It had a tiny school filled mostly by the children of middle-class parents in Lancashire; all the boys were Church students. In 1812 the Benedictines advertised in *The Laity's Directory* that 'a limited number of young gentlemen not designed for the ecclesiastical state will be admitted'. By 1815 Baines was headmaster and determined to make a bid to capture the sons of the gentry in large numbers. He had the noviciate separated from the school, devised more and more elaborate syllabuses and thoroughly alarmed his colleagues by his rapid success. In 1817 he was packed off as a missioner to Bath. This was a great centre of fashion and Baines soon made his name as a preacher. In 1829 the Franciscan Vicar-Apostolic of the western district died. Rome had long ago fixed a principle that this district, now the poorest, should always have a bishop belonging to a religious Order. By this time the Orders were so short of men that the choice was limited. Baines, aged only forty-one, voluble, persuasive, self-confident, was chosen as bishop. With typical speed and daring he surveyed his district and estimated its needs. He even supplied *Propaganda* in Rome with a statistical table of missions in England and Wales.

Any other bishop than Baines would have been depressed by

the results of the survey. Of approximately 390 missions in the country, there were only forty-seven in his district, many of them small and decrepit country ones. The only industrial areas were in Somerset and the Mendips, both declining, and in South Wales, growing but as yet with few Catholics. He warmly invited the Jesuits in, braving the disapproval of most of his fellow-bishops. He used his scanty district funds to buy Prior Park, a majestic folly near Bath. There he proposed to establish a school and a diocesan seminary, both closely under his direction. He needed experienced clerical teachers, and he needed them quickly. So he approached his own Benedictines and proposed, with all his persuasive skill, that they should shut down their struggling little schools at Downside and Ampleforth and place their staffs, pupils and funds at Prior Park. He talked so fast and impressively to the two communities and to the authorities in Rome that most of the Ampleforth community and Rome succumbed to his charm.

Baines produced so many fascinating prospectuses and ideas ahead of his times that it is depressing that he achieved so little. Prior Park never developed into a real seminary and its success as a school was short-lived. Baines nearly destroyed Ampleforth and his old Congregation henceforward had little good to say of him. In his own curious way he subscribed to Milner's authoritarian views. But in almost every other way he was a child of late-eighteenth-century practical liberalism. He delighted in English prayers. He got on famously with Protestants. He privately considered that the traditional forms of the religious life were obsolete. Like Lingard and Milner he never wanted to convert the mass of Protestants: he sought only to put the old Catholic house in such good, Christian order that Protestant prejudices against it would die a natural death. It was not surprising that in 1862 Acton put a 'Life of *Baines*' into his reading-list for Richard Simpson's proposed article on the state of Catholic parties, but that he did not find a neat pigeon-hole place for him in his suggested outline of them. Baines was not exactly and simply of the old school, and yet he was also not a forerunner of the new school of the enthusiastic, romantic Romanists.

Epilogue

No longer the Catholic Church in the country; nay, no longer, I may say, a Catholic community—but a few adherents of the Old Religion, moving silently and sorrowfully about as memorials of what had been. 'The Roman Catholics'—not a sect, not even an interest, as men conceived it—not a body, however small, representative of the Great Communion abroad —but a handful of individuals, who might be counted, like the pebbles and *detritus* of the great deluge, and who, forsooth, merely happened to retain a creed which, in its day indeed, was the profession of a Church. Here a set of poor Irishmen, coming and going at harvest time, or a colony of them lodged in a miserable quarter of the vast metropolis. There, perhaps, an elderly person, seen walking in the streets, grave and solitary . . . An old-fashioned house of gloomy appearance, closed in with high walls, with an iron gate and yews, and the report attaching to it that 'Roman Catholics' lived there . . .

John Henry Newman; sermon on 'The Second Spring', preached at Oscott, 1850.

Who is she that stands triumphant,
Rock in strength, upon the Rock,
Like some city crowned with turrets,
Braving storm and earthquake shock?
Hers the kingdom, hers the sceptre;
Fall, ye nations, at her feet . . .

Aubrey de Vere (Tractarian convert).

Robert Hugh Benson, a late Victorian convert (and, like so many prominent Catholics since the 1570s, bred in Anglican vicarages), wrote two popular novels. In one he imagines a future in which all Britain has become Catholic; in the other the world has completely fallen away from Catholicism, and the Catholic Church is reduced to one person, the Pope, a hunted fugitive. The most popular of all

Victorian Catholic hymns, written by a convert clergyman, Frederick William Faber, in a time of great triumphalism, runs like this:

> Faith of our fathers, living still
> In spite of dungeon, fire and sword . . .
> Faith of our fathers; Mary's prayers
> Shall win our country back to thee . . .

All of these writers were vividly aware of the immense changes in the fortunes of the Catholic community and the possibility of further disasters. Even Faber—sentimentally and without conviction—suggested the possibility:

> Our fathers chained in prisons dark,
> Were still in heart and conscience free:
> How sweet would be their children's fate,
> If they, like them, could die for thee!

The Catholic community was built up and sustained by a long succession of influxes of converts and foreign Catholics. It began with the student converts of the 1570s, was swelled by a second wave of them in the 1590s and the crowd of gentry converts of the early seventeenth century. There followed the small but steady irruption of middle-class converts in 1680–1720 and then the Irish flood from the 1780s, mingled with the Italians and the French. Lastly from the 1840s came the largest irruption of Irish immigrants and Tractarian Anglicans. The other side to the medal was the great losses from the Catholic community by defection or emigration. These began with the huge defection of 1534–53. It continued with a rain of apostasies, temporary or permanent throughout the Elizabethan period. The decline of the Catholic gentry—by natural extinction, bankruptcy, apostasy or, in a few cases, emigration to the Continent or America—began by 1640 and ran fast in the later seventeenth century and on into the eighteenth. From the 1760s, as the country missions declined, an unknown but certainly considerable number of poor Catholics abandoned their religion. A large proportion of the Irish immigrants rarely went to Mass-houses and lapsed. In the early nineteenth century, especially in South Wales, the bishops and missioners were often unable to establish chapels fast enough to cope with the irruption of Irish and shifts of industrial population caused by booms and slumps. The triumphalism of the 1860s and 1870s to some extent grew out of the experience of steady expansion of Catholic numbers and crowded churches. But the bishops and priests were more preoccupied with desperate efforts to reclaim hosts of lapsed Catholics than with conversions from Protestantism. Even the story of the Tractarian converts was not without its black side of reversions to Anglicanism or apostasies to unbelief. In September 1851, when Newman had announced the beginning of the glorious 'Second Spring', Henry Charles Howard, Duke of Norfolk abandoned Catholicism for the Church of England and sent his son to Eton. Also, from the later eighteenth century there had been a steadily increasing flow out of England of Catholic emigrants and remittance men. William Mawhood in the 1770s was trying to place his wayward son Charles in the Army or the colonies and eventually despatched him to America in the Army with many tears, a copy of *The Imitation of Christ,* and anxious, but not very confident, exhortations to be true to his religion. In the 1840s William Bernard Ullathorne was facing the grim realities of lapsed Catholics and irreligion in the convict settlements in Australia. By the 1860s the Maxwell-Constables of Everingham, Yorkshire had a string of wild younger sons and nephews as Papal Zouaves defending Rome, cattle ranchers in Wyoming and settlers in New Zealand, where the Welds of Lulworth ran a service for placing Catholic youths 'of good family'.

The English Catholic community persevered tenaciously 'braving storm and earthquake shock' while its human material was constantly arriving or departing. In theory, and occasionally in practice, Catholicism was a hereditary faith, the faith of our fathers, transmitted by parents and sustained unwaveringly. But for the most part in reality it was a religion of converts and conversion and Confession was its greatest bulwark. From Augustine Baker (and, before him, Robert Persons) to the correspondence of Catholic gentry families like the Salvins of Croxdale and Constable-Maxwells of Everingham in the 1860s. English Catholics marvelled at the vagaries of the course of the faith. There were families who embraced Catholicism with fervour in one generation and rejected it with equal fervour in the next. Yet, one by one, in the third generation, they returned to the fold.

Why did Catholicism attract so many converts? According to the apologists the reason was always the same, departure from 'the Egyptian darkness' (to use Benet Fitch's term) of Protestantism into the plainly obvious truth of Catholicism which had a monopoly of Christianity and holiness and which was the old religion of England. Where Protestants had Christian truths and an integrity of life, it must be a remnant of the old Catholic past. In the 1720s Stephen Tempest of Broughton's conviction that he and his Protestant gentry neighbours shared most Christian beliefs went with a certainty that Catholicism was natural, Protestantism unnatural, and so his neighbours unconsciously part-Catholics. In the 1840s John Lingard's intimate friendship with the Protestant Murrays and Unitarian Shepherds was, consciously and unconsciously, based on the same feeling as well as on a warm humanity. For their part, since they identified Popery with formalism in religion and image-worship, Lingard's cheerful informality and his broad jokes about Roman superstitions—his broadest about a flea he caught in the Papal Audience Chamber, enclosed in a quill, and despatched slyly to a convent to be kept as a holy relic—convinced them that he was at heart a good Protestant.

As we have seen, the real reasons that brought about conversions to Catholicism were almost as various and mixed as the converts themselves. There were certainly many reasons which had little to do with religion. There were the gentry survivalists of the 1570s, intensely social conservatives and the enemies of expanding court influence. There were Catholics who stuck to their religion glumly, held there by family honour and *pietas*. As Alexander Pope wrote to Atterbury: 'I am not a *Papist*, for I renounce the temporal invasions of the Papal power . . . I am a Catholic in the strictest sense of the word . . .' Anyway, he added, his apostasy would probably kill his old mother, to whom he was much attached. There were converts, like Andrew Marvell, Boswell and Gibbon, who seem chiefly to have been in revolt against parental influences. Robert Persons suspected that many English Catholic clerical students were primarily converted out of a typical, perverse English hatred of the magistrate. As for the Welsh Catholic students, they hated the English and associated them with Anglicanism, and, as university graduates, had little chance of competing with Englishmen for Anglican livings. There were Protestants, even Dissenters, who became Catholics temporarily in James II's reign to gain office. There were some (not many) early-eighteenth-century noblemen and gentry who, like the poor Duke of Wharton, became Catholics primarily because their emotional revolt against Whiggery drove them not only into Jacobitism but into its purest heart, Catholic Jacobitism. Lastly there was the unnumbered host of Catholics of all classes who were nudged and persuaded into conversion by Catholic spouses, relations, guardians or masters, and who were kept in it merely by family convention, education and clerical pressures. In the days of mass religious practice, Catholics, like Protestants, accepted such motives (however much they regretted them and sought to transform them into real religion) as a fact of life and often Providential. Augustine Baker's 'map' of his own religious history frankly recognises the part played in it by accident, material motives and apparent 'cross-currents to the main chance'.

Beneath, and often interwoven with, these material reasons were religious ones. These also were more various than the apologists conceded. There were converts whose primary religious motive appears to have been a panic fear of damnation. Tortured by uncertainty of their salvation, they hunted round preachers, ministers and sects seeking peace. Such seekers were common from the 1580s. They existed in the eighteenth century and crowded to hear the Wesleys. Even Dr Samuel Johnson had a trace of 'seeking' in him. The Evangelical movement in the early mineteenth century produced a fresh crop and many Anglican Tractarians, like Faber and Newman, passed from the Evangelicals through Tractarianism into Catholicism. As Acton wrote to Richard Simpson in 1862 'converts are an element, a leaven, not a party' since they differed widely in the religious attitudes they brought from Protestantism and retained as Catholics. But, he considered, far too many bore the 'sickly, one-sided' taint of an Evangelical upbringing. But this had been true ever since the 1570s and the rise of English Puritanism. There was a long line of ex-Puritan Catholics from Robert Persons, through Augustine Baker, Benet Fitch, John Gother and Richard Challoner to Newman, Faber and Manning.

Down to the 1670s one leading motive for conversion was superstition. As John Aubrey observed, the medieval thought-world of superstition lasted strongly in England down to the mid seventeenth century, with ghosts, portents, fairies, witches and wonderworkers. From the 1570s there were converts who maintained that they had seen Christ in the elevated Host at Mass, or experienced there a light and sweetness totally unknown at Anglican services. Amongst even educated Protestants, Catholic priests, relics and rites still had a magic, wonder-working power. As late as 1679 Shropshire Protestants firmly believed a story that the Catholic Mr Plowden, being forced by law to attend Anglican Communion, touched the Communion cup and at once its stem snapped. According to the Jesuit *Annual Letters* many of their converts came to them because of dreams and portents. Many others were deeply impressed by the part which the Fathers played as exorcists during the great witch-scare of 1590–1620. On some occasions the Fathers provoked tournaments of exorcism with Anglican clergy. The Jesuits and some pious Catholics found the confessors and martyrs great wonder-workers, able to strengthen weak faith or even convert their persecutors and casual Protestant spectators of their executions. Catholic shrines had, even in the eighteenth century, a hold over local Protestants. The Lady Chapel at Mount Grace in

north Yorkshire attracted many Catholic pilgrims: it also had
Protestant visitors who did not always come (as the Herald
Warburton did in the 1720s) out of secular curiosity. Catholic
sacraments long had a wonder-working reputation. Even so educated
a Catholic as Augustine Baker sought a private monastic profession
and, later, ordination as a priest, mainly as specifics against depression and his numerous strange bodily ailments. So also the Protestant
Benet Fitch was sure that only reception of the Catholic Eucharist
could heal his manic depression.

But by the 1670s this medievalism was perishing. It was preserved,
rather artificially, in some pious Catholic circles, especially amongst
Jesuits and nuns, and it survived as a kind of folk-memory amongst
country people, Protestant and Catholic, in the remoter areas. In
the 1870s and 1880s Protestant farm people in Leicestershire had
a habit of attending the very flowery High Masses sung on the
greater festivals by the Rosminians at their church in Ratcliffe.

Other converts were primarily attracted by the Catholic system
of Confession. This may seem strange, since traditional Protestant
apologetic particularly abominated auricular Confession as mercenary priestcraft and the source of much immorality. Yet educated
Protestants, even seventeenth-century Puritans, had a hearty respect
for Catholic casuistry. William Perkins, Ames and the Anglican
Caroline divines bitterly criticised it, but nevertheless made lavish
use of its manuals. Auricular Confession in some form or another
(to ministers, congregations, parents) was an enduring, and sometimes prominent, feature of the life of most Protestant religious
societies and sects. Hence converts to Catholicism from an Evangelical background (for instance John Gother and Edward Manning)
particularly appreciated Confession, especially its humiliating and
penitential side: Manning went to Confession daily.

Other converts were attracted by the reputation Catholics had as
masters of prayer, ascetic or mystical. The reputation was often
undeserved, but it endured amongst devout Protestants. A long line
of Protestant spiritual writers down to the Non-Jurors and the
Wesleys made a selective use of Catholic devotional books.
Crashaw's devotion to St Teresa of Avila long preceded his conversion. The Calvinist Joseph Hall openly admitted his dependence
on the old monks. Defoe, the Dissenter who hated idolatry,
approved of the quiet Benedictine community in Winchester. There
were Catholic books of devotion (by Robert Persons, Benet Fitch
and the Jesuit Père Grou of Lulworth) which were far more widely
read amongst Protestants than Catholics.

Most educated converts from the 1570s to the nineteenth century
owed their conversion at least in part to reading Catholic books.

The appeal of Catholic works of apologetic was extremely limited. Most of them were cut-and-dried and syllogistical in form: their simple line of argument was that Catholicism was the old religion and the one true Church. The force of this was cancelled out by several factors. Before the later eighteenth century few of even the educated had much knowledge of history. Protestant apologetic was far weightier in quantity and quality. Moreover Catholicism then had no monopoly of a claim to an absolute authority in religion: most denominations in some way claimed infallibility for their formularies or interpretation of the Bible. As early as the 1630s the 'Great Tew Circle' (Lord Falkland and William Chillingworth) were criticising the absolutist claims of all Churches. Hence the reading of old-fashioned Catholic apologetic probably did no more than ease a decision already made for quite other reasons. In the later eighteenth century came new and more sophisticated styles of Catholic apologetic, devotional from James Archer, and historical-Tory from Milner and Lingard. But the Tractarian converts had never read Gother, Manning or Archer, and, when Catholics, equated them with a debased, almost Protestant Catholicism. The historical-Tory converts of the 1830s and 1840s, Pugin, Digby and Phillips De Lisle certainly did not owe their conversion to reading Milner and Lingard.

It seems therefore that the great majority of converts to Catholicism from 1570 came uninvited and by many different paths. Some were brought in by their Celtic nationalism—the Irish and, though only in the sixteenth and early seventeenth centuries, the Welsh and Cornish—some by the tradition of aristocratic dissidence, some by Puritan heart-searching, some by Tractarian idealism, some by medievalist-Tory reaction. Each lot of converts was drawn by its own vision of Catholicism, found the reality disappointing, and, consciously and unconsciously, attempted to remould it in some degree into the shape they wanted.

So we come back finally to 'the handle and the axe', the problem of the identity of English Catholicism. Ever since 1570 it has, chameleon-like, constantly changed its personnel and its characteristics. Its apologists, at least before Newman, claimed for it a monolithic, unchanging character as the faith of our fathers. They made this supposedly unchanging character the community's main claim to Catholicity. As Bossuet said, other Christian bodies were man-made and so inevitably had variations. Catholicism, the true Church, by definition could not change. But when we examine in turn each of the characteristics traditionally regarded as essential

M

to Catholicism and so unchangeable, we discover that English
Catholicism had it, but in ways and degrees which varied greatly
from age to age.

The English Catholics from 1570 inherited a great accumulation
of Church laws, theological and liturgical texts, traditions and
customs. Some of these were obsolescent, some long ago overlaid
by quite contrary customs, some had long been interpreted amongst
Catholics in widely differing ways, and some were more pagan than
Christian. Medieval English Catholicism had been a great, loose-
jointed, sprawling system comprehending in itself a wide variety of
differing approaches and schools of thought. On the Continent the
Catholic Council of Trent had already met and started processes
designed to prune, unify and reform the system. But the decrees
of the Council could not be executed in Protestant England. The
restored English Catholic community inherited a rambling, ramshackle house in which there was plenty of room and precedent for
its separate parties to occupy separate parts. They were all Catholics,
but differed greatly on many vital matters. Meanwhile, living in a
Protestant country, in circumstances for which neither the old
Catholic system nor the new Tridentine one made provision, there
had to be a considerable element of improvisation. Again and again
English Catholics had to take actions that seemed necessary and
only later try to square them with their confusing textbooks and
with Rome.

In the early seventeenth century this situation of (in the eyes of
Continental Catholics) Catholic chaos gave place to one of part-
chaos. The establishment of English Catholic institutions abroad
brought some elements of Tridentine order into the muddle. But
at no time before 1798 was it possible to make this order effective.
As Newman said in his Oscott sermon in 1850, English Catholicism,
hitherto an anomaly, could now become a Church.

The interpretation he and the men of the Second Spring imposed
on history since 1570 dismissed it as a dark age of semi-Catholicism,
heroic, even admirable, but not to be copied and best forgotten.
This judgment was in part right, in part wrong. It was right in
seeing the English Catholicism of 1570–1850 as a swirling mass of
inconsistencies and changes. It was wrong in regarding such a state
as uncharacteristic of Catholicism. The orderly English Catholicism
of 1850–1950 was itself a period-piece about which there was little
intrinsic permanency. Catholicism is a 'thing' with a character and
an identity, like a person, but it is unwise to identify it with
particular characteristics, even if, for some long periods of its
history, they have been sharply predominant. The swirling, chaotic
character of English Catholicism between 1570 and 1850 most

probably reflected better the inner character of what Newman called the Great Communion than the apparently apple-pie order and oddities of Second Spring Catholicism.

In Britain Protestants have insisted that Catholics are primarily the Pope's men, Papists, *Roman* Catholics. Between 1570 and 1850 educated English Catholics held a wide variety of opinions about the Papacy and its place in the Church. Indeed the jumbled accumulation of medieval texts they had inherited fully entitled them to do so. They all accepted that unbroken Communion with the other Catholic Churches and therefore the Pope was essential. But, as their experiences during the period of most chaos (1570–90) showed, this Communion might be very informal. During this period there were distinguished English Catholic clergy who maintained that simultaneously Catholics might remain members of the Church of England. It took a great deal of persistent pressure by Rome, Romanising English clergy and the Anglican authorities also to render this position untenable. From this time the English Jesuits associated themselves with high Papalist theories, while the secular clergy and Benedictines were distinctly minimalists. 'Ultramontanism' of the type popularised in England after 1840 was, however, so novel and extreme that it deeply shocked the traditionalists of all schools of thought. Indeed before 1840 English Catholics took the Papacy for granted in a medieval fashion without particular interest, reverence or romanticism. The cultured amongst them, like their Protestant contemporaries (who were often more familiar with the topography of Rome than were Catholics), had a romantic feeling for the classical and Christian antiquities of 'the City', but none for its Byzantine, devious, ineffectual Curia, its *banditti*, prostitutes, fleas and corruption. We today find it difficult to understand how men could cling so stubbornly in allegiance to an institution they either disregarded in practice or spoke of with such frank cynicism. But they and their Protestant neighbours lived in a mental world where great principles—for instance the primacy of God, the hierarchy of Orders in society, the absolute necessity of a monarchical authority at every level in society—were believed with great simplicity and the actual absurdities, perversities, cruelties and immorality of Popes, kings, bishops, landlords, husbands and parents endured with a stoical, even fatalistic, constancy.

Episcopacy bulked large in the Second Spring view of true Catholicism. Yet from 1558 to 1686 English Catholics did without bishops, and from 1686 to the 1790s had ones with little power. Throughout these years the idea, and even the necessity, of episcopacy was debated amongst Catholic divines with extraordin-

ary freedom. A wide spectrum of diverse views existed, ranging
from the near-Presbyterianism of many Jesuits to the highly constitutional bishops favoured by the secular clergy. But hardly a
single Catholic before the 1830s defended the idea of an absolute
prelacy, linked to an all-powerful Papacy, which took flesh in
England after 1850.

The Second Spring theorists also greatly exalted the priesthood as
not merely the backbone and soul of Catholicism but as the Church
itself. Manning's extraordinary flight of fancy, *The Eternal Priesthood*, imagines a Church in which all alike are bound by the
discipline of a strict religious Order. In each parish the Father is,
in miniature, a Pope or bishop, even an Abbot. The laity must
leave everything to him, be silent before him, doff their hats and
kneel for his blessing; Mass servers must repeatedly kiss his hand.
For their part the religious Orders of the period liked to treat their
schoolchildren and parishioners as quasi-religious. This extreme
clericalism had flourished in earlier ages, but now, as then, good
Catholics were simply drilled in strong physical and mental habits
of conformism; religion was standardised and sterilised and a deep
anticlerical backlash fostered. But this sort of thing was novel to
English Catholics. From the early seventeenth century to after 1880
the mystique of clericalism was at a low ebb; the Catholic laity
treated their missioners much as their Protestant neighbours treated
clergymen. Missioners were generally regarded, without enthusiasm,
as necessary evils.

Again in Second Spring theory, Catholicism was, *par excellence*,
an intensely sacramental or 'Incarnational' religion which, unlike
Puritanism, found God in and through an abundance of sacraments,
sacramentals, rituals, blessed objects, saints, shrines, rosaries,
medals, scapulars and Indulgences. To classical Protestantism the
nature of popery was to be an idol-worship. In reality the history
of Christianity has been a complicated interaction between ritualism and Puritanism. The Protestant Churches have shared the
pattern and from their early reaction against late medieval Catholic
folk-religion they rapidly fell into an intense, if different, ritualism
of their own. From the 1570s English Catholicism lived through
a swirling interaction of the two strands. Even the Jesuits had in
their ranks austere Puritans and lush ritualists. In general folk-
ritualism was in the ascendancy down to 1660. But a Puritan
(Blacklowist, Jansenist) reaction was gaining ground and prevailed
throughout the eighteenth century, shying away from sacramentalism and rituals. A devout Protestant could object to very little in the
teaching of the *Manual for Interior Souls* of the exiled French
ex-Jesuit, Jean Grou, missioner at Lulworth Castle in Dorset. In

the early nineteenth century the Second Spring coincided with a Catholic reaction into high sacramentalism which dismissed Grou, Archer, Gother, Robert Manning and even Milner as Jansenists, almost Protestants. These vagaries of English Catholic history have produced some strange conflicts. Between 1660 and 1800 Catholics with an old-fashioned piety were outraged by the 'Protestantism' of their fellows and there were, for instance around the Bar Convent at York and the English Carmelite convents, islands of lush super-stition. Again, in 1800–50, there were priests like Lingard and congregations who reacted with equal ferocity against the reintro-duction of Catholic ritualism. Faber's Brompton Oratory caused much savage comment and there were congregational riots at Coventry when a statue of our Lady was set up in the Catholic chapel.

In theory true Catholicism is a religion in which the contemplative life and religious Orders must needs play a prominent part. Late in the sixteenth century the Puritan Anglican divine, William Perkins, and the radical Catholic missioner, William Watson, both simul-taneously perceived what an odd part monasticism had played in Christian history. Perkins saw that it had repeatedly been a radical, Puritan movement of protest against Catholic ritualism and Pharisaism: he noted that many of the founding fathers of Protestantism had been monks or friars, For his part Watson noticed how religious Orders, down through history, have repeatedly mushroomed, grown corrupt and institutionalised, and then have faded away or have been forcibly dissolved by Catholic authorities. Catholicism has always needed monasticism as a purgative but has been for ever discarding worn-out Orders as scandalous and offensive. Modern English Catholicism was born in the 1570s at the height of a general Catholic reaction against a corrupted monastic-ism. Hence before the 1620s there was little desire to form new Orders or revive old ones and the pious were content with informal communes. From the 1620s there grew up a monastic movement and the rapid establishment of mostly conventional Orders which just as speedily, if with a lively radical protest from some members, hardened into self-perpetuating and highly clericalised institutions. By the 1770s and on to well after 1850 English Catholic opinion was generally hostile to monasticism and the Orders in full decay. From the 1860s came a new and large rush into religion. But, for the most part, this movement was not a real wave of contemplation and radicalism of the kind which begot earlier monastic revivals. It was, like the contemporary, and much smaller, phenomenon of Anglican monasticism, powered by Second Spring (High Church) devotion and the dominant clericalism seeking to gather into useful

Institutes the pious laity needed as auxiliaries of the clergy to service the schools and parishes.

The last essential feature of a true Catholicism in the Second Spring picture was a rigid segregation of good Catholics from the infection of Protestantism. Mixed marriages, mixed schooling and even social contacts with Protestants were discouraged. Catholics should live in tight parochial communities, read Catholic literature and see everything the Catholic way. In penal times (1570–1829), some degree of religious segregation was obviously dictated by circumstances. Medieval Catholic tradition contained strictures on contact with heresy and a rich mythology about the despair and moral degeneration of heretics and the fallen. The Common law and Anglican Church law enforced segregation. Most Catholics were converts and so expelled by their families and local communities. A rabid and bitter anti-Catholicism flourished amongst Protestants. Yet in spite of all these factors only a minority of Protestants and Catholics wanted, or practised, a strict segregation. The survival of English Catholicism and its harvest of converts were largely made possible by this general acceptance of Catholics as licensed Dissenters *within* a Protestant society. A figure like 'Squire Mannock' (an eighteenth-century Jesuit who, with the leave of his superior, inherited a baronetcy and family estate in Suffolk along with a subordinate but real place in county society) became unthinkable after 1850. After 1850 it became just as unthinkable that Catholics had once been married and buried by Anglican rites, used inn rooms and public halls for Mass, allowed Dissenters to attend their chapels on occasion, let Catholic children go to Protestant schools and universities, let nuns go about in secular dress. After 1850 these informalities faded and a grim tension set in between Catholics and Protestants.

The historical line of continuity of the materials of my handle and axe may be thin. But at least I have always had some sort of axe, effective enough to do the jobs required of it. The English Catholic community's line of continuity, as we have seen, has been bent and thin, through many profound shocks and subtle changes of outlook. Its sufferings have reflected in miniature the far greater changes endured by the 'Great Communion' of which it is an integral part. Yet, like the axe, some sort of English Catholic presence has existed since 1534. Through all its changes of form, it has undoubtedly retained a recognisable identity and constant function. On the one hand it certainly has always had something about it which has made it the most doggedly parochial and local of Christian Churches.

English Catholics have been always stubbornly devoted to particular sites, buildings, rituals. Their aggressive Englishry has been the despair of reformers and of the Popes. Yet, paradoxically, their other great enduring characteristic has been their sense of catholicity, of having an allegiance which is more than local or English, more important than cherished sites and rituals, an allegiance and openness to (again using Newman's phrase) 'the Great Communion'.

Bibliography

1. *General Histories*

A. *1534–58*

This is best covered by A. G. Dickens, *The English Reformation,* London, 1972; G. W. O. Woodward, *The Dissolution of the Monasteries,* London, 1966; D. Fenlon, *Heresy and Obedience in Tridentine Italy: Cardinal Pole and the Counter-Reformation,* Cambridge, 1974. The literature on Thomas More is enormous and enthusiastic, but see R. W. Chambers, *Sir Thomas More,* London, 1935; R. Pineas, *Thomas More and Tudor Polemics,* Bloomington, Indiana, 1968; and essays on More by G. R. Elton in *Studies in Tudor and Stuart Politics and Government,* vol. I, Cambridge, 1974. Also, with caution, P. Hughes, *Rome and the Counter-Reformation in England,* London, 1942.

B. *1558–1603*

W. P. Haugaard, *Elizabeth and the English Reformation,* Cambridge, 1968; C. G. Bayne, *Anglo-Roman Relations, 1558–1565,* Oxford, 1913; J. Bossy, 'The Character of Elizabethan Catholicism', in *Crisis in Europe, 1560–1660,* ed. T. Aston, London, 1965; P. McGrath, *Papists and Puritans under Elizabeth I,* London, 1967; A. J. Loomie, *The Spanish Elizabethans,* Cambridge, Mass., 1965.

C. *1603–1714*

J. Bossy, 'The English Catholic Community, 1603–1625', in *The Reign of James VI and I,* ed. A. G. R. Smith, London, 1973; G. Albion, *Charles I and the Court of Rome,* London, 1935; M. J. Havran, *The Catholics in Caroline England,* London, 1962; K. J. Lindley, 'The Lay Catholics of England in the Reign of Charles I', in *Journal of Ecclesiastical History,* XXII, 1972; K. J. Lindley, 'The Part Played by Catholics', in *Politics, Religion and Civil War,* ed. B. Manning, London, 1973; P. H. Hardacre, *The Royalists during the Puritan Revolution,* The Hague, 1956; T. Birrell, 'English Catholics without a Bishop, 1655–72', in *Recusant History*, IV, 4; T. H. Clancy, 'The Jesuits and the Independents, 1647', in *Archivum Historicum Societatis Jesu*, XL, 1971; J. Miller, *Popery and Politics in England, 1660–88*, Cambridge, 1975; J. P. Kenyon, *The Popish Plot*, London, 1972.

D. *1714–1850*

B. Hemphill, *The Early Vicars-Apostolic, 1685–1750*, London, 1954; J. Kirk, *Biographies of English Catholics in the 18th Century*, ed. J. H. Pollen, London, 1924; G. H. Jones, *The Mainstream of Jacobitism*, Cambridge, Mass., 1954; E. Duffy, unpublished Cambridge Ph.D. thesis, 1973, 'Joseph Berington and the English Cisalpine Movement', and 'Ecclesiastical Democracy Detected', in *Recusant History*, X, 1970; E. H. Burton, *The Life and Times of Bishop Challoner*, London, 1909; B. Ward, *The Dawn of the Catholic Revival in England*, London, 1909, and *The Eve of Catholic Emancipation*, London, 1911–12, and *The Sequel to Catholic Emancipation*, London, 1915; F. C. Husenbeth, *The Life of John Milner*, Dublin, 1862; R. Simpson, 'Milner and his Times', in *The Rambler*, II, 1863; M. Haile and E. Bonney. *The Life and Letters of John Lingard*, London, 1912; E. Towers, *Lingard and Ushaw*, and R. Bilsborrow, 'The Lighter Side of Lingard', in *The Ushaw Magazine*, July, 1951; J. B. Dockery, *Collingridge*, Newport, 1954; C. Butler, *The Life and Times of . . . Ullathorne*, London, 1920; W. B. Ullathorne, *Cabin-Boy to Archbishop*, ed. C. Butler, London, 1922; B. L. Kentish, *The Chronicles of . . . the Ullathornes*, privately printed, 1966; J. L. Altholz, *The Liberal Catholic Movement in England, 1848–64*, London, 1962; A. Watkin, 'Gasquet and the Acton–Simpson Correspondence', in *The Cambridge Historical Journal*, X, 1, 1950.

E. *1534–1850*

See C. Dodd, *The Church History of England*, 5 vols., ed. M. A. Tierney, London, 1839–43; J. Berington, *The State and Behaviour of English Catholics from the Reformation to the year 1780*, Birmingham, 1780; J. Knaresborough, *The Sufferings of Catholicks* (?1714, MS, Constable of Everingham MSS, County Record Office, Beverley); D. Mathew, *Catholicism in England*, London, 1948; M. D. R. Leys, *Catholics in England, 1559–1829: A Social History*, London, 1961; J. Bossy, *The English Catholic Community, 1570–1850*, London, 1976.

2. The Catholic Aristocracy

A. General

L. Stone, *The Crisis of the Aristocracy, 1558–1641*, Oxford, 1965; G. E. Cokagne, *The Complete Peerage*, London, 1910ff.; G. E. Mingay, *English Agricultural Society in the 18th Century*, London, 1963; F. M. L. Thompson, *English Landowning Society in the 19th Century*, London, 1963; A. Simpson, *The Wealth of the Gentry, 1540–1660,* Cambridge, 1961; H. E. Bell, *An Introduction to . . . the Court of Wards and Liveries*, Cambridge, 1953; *The Agrarian History of England and Wales, IV, 1500–1640,* ed. J. Thirsk, Cambridge, 1967; H. J. Habakkuk, 'English Landownership, 1680–1740', in *The Economic History Review*, X, i, 1940, and 'Marriage Settlements in the 18th Century', in *Transactions of the Royal Historical Society*, 4th series, 32, 1950; J. D. Chambers and G. E. Mingay, *The Agricultural Revolution, 1750–1880*, London, 1966; G. Hammersley, 'The Revival of the Forest Laws and Charles I', in *History*, June, 1960; H. J. Habakkuk, 'Economic Functions of English Landowners in the 17th and 18th Centuries', in *Explorations in Entrepreneurial History*, London, 1953; P. Roebuck, 'Absentee Landownership in the late 17th and early 18th Centuries', in *The Agricultural History Review*, XXI, 1973; J. O. Payne, *Records of English Catholics of 1715*, London, 1880.

B. Westmorland and Cumberland

M. E. James, *Change and Continuity in the Tudor North*, York, 1965; 'The Household Books of Lord William Howard of Naworth', *Surtees Society*, 67, 1877; D. Scott, *The Stricklands of Sizergh Castle*, London, 1908; H. Hornyhold, *Genealogical Memoirs of the Stricklands of Sizergh,* London, 1928.

C. Northumberland and Durham

Northumberland County History, ed. J. C. Hodgson, Newcastle, 1893; M. E. James, *Family, Lineage and Civil Society . . . a Study of Society . . . in the Durham Region, 1500–1640*, Oxford, 1965, and 'The Concept of Order and the Northern Rising of 1569', in *Past and Present*, LX, 1973; E. Hughes, *North Country Life in the 18th Century: the North-East, 1700–50,* Oxford, 1952; W. V. Smith, *Catholic Tyneside*, Newcastle, 1930; 'Durham Recusants' Estates, 1717–78', *Surtees Society*, 173, 1962; A. M. C. Forster, 'Catholicism in the Diocese of Durham, 1767', in *The Ushaw Magazine*, 72, 1962; 'Description of Catholic Missions in the county of Durham', in *The Catholic Magazine*, ii, 1832; W. Palmes, *Life of Mrs Dorothy*

Lawson, Newcastle, 1851; R. Arnold, *Northern Lights* (Earls of Derwentwater), London, 1962; J. Bossy, 'Four Catholic Congregations in Rural Northumberland, 1750–1850', in *Recusant History*, IX, 1967; *Memoirs of a Northumbrian Lady*, ed. L. E. O. Charlton, London, 1949; A. Forster, 'The Recusancy of the Brandlings', in *Recusant History*, X, 1969; F. J. A. Skeet, *History of the Families of Skeet, Widdrington & Others,* London, n.d.; Salvin MSS (Croxdale Hall, Durham); Selby of Biddleston MSS (some transcripts); Lawson of Byker and Newcastle MSS (Brough Hall, Yorkshire); Correspondence of Sir Carnaby Haggerston, in Constable of Everingham MSS, County Record Office, Beverley.

D. *Lancashire and Cheshire*

'Lord Burghley's Map of Lancashire', in Catholic Record Society, *Miscellanea,* 4, 1907; J. S. Leatherbarrow, *The Lancashire Elizabethan Recusants,* Manchester, 1947; C. Haigh, *Reformation and Resistance in Tudor Lancashire,* Cambridge, 1975; K. R. Wark, *Elizabethan Recusancy in Cheshire,* Manchester, 1971; F. O. Blundell, *Old Catholic Lancashire,* 3 vols., London, 1925–41; Borthwick Institute, York, R.VII/G.897, 1572, the conversion of Anthony Travers of Preston; Catholic Record Society, *Miscellanea,* 53 (Lancashire and Cheshire recusant lists, 1595 and 1629–41), London, 1965; *Registers of Estates of Lancashire Papists, 1717–88,* 2 vols., ed. R. S. France, Record Society of Lancashire and Cheshire, 1964–6; J. Gillow and A. Hewitson, *The Tyldesley Diary, 1712–14,* Preston, 1873; *The Great Diurnal of Nicholas Blundell, 1702–28,* 3 vols., ed. F. Tyrer, Preston, 1968–72; *Crosby Records,* ed. T. E. Gibson, London, 1880; *Crosby Records,* Chetham Society, Manchester, 1887; *Cavalier: Letters of William Blundell, 1620–98,* ed. M. Blundell, London, 1933; MS *Diary* of William Dicconson, 1690–1700 (Ampleforth Abbey); C. Webster, 'Richard Townley and the Towneley Group', in *Transactions of the Historical Society of Lancashire and Cheshire,* 118, 1966; MSS of the Towneleys (County Record Office, Preston), Sherburnes of Stonyhurst (Weld MSS, Preston), Dicconsons of Wrightlington (Preston).

E. *Yorkshire*

J. C. H. Aveling, *Post-Reformation Catholicism in East Yorkshire,* York, 1960, *Catholic Recusancy in the West Riding, 1558–1791,* Leeds, 1963; *Northern Catholics: Recusancy in the North Riding, 1558–1791,* London, 1966; 'Catholic Recusancy in York, 1558–1791', Catholic Record Society, Monograph 2, London, 1970, 'Some Aspects of Yorkshire Recusant History', in *Studies in Church*

History, IV, ed. G. J. Cuming, Leiden, 1967; *The Meynell Family Papers*, in Catholic Record Society, *Miscellanea*, 56, 1964; 'The Recusancy of the Fairfax Family', in *Biographical Studies/Recusant History*, 3 (ii), 4 (ii), 6 (i), 6 (ii), 1956–62; 'The Marriages of Catholic Recusants, 1559–1642', in *The Journal of Ecclesiastical History*, XIV, i, 1964; J. W. Wardell, *History of Yarm*, Yarm, 1957; *The History of Nidderdale*, ed. B. Jennings, Huddersfield, 1967; MSS of the Bellasis and Fairfax families (Newburgh Priory), Gascoigne, Hammond and Hungate families (Leeds City Library, Archives Department), Trapps family (Trappes-Lomax family), Lawson family (Brough Hall), Tancred family (Leeds Diocesan archives), Constable of Everingham, Constable of Burton Constable (County Record Office, Beverley), Danby family (Cartwright Hall, Bradford), Tempest family (Broughton Hall), Stapleton family (Beverley), Crathorne family (Dugdale MSS, County Record Office, Northallerton), Scrope family (Danby Hall), Worsley family (Hovingham Hall), Swale family (Northallerton).

F. *West Midlands*

See *Staffordshire Catholic History*, 1961ff.; *The Worcestershire Recusant*, 1963ff.; *Victoria County History, Staffordshire*, vol. iii, 1970, *Warwickshire*, vol. ii, 1971; *The Tixall Letters*, 2 vols., ed. A. Clifford, London, 1815; E. A. B. Barnard, *A 17th Century Gentleman: Sir Francis Throckmorton, 1640–80*, Cambridge, 1948; M. Jones, *History of the Fitzherbert Family of Swynnerton*, n.d.; MSS of the Throckmorton family (Coughton Court).

G. *East Midlands*

G. A. Hodgett, *Tudor Lincolnshire*, Lincoln, 1975; MSS of the Young family of Market Rasen (the family); M. E. Finch, 'The Wealth of Five Northamptonshire Families', *Northamptonshire Record Society*, 19, 1956; J. Wake, *The Brudenells of Deene*, London, 1954; G. Anstruther, *Vaux of Harrowden*, Newport, 1951; R. Meredith, 'The Eyres of Hassop', 1470–1640', in *The Derbyshire Archaeological Journal*, 84, 1964, and 'A Derbyshire Family in the 17th Century: the Eyres of Hassop', in *Recusant History*, 8, 1965 and 9, 1967; M. Doughty, 'The Poles of Spinkhill', in *The Mountaineer* (Mount St Mary's), 1958–9.

H. *Berkshire, Buckinghamshire, Oxfordshire, Hampshire*

J. E. Paul, 'Hampshire Recusants in the time of Queen Elizabeth', in *Proceedings of the Hampshire Field Club*, 21, 1959; T. Atkinson,

Elizabethan Winchester, London, 1963; G. N. Godwin, *The Civil War in Hampshire,* London, 1904; for the Calvert family see T. Hughes, *History of the Society of Jesus in North America,* New York, 1908; Calvert MSS in the *Maryland Historical Society* publications, and the Kiplin and Turner MSS, County Record Office, Northallerton; B. Stapleton, *History of Post-Reformation Catholic Missions in Oxfordshire,* London, 1906; R. J. Stonor, *Stonor,* London, 1952; G. P. Crawford, *Notes on the Family of Englefield* (of Whiteknights, Reading), n.d.; A. M. Sharp, *History of Ufton Court* (Berkshire), Reading, 1892; G. Sherburn, *The Early Career of Alexander Pope,* Oxford, 1934 (for the Englefields, Blounts and Binfield); Yates of Buckland, Berkshire MSS (Coughton Court, Warwickshire).

I. *East Anglia*

A. Jessopp, *One Generation of a Norfolk House* (Walpoles), London, 1913; P. MacGrath and J. Rowe, 'The Recusancy of Sir Thomas Cornwallis' in *Proceedings of Suffolk Institute of Archaeology,* 28, iii, 1961. K. Bedingfield, *The Bedingfields of Oxburgh,* 2 vols., London, 1915; E. Castle, *The Jerningham Letters, 1780–1843,* 2 vols., London, 1896; *The Life of Lady Warner,* St Omer, 1691; G. H. Ryan and L. J. Redstone, *Timperley of Hintlesham: a Study of a Suffolk Family,* London, 1931; 'The Essex Recusant', 1–2, D. Shanahan, 'The More Family in Essex, 1581–1640', 5 (i) 'The Wrights of Essex', 6 (i) P. Knell, The Mores in Hertfordshire, 1617–93, 7 (i), M. Nolan, 'The Whitbread family'; C. Clay, 'The Misfortunes of William, 4th Lord Petre, 1638–55', in *Recusant History,* XI, 1971; W. R. Emerson, 'The Economic development of the estates of the Petre family in Essex in the 16th and 17th Centuries', Oxford Ph.D. thesis, 1954; D. Cecil, *The Cecils of Hatfield House,* London, 1973.

J. *The West Country*

A. L. Rowse, *Tudor Cornwall,* London, 1941; W. G. Hoskins, 'The Elizabethan Merchants of Exeter', in *Old Devon,* London, 1966; R. Lloyd, *Dorset Elizabethans,* London, 1967; P. Walsh, *Lanherne,* n.d.; A. C. Ellis, *The Story of Torre Abbey,* n.d.; F. Harrison, *The Devon Carys,* 2 vols., New York, 1920; G. Oliver, *Cliffordiana,* Exeter, 1828, and *Collections illustrating the History of the Catholic Religion in . . . Cornwall, Devon, Dorset, Somerset and Gloucester,* London, 1857; Lord Mowbray, *History of the Noble House of Stourton,* 1899; J. A. Williams, *Catholic Recusancy in Wiltshire, 1660–1791,* London, 1968, and *Bath and Rome,* Bath, 1963; K. MacGrath, *Catholicism in Devon and Cornwall, 1767,* Buckfast, 1960.

K. *Sussex, Middlesex and Kent*

R. Manning, *Religion and Society in Elizabethan Sussex*, Leicester, 1969, and 'Catholics and local office-holding in Sussex', in *Bulletin of Institute of Historical Research*, 35, ix, 1962; J. Mousley, 'Fortunes of some Gentry families in Elizabethan Sussex', in *Economic History Review*, II, ii, 1959; *An Elizabethan Recusant House* (Montagues), ed. A. Southern, London, 1954; M. de Trenqualéon, *West Grinstead et les Caryll*, Paris, 1893; H. Knatchbull-Hugessen, *A Kentish Family* (Knatchbulls), London, 1960.

L. *Wales*

G. D. Owen, *Elizabethan Wales*, Cardiff, 1962; A. H. Dodd, *Studies in Stuart Wales*, Cardiff, 1952; M. O'Keeffe, 'The Popish Plot in S. Wales', M.A. thesis, University College of Galway, 1969; R. Mathias, *Whitsun Riot*, Cambridge, 1963; A. Clark, *Raglan Castle and the Civil War*, Chepstow, 1954; H. Lloyd, *The Gentry of S.W. Wales, 1540–1640*, Cardiff, 1968; J. Cleary, *Recusancy of the Barlows of Slebech*, Cardiff, 1957; M. Blundell, *St Winifred and her Holy Well*, London, 1954.

3. *Court Catholicism*

P. Thomas, 'Two Cultures? Court and Country under Charles I', and N. Tyacke, 'Puritanism, Arminianism and Counter-Revolution', in *The Origins of the English Civil War*, ed. C. Russell, London, 1973; C. Oman, *Henrietta Maria*, London, 1936; M. A. Gibb, *Buckingham*, London, 1935; M. Havran, *Cottington*, London, 1973; G. Huxley, *Endymion Porter*, London, 1959; Strafford Correspondence, in Wentworth Woodhouse MSS, Sheffield City Library; 'Registers of Catholic Chapels Royal', in *Catholic Record Society*, 38; D. Lunn, 'John Huddleston and Charles II', in *History Today*, April 1975; *Pepys' Diary*, ed. H. Wheatley, London, 1904; R. T. Peterson, *Sir Kenelm Digby*, London, 1956; J. Evelyn, *Diary*, Oxford, 1955; C. Hartmann, *Clifford*, London, 1937; A. Browning, *Danby*, Glasgow, 1951; V. Barbour, *Arlington*, Washington, 1914; F. C. Turner, *James II*, London, 1948; J. P. Kenyon, *Sunderland*, London, 1958; C. di Cavelli, *Les Derniers Stuarts à St Germain*, London, 1871; D. Daiches, *Charles Edward Stuart*, London, 1975; S. Baxter, *William III*, London, 1966; S. Leslie, *Life and Letters of Mrs Fitzherbert*, London, 1939–40; J. Stoye, *Europe Unfolding, 1648–88*, London, 1973. (Hanover).

4. *The Gentry, Science, the Arts and Professions*

A. *Science*

Aubrey's *Brief Lives*, ed. O. L. Dick, London, 1972; C. Hill, *Intellectual Origins of the English Revolution*, London, 1965; R. S. Westfall, *Science and Religion in 17th Century England*, New Haven, 1958; H. Hartley, *The Royal Society*, London, 1960; F. van Beecke, *Sir Edward Sherburne*, Amsterdam, 1961; D. Glass, 'John Graunt', in *Notes and Records of the Royal Society*, 19, 1964; Towneley MSS (Preston); Gascoigne MSS (Leeds: Sir Edward Gascoigne's Notebooks).

B. *Writers*

The Metaphysical Poets, ed. H. Gardner, London, 1974; C. E. Ward, *John Dryden*, Chapel Hill, 1961; L. Bredvold, *The Intellectual Milieu of John Dryden*, Ann Arbor, 1956; G. Sherburn, *The Early Career of Alexander Pope*, Oxford, 1934; Boswell's *Life of Johnson*, London, 1906; *Thraliana*, ed. R. Balderston, London, 1951; E. Mavor, *The Ladies of Llangollen*, London, 1971; F. Burney, *The Diary of Mme d'Arblay*, London, 1876; G. de Beer, *Gibbon*, London, 1968; T. Wright, *William Cowper*, London, 1921.

C. *Musicians*

W. Woodfill, *Musicians in English Society, 1558–1642*, Princeton, 1953; E. Cole, 'Francis Tregian', in *Music and Letters*, 33, 1952; P. Platt, *Dering, ibid.*, January, 1952; 'Peter Phillips', in *Recusant History*, IV, ii; E. Fellowes, *William Byrd*, Oxford, 1963; A. Lewis, 'Matthew Locke', in *Proceedings of Royal Musical Association*, 1947–8; J. Westrup, 'Foreign Musicians in England', in *The Musical Quarterly*, January, 1941; H. Langley, *Dr Arne*, Cambridge, 1938; P. Scholes, *The Great Dr Burney*, London, 1948.

D. *The Stage*

G. Bentley, *The Jacobean and Caroline Stage*, Oxford, 1941–68; C. J. Sisson, *Lost Plays of Shakespeare's Age*, London, 1936; S. Rosenfeld, *Strolling Players and Drama in the Provinces, 1660–1765*, London, 1939; H. Baker, *John Phillip Kemble*, Harvard, 1942.

E. *The Professions*

W. Prest, 'Legal Education of the Gentry, 1560–1640', in *Past and Present*, 33, 1966; R. Robson, *The Attorney in 18th Century England*,

Cambridge, 1959; J. Raach, *Directory of Country Physicians, 1603–43*, London, 1962; B. Hamilton, 'The Medical Profession in the 18th Century', in *Economic History Review*, iv, 1951; J. Miller, 'Catholic Officers in the Stuart Army', in *English History Review*, 88, 1973; Earl of Castlemaine, *The Catholique Apology*, London, 1674; Catholic Gentry Pedigrees, in Lawson MSS (Brough); G. E. Aylmer, *The King's Servants: the Civil Service of Charles I*, London, 1961; D. C. Douglas, *English Scholars, 1660–1730*, London, 1951; H. Furber, *John Company at Work*, Cambridge, Mass., 1948; A. D. Francis, *The Wine Trade*, London, 1972; Henry Scrope's Leghorn MSS, in Scrope MSS, Danby; Correspondence of Thomas Tankred, draper and Hon. Charles Widdrington, 1729–39, in Towneley MSS (Preston); Henry Maire-Lawson's banking business accounts, in Lawson MSS (Brough).

5. *The Middle Class and Lower Orders*

J. C. H. Aveling, *Catholic Recusancy in York*, London, 1970 (pedigrees and records of a dozen Catholic middle-class families); 'The Mawhood Diary', in *Catholic Record Society*, 50; Bishop Walton's MSS, Leeds Diocesan Archives; MS Notebook of John Fisher, The Presbytery, Holme on Spalding Moor, Yorkshire; letters of Father Mannock, S. J., 1737, Birmingham Archdiocesan archives, C/444; Catholic mission registers, Somerset House (some printed by the *Catholic Record Society*); J. H. Harting, *London Catholic Missions*, London, 1905; T. Burke, *Catholic History of Liverpool*, Liverpool, 1900; R. J. Stonor, *Liverpool's Hidden Story*, Wigan, 1957; C. S. Davies, *History of Macclesfield*, Manchester, 1962; H. Clemesha, *Preston-in-Amounderness*, Manchester, 1912; R. Billington and J. Brownbill, *St Peter's, Lancaster*, Edinburgh, 1910; M. Rowlands, 'Staffordshire Papists in 1767', in *Staffordshire Catholic History*, 6 and 7, 1965; S. Shaw, *History of the Staffordshire Potteries*, Hanley, 1829; W. Waugh, *History of the Leeds Mission*, Leeds, 1910; C. Hadfield, *St Marie's, Sheffield*, Sheffield, 1889; A. Briggs, *History of Birmingham*, ii, London, 1952; R. Church, *Economic and Social Change in a Midland Town: Victorian Nottingham*, London, 1966; H. J. Perkin, 'The Development of Modern Glossop', in *Small Town Politics*, ed. A. Bush, Oxford, 1959; J. Hickey, *Urban Catholics* (Cardiff), London, 1967; M. J. Rowe, *Catholic Bury St Edmunds*, 1959; J. H. Harting, *London Catholic Missions*, London, 1905; B. W. Kelly, *Historical Dictionary of Catholic Missions*, London, n.d., and *Old English Catholic Missions*, London, 1907.

E. P. Thompson, *The Making of the English Working Class*,

London, 1974; K. H. Connell, *Irish Peasant Society*, Oxford, 1968; S. Gilley, 'The Roman Catholic Mission to the Irish in London', in *Recusant History*, X, 1969; *Census of Religious Worship, England and Wales, Report and Tables,* London, 1853.

6. *Recusancy, Legislation and Fines*

J. A. Williams, 'The Recusant Rolls', in *History*, L, 169, 1965; H. Bowler, 'Some Notes on the Recusant Rolls', in *Recusant History*, 4, 1958, and *Catholic Record Society*, vol. 57; J. C. H. Aveling, *The Northern Commission for Compounding, 1626–42* (with introduction on the history of fining), *ibid.,* 53; M. Rowlands, 'The Iron Age of Double Taxes', in *Staffordshire Catholic History*, Spring, 1963; J. C. H. Aveling, 'Catholics and Parliamentary Sequestrations', in *The Ampleforth Journal*, June, 1959; *Statutes of the Realm*; A. W. B. Simpson, *An Introduction to the History of the Land Law*, Oxford, 1961.

7. *Religious Practice*

A. *General*

A. Allison and D. Rogers, *Catologue of Catholic Books in English, 1558–1640*, Bognor, 1956; J. Gillow, *A Biographical Dictionary of English Catholics*, London, 1885.

B. *16th and 17th Century Traditional Practice*

(i) *Primers* and *Offices of Our Lady*: Miss Littledale, Oxford (Pudsey family, 1576); Exeter College Library, Oxford (Winchester, 1570–80); York Minster Library, XVI.G/5 (Pulleins, 1597–1616); Ampleforth Library, Codices, 704 (Middletons, 1643–53).

(ii) *Sarum Missals: Catholic Record Society*, vol. I (Huddleston); Ampleforth Library.

(iii) *Chapel fittings*: Ushaw College, XIX.F.7/14 (Yorkes, 1620s); County Record Office, Northallerton, Minutes and Orders, 1656 (Lord Eure); Newburgh Priory MSS (Gilling); 'Household Books of Sir Miles Stapleton, 1656–1705', in *The Ancestor*, III, 1902; 'Fowlers of St Thomas, 1684–8', in *Staffordshire Catholic History*, 2, 1962.

(iv) *Confession: Enchiridion sive Manuale Confessariorum . . . Doctoris Navarri*, Antwerp, 1601 (standard work used at Douai); *Casus Aliqui ad Angliam Spectantes* (*c.* 1650), Ampleforth MS. 9; Cecil MSS, Hatfield, 118/67.

(v) *The Mass and Prayer*: Borthwick Institute, York R.VII/G, 824, 902,1297; Cecil MSS, 141/165–6; John Brerely, *The Liturgy of the Masse*, Paris 1620; Richard Lascelles, *A Little Way how to Heare Masse with Profit and Devotion*, Paris, 1644; Thomas Worthington, *The Rosary of our Lady*, Antwerp, 1600; *Certaine Devout and Godly Petitions commonly called the Jesus Psalter*, Louvain, 1578; *Notes & Queries*, N.S. XII, December 1861 (pilgrims); K. Thomas, *Religion and the Decline of Magic*, London, 1971.

C. *'English Prayers'*

M. Norman, 'Gother and the English Way of Spirituality', in *Recusant History*, II, 1972; M. Rowlands, 'Education and Piety of Catholics in Staffordshire in the 18th Century', *ibid*. X, 1969; J. Gother, *Instructions and Devotions, for Hearing Mass, for Confession*, London, 1744; *The Manual of Devout Prayers*, London, 1728; Richard Challoner, *The Garden of the Soul*, London, 1740; *The Divine Office for the Use of the Laity*, London, 1768; *The Complete Catholick Manual*, London, 1770; *The Layman's Afternoon Devotion*, Preston, 1778; J. Lingard, *Manual of Prayers*, York, 1844.

D. *The 19th Century Liturgical Revolution*

Prayers before and After Mass, Wolverhampton, 1792; E. Purcell and E. de Lisle, *Life and Letters of Ambrose Phillipps de Lisle*, London, 1900; A. W. Pugin, *Contrasts*, London, 1836; B. Little, *Catholic Churches since 1623*, London, 1966; R. Chapman, *Faber*, London, 1961; E. Larkin, 'The Devotional Revolution in Ireland, 1850–75', in *The American Historical Review*, LXXVII, 1972.

8. *The American Connection*

J. Hughes, *History of the Society of Jesus in North America*, New York, 1907; J. T. Ellis, *American Catholicism*, Chicago, 1956, and *Catholics in Colonial America*, Washington, 1964; P. Guilday, *Life and Times of John Carroll*, New York, 1920; R. C. Madden, 'Catholics in Colonial South Carolina', in *Records of the Catholic History Society of Philadelphia*, March–June, 1962; M. Trappes-Lomax, *Life and Times of Challoner*, London, 1957.

9. *The Catholic Clergy*

A. *Bishops*

See section I. above; J. A. Williams, 'Bishops Giffard and Ellis and the Western Vicariate' in *Journal of Ecclesiastical History*, XV, 2; G. Anstruther, 'The Appointment of Bishop Williams', in *Archivum Fratrum Praedicatorum*, Rome, XXX, 1960; W. M. Brady, *The Episcopal Succession,* Rome, 1877; Leeds Diocesan archives, Matthew Gibson's Notebook, 1787, William Gibson's Diary, 1792.

B. *The Secular Clergy*

L. Halkin, 'La Formation du Clergé Catholique après le Concile de Trente', in *Bibliothèque de la Revue d'Histoire Ecclésiastique*, Fasc. 50, iii, Louvain, 1970; T. F. Knox, *1st and 2nd Diaries of the English College, Douay*, London, 1878, and *Letters and Memorials of William, Cardinal Allen*, London, 1882; *Catholic Record Society*, vols., 9 (Allen); 58 (Allen and Barret); 10–11 (Douai Diaries, 1598–1654); 63 (Douai, 1639–1794); 27 (Douai Diaries, 1715–78); 30 (Valladolid); 14 (Seville); 40, 54, 55 (English College, Rome); 22 (Archpriest Controversy); 51 (Wisbech 'Stirs'); A. Kenny, 'English Hospice, Rome', in *The Venerabile*, Rome, XXI, 1962; J. Croft, *Lisbon College,* London, 1901; G. Anstruther, *The Seminary Priests,* vol. 1, *Elizabethan*, Ware, 1968, and vol. 2, *Early Stuarts*, Great Wakering, 1975; R. Challoner, *Memoirs of Missionary Priests*, London, 1924; T. G. Law, *Conflicts between Jesuits and Seculars*, London, 1889, and *The Archpriest Controversy*, London, 1898; W. Watson, *A Decachordon of Twelve Quodlibeticall Questions*, London, 1602; J. M. Cleary, *Checklist of Welsh Students in Seminaries*, Cardiff, 1971; Thomas Stapleton, *Opera Omnia,* Paris, 1620; T. Veech, *Nicholas Sanders*, Louvain, 1935; J. Booty, *John Jewel,* London, 1963; J. Sergeant, *Account of the Chapter*, London, 1853; R. Bradley, 'Blacklo and the Counter-Reformation', in *From the Renaissance to the Counter-Reformation*, ed. C. H. Carter, London, 1966; Thomas White, *On Purgatory*, Paris, 1659, and *Apologia pro Doctrina Sua*, Paris, 1661; R. Clark, *Strangers and Sojourners at Port-Royal*, London, 1932; J. Orcibal, *Saint Cyran*, Paris, 1947; J. Dagens, *Correspondance de Bérulle*, Paris, 1939; L. Cognet, *Le Jansenisme*, Paris, 1961; *Blacklo's Cabal Discovered*, Liège, 1680.

E. Duffy, 'Ecclesiastical Democracy Detected', in *Recusant History*, X, 1970; J. Berington, *The State and Behaviour of English Catholics*, Birmingham, 1780; *History of the Lives of Abeillard and Heloissa*, Birmingham, 1787; *The Memoirs of Gregorio Panzani*, Birmingham, 1793; A. Geddes, *Carmen Saeculare*, London, 1790, and *Critical Remarks on the Hebrew Scriptures*, London, 1800; W. J. Anderson, 'The College for the Lowland District' (Alexander Geddes), in *The Innes Review*, Autumn, 1963; F. X. Plasse, *Le Clergé Français Réfugié en Angleterre,* Paris, 1903; M. Weiner, *The French Exiles, 1789–1815*, London, 1960; D. Milburn, *History of Ushaw College*, Durham, 1964; B. Ward, *History of St Edmund's, Ware*, London, 1910; *The English Catholics, 1850–1950*, ed. G. Beck, London, 1950.

C. *The Religious Orders of Men*

(i) *The Origins*
P. Guilday, *English Catholic Refugees on the Continent, 1558–1795*, London, 1914; R. Lechat, *Les Réfugiés Anglais dans les Pays-Bas Espagnols, 1558–1603*, Louvain, 1914.

(ii) *The Jesuits*
H. More, *Historia Missionis Anglicanae Societatis Jesu*, St Omer, 1660; 'Letters and Memorials of Robert Persons', *Catholic Record Society*, vol. 39, and 'Memoirs of Robert Persons', *ibid.* vol. 2; H. Foley, *Records of the English Province of the Society of Jesus*, 7 vols., London, 1875–1909; H. Chadwick, *St Omers to Stonyhurst*, London, 1962; B. Basset, *The English Jesuits*, London, 1967; P. Caraman's lives of: *John Gerard*, London, 1956; *Henry Garnet*, 1964; *William Weston*, 1953; *Henry Morse*, 1966; R. Simpson, *Edmund Campion*, London, 1867; C. Devlin, *Robert Southwell*, London, 1956; W. F. Rea, 'John Gregory', in *History Today*, March, 1966; C. Reilly, 'Francis Line', in *The Month*, May, 1959; R. F. Doublet, *Thomas Faulkner, ibid.*, April 1960; John Warner, 'History of the English Persecution of Catholics', in *Catholic Record Society*, vols. 47–8; L. von Pastor, *History of the Popes*, London, 1923–53; F. Nielsen, *History of the Papacy*, i, London, 1906 (the suppression and restoration of the Society); Stonyhurst College, Anglia MSS; Jesuit MSS, Farm St, London; J. C. H. Aveling, 'Jesuit History' in *Ampleforth Journal*, June, 1965.

(iii) *The Benedictines*
D. M. Lunn, 'Origins and Early Development of the revived Benedictine Congregation, 1588–1647', Cambridge Ph.D. thesis, 1970; Y. Chaussy, *Les Bénédictins Anglais réfugiés en France au XVIIe. siècle*, Paris, 1967; A. Allanson, MS *History, Records, Chapters* and *Biographies*, Ampleforth Abbey; Weldon MS, Douai Abbey; Provincial Account Books, Downside Abbey; 'Memorials of Augustine Baker', in *Catholic Record Society*, 33; *Sancta Sophia*, ed. S. Cressy, London, 1948; *Ampleforth and its Origins*, ed. J. McCann, London, 1952; G. Sitwell, 'Leander Jones' Mission', in *Recusant History*, V, 1962;

M. Nedoncelle, *Trois Aspects du Problème Anglo-Catholique*, Louvain, 1951, and 'John Barnes', in *Revue des Sciences Religieuses*, 86, 1960; J. Barnes, *Traicté et Dispute contre les Equivoques*, Paris, 1625; J. C. H. Aveling, 'The Education of 18th Century English Monks', in *Downside Review*, Spring 1961.

(iv) *The Franciscans and Dominicans*

'Franciscana', *Catholic Record Society*, 24, 'Dominicana', *ibid.*, 25; Thaddeus, *Franciscans in England, 1600–1850*, London, 1898; Franciscan MSS, Forest Gate, London; G. Anstruther, *A Hundred Homeless Years*, London, 1958; G. Gumbley, *Notices of English Dominicans, 1555–1952*, London, 1955; J. Dockery, *Christopher Davenport*, London, 1960; Sancta Clara, *Deus, Natura, Gratia*, Douai, 1634; C. Palmer, *Philip Howard*, London, 1867.

(v) *Other Orders*

C. de Gamaches, *La Mission des Capucins*, Paris, 1881; J. Brousse, *Ange de Joyeuse et Benet Canfield*, London, 1959; O. de Veghel, *Bénoit de Canfield*, Rome, 1949; B. Canfield, *Règle de Perfection*, Paris, 1608; B. Zimmerman, *Carmel in England*, London, 1899; E. M. Thompson, *Carthusian Order in England*, London, 1930, and Parkminster MSS, Sussex; J. R. Fletcher, *The English Bridgettines*, London, 1920.

D. *Religious Orders of Women*

(i) *Benedictines*

Annals and Registers (Ghent: *Catholic Record Society*, 6, 19, and *Annals*, East Bergholt, 1894; Cambrai: *Catholic Record Society*, 13; Paris: R. Eaton, *Benedictines of Colwich*, London, 1929; *St Benedict's Priory, Colwich*, Colwich, n.d.; *Dunkirk: History*, Teignmouth, 1958; Pontoise: *Catholic Record Society*, 17; Brussels: *Catholic Record Society*, 14); Toby Mathew, *Life of Lady Lucy Knatchbull*, London, 1931; Augustine Baker, *D. Gertrude More*, Edinburgh, 1910; *The Holy Practices of a Divine Lover, or the Sainctly Ideots Devotions* (Gertrude More), ed. H. Lane-Fox, Edinburgh, 1912, and her *Confessiones Amantis*, Paris, 1658.

(ii) *Franciscans*

Annals and Registers (Poor Clares of Gravelines: *Catholic Record Society*, 14; Dunkirk: Dunkirk MSS, Ushaw College; Rouen and Aire: Poor Clares, Darlington; Franciscans of Brussels, Nieuport, Princenhoff and Bruges: *Catholic Record Society*, 24).

(iii) *Dominicans*

Annals and Registers of Vilvorde and Spellekens, *Catholic Record Society*, 25.

(iv) *Canonesses*
Annals and Registers: Paris: *Catholic Record Society*, 8; F. Cedoz, *Un Couvent de Religieuses Anglaises à Paris, 1634–1884*, Paris, 1891; MSS at Ealing Augustinian convent; Louvain: *The Chronicle of the English Canonesses of Louvain*, ed. A. Hamilton, London, 1912; Liège: *Catholic Record Society*, 17; Bruges: *Flemish Mystics & English Martyrs*, London, 1925, and MSS at the Augustinian convent, Newton Abbot.

(v) *Carmelites*
Annals and Registers: Antwerp: MS at Lanherne Carmel, Cornwall; Lierre: MSS at Darlington Carmel, Durham; Hoogstraet: MSS at Chichester Carmel, Sussex; J. Hardman, *Two English Carmelites*, London, 1925.

(vi) *Mary Ward Sisters*
Annals and registers: Bar, York: *Catholic Record Society*, 4; M. C. E. Chambers, *Life of Mary Ward*, London, 1882; *Life* by Winifred Wigmore, Bar Convent; M. Oliver, *Mary Ward*, London, 1960; L. Hicks, 'Mary Ward's Great Enterprise', in *The Month*, CLI, CLII, 1928–9; H. Coleridge, *The Bar Convent, York*, London, 1884.

Index